Grimoire of Arts

Bryan S Lovering
Edit by Strix

Conjuration of the Vessel

Anoint with consecration oil under the light of the full moon.

Blood of my blood

Flesh of my flesh

Light of the moon

The gate is open

The key is made

That the thought made word

The word made made flesh

The flesh made manifest

That the world be changed

The vessel is prepared to recieve the spirit

The vessel is prepared as the way

To the will made manifest

The thought made word

The word when spoken made flesh

The flesh to be what manifests

That what manifests shall change the worlds

Dedication

To my dear mother, Jan Lovering, who put up with the odd hours, and to my friends, those of you who never who gave up in helping me write this work, as well as putting up with the crazy experiments I have attempted over the years, and will yet attempt for the next volumes.

To my Dad, Scott Lovering, who has inspired many journeys into the natural world.

My roommates over the years Nate, Christine, and all those who have stood with me.

Specifically, for putting up with me for so many years;

Lady High Warlock Minmunte Woerelak

Senior Warlock Kli Woerelak

Senator Rage Warlock

Strix, for her edit job.

As well as H.P Lovecraft, and Simon, for his version of the *Necronomicon*, a work that has inspired me since the beginnings of my studies.

Thank you all.

Disclaimer

There is nothing more dangerous than seeking your own path to the source. Law must be natural law, and balance, any references to violation of a law of your land is one you undertake at your own risk. It is yours and yours alone, not anyone associated with the creation of this work. All herbal recipes are for notes and references only, do not use them.

Always consult your doctors when doing anything that would be considered medicinal or medical. This work is not for the ego. Not for those who would become arm chair magicians, and waving this text around as a mark of status. If you would misuse this work, then on your own head be it.

This work is considered to be a curio in all reference to any recipe incense, and should not be re-created under any circumstance where any and all local laws would prohibit such actions, or the risk of bodily harm of any form is mentioned.

Do not use this if you're going to go blame others for your own weakness of character that results from the misuses of the things contained herein. You have been warned.

Why This Work?

There is a world of the arts which no one gets to see. This will show some of the things that are out there. It is for those that see the higher forms of the art beyond witchcraft or other religious dogma. This a tool crafted by a Warlock, for the Warlock community. This is what I brought to the table of our community, this is what has been birthed of my times of study within this community. May it help to guide others further upon the path as we guard the gates, and protect the knowledge of the ages.

How to use this Book:

Copy all seals into your own hand when needed,

Add colors where applicable.

More is unsaid about things described than what has been written.

Use your intuition to find the "Truth" in what has been recorded.

Copyright 2012

Only passages may be copied. For personal use only.

Any reproductions must not be used for the profit of the individual copies.

All original copyright is maintained by the author.

Table of Contents

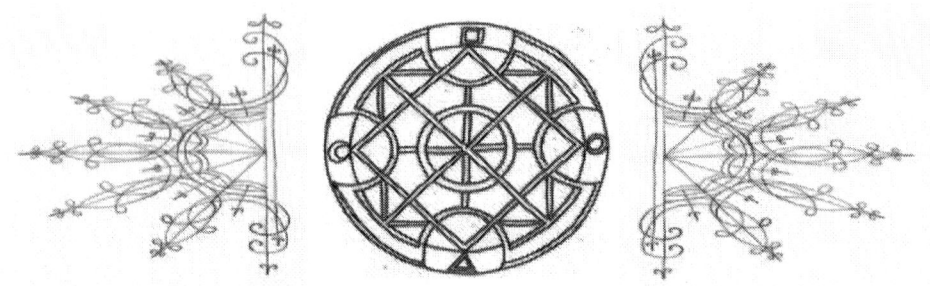

Conjuration of the Vessel 3	Divisions of Creation... 53
	The Supernal Realms 53
General Mechanics.. 12	The Bestial Realms 53
Key of Creation.. 13	The Celestial Realms 53
Key of the Arrays.. 18	The Infernal Realms 54
Exercises for Manifestation................................ 23	The Elemental Realms 54
Key of the Word... 24	Recreating a Living Mind.. 55
Key of Perceptive Mytho-geography 26	Greater Modifying of the Living Mind....................... 56
Key of Union... 28	Demonic Creation from a Person............................... 57
Key of the Funerary Arts... 29	Nesting Consciousness.. 58
	Creation of the Homunculus 59
Creation Magick... 30	Humanoid qualities 59
Of Creation... 31	Spatial Distortion 60
The Sources of the Singularity................................ 35	Remote Spatial Distortion.. 60
The Sources and the Planets.................................... 38	Reality Blending... 61
The Source Seals... 39	Conjure of Linking 61
Conjuration of the Sources :.................................... 39	Of the Internal View 62
Watchtowers... 40	Divisions of the Mind... 63
The Tower of the Arts... 41	Developing the Core 64
Call of the Tower.. 42	Daily Exercise 64
Anchoring of the Spirit 43	The Spoken Word 64
Created Beings... 44	The Unspoken Word.. 65
Creation of the Elementary..................................... 45	Conjuration Quick Reference...................................... 66
Basic construction:... 45	Passive Manifestation....................................... 66
Exercises for Creating an Egregore..................... 46	Neutral Manifestation.. 66
Application for Creation:................................... 46	Active Manifestation... 66
Creating Demons.. 47	Types of manifestation.. 67
Cairns, Nodes, & Ley Lines.................................... 48	
From a Person.. 49	Ascension Magick.. 70
From Oneself.. 49	Ascension of the Body.. 71
From a Grouping of People..................................... 49	"Awakening"... 72
From the Singular Collective 49	The Hierarchies... 73
From the Human Unconscious Collective 49	The Oath of Service.. 75
Conjuration of the Familiar Creatures.................... 50	Pacts of the Divine.. 76
To Call the Red Dragon...................................... 50	Pacts of Spirits... 76
Calling of the Black Dragon............................... 50	Pacts of the Elements.. 77
Dragon of the Ages... 50	Pacts with Places... 78
Conjuration of the Hounds of Hell..................... 50	Awakening of the Spirit.. 79
Creation of the Archetype....................................... 51	Invocation of Power Of Consciousness...................... 79
Creation of Realms.. 52	To Align to the Darkness of the Soul......................... 80
Application... 52	Rite of Transformation 81
On Conjurations.. 53	Invocation of Becoming.. 82

Summons of the Draconian Spirit.................................88
  Ceremony of Removal 91
  Ceremony of Return..93

"So how far down does the rabbit hole go?".......................94

Elemental Magick...95
  Union of the Elementals 96
    Earth...96
    Water 97
    Air...97
    Fire..97
  Elemental Forces..98
    Exercises of Elemental Magick..................................104
  Time..105
  The Elemental Divisions..106
    Exercises on Correspondences..................................107
  Elemental Seals 108
    Structure of the Seals 108
    Dimensional Seals of the Elements 108
  Elemental Seal Design..111
  Seals of the Elements...112
    Exercises on Seal Creation.......................................112
  Elemental Energy: Defensive Techniques....................113
    Basic Shielding...113
    Elemental wards...113
    Auric Hardening..113
    Auric Mirrors..113
    Geometric Shield..113
    Cross Shield..113
    The Spiral Shield...113
    Braided Elemental Shield..114
    Singular Elemental Shield...114
    Multiplied Elemental Shield......................................114
    Greater Auric Mirror 114
    Charge of the Waters...114
    Charge of the Fires for Protection............................114
    The Twin Pentagrams...115
    To Protect A Space...115
    To Protect A Fixed Loci..115
    The Dream Catcher..115
    Crystal Barrier...116
    Mirrored Aura..116
  Ex Nul...117
    Bringing Down the Barrier of Gaia...........................117
    To Dissolve Spiritual Walls..117
    To Dissolve Spiritual Shields....................................117
    Removing Power from Exorcisms............................118
  Offensive Elemental Techniques...................................119
    Offensive Mirror Shield..119
    Greater Mirror...119
    Destruction of the Greater Mirror.............................119
    The Perpetual Energy Construct...............................119
    Ovum Udinbak...119
    Nightmares of the Soul...120
    To Magnify Discord...120
    Chains Of Eternity..121
    Rite of Decimation...122

"Where is the rabbit,..?"..125

Alchemical Arrays..126
  On Creation..127
  Materials..129
  Circles of the Art...132
    Exercises of Circle Construction..............................133
  Array Mechanics 134
  Terrestrial Array Foundation..135
  Sacrificial Array...136

  Generation...137
  Barrier...138
  Gate of the Inner World..139
  Celestial and Abyssal Seal...140
  Active and Passive Seal...141
  Array of the Doppelganger...142
  Blood Circle of Summons...144
  Blood Circle of Binding...145
  Blood Gates..146
  Dream Array...147
  Elemental Gate..148
  Integration Array...149
  Elemental Stasis..150
  Opening Seal..151
  Storage Array...152

Gate Magick..153
  The Nature of Gates 154
  Portals...156
    To Open Portals...156
  Vortexes 157
  The Opening of the Way...158
  Conjuration of the Elemental Seals..............................159
  Conjuration of the Gate..159
  Conjuration of Celestial Gates 160
    The Lunar Gate..160
    Gate of Mercury..161
    Gate of Venus..161
    Gate of Mars..161
    Gate of Jupiter...162
    Gate of the Sun...162
    Gate of Saturn...162
    Gate of Neptune..163
    Gate of Uranus..163
  Conjuration of the 72..164
  Conjuration of the 1728 Gates......................................166

Blood Magick..214
  Of Blood..215
  Bloodless Sacrifice..216
  Awakening the Inanimate...217
  Marking the Blood...218
    The Rite of the Marking...218
    Rite of the Unmarked...218
  Blood Substitute Condenser..219
    Table of Condensers..219
  Clone Generation...220
  Conjuration of The Beast Bird of Paradise..................221
  Mounting of the Familiar's Spirit...................................223

Shadow Magick...224
  Basic Technique...225
  Advanced Manipulation..225
    Basic Tendrils..226
    Complex Tendrils..226
    Terrestrial Tendrils...226
    Shifting shades...226
  Remote Tendril...226
  Spelled Tendrils...226
  Basic Shadow Servitors..227
  Advanced Shade Servitors...227

" Was there even a rabbit?"...228

Daemonic Magick	229
Of Archetypes	230
Of Demons	231
The Source	231
Invocations of Elemental Forces	232
Invocations of Planetary Forces	232
Invocations of Deities	233
Invocation of the Spirits of Places	233
Evocations of Elemental Forces	234
Evocations of Elemental Powers	234
Evocations of Planetary Forces	235
Evocation of Planetary Spirits	235
Evocations of the Forces Within a Place	236
Evocations of the Spirits of Places	236
Evocations of the Bestiaries	237
Evocations of Deities	237
Living Evocations	238
Greater Summons of the Living Spirit	240
Essences	242
Of Souls	243
Spirits of the Departed	244
Soul Entrapment	245
Conjuration of Entrapment	246
On Possession	249
On Spiritual Consumption	250
Devouring Spirits	252
Greater Devouring	253
Of Demons	254
Summons of demonic Forces	255
The Summons of Djinn	255
Of Archetypes	256
Patrons	257
Source	258
Animation	259
To Bring Life	260
To Take Life	261
Resurrection	262
Restoration of life	264
Restoration of Life – English	265
Spirit Objects	266
Summons of power	267
Conjuration of the vessel	269
Summons of the Spirit	269
Return of the Spirit	269
Sealing of the Spirit	270
Naming the Spirit	270
Conjuration of Containment	270
Spirit Traps	271
Conjuration To Bind Spirits	272
Transference of Power	273
Rite of Restoration	275
Rite of Forgiveness	276
Conjuration of the Release	277
Conjuration of Service	278
Conjure of the Light Fire	279
Union Rites	280
The Union Ceremony	281
Demonic Union	281
Archetypal Union	282
Soul Binding	283
The Ritual	284
Blessing for the Candles of the Fates	286
Elemental Union Ceremonies	287
Union of the Air	288
The Union of the Water	291
Union of the Earth	294
Union of Fire	297
Unions by Caste	300
Light Union	301
Shadow Union	304
Dark Union	307
Funerary Rites	310
The Funerary works	311
Passing of the Air	312
Passing of the Water	314
Passing of the Earth	316
Passing of the Fire	318
The Opening of the Way	320
The Ascending of the Way	326
Tabula Rasa	328
Exorcism Rites	330
The Fundamentals	331
Exorcism of the Air	332
For a Place	332
For a Person	333
Exorcism of the Water	335
For a Place	335
For a Person	336
Exorcism of the Earth	338
For a Place	338
For a Person	339
Exorcism of the Fire	341
For a Place	341
For a Person	343
Conjuration of the Fall	345
Exorcism of the Divisions in the Mind	347
"That was tasty rabbit..."	348
Lapidary Magick	349
Ring of the Red Queen	350
Ring of the Guardian	352
Ring of Transmigration	353
Herbal Formulary	354
Medium of Transference	355
Greater Transference	356
Conjuration of Desire	357
Relaxation	358
Vision/Trance	358
Projection Awareness	358
Astral Vision	359
Projection	359
Healing Projection	359
Hang-Over Relief	360
Speedy Relief	360
Elemental Blends	360
Earthy Blend	360
Watery Blend	360
Airy Blend	360
Fiery Blend	360
Gender Blends	361
Masculini-tea	361
Femini-tea	361
Planetary Blends	362
Sun	362
Mars	362
Moon	362
Jupiter	362
Mercury	362
Saturn	362
Venus	362
Miscellaneous Blends	363
Exorcism Blend	363
Protection Blend	363

- Longevi-Tea..................363
- Immortali-tea..................363
- Luck & Wishes..................364
- Purification..................364

Sex Magick..................365
- Masturbation..................366
- The Great Rite..................368
- To Give Birth..................370
  - The Summoning of a Human Soul Into Incarnation:......371

Art of the Mind..................373
- To Evoke Truth..................374
- To Forget..................375
- The Greater Seal of the Mind..................376
- To Restore the Mind..................377

Time Magick..................378
- The Clock..................379
  - Setting the Clock..................379
  - Uses of the Clock..................379
  - Layering the Clock..................379
  - The Source Clock..................379
- Sphere of Premonition..................380
- Conjuration of The Greater Seal of Twelve..................381

Blades of the Art..................386
- Conjuration of the Blade of Oblivion..................387

Bibliography..................388
- General Reference..................389
- Right Hand Path..................389
- Crowley..................389
- Witchcraft..................389
- Taoism..................390
- Left Hand Path..................390
- Divination..................390
- Alchemy..................390
- Regional..................391
- Grimoire Texts..................391

Appendix..................392
- Of Locations..................393
- Circles..................395
- Cleansing..................396
- Banishing..................397
- Incense..................398
- Candles..................399
- Music..................400
- Of Stones & Metals..................401
- Blades of the Arts..................402
- Working the Rites..................403
- The Great Art..................403
- Paths of Practice..................405
  - Folk Magick..................405
  - Shamanism..................406
  - Witchcraft..................406
  - Necromancy..................407
  - Sorcery..................408
  - High Magick..................409
  - Demonic Magick..................410
  - Chaos Magick..................410
- Tools: A Primer..................411
- On Consecration of Tools..................412
- Cleansing Charged Tools..................414
  - Exercises..................415
- Blades of the Art..................416
- The Chalice..................416
- The Wands of the Art..................416
- Skull of the Art..................416
- Box of Containment..................418
- Seal of Perpetual Creation..................420
- Seals of the Gates..................422
  - Gate of the Earth..................422
  - Gate of the Darkness..................422
  - Gate of Light..................423
  - Gate of the Summer Solstice..................423
- Creation of Tools..................424
  - Exercises for Tool Creation..................426

Creation of the Grimoire..................427

General Mechanics

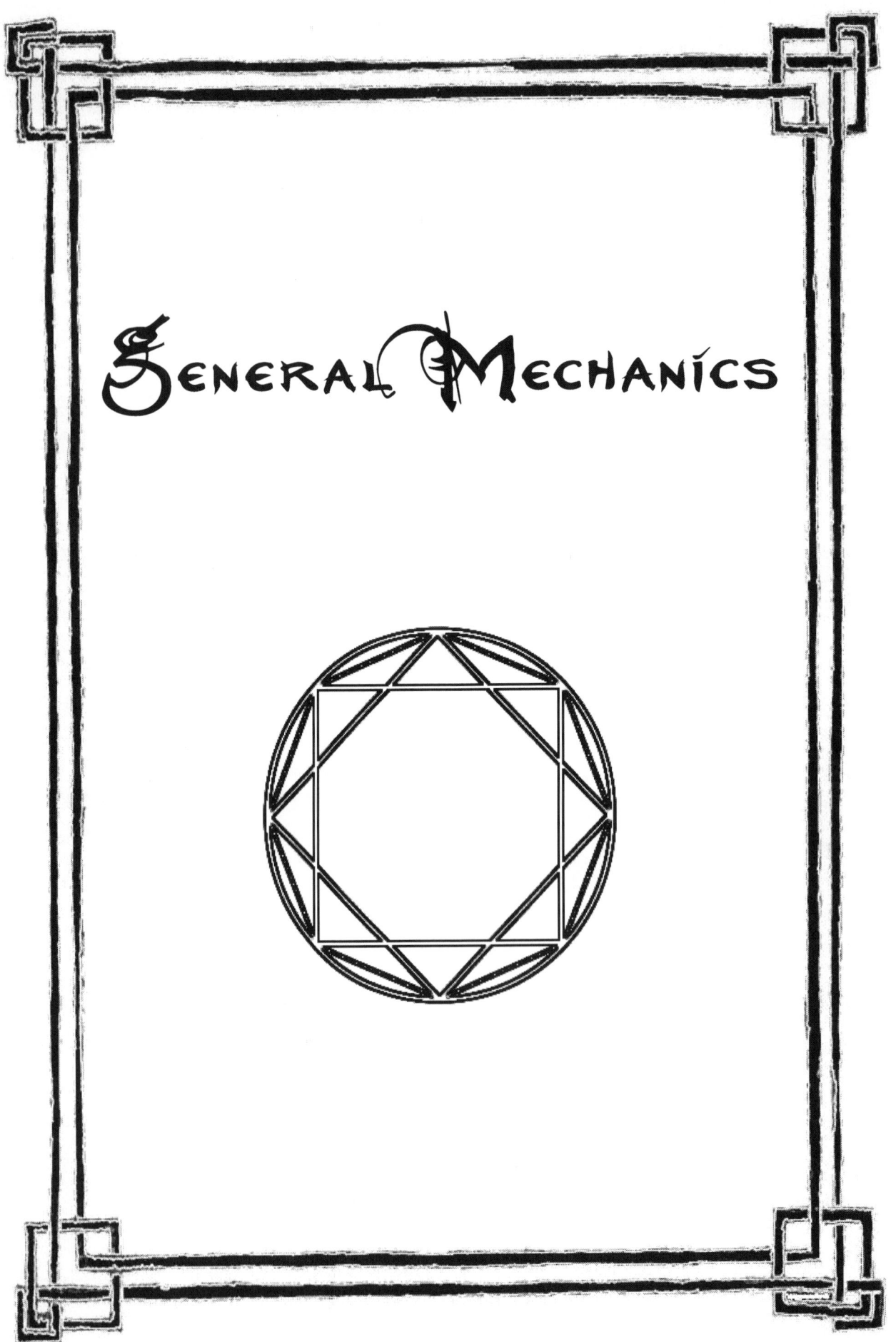

Key of Creation

The foundations of this viewpoint are simple to understand, but their application applies to all things found within the inner nature of this work. To apply these practices is to study and develop oneself in accord with their foundation, their source of being.

It can be described simply as a path that brings all together for the balance of the soul. To find the roots of this idea would mean to study all of the major religions of the Eastern and Western traditions. To look towards history to find out ways to develop the future of our world. This work expresses the following concepts:

- *Everything has the potential to become as a god-force, a Kami.*

- *The elements of the natural world and the celestial environment are what connect our internal power to the external manifestation*

- *Within every person there is a search for the inner world to unite with the outer world. When this is done, the being is complete.*

- *The elements have their places; the stars in theirs. The gods have the ceremonies which they respond to, however, they must be developed and worked in a way that pushes one's own understanding of what it is to be Divine.*

Magick, under this title, is the definition of natural forces which have no other classification so they shall be called magick. It is something you become part of, you do it to evolve, to be different. Every aspect of yourself will change. Other authors on the subject have said the same thing. I did not believe them, until I looked back. It is what you do to command the forces of nature, the price you have to pay is your transformation, more often than not. Having to live through what you wish for, what you cause to be, what you evoke of the raw threads of creation, this is generally the greatest price of all the works. These are no simple acts of a Wiccan willy-nilly wishing to cause something to occur by lighting a candle in the dark spaces. These are not so complicated as to have to have the pomp and pretension of the rhetoric passed generation to generation. However they can be, depending on how the depth of dedication.

In the following works, the journey will take you through the mechanical application of how I have used these works. You might find yourself breaking away from any system contained, which is the point. The spells, rituals, and arrays contained there are application of the material here.

If in your studies and doings you have come across it, great. If you have not, great, have the blank slate use it as a paperweight. I have been in correspondence with people from various traditions, and those who are of the "scholarly" approach to the grimoire tradition find flaw in the work, because it does not hold to dogma. To them it lacks cohesion, protocol for being in contact with the greater forces in a safe manner. That is the point of that work. It is hands-on; you need no introduction to the work.

In the course of this work, I will discuss and show the diagrams through what I feel show the best manifestation of these ideas. How the order of the strata of the cosmos flows in union with the elements of nature, brings for the greater whole of understanding to be able to work from levels akin to the gods. If we are to become gods, why not have the power at our fingertips to be as they?

We, who are at the beginning of this, have only a need to look at the foundations. Where does it begin? What manner does it serve? Do we instead work from the terrestrial level of power upwards to the divine, or do we start with the farthest reaching aspects of self to the greater mind of the whole collective? To you, I say that we will begin outside of ourselves. As much of the work, if not all of the work, is contained within our minds and personal gnosis. We must have a foundation that is external to the body, if we would build the inner world of the microcosm accordingly. What is our cosmos, according to this view point?

I say it resembles this diagram, in as best of terms as I can attempt to show at one time.

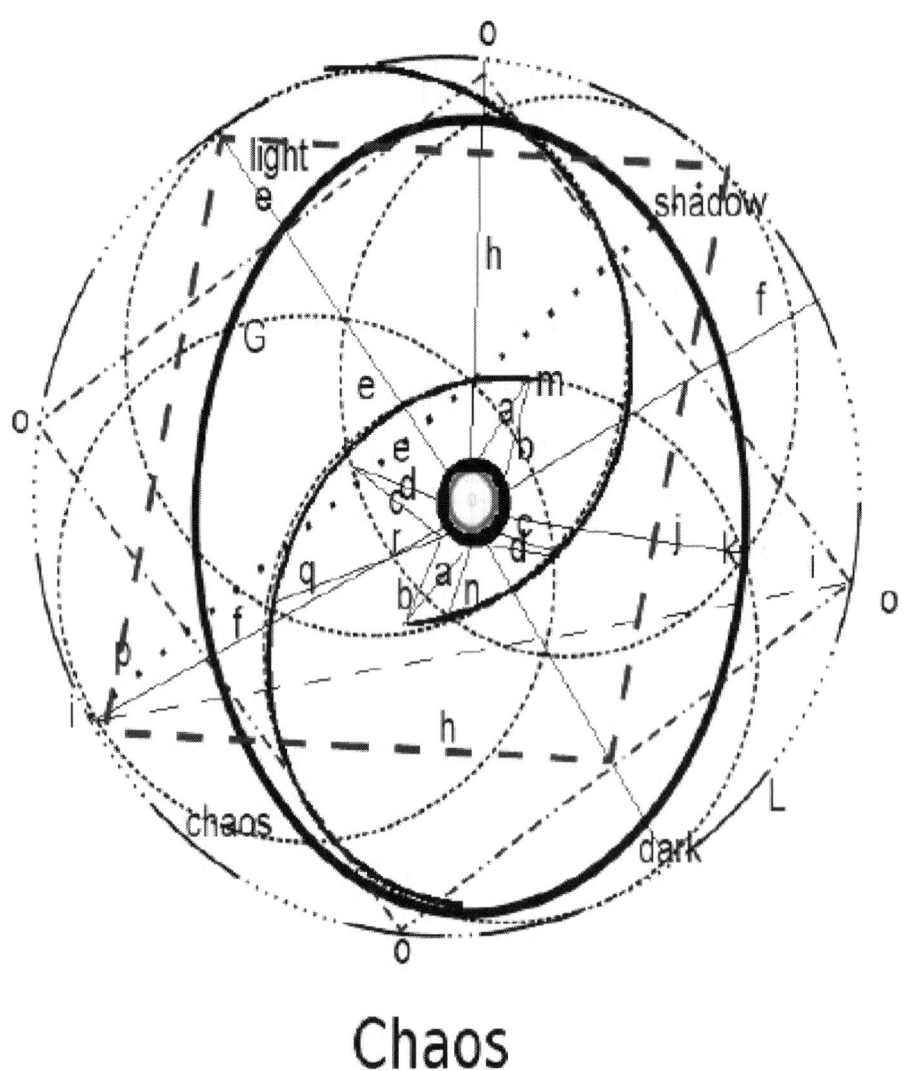

Chaos

Let us begin to define that structure we see. It is the central point of the 8, supported by the 4x2 the elements of the physical world with the alchemical nature of each; earth, air, fire, water, hot, wet, dry, cold. When we manipulate the physical state of a thing, it is based on the interaction of those states with one another. We then expand outwards from the central point. The broken grey around this circle is left there to represent the shell of the natural world, in which we find ourselves. The best way to put it might be: the veil that divides the world of the physical from the mental world of gnosis, which is the foundation of all the mechanics. Based on this, we have the establishment of the system presented henceforth as the working model on which my work is founded.

(a) are the lines connecting to the currents of light and dark,

(b) lines are the connection between the light and dark currents to the microcosm within the realm of 8. It is through the night and the gates thereof that the initiate becomes able to enter into the world's exterior.

(c) and **(d)** are then the reactions between the dark world and the shadow worlds, as well as the shadow worlds and the light worlds.

(e) connects the worlds of light and dark. Just like there is also a line which connect the source of the shadow to the source of the chaos, the shadow realms and the chaos realms also encircle the sphere of eight. Each of these are the four primal sources. The line **(e)** is the link of the gates between the space of all of the overlap of these spheres.

(f) is the rotational f-e motion, the horizontal axis.

(G) is the inner circle were in is the rotation of our cosmological sphere the sphere of time as it is where our consciousness exists.

(h) is the line of influence from the 0 elements.

(i) is the integration of gates/seals on the relation of the source and the sphere of **L**.

(j) the line of action from point k to the seal of 8 when conjuring from that point.

(k) is the inner degree of the circle **G** the sphere of time interacts and opens a gate from the darkness into the shadow realms.

(L) is the cosmos as it is connected to the mind of all.

(m) is the point of interaction from the sphere of darkness with the choices of **a/b** unto the sphere of eight. In the relation to the spheres in their rotation, and their place in between the gates of the four,

(0) is one of the origin source/primal elements. As there are four, there are four represented as the seals which balance the world structure. **(i)** interacts with all the elements. from this source.

(n) is the point of interaction of the light and shadow within the dark overlap with chaos.

(p) is the connection of the chaos to the shadow, like e connects the dark and light. q is the relationship between a gate/seal/portal and the plane of creation from the seal of creation of the 8 point array.

(r) is the gate of interaction between the points **(q)**, **(f)** and the shadow realms upon its relationship with the point of origin in the center.

The red trapezoid is the means of conjuration as it is related into the sphere of creation.

The blue is the relation to the primal elements

The External Chaos is the classical "Space" of potential energy of manifestation.

From this, you build the correspondences to opening any sphere within any realm within in the spheres of creation with application of the 8 primal element array. You have what is the source currents of light, dark, chaos, shadows. The neutral point between the others. In this method, the shadow has been given its separate position as neither belonging wholly to the light or wholly to the dark; it is the grey line which has been the source of many hours of lamentation to try and explain why it would be considered a point of the source.

What we have above it is the elemental viewpoint of the world. What we then must do, is say, "Alright, that is how the elemental world interacts with the physical." So, when you have done this, say that every point of interaction occurs 8 times over. So you have the above points, in a superstructure of the light nature of things, the dark nature of things, the living nature of things, the dead nature of all things, you have the mind of all things, and the spirit that the things contain. You have the Time in which those things exist, and you have the chaos/potential those things have by their relationship with the other seven aspects of the source current.

When I say source current, I mean exactly that; a part of the integral essence of a thing which when removed causes that thing to cease to be what it is. Essence manipulation has been the root of what I seek to accomplish by the nature of this work. To change the very center of the thing, so that the change is absolute, the manifestation is precise. All things contain the following:

Light - both in the physics sense of the term as the reflective quality of the matter as it has come together, and the alchemical highest possible attribute of becoming like unto the gold.

Dark - both in physics as the density, as well as its basest alchemical attribute.

Mind - the mind of a thing is its nature, its interaction with creation on the level of manifestation according the nature which it is compelled to be. Ex : Flames are hot, and consume wood; the mind would be the will of consumption where it reaches for the next material to draw into itself.

Life - while it exists with a light and dark nature, as well as a with a mind, there is a life about it; an energy of the natural which gives it form, and action which can also be expressed as the union of these things in terms of the Spirit quality.

Death - when the energy of the thing when it changes form and ceases to be alive in the form it was in before hand. The thing in question can undergo change many times through fixed points, and little deaths of what was, so that it can grow to become.

Spirit - the behavior of a thing, its actions, its sympathy and antipathy to the things which come to the interaction with creation as a whole. What is determined by its natural proclivities of being; what does it like? What doesn't it like? What does it hope for? What does it fear? These are the spirit of a thing.

Time - these are the consecutive moments that exist when the thing aforementioned interacts with the environment, in the manner of behavior, it is the line of connection that carries it from one perceivable moment to the next.

Chaos - the potential of a thing, the evolutionary process, the rising of a thing to any challenge it comes across, or the collapsing of it, under pressures which cause its death of form, to be made or broken by its essence.

Within every singular force in creation, be it a rock, a metal, a god, a plant, a demon, a spirit, fae, or some egregore/critter, there are these sources that make up its essence. If you manipulate these threads common within all things, you can command the very essence of the gods, or man itself. You need not work with the dogmatic approaches of so many people in the past, and current times who feel that the power of creation is the domain of a god-force alone.

It is this that is the key of foundation of creation. So that any work, so long as you address the point of manifestation, you have the necessary familiarity to duplicate any force, or experience in creation via your chosen outlet of manifestation. The trick from here is to understand this idea, integrate this idea, and work it like a whore works a street corner.

Every word, every thought right on up to the great moving balls of gas, fire & ice in the sky have each of these 8 aspects. Without them, you have no creation, you have no foundation on which the essence of a thing can exist. In terms of philosophy, we will build upon the platonic elemental world, and we embrace physics and its understanding, with all the quantum theory on the physical. However, the essence of the thing is what to focus on. What is inside the zero point current that exists in all things, the DNA of DNA? I would say it is to my understanding of particulates in creation the above. I am sure someone else out there down the line will have their own take. Wonderful, by all means, pick it apart, tear it down, but at least you are pushing beyond the current status quo. Challenge the "what is," make it become the greater possible result. But with that said, it is the creation magicks, the elemental, shadow manipulation, and other works in which the essence of the physical world, is bent to the will.

Key of the Arrays

It's time to discuss the methods of manifestation as they apply to the work. We have the external world view, which gives the form to the foundation. Now let's get it to where we can use it.

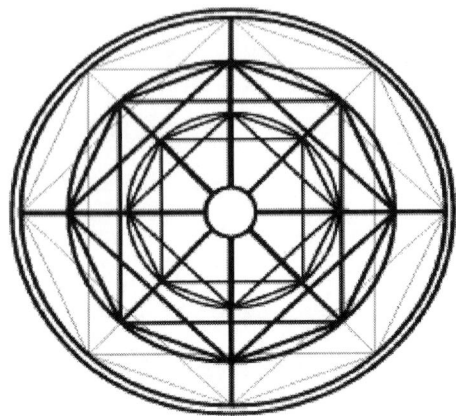

This compatible view of the central points of the above discussion on the 8 sources of creation; 8 planetary forces of the Moon, Sun, Mercury, Venus, Mars, Jupiter, Saturn, and Uranus; and the four physical elements and their alchemical states of being.

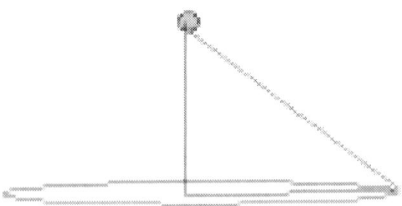

When you have the point of origin from the center of the circle of manifestation, the external energy which you would draw or entrain to your array of manifestation. It establishes the angles of flow and action, within the space of the array. Every level of gate that is opened, every force that is conjured by this method, acts as the point of generation for the overall impact of the current. Like when one draws down a divine force, celestial force there is the external energy current that exists, and then its duplicate is drawn upon the earth or in the ritual area, and is aligned with and pulled downwards towards earth in a vacuum chamber such as to allow the energetic particles that flow through the void to not be disrupted by the terrestrial current.

So with this, you have the singular point of origin to which the central point is meant to pull. When you begin opening the gates within the array for any of the eight, or however many you are working with, there becomes many points of interactions. For a primary 8 point array like this:

So you have the gate of the 8 with the central focus point. When you look at it from the viewpoint of manifestation you have the following energetic structure :

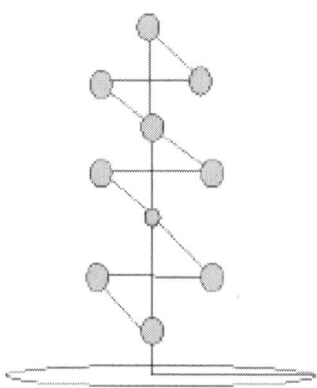

It is the Central point and its correspondence to a point of origin for the energy to be manipulated. Where the eight supporting points come in, to balance the flow of the central current. If you use the seals of the source, they will balance out the current to be.

The Source Seals

Ascribing sigils to the work is for the purpose of giving us a focus for the construct that we would have as the balancing agents in the work. Things that make up the essence for manifestation.

With the points of balance within the array already mentioned, we then move onto each of the angles, and corners and angles that flow.

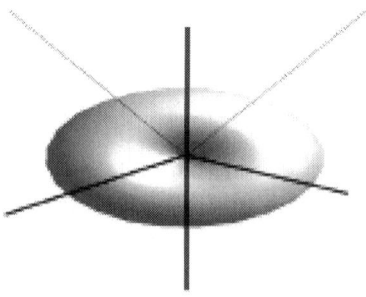

The angles and their corners have specific flow patterns; each creates a bubble, a doughnut through which the energy of the seal is created and pulled through its rotation, being affected by the frequency of the "source current".

In this manner, we progress into the understanding of the seal's elements. From here, it helps our case in understanding the rotations of the elements within the array of manifestation.

With this form we have an understanding of the flow and interaction of the 8 points along the outer ring, and their interactions within the greater whole of the work, bound up as a single current. We look at its 3 dimensional rotation through the use of modern computer programs to discern the nature of the energy flow within the space. Lines, and outside the lines focus things away. The obtuse angles focus the energy of the outer side of the lines to the inner sides of the lines towards the center point. Each point on the edges then forms a sphere of currents which all become unified into the current one is working on.

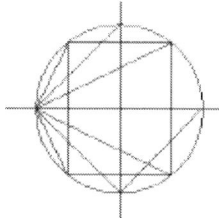

These angles will flow around the space within the circle, and condense at the center point. The energy will flow around the lines spiraling inwards, and upwards to the horizon from the point of origin, which is the center of the array. However, subtleties exist within the array that any point on the outer edge will encompass the energy represented either in element, or word, or symbol to the currents that it is supposed to represent. These spheres will condense themselves down and form the foundations of the array. Each of these secondary points will be the channels for the current in a repeating pattern. At every horizon point there will be another circle formed equivalent to the circle which originates. This means that from the floor, at equal distance from the radius to the center point, there will be from the center point above.

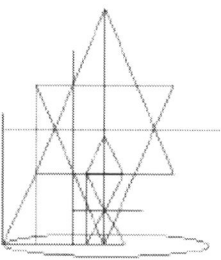

These flattened points of the array expand upwards creating the column into the dimensions. All of these will be in equal measurements to the array on which it was created.

r - radius of C1
r + r = C2
C2 = height of the new circle.

The more current put into the generation of these patterns, the greater the channel becomes. If the astral plane sits just about 9.8 feet above the ground, then a circle of 9.8 meters in diameter will reach directly into it at its center point. Using the Pythagorean theorem of $a^2 + b^2 = c^2$, we are able to determine that the center point for the primary point of manifestation is about 4.5 meters, which puts it roughly inline with the central heart Chakra/pranic root. With a secondary invocation/charge to these forces, the circle will then double on itself forming the third array and successfully reach exponentially its target, if one wanted to work on a plane.

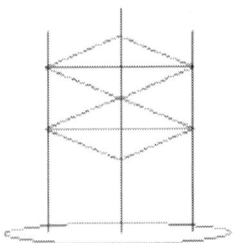

The figure to the right is a bigger view of the circle of image above. However in this one, the horizon point is where the array begins again. Exponentially going inwards, and outwards based on the level of the charge that has been channeled into the array down the center columns. So if a single charge of the current creates at least 3 equal circles to the original, then that would be a channel of current 13 feet in the air. Thus continuing exponentially.

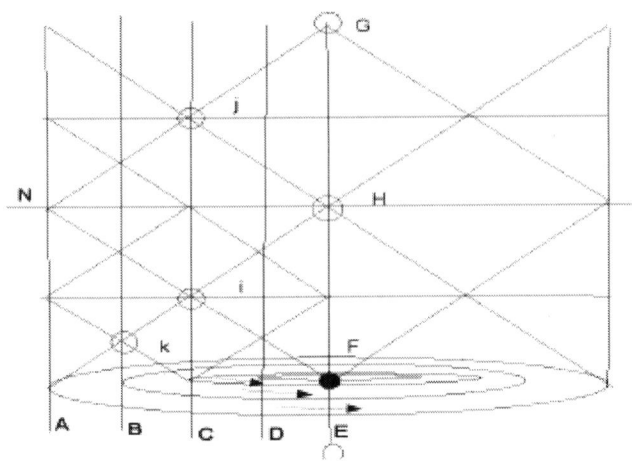

On the chart above the circles correspond to the differing circles drawn within a circle.
    The Lines:
        A – First current
        B – Secondary current
        C – Tertiary current
        D – Fourth current
        E – Fifth current from the plane of origin or the union between the circle and the plane/force of desire.

It is to be assumed in this description that the circle is a standard one, with the four circles layered within themselves at equal distance.
    The Points:
        (F) – Event Horizon
        (G) – Total Output
        (M) = $a^2 + b^2 = c^2$ of the distance between (A) and (F)
        (A) + (B) + (C) + (D) +(E) = energy input
        (A+B) + (B+C) +(C+D) + (D+ E) = total energy = (F)
        A(F) +B(F)+C(F)+D(F)+E(F) = total output =(G)

The sphere below the F represents the plane that the circle sits upon. As one is using the grounding currents to create a new sphere of working.

Plane N is equal distance from point (F) to point (H)

This is the point of the reflection and creation of the new planar scope as per the ratio of the initial of the distance between line (A) and line (B) have their point of reflections.

Plane (G) sits is the equal distance from the circle (A) to (F)

It is within the construction of these forces that gives the individual the standpoint of the link between this plane and other planes. The frequencies generated herein are the construct of the initial method. It then should be assumed that the energies are all flowing with the rotation of the space, layering and overlapping each other. That there becomes a solidification of the frequencies upon their union at point (F), which then creates the gate from the point of desire, to the plane of origin. In this moment you develop a "gate" effect between what you would achieve through connecting to the powers that the circle is meant to become one with and the other energies you are going to be working with in this space.

Using this sort of current is expanding upon the space, and creates a void space within the points as the currents overlay and build within each other, creating a frequency that resonates within the soul and outwards with the macrocosm, in a sense creating a form of "Zero Point". This then can transcend through to the illusory manifestations that you would have caused through creating separate planes for manifestation.

Exercises for Manifestation

Find old spells/ceremonies/rituals that you have written or found and identify the Formula of Manifestation found within them. Note any observance of them not being successful or missing parts of the formula if the spell was not successful.

Compare then 3 spells written from other sources that you have found not containing all parts of the formula of manifestation.

Write corrections of the spells for the 3 you have found that were "incomplete" and finish them to make them possible for manifestation. Explain the breakdowns, and why you chose to add the parts you did.

Write one new spell using the format discussed in class and identify its parts. Scan or render using software for graphic design any images, or links to the imagery required for the use of the spell.

If you have never used spells or written them down previously, then you are to find 3 spells written by other sources and identify those parts that correspond to the format, but you must cite your sources properly.

Key of the Word

Words have a frequency, power, and meaning. There is a way to use them which can inspire people, hurt people, and command the very essences of creation. From what we have available to us. There are a vast number of books available to us on how to use power via speech to work the world around us. It is not for the faint of heart. However, in my work there is a difference to the usage of words. There are roots to every word. As discussed, everything, even words, have their 8 sources to the essence.

So, with this understanding, I will attribute this key to a friend of mine from before I began traveling. His name we shall call Raven, as that is how he was known to me. He had a method of magick that was the unspoken syllable. This syllable moved with all syllables around the mind of the body in what he would term the library. From this library, with gesture, those syllables are pulled together to form barbaric word constructs. It is those word constructs which vibrate and call out to the spirit of the root.

That spirit of the root is bound by the root of the word, through the power of every time that word is spoken. So with my work, instead of using gesture to command the raw forces of creation, you use the array to support the frequency of movement by the way the energy. Words for us, are spirits. Every word spoken, every syllable that rolls across the tongue.

> *It* - becomes all things which have no gender, all inanimate things which ever have been, all nameless forces which have attribute but no conceivable name.
> Common names of deity - being spelled by modern tongue or not give to the archetypal spirit that would command it.
> Uncommon names are created and made by the random assorted application of letters and phrasing from different cultures.

If, in your work, you must come up with a name to command a spirit by, then you would have to either force the spirit into giving you its name, or you bind it by a force which is unable to be broken, and then command its name be remade to what you were doing. Scrabble tiles thrown in a runic method over an array. Whichever ones feel and flow right together, that are closest to the center. Clockwise for the more angelic critters, counter clockwise for the less savory.

> The words are manifestations of united source current
> The syllables have a spirit which affects the whole
> The words have a spirit in the memory of all who have said them
> There is a time in which is given life to the meaning behind the words
> The inner world thinks of the words, and draws in its association
> The outer world speaks the word into the world

All of these together form the power of a single spoken word. When you string these along in sentences and paragraphs, you build the web by which the words you use can command, and conjure the forces of creation.

So unlike words on a page which are infinite in their saying, to have read them you have put time into them, into their spirit. It is our words which will outlive us. So, the frequency of them must be embraced with that level of reverence. Command the word, the very heart of every sound, and you have the power that is in the spoken conjuration.

When you couple this with the unspoken mind that you have, the little voice in your head that reads or thinks more or less when you are absorbed in a conversation. When you do this and you speak with both minds as one, you are bridging the inner world, and the outer world, by your thought, your voice, your will, the very time in which you have here on this rock, to become and change towards something greater.

However, you are taking time of your own life away with every word you speak. It's one more closer to the end of your existence as meat. From this, it takes on the perspective that for every act of magick that you do, for every spell that you would work, you are taking from your time line what is otherwise time that could be spent doing something else. So you are putting your very life on the balance of every single conjuration you have spoken. Every word is a syllable that resonates with every single thing you are, and the potential you have to be more.

Key of Perceptive Mythogeography

I mention this under perception, because it comes with the territory. In planar work there is a lapse of perceptions; it is good to be aware of distance/time ratios when working with entities on their own planes of existence.

We will say that a conjuration of a living person, roughly 2000 miles apart, takes about 6 minutes for the summons to take effect, as well as a dismissal.

Likewise, we can say that the average time spent in meditation or projection to, say, the Infernal realm of Hell, equates to roughly 6 hours there for every hour spent here on earth, so if you were to project for a night of 6 hours on earth, it equates to a full 36 hours spent in Hell.

So we will say that for every hour on earth, in the realms of the Seelie and the Unseelie planes the distortion is about a day. So if you were to project for 8 hours you have spent 8 days off world.

Planes of the underworld time goes slower, more like a month for every 5 hours.

Planes of the heavenly hosts, angels and the like do so at about the same dilation as their underworld counterparts. Being more removed from the earth spheres, farther than the celestial worlds of the archetypes, puts things at about hour on the angelic planes is about 2 days earth time; slow moving sense of time.

The Archetypal world also moves in a different space of perception on earth time, with the space of an hour, can be anywhere from a day there, to 3-6 months depending on what place you are visiting.

This difference in time should be something that you should explore for yourself. You should be aware of its impact on your timing here on earth. If you are doing the gate ceremonies, or creating a space that is moved from different places, it's like you're folding time and traveling within the slower moments of the passing seconds. It's in those places where you find the greatest distance of space the farther away you move from the earth sphere.

I read once that there is a thing called mythic time, and earth time. It's a lot in the same way that there is the life of a rock which is billions of years, compared to a tree which is hundreds, compared to a human which is about 80-100 years; then you have a cat, or a dog which is ten or twenty years. Time moves differently depending on what it is you're doing. If you can gauge your perception and project your will to those times when you seek manifestation, then in ritual, a moment can seem like an hour, and an hour can seem like you were reading off a conjuration for a week. So again, it is good to be aware that you can also in the course of later workings directly with the source current, in the period of time, it's about your perception which allows you to work more directly with it, or less directly with it. Really nasty things, like speeding up a persons 100 years of life into a single moment, or really useful things, like cultivation of skill in working with an energy current can be done in the space of a few hours and it will be like one has lived for 1000 years. Granted, it's all about perception. The more you know and work with how time flows, the more you will be able to observe its tides and ebbs.

In the space of life, there is also blending of the conscious mind with the unconscious mind in perceptive ways. Many of these ways are common to say deja vu, or what could be considered a precognitive vision. In these points there is a fixed time. *Dr Who* is a better reference for fixed time. However, we will say that it is exactly that; where all moments in space/time/perception have landed you in a circumstance for whatever reason, and you have to figure out where the hell you have to go from there.

Your choices, actions, all of it, have led you to that point in your line. That reflection of understanding that you have of that is when you reflect on your marker. When you can sit down rationally and calmly and understand what it is. Know that in that moment, you are exactly where you need to be, feel what you need to feel, and observe it, so where ever it is, life or creation will take you. Whatever the form you are to manifest in next will be. Those memories, those points of fixed time are etched in your time line of existence. So that in those moments when you would overcome your personal limitations on temporal awareness, you can look back, and see those defining moments. Those moments in your history which make you cringe, those which make you cry of joy or immense sorrow. They are the periods where your spirit is determined through the actions you have taken after.

So, you say to me, "Does that mean that I can look back on my time line and alter it?" Perhaps with the right system in place, the right spirit of conjuration that would allow you to force the events of a situation in the past to be altered. However, it does mean that you can alter the spirit of a situation to come. It's much easier to affect the probability using fixed outcomes. If you have the fixed event in mind say for a job, place to live, or experience you would have brought about. It is much easier to work on altering the perception of how those events will come to be by pulling the right strings. However, if you are looking to manipulate perceptive outcomes on a larger scale, say cities, or towns or regions, whatever, then you have their possible times, all the possible events that come together, all the little choices that you have to modify. The focus and awareness it takes to modify just one external perception is enough to pack it in, and say, "I'm not doing that shit." In extreme cases, however, it's dependent on the needs.

If you are going to be undertaking a ritual that will recreate a person's perception of an event, a person, or a thing, and removing all of the things associated with it, this requires timing, care and an exact intent on the thing being changed. I have only ever done this work when it has been requested of me, generally. The perception on a person and the removal of immediate pain, is that there can be growth past it.

It is all perception; how the energy flows, the ratio of time distortion across geographic lines, to the impact of time and moments in time upon your life as you read this. As with the true fashion of this work, it starts with the exterior dimensions and works its way into the center of the very person. How we exist and move within a perception of time. This discussion, then, can only be concluded by someone who goes out and experiences it, seeks it out, and finds the similarity of these words to their own findings.

Key of Union

It is the marriage of a thing, the bond of a thing, the pact of the thing which defines itself as a married union, a bond of alliance. It is a mutual thing done as a way to ensure the development of both parties. It is an act of passion, or promise, that is set into a stone of commitment. Generally there is a symbol of such bonds; rings are great examples of this. There are also rings that can be charged with properties to bring out the natures of the persons to be balanced.

The principal to maintain with the understanding of a union, is about uniting the two separate forces resident with the two bodies, to find their best or worst attributes and make them whole and balanced by the nature of the relationship. If there is a union done, and there is not one bringing strength to the weak parts of the other. With what is found within the grimoire, there are elemental unions, perspective union, and soul binding works. These works are examples of things which can be done with people, between people, spirits and people, and spirits with spirits. The point of this key is that it is a spiritual bond more so than the legal one our societies are concerned with. They are about the development of people and spirits through an agreement of partnership.

There are things to consider when you embark on a union. With people, it can be that their natures are more watery, airy, fiery, earthy, etc. However, with spirits, it's about finding the balance that you seek within the soul of the other creature. Spirit unions have a way of bridging the planes. Some of the old rules are still in place with some of the creatures that you find in creation. Legends of the fae expanding their number through unions with humans. Legends of gods marrying the mortals to create their offspring. Angels with humans to create the Nephilim. These unions still occur.

Incarnating in the human world also occurs through the use of unions to create suitable progeny. If you bind with a spirit, you then have the plane which created the spirit flowing through you, so you likewise become of that plane. Sometimes we find examples of this in history, where those who bond become fae, or djinn, or demons. They can then become suitable carriers in the blood to be able to bring these spirits into our world. The ritual of Great Rite, is exactly the way of consummation of such unions. The Rite is designed to be the controlled possession of a lover, to copulate to orgasm both the human and the spirit. There are many ways this can be done, but generally in a few days of the union, around the days of the full moon are best. However, these things will have a way to work out naturally.

After orgasm, the possession is generally lifted, as the energy from the act has been spent. From this, if you are able, you can stack the spell with the one to summon a soul into human form. Then you can copulate with the spirit, and bring through the blood and union any spirit in creation into living flesh. Even if it is an elemental egregore, it can be birthed in this manner. There are plenty of things with which one can do as far as taking on spirit lovers, demon lovers and the like. However, a word of caution should be said that intercourse with such spirits is not safe, as it exposes every single current that exists within the mind and psyche. This can be used against the one who is interacting with the spirit to cause madness, insanity, or death. If it is encroaching upon madness or it has occurred and there is a secondary spirit that has taken possession of the host then that inflicting spirit shall need to be removed. This can be accomplished by use of a ceremony of exorcism matching or polar opposite of the essence of the spirit.

Key of the Funerary Arts

It's a common stretch to take it as a divorce in being from the state of life. It is a primary one which embodies the truest sense of the source of death. It is the period of change. The rituals of such are what helps the living accept the state of change in the person who has departed. However, funerary rituals can also be used to cause great and sweeping change in a situation. There have been hundreds, if not thousands, of examples provided by the use of the Catholic, Christian, Egyptian and other funerary rites to cause both death of people, spirits and things which affect the human condition. Like with the exorcism, there can be effects on both things, people and spirits. However, the work which is included in the Grimoire is focused on the human rites of passing. Modification of the ceremonies is possible to be focused on an issue one would have be put to rest.

There can be many forms which you will need to take the time to examine as part of the greater work in your progression. From this point on, everything can be found in their respective sections.

Creation Magick

Of Creation

In the discourse of cosmology, the student is referred to religious models and assorted other dogmatic structures of the world view and creation. It's a matter of choosing what model, what structure, works best for your world view. What is presented here is my version of the cosmos. One model is not better than any other., to a Warlock there is the Singular Collective and everything else is an extension of it. You must develop or adopt your own model that you think the world operates by, and live your life by those views. You must build your world view on your own form your understanding. Here is an example of what the cosmos would be like based on the mechanics of this text. To have greatest success from the outset, your view must encompass everything: from the smallest grain of sand, to the trash in the alley behind an apartment complex in the city which is on the other side of the world from where you sit. You must be aware of all of it, you must be able to feel the currents and work with them. This is the simple part of building one's own system of cosmology. The method for doing this is not more or less complicated than breaking down every religious text and scientific model that has ever been.

From this we begin simply. In the beginning, or what I consider to be the beginning, there was a source, a singularity of current. The Singular Collective became conscious. Not to say that this is god, as this force did not have consciousness. Then something happened, be it of its own development or because it had a will. This source developed into active and passive sides. In four variations this manifests. One side of the source is light, this is the active current. One side is dark, receptive. One side is a shadow is the balanced between the two, the other way which is where the development only reached so far, is the chaotic blending of the active and passive sides into overtly active yet neutral currents. Like the shadow which is more receptive than active, the chaotic current is more active than receptive. Yet these quasi aspects balance out and form sources of their own from the singularity in its dark and passive aspect, and the light, active aspect. Each aspect revolves as its own currents exist as a fractal spiraling, into and out of some center point, eternally. This is the same on every level of creation. Not a single way, but not many ways. Always both, as it manifests, and the thing which manifests because of it.

From this source fractal, which operates on all planes, in all ways, we have then the elemental forces. The earth, the air, the fire, the watery forces which manifest in both light, dark and shadowy, and chaotic forms. Every world, made up of gases or rocks, all of these energies this "Chi" current which flows through all things. Thus forging the planets, the physical planets, and the stars as we see them on this world. We have now the four elements, originating in their aspects of dark, light, and neutral currents. Every element has an active side, and a passive one. Forth from the elemental qualities we develop along the threads to the planetary forces, each having their own energy, a spirit to contribute to the flows of creation. Justice, love, transformation, war, death, power, knowledge, wisdom, and so on. These manifest as the elemental energy coalesces into the different forms. Each theme such as wisdom, war, transformation, manifests through the interaction and reception of each of the elements. It is through their blending that these structures exist. As these interact with each other they form the celestial spheres, these planetary and starry bodies in the night sky. Every star, planet, and celestial body has a spirit.

The primal elements which flow directly from the source current do not necessarily have a spirit of their own, but do have a natural will which is to exist in their form, to flow to their natural capacities. It is this will which when interacting with the other elements formed the planets, and the celestial "wills" which can be called down through sympathy or antipathy from the micro and macrocosm, the inner and outer worlds, so to speak. It is this "celestial will" we shall say, that gives us the spirit of the planet. If the primal elemental force of fire interacts with the water, and a little more air, then earth it generates a celestial force. This can of course be called on to fill a certain end that one would desire to work with, and evoke, summon, conjure with, or invoke into their lives. This is a macro cosmic scale of creation. The outer world as it were. It is from these celestial wills that angelic forces, or lighter force, or active forces are created and can be worked with. For example, calling down the angelic hosts or the active forces from the lighter perspective. There are also the darker, or receptive currents of this outer world which manifest themselves as the darkness, the spirits and the demons. These forces by the nature of their existence are not just passive, nor just active, but they are all a blend of some element, or perspective which created them. So you have a demon which is made of up neutral currents, active currents, and passive currents which is made of fire, water, earth and airy currents. Same with the angelic currents. It's not like one is strictly composed of fire, composed of water, composed of air, receptive, active, neutral or chaotic.

Those beings are what were considered the ancients, those of the first time. Each are made of their source currents, those spiritual beings which are the ancestral currents of all "spiritual life". These ancient forces are not subject to those things which come later. The ancient spiritual forces are raw and unyielding, they are not subject to constructs of good and evil. Like the water, they exist because that is their purpose.

To be the spirit of their source, to be the hand, body, and will of the thing which created it. By its creation it is. Forth from this comes their interactions with the other elements, and the other currents which are present within the worlds. In mythology the Titans would be the children of the ancient forces. Only Gaia and Cosmos are named as the progenitors of creation. From the structure of nature this view is limited and incorrect.

There were enough to equal the manifestation of the triumvirate and abstracts in pure form. These are the First creation. The dragons, if you will. From the draconian forces of creation, come the Second creation. These forces are the offspring of the interacting between the source, the primal forces, birthed the elemental forces, the natural forces and the celestial beings in their origins. Designation of things like night, day, twilight, justice, order, chaos. These are the offspring's of the first creation. For those clever readers, yes chaos is listed twice. It's one of those abstracts which has no place in one or the other, belonging really to its own development and evolutionary path. But such is the nature of chaos.

From the Third creation which is the resultant intermingling with the Forces of the second creation with the subdivisions, from war comes vengeance, murder, hatred, death. This would be the respective children of the Titans. The "elder gods" in Sumeria. The Marduk, child of Enki who split the Dragon Tiamat and made from its flesh the earth and the sky, mixing its blood with the earth to give life to the human race. However humanity comes a bit further down the line from where we are at, so we will get back to this later. We now have the "elder gods" those forces which are the actions of what is considered acts of love, justice, war, peace, hope, kindness, music, fertility, knowledge, wisdom, magick, and every other "theme" that manifests itself on the worlds. From these we have the offspring of the elementals which were made of the second creation. As a natural progression from source, the Chi developed in its own ways, each force independent and growing, these mindless forces have thus developed a mind.

Fire wants to burn and reaches beyond itself to consume those things which sustain it. Water flows regardless of its obstacles, carving out the rock itself. The Air will cut through it, the Earth will move through it. There however was not a peaceful progression. To serve the Ancients, the "Elder Gods" as they shall be called were created from the "will" of the Ancients.

If the Ancients were the hands of the Perspectives, then the Elders were the fingers of those hands. They in turn created of their will, what would be considered the powers, the angelic forces, which served the will of their creator; like their will served the will of the things which created them all the way back to the source. These "angelic forces" are of the Fourth creation. These forces served the will of the Gods which created them, these forces became more specialized, and the Elder Gods expanded their numbers, creating other things within creation. The microbial organisms, the animal life. These things extended as part of the Fourth creation. Not as we see them, know them and touch them today, but in a form that they did come to be. However forth from this model, we have that Chaotic current, which evolved separately as chaos, especially primal chaos is wont to do. The mentality of "I wonder what would happen if..." Chaos of course created of itself, and by its own will from the beginning; it always creates, destroys and comes and creates again. When chaos by this time has intermixed into the very natures of the Elder gods, and thus into their creations, a Mind was created in each creation. The evolutionary tracks had begun. But with the mind also came the reflections of the forces which were not of the original source. War was created. When War came, it caused the first fall.

For lack of a better term, the Primal source of conflict came about and the balance was not maintained. This then caused the Ancients to war with their sources, the forces which they were created by, the balance of the the passive, active, balanced, and chaotic currents within creation. When this occurred, the fractals became different, and the energy warped, evolving and mutating. The children take over for their parents. The Elder gods warred with the Ancients, causing the second fall. When the Elder gods formed the councils and covenants with each other, they established the roles of hours in the days, and the nature of how creation shall be. The Fates were created of this, as was Death, to ensure the tide of everything. Then the Fourth creation which were the children of the Elder gods, observed this behavior and warred with their parents. They cast them out of their places and took upon themselves their thrones, their orders, their powers.

Humanity was created in what could be a Sixth creation: as the elder gods created the angelic powers, they created the animal lives, and thus the Human, or what is considered to be a fleshy body. They established the rules and laws by which the operations of things such as incarnation, death, and every fundamental existence of the world was to be observed by. However the elder races didn't bestow to the Fourth and Fifth creation the capacities to create outside of their own existence. They can propagate the planes which were already created by the Elder gods and the Ancients with themselves and their offspring. The mixing of the blood of the ancient force of Tiamat with the elemental sand to create life, gave a connection to the primal currents to man, or the Sixth creation. Giving them, in a sense, equal footing with the Elder Gods and those who develop their energies as such, as the Ancients themselves, because of the inherited spark of the divine which is on this plane "human". A flesh body which contains the spiritual body. With the spirits of the Fourth creation, they lacking the abilities to command the power of creation themselves, they found ways of "breeding" and entering and gaining for themselves some capacity of creation.

The Nephilim were an example of this. When the Elder gods observed this, they considered such beings corruption of the powers, and wiped them off the face of the earth. This caused their powers, which they created to serve them, to rebel. Like they did to those powers which created them, having against the ancients to establish such orders which the ancients had no want for. Thank Chaos. This caused the Third Fall. Those Elder gods, died, or fell into the shadows like the Ancient ones they "dethroned" or imprisoned. They become the infernal forces, they became the things which lurked in places that "angels" fear to tread. The angelic hosts have fought wars between themselves for the order of the worlds, they have given us prophets, and called demonic the things which come before them. They build themselves up as the elder gods which created them, lacking the connections to the source currents. Fighting pointless wars, and causing endless crusades against the things which existed before them. This is where we sit. Between them and their petty fighting. We can break it down further into what has occurred as a resultant of each fall. With every fall, new things occur, new things take the place of old things. Yet those things which are swept up under the carpet are also preserved by said carpet.

Even in the deepest abyss there exists places where the Ancients have survived, not having to adapt, but they still exist. Elder gods have created planes where the old covenants and councils still exist and operate. Not necessarily the "hell planes" and "abyssal places" but more like the shadow planes, things which exist in neither one nor the other. You have to be a part of those places in order to get into them. Elder Gods can pass through because they are both, but the specialized forces of the angelic/demonic hosts which have arisen, lack said capacities.

Man, because of the connections to these forces, has the capacity to fit into the places between, where the ancients and elder gods still exist; and develop his desires, and create the powers to serve him, albeit in a more limited capacity. Man is also able to create such things as demons, elementals, and thought form servitors out of the primal elements. This is because of our connections to the primal source through the blood, thus the nature of our existence. We do not need religion, we do not need gods, because we are of them already, we have within us the spark of the divine. We only need to awaken it. Yet this being said it is not the only option open to those forces which exist, in these in-between places. As the Elder gods established the laws of nature, those created afterward and cannot violate the laws of nature, and become limited to the capacities of such things. To be flesh is to gain for a lifetime the means to awaken the blood, and thus the spirit, a force like unto the Ancients; allowing for said lifetime, and even possibly after, the capacity to become like the force which it aligns with.

The law of incarnation states that possession only secures a line for the spirit to come into the body at a later date for those "demons/angels" which would have their will done on this plane. The Christ concept is such a force, where the body must become "impregnated" before hand, to be able to "host" the spirit which established the bloodline. It doesn't matter if the body which was "possessed" was physical or not but that it was a body, which had to impregnate flesh in order to create. Thus showing the studious that said body, is from the Fourth creation. Elder gods were the "gates" to the Ancient ones, just as the Ancient ones are the gates to their sources, and the primal elements in each perspective. It is accepted by authors such as Sepharial, who wrote the Manual of Occultism in the early 1900s, that there are classes of souls. These souls can choose to take possession of the body, and are divides into different classifications. Those mentioned by Sepharial are described hence, but his are found incomplete to this model. The Human Soul, which is the once born soul, the empty vessels of man which live, eat, breed and die like any animal and is thus the animal soul, the thing which moves the body towards life breath, but doesn't give any form to life other than the fact that it lives. The Elemental Soul which cause the different personalities atop the animal soul, giving to the life through personality. There are also Celestial Souls which come and go of their own accord, lacking a body, they take one up temporarily. This commonly occurs in the forms of possessions, and those possessions can occur to various ends. Temporarily or for entire life times, there will be more discussion of the types of souls which are found in human form later.

It is only the capacity of the body which we are discussing at this point. The world as it stands now, and what it has the capacity to become is the time we are in now. The Seventh creation as it were, as humanity, in fleshy form, made of material the worlds become as we create them. It is remarkable what significance such consciousness might bring, it doesn't matter the perception of the "intelligences" from other star systems, or from angelic or even demonic hosts. But that humanity develops its own nature, capacity to create, thus allowing anything which takes up the humanoid form to have a chance to create a world or worlds of their own. Becoming like unto the gods, and the primal forces if they wish it, through the development of their connections with the currents, those essences which flow through nature. Good or evil are perceptions, or points of view, and what is written here is not "truth" in the literal sense. It is because this is what I have observed to be true for my own working when needing to make use of a cosmological system. At least this is one that I have created to make it a personal experience in working with it.

This is neither right nor wrong, but a point of view which allows an understanding of the mechanical natures in things, as well as a chance to study the themes of these great falls, and know the lesser works of the celestial forces. For me it's about being able to recognize which soul is doing what function, and how that function can be employed to better suit the needs I have in my own life/existence. If I have the capacity to be like the Ancient ones, then I have within me the route to become one with the source current, and unify out those aspects of my essence which will allow me to develop as I see fit.

The Sources of the Singularity

Each of the sources can be found in the other. Every aspect has all eight aspects within them. As would be expected of ways to discuss the singularity. The singularity has no name, no form, yet it is all forms, all names. We can name the things which extend from it. We can give reference to it, and what we can discuss so as to better learn its nature. For those of my readers who say "why?" I say, so that we can discuss something greater than our understanding. If you disagree, then it's not your place to be able to discuss the things beyond your own frog pond.

In the beginning all is dark, all is formless and it is void. If this sounds familiar it is because this is where everything begins. In some manner or another. It is without form, it is post-natal. It is the oldest of the old currents, and it is in this world is the space between spaces. The area where the Yin current, can manifest. It is both action in formation, and it is self propagating, needing nothing to sustain it. It is this aspect which is why I am classifying this as a source of the singularity. Because it is a way to discuss the singularity. We, being human, require point of reference to begin or enter into dialog about the forces that we observe. So we will do what we can, describe the faces, using the best terms at our disposal.

The light is the force which takes all into itself, and penetrates through all things. Destroying that which is not of itself. As a fire consumes the wood. It devours, it seeks to propagate as it in its own way is an unnatural elemental of being non-sustaining origin. Relying on external forces to cause it to survive. We have the supreme Yang principal, the generative. The formative. The world of being, causation and matter. All things which are stirred to formation. Yang in its most active form pulling the dark matter into shape.

The animation principal which we have discussed through this work as the means by which the spirit of life is injected within the body which we have discussed the methods to create. Primal Chi is the foundation of what is classified as "Life"; *anima*, the living breath, whatever path you follow this is the breath that infuses the vital aspects of those whose bodies are crafted of the elements. The essence can be described as all the elements that combine emotion, with the chemical process that exists as development, growth, moving, learning, doing, action. All things which exist, have a life or some impact of action, or motion.

To the Taoists, this principal is the post-natal Chi, and the Yang principal of growth, moving, and motion. It is what stirs the dark, creative principals into action and union of its elemental quality. The vital awareness which gives the motion to the organs to set about their functions, the trees to self replicate. We can describe the nature surrounding these attributes of the source of life, as we can only classify these things towards their relation to other things. It is a face of the Singular Collective. We can say these things are "life-like" and so we describe what would be falling into that category would be considered to be a "life" source.

The union of the physical world and the spiritual world has a point of interaction, and through this interaction, it gives us action. This action causes perceptions. This perception breeds a concept of what was past actions, current action, and the next possible outcome. It is this case which we see time, as time is a side effect of life. However, it is perception. Anything which can be perceived falls under the purview of a sense of time. So if you eliminate perceptions of a thing, you have something which exists in a timeless space. Schrodinger's cat exists simultaneously dead and alive at the same time, as there is nothing to perceive what it is within that box. There exists time, and timelessness, and scales and measures by which we can observe what would be the time, the changing and motions. We have the mythological time frames of the gods, titans, and the elder spirits which move as great strokes over hundreds of thousands of ages, we have the terrestrial time which lapses billions of years as the rocks, trees, and waterways flow. We have the animal life which has set spans of time it interacts upon this earth. We have mythic time which we call the time before creation, which also can overlap with the time-frame of the gods, or at least what would be described as gods. As the manifestation of the singularity and its awareness. When the singularity came forth to realize itself, we have the beginning of "time". From this we move into death, the state of return, change, transformation and desiccation.

What is transformed goes through an act of death. It is the change in one state, the mutation of it, from one state of matter to another. One process of awareness to another. One moment to the next. Every second we live, we die, under the motion of time. One hour changes and our senses of life are taken, changed if ever so slightly, and we have this death. We have the death of bodies, celestial, terrestrial, animal, mineral. All things change, under the influences of time. And it is through this that the singularity manifests through its interaction with the mind. To which we give our awareness of remembering the history.

We have our history, the record of what occurred before, from the geological histories of minerals, to the rings of trees which show how much life they lived within a time, and period of changes that they endured. It gives us a record of what occurred. A means by which we can process what we experience as some marker. Some means by which we are able to learn, develop and push beyond the limitations found within nature, by integrating our ability with a controllable sense of death, to force the change necessary to push us along what ever path we walk. From this change we remember, and it is our memory which gives rise to a sense of a spirit.

A body which exists beyond the temporal, the ability of a mind to collect the memories of the ageless, and store them in an undying form. This spirit is the animating force that pulls together the emotions of the mind, the recollections of the time, and the impact of life and death upon the body. It shapes how we behave, how we understand what will occur next, and how we can balance. What we view as ourselves, our "will" within the connection to the singularity. So from the spirit of the thing, it begins to move us in ways which will shift how we interact. When we become shaped by our memory we then can choose to move within the elemental properties. These properties are the Light and the Dark. So it is that the sources circle themselves all are contained within the other, as they form the structure of the singularity.

When we make conjuration, of any force of the sources, we do so manipulating one or all of each of these. They exist in all actions, regardless of focused intent or not. If you observe the active and passive nature, the actions it has within perception and its perceived changes, as well as the record of those changes upon it, and its ability to persist in such a away as to seemingly impact the world around it. Then you have witnessed the sources at play in the thing. These are the fundamental building blocks of what we can think of to be the singularity in action. So when you draw a circle of 8 divisions.

Chaos is counted as one of the sources, as it is the means by which it acts as though pulled by some unknown destiny. It is the unknowable aspect of the singularity. It's paradox in manifestation. What should not exist but does anyway. Simply because it chooses to make it manifest. The singularity loves paradox, it encourages it and will not fight if a paradox occurs. It is the other things which cannot place such a paradox where they rebel against it and cause the break down of it, until nothing remains, yet it's in the unknowable outcomes where chaos finds its place. What comes about because of its nature, its internal, unknown drive. If it works, it works, if it doesn't it doesn't, and if it shouldn't yet does, or if it should yet doesn't. Is all under the dominion of this source.
Say for example this:

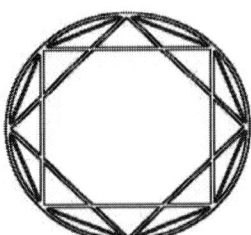

We have the origin point in the center as the blank spot. It is this from which the 8 come forth. It is the point of origin and the circle which unites the sources as they manifest. The outer band which unites the sources of 8 we have the effect of the whole upon the thing. The division of the current, into its pieces as to focus on the manipulation of the internal nature. Or the drawing of the internal nature out, or upon what we desire to effect within this construct.

When you make such a creation out of a controllable media such as a blooded ink, herbal condenser, elemental compound, you give the external stimuli needed to cause something to stir in the free energy. In manipulating the 8 sides of a thing, you enter into the shifting of its connection to the singularity. With this connection manipulated you can control to extent the effects it has upon the environment if you can include what would be its body, mind, spirit, so as to unite all separate aspects to the sources on their own. This would be the pinnacle seal of all works contained herein. It can cause generation of the media externally, from the internal array. All arrays herein contained can be used with this as the boundary point to it. As this is designed to unite the seals of the 8, the 8 trigrams of the post-natal and the 8 trigrams of the prenatal Chi flow. From this you can inscribe the seals of the 8 planets, and from these planets you can extract the forces of the elements, and the natures you would command by balancing them to the void space.

Made of condensers which by their nature are extensions of the sources, because they have experienced a life, death, mind, spirit, darkness, light, time, and chaos. You will have a perfect root to pull upon the sources of the singularity and thereby be able to tap directly into the singularity in a stable manner so as to make manifest any force which you require. Be it a formative current, or destructive current. Be it a banishing of current, or a drawing of current. It is in the interplay of what kind of working you seek to manifest that your will will draw upon this external media and pull from within you, your own connection to the singularity, and you and your environment will be changed for the interactions.

Western magicks is based on pulling in celestial alignments to set about the pathways for manifestation. Calling upon the 8 planets to do what it is you would have them do. Eastern magicks is about pulling them up from inside the body, to give them manifestations through the use of meditation, words, thoughts, vibratory sounds to unify the body to bring about the desired result. With this, you will be able to blend the living catalyst of the external world, to the internal world. By identifying the sources of the thing which you would manipulate or influence. Through this work, when you add a living catalyst to the seal or array, you would be able to pull forth its connection to the singularity, and it is this current, or free energy, which you will effectively shift, or change dependent on what it is you need to work with.

To make use of such an array, you will need the catalyst with which to connect yourself to the external media. In this, blood works the best. If you haven't got blood, then use the blood substitute condenser which duplicates blood. However, this requires use of a component which originates from the subject of influence. You need to be able conjure, channel, or make manifest your work from within this array point. As it is in this space that the current you would have make manifest comes forth. When you can place an element of yourself within the work, using frequencies of generation. Words of power, loaded with intent that blends the inner world, and causes motion to the external world. You give yourself an "altar" where the worlds meet. You build the rifts, you cause the veils between time-space to fold, or move according to what it is you need, or require.

The Sources and the Planets

Now the thing is, we all understand there are planets, the big balls in the sky of gasses and what have you. In this point of the discussions and workings, we have to come to a union of what is presented here with all of your already accessible information from other texts/experiences. When I refer in this work to a source, it is an indivisible essence from which one thing is inexorably a foundation to one side of its nature. Like breaking apart a conception and finding within it, the *light, dark, mind, spirit, life, death, time, chaos* which exists in some degree in all things. Such promise does this line of correspondence hold, that it will give nicely to coming volumes of work based on such things.

All of these center around the earth. As we are based here and the sources flow about the systems of the cosmos; things like the meaning and nature of the cosmological structure of Ptolemy, which placed the sun at the universal center. In our work, the earth is central. From there we now have the modern science and development of the accurate physical bodies. It is their spiritual property we seek to understand. Not the relation of their locations in space. This is so because we are here, our spirits are tethered here, so what we have in the placement of these concepts around the center point is based on perception and degree.

Light, Dark, Life, and Death are variations of degree. Based on these degrees, we can gauge what it is to be dark, or light. What constitutes being of the living and being of the dead. Two of these being the inner universe, two of them being the Outer Universe in balance.

Mind, Soul, Time, Chaos are variations on Perception. These give us the measure of actions, and reactions within the degree of experiences granted us by those things of light, darkness, life and death. Again, here we have the inner universe, and the outer universe in balance.

We give the concepts anchor points, we give the degree of our perceptions, and we can alter the environments based on the fluid states of the macro and microcosmic worlds. From these correspondences we are then free to create, re-create from our own connections to the singularity. From here we have no need of gods, demons, or what have you, other than as the aspects of the self/singularity in unison. Sure, they exist as fragmentation out in the void/space; it is up to us whether or not to employ such things in our work.

There really is no importance in the motion of the bodies of the stars in relation to our work. However, there is a path they that take us on. *Sun, Mercury, Mars, Venus, Jupiter, Saturn, Uranus, Neptune,* shall thus be *Light, Spirit, Mind, Life, Time, Death, Chaos, Darkness.*

If you follow this path in the setting and the opening of the seals, your work will be able to duplicate the flow of those as they exist within the body as the Chakra points, as well. From this, you can have a working structure inside as well as outside, in unison with both the Ptolemaic view, and the Copernican structures. The reason we do not use the earth, is that we are located on the earth. If we originated off world, and we were on a distant planetary body, then we would have to have correspondence as such. However, since we are here, we have not the need. Yet, if you combine the elemental seals with the 8 seals, you will be able to create a terrestrial tether point. So your projection can be anchored to the creative earth energies.

The moon, in its relation to the earth, is used as opposed to the earth directly as a staging ground. It is a barren wasteland of frozen, dead rock. However, it is close enough for the body to project to, and deal then with the super-celestial currents. So, if you use the moon as your central point of origin, you will have the 4 seals of the earth that surround the moon seal as the foundations of the staging ground. In this manner, you must tie the earth's stability to the lunar gate, and from there, use the conjurations to pull forth the power of the celestial bodies.

As they will manifest on a void-space plane, there is no risk of impact upon the physical unless that is where your aims are directed. From this, you can use lunar components to tether planes of creation to the moon, and the ley lines of the earth can be tied accordingly to create a path to the plane of creation. In this way, you can tie the physical component to the moon and cosmological currents.

The Source Seals

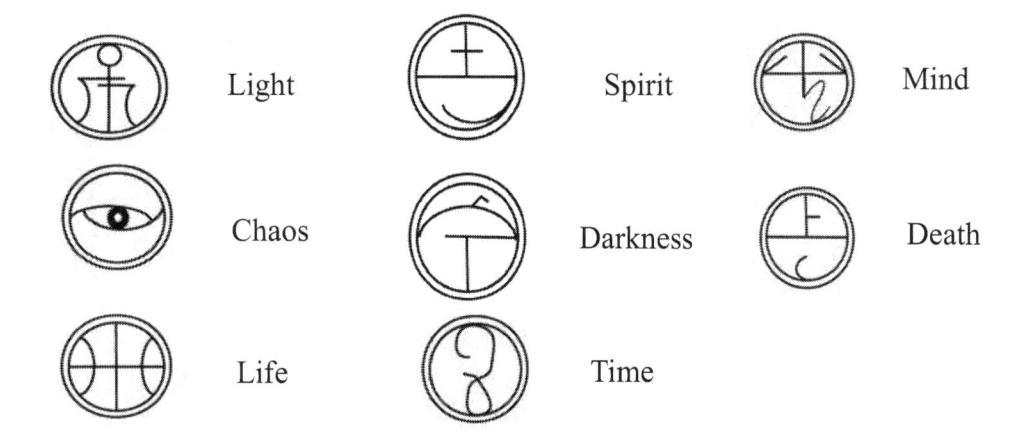

- Light
- Spirit
- Mind
- Chaos
- Darkness
- Death
- Life
- Time

Conjuration of the Sources :

That which is not of the living
That which is neither of the dead
That which never has been born
That which shall never die
Hear now my words and thoughts
Be summoned forth
The gateway is ready
Seal of the source of (name the source)
Be opened before me and the raw power be brought forth!

Watchtowers

So if you read that, and your first thought was the movie **The Craft**, good for you. Based on ideas that there are guardian forces at the cardinal points so as to protect the entry and exits in works dealing with celestial magicks. With *Transcendental Magic* by Levi, the author gives methods to call upon the gates of the north, south, east, and west. In Simon's *Necronomicon,* he gives the process for summoning a Watcher, the egregore to protect the Magus, as the familiar spirit. Our work has covered creating familiars, and so we do not need to discuss one such as this. However, in that work, there is also the calling of the quarters, drawing in the ancient lords of the directions.

Gates such as the north, south, east and west provide a two way street based on when they are used. There is some archetypal force that you create to set at the pathway to keep things that would otherwise be safely outside and away from you, your work etc. These are done to provide a safety net to your consciousness. If you open the flood gates of energy and everything associated with that power, sources comes through, then you're in for a ride of spirits, demons, energy, angels, gods etc. Creating points of barrier such as the Watchtowers will allow you to control what comes in and out of your work space. You do this in order to keep any unwanted energy from disrupting your work, or harming you when your psyche is most vulnerable during open acts of creation.

What most of the books out there don't tell you is that these gates are also a safeguard for the doings on this plane. If you summon gates of the four directions, and their sub-directions NW, SW, NE, SE, then you have also placed limitations on what you can achieve in this plane. So when you use the conjurations of the terrestrial gates you are limiting what energy will flow from your point of working into the natural world, preventing any unnecessary bleed-off. In this work, it is a good thing, as we have discussed how to channel directly from the singularity without any of the safety measures that traditions give to us. This protects our environments when we are working, so as not to cause any unneeded shifts in the consciousness of those around where we work. If they become influenced by ebbs and tides of energy, then it will push regions out of balance. It also protects you from being harmed directly by the celestial power, as it forces the power to come through the gate to you, filtering in what you want. So it's good on both sides of the gate, coating your work in the energy of the plane of origin.

When it comes to the protections of a Watchtower, you have to consider what it is that will be your guardian force. If you summon up monsters to watch the gates, you must be more monstrous in order to keep them in line, and force them to do their job. If you are using holy angels to do so, you must be more godly in order to keep them in line. However, if you're keeping true to the work, and you would be using the direct sources of creation to do the thing, it will be easy to craft of the direct sources you would use. You could even set it up so that the sources of the 8 act as the gates of the terrestrial current in each of the directions when you are working source magicks.

For every Chakra point, for every union of planetary force to that point, we have the manifestation of the macro cosmological structure manifest in miniature. If you have done the R.o.T., it will allow you greater ease when working these forces. In the beginning, while you adjust to having all the currents of the 7 spheres passing through your body in such a balanced force, there are then divisions to those points. You will experience the split within your body, your psyche. You will come face to face with what are the spheres of the Tree of Life, and the spheres of the Shells of Knowledge. You must come to balance with these forces. Working path structure, and following along in the *Liber IHVH* by Michael Ford, is a good way to connect with the shells, their demons, and their monsters.

Through using the Watchtower idea, to protect yourself, you can face them one on one. It is why the old grimoires demanded no less then a months space, or years of training the mind of the plucky Magus when working the great gates. In our work, by circumventing the need for the structure of waiting, you will align within yourself through your strength of will alone, in its connection to your nature, and how you would manifest yourself through your ritualized death and rebirth.

This way, you can maintain a rational control over your environment. Through the assimilation of the god-form you become united with the demonic, and the celestial aspects resident within your own psyche. From here, you pull with full awareness your magicks of the celestial pantheons, or infernal pantheons according to how far you develop. While you haven't endured the years of path working that say a witch, or shaman has, and lack the awareness of the singularity that the Warlock has, it gives you a means by which to face yourself. Facing your inner worlds, where your body then becomes host to the creative power of the universe. After the working of the Rite of Transformation, you have at your disposal the internal energy structure to affect the external world in greater capacity. So, you must use gates to affect the physical world. As your origin energy is celestial, it doesn't translate all too well upon the physical. There needs to be a frequency shift in order to achieve the level of control and finesse required by working magicks.

You must in this way build your cosmological correspondences. In doing the building of a world view, it gives you point of reference to draw those forces from. When you use the gates, you send the energy through them to affect the physical world. So in this way, you must find your own connections to the gates of the directions, and use them as you would see fit. It is through these gates, that the super-celestial current, and the energies of the macrocosm can affect the greater external environments in which we live, so as to cause the desired outcomes. This is the point when all of our internal workings become the external free energy manipulation, achieving greater working beyond what ordinary conceptions of the Watchtowers would be. Move to the seal of the elements. From those seals, you have the means to open the gates of the elemental force directly upon this plane, so as to achieve a non-limited effect.

The Tower of the Arts

The body upon an array, or using the art of the soul, can form the pillar of the Ars. From this, one is able to call upon the forces of the earth and the heaven.

The tower represents the soul's current and its place in creation. From the use of this conjuration, one calls upon all they are, from the deepest points within their essence that connects to the source. The tower manifests as the order which they are a part of.

The different orders of the soul are infinite, because every one has a different current flowing through them. Some of the orders are:

Elemental:
    Earth, Air, Fire, Water, Ice, etc.

Celestial:
    Planets, Stars, Angelic, Demonic

Temporal:
    Hours, Zodiac, Day, Night, Twilight

Primordial:
    Gods, Titans, Chaos, Raw Elements

The orders of the soul are what determines the kinds of Art one is most familiar with naturally. For some it is Dark Fire, some it is Ice, some it is Water, others Air. It's not just about alignment with the elements, but also a point of the celestial hierarchy where one has more influence over the spirits of that particular element, and a kinship with them.

This would allow them the ability to become like a lord or Priest of some force, but all in all, it is that they become the living extension of the plane. As such you become the living conduit of that energy.

Call of the Tower

Source of the Deep Eternal
Nameless beyond Name
Creator of the All
I do hold thee in my center
I hold the keys to the gates of creation
I open the gates of the earthbound
I open the gates of the celestial
The pillar of my soul, Come Forth!

Anchoring of the Spirit

In the body, there exists organs which keep the animal life in the body, and those which keep the spiritual life in the body. The Prana/Chi current which is the same moving force upwards and downwards in the eternal spiral. The energy forms itself along the Kundalini path, the dragon current within the body. Flowing through the Chakras and outwards into the organism, then into greater worlds. The world within the body is considered as the microcosm, the cosmos in small form. Forming itself from the egg and sperm, separation of cells and DNA into the organism, then when it is "born," becoming alive. Thus, it is a depiction of each stage of the greater world. This is just a significant fact if you hold that the cosmological viewpoints in the previous pages are in fact what you chose. If you have not yet chosen, it can be an observation which is not going to be discussed further. The microcosmic world within the body operates much like this world, with the 7 major centers, and the minor currents within each flowing a different form of energy, while the body itself is sustained both by chemical reactions and the subatomic energies which form all matter.

Everything is made up of particles, and energies, and wave lengths, you know then that such things are altered by vibrations. Thus, you have the vibrations of the inner organs and the Chakra points. You then have the worlds within, meeting the outer worlds. Breath, sight, hearing, reproduction, evacuation, touch, taste. There are 9 gates from which one can observe this world. 7 major energy centers of the Crown, Third Eye, Throat, Heart, Solar Plexus, Navel, Root. The minor Chakra of the fingers, the palms, the wrists, the elbows, the shoulders, the hips, the knees, the ankle, the heel, the center of the foot, the toes. The smaller points represent what is to be considered as the stars, each having their current which contributes to the nature of the body, its well being or ill. To work within this inner world, you must awaken and know each internal current and how it responds under the different perspectives.

Now comes into the concept of the mind which is within the body. The body itself will breathe, relieve itself, hear, see, taste, and feel every day, if the energy which allowed for such things to be remains a constant. This is what is considered by some to be the animal mind - the instinctual process where breath needs not be taken on thought, but is done automatically. The primal will which pushes the body to survive. That gross animal, infernal mind which operates not on concepts of justice, honor, or loyalty, but seeks only to survive to continue those breaths. That which connects the body to the natural forces in the creative scheme. Next comes the mortal mind, the elemental waking mind. That which gives the color to our perceptions allowing us to act on our primal or supernal natures, responding to the "angelic" active or the "demonic" passive or shadow situation as it presents itself in the chaos which is this life. From this we have our supernal mind, which originates the ultimate actions we choose. Those actions which are neither belonging to ourselves or the thing being acted upon, but in the action awakening that elder god force which that action represents.

To bridge the world of the mortal and the immortal, we venture into discourse of the body, to understand that its mechanics hold the fundamental materials required to bridge worlds and create. As above, so below, as below, so above. These things are known. We must remember and think to apply when it comes down to our physical work with these concepts.

Vibrations travel through even the deepest void. So too does the thought within the space of the mind, vibrating out the will to the outer world. Ancient sages from different paths have understood that it is these vibrations which allow the manipulation of the physical world. These perceived thoughts from other star systems, communicating messages, and methodology have origins both in the internal world, and the external world.

When the life leaves the body, it is a shock to the spirit to be stuck in the corpse for an extended amount of time. To return it puts it in a state of panic, especially since the body though dead and sensations of pain have ceased, still retains an internal awareness. To abuse the corpse is to damage the spirit. Those collections of memory, pain, longing, and loss are the things which tie the spirit to a location. It is the feelings of love, completion, and peace that set the spirit free from its body.

Use this with the creation of nodes, to create land spirits, use this with symbols of power to create mass archetypal anthropomorphic personifications.

Created Beings

When you create a being, you expand part of yourself. I read a story in my youth about the Buddhists who require the initiate to go to a secluded cave and draw out the mandala of the summoning for their egregore. It was required that they had to see this thing, that they had to converse with it, that they had to understand what it was. Being an emanation of their own mind, a perception to their inner nature in their subconscious mind, the monk returns to his master and tells him what he finds. It is only after months does he come to the above realization about it being a manifestation of Self. Like unto the demons and angels we have described in above chapters, how they are the outer world's perception in relation to the area of the brain which cause their manifestation in the lives of those who call them forth or experience those thoughts. Here we take now a greater study into these things which the mind creates.

To be successful at achieving manifestations of the subconscious that act independently from the will of the mage to do the required tasks, is a sure sign of mastery. But above all, caution is suggested, because your thought forms will turn against you; what they were designed to do will return in on themselves, in on you, if you do not dispatch the energy used to pull them into manifestation. Chaos magick has some excellent techniques for working with the raw energy required to make use of successful thought forms and servitors. What we will do however is take and expand upon these concepts. In the coming passages we will have explored recreation of the living soul within someone, as well as creating a servitor from the raw physical remnants of animals and creatures whose traits are desirable in having in the resulting creation. But now we must progress into the creation of those angels and demons. To make them spiritually corporeal in order to achieve the utmost control over your environment. When you master your demons through path-working of the inverse tree, you will be able to command your demons at will, and you will be able to send them out with remarkable results.

Creation of the Elementary

In the Judiaica it's the Golem, in the Buddhist it's the Egreore, to the alchemist it's the Homunculus, to the witch it's the Familiar, to the Ceremonial Wizard it's the Servitor. These are the things which we create to serve our needs, to be independently made from our own mind so as to act as the guardians, seekers, and other aids to our practices.

Made of the elements, these are the forces we weave to serve us, and watch over us when we sleep. They can be for defense, or for offense depending on the need, and they shouldn't be allowed to gain independence unless you have the skills to maintain the construct.

When it comes to creation of a construct like this, there are steps required across all religions and paths of study. They are easy to understand and simple to apply.

Basic construction:

1) Give it a Place to reside.
   This can be a symbol you draw in ink, paint, or carve into wood. It can be a stone, or object.

2) Give it a task.
   This is the most important part of your construct, why it functions and how.

3) Give it a name.
   Giving it a name ties it to the task you are setting it for, as well as binding it to service. If you know the name of the thing, you know its spirit, and can command it as such.

4) Give it a lifespan.
   When making a servant of this nature, it is important to give these things a limit; common sources say that one month is enough time, from full moon to full moon. They can be recreated every span or as need requires.

5) Give it a form.
   It is good when you are calling it by name that you can focus of its form, be it animal, or some hybrid of forms like the Sphinx. It doesn't matter the form you use, but if you can attach to it some image of how you would make it, then you can conjure it forth at will.

6) Give it a source of energy.
   This is a good way to ensure that it has a controlled life span, by being able to deprive it of a needed energy source. This source can be a drop of blood on the seal, it can be a special blend of incense, it can be a rain storm or it can be a candle flame. It all depends on what you would create it to do, and what element the element of its creation is.

When you would embark upon the creation of the elemental, you should have a good idea why you need this form. It is always handy to have one on hand when you are working on a ceremony, as it can take the place of having a "watcher" or "guardian" of the circle. If you can make it yourself, then you know you can trust it to do the job. Assuming that it is suitable to defend your space when you are working.

I have found that in the beginning studies of ceremonial arts, there are a lot of seals and symbols for spirits, but this is the best way to practice the arts of evocations when you have "created" one yourself; that way you won't be subjected to the adverse side effects from attempting to conjure something up out of the Goetia or something like that. In regards to the elemental forces, they are excellent to have as constructs that are the "spirit" in the seal of the element, so when you would call upon the power of the elemental forces you can channel that current through this medium externally from your own body, giving you the extra focus for directing the other currents present in the work.

When creating something, you can also use physical items from animals, or nature to "tie" it to that element or form. Such things can be a piece of bark from a tree of power, or a leaf, or a seed, or claws, hair, or teeth from animals. It doesn't usually matter the manner in which the item is in, as it should be burned to ash and mixed into what ever medium you will be using to craft the seal.

There is a also a good way to maintain extra control over the familiar by blending three drops of blood, one drop for the mind, one for the spirit, and one for the body of the construct. This, however, is not necessary and requires a focus on the mind (task), spirit (elemental source in union with the task), and the body (form). Upon the creation of the construct there should be an animation of the spirit, and this would require the calling upon the elemental force from the seal, or elemental tool to have the current flow into the construct.

Exercises for Creating an Egregore

Write out a method of servitor creation for a servitor of a single element for a specific purpose. Explain your choice of purpose and what you would include in the ceremony. Explain any color correspondences, what tools would you make use of. Then create a spell of animation that will channel the current into the form to give it life to your purpose.

Like above, create one for each element including both eastern and western charts, earth, air, fire, water, wood, metal.

The properties that you give this, as well as every other reader who employs this particular servitor, will give it a greater consciousness than one individual singularly. Each will have their own manifestation of the greater whole. For everyone who employs this critter to their own ends, when it is not in use, the energy will transfer to the collective construct of the sigil to create a force greater than one on their own. This is how a collective works; in a sense one can create a god-form manifestation of a singular sigil, with enough people putting power behind it. The Liber Sigilium does this with the Grimoire of the 8 Gods of Chaos.

Application for Creation:

Take horn shavings, claw shavings, fur from an animal, and burn the mix to ash. Mix this ash with clay and sculpt a creature that has the claws of the animal you have used, antlers/horns in used in the construction, with the body the style which you have used. Upon its body, in the center, carve the sigil. This is one that can be made:

Use the Conjuration of animation, while you bleed upon the form to give it life from your blood. Choose for it a name. Use a quartz crystal as its home. Under the light of the full moon charge the crystal and read the Conjuration to bring life.

Creating Demons

Pull from yourself all emotion that you wish to be present in your creation. Bring together thought, material components, and fresh blood. To fuse the whole together, burn everything, and mix your blood with the ashes.

Give it a name, and a symbol by which you can call it forth. Designate to it a source of power outside your being so it doesn't drain you, and give it the means to sustain itself so over time it can become an entity of its own, a true demon. Give it life, and weave into its essence a way to destroy it, if it decides of its own volition to become more problems than it's worth.

Craft a sigil, engrave it on the body you have created, that has been mixed with the blood and ashes. Burn everything for the third time, and place the ashes in or by an elemental body that represents the elements and emotion that best fits for the nature of this demon.

Demons are comprised of raw emotion, they are on overload of senses. Built with elemental bodies, they are then subject to the nature and inherent emotions of the elements which animate them. Scatter the ashes, leave nothing but the glyph, and its information within these pages; summon it forth in the spot where its body may be composed of the elements where the ashes were dispersed. Angels can be created in the same manner but they must contain no emotion and are created from the celestial elements instead of terrestrial.

You must also bring these to life as with the same animation of the spirit. Breathe the vital breath into these creations; they are of you, your thoughts made flesh, your will made flesh. Keep in mind that you have to destroy these thought forms eventually when they have served their purpose. It is unwise to keep them longer then deemed necessary for your own sanity. Do not give into your pride, do not tell others what you are up to when you are working on these forms. They are personal, as emanations of your own mind and soul and thus are no one's business. Of every member of the temple, it will be required that you demonstrate this ability, and the ability to successfully banish it.

Gather the components of the raw element from which you would shape the servitor. Draw or sculpt the servitor on clay, or paper. Mix the clay with blood, or mix the ink with blood. Only yours will do, as it is you who assumes the god-head to bring this thing to life.

Burn everything to be subsumed into the elemental body as the ashes are mixed. Name it, give it life. Bottle the element if it is water, and paint upon the vessel its symbol and its name. If it is fire then inscribe it on a candle; when it is about to go out, light another candle of the same make to carry the spirit. The wax should be mixed with blood as well. Should the spirit be made of earth, then ashes, mixed with earth corresponding to the type of elemental, shall be in an urn inscribed with its name, and glyph. If it is to be of air, then the ashes should be mixed into an incense. Should you need to recreate the elementals from spent components, then simply mark their glyph parchment and summon them forth as you would a demon, either created or not. Destruction of this comes when life is removed, and the elemental base is consumed in the contrary element.

The use of these elementals should be in the ceremonial rites that you construct. You should build and design everything about your rituals, down to the last elemental which gets absorbed into the circle on which you do the work. It is thus that everything will be of your own consciousness, as such the resultant work will be the mastery of your own concentration and focus.

It is good if you understand the lengths to which this is required. If you can make your demons and your angels manifest themselves to serve your desires, then you can make sustainable elementals from which you can build successful mediums of working, and solidifying in their power so even greater works can be attained from these entities. If your work requires the elemental sacrifice of something, then you have the energy already in place which would be a "bloodless sacrifice".

Cairns, Nodes, & Ley Lines

What the earth has given to those who would use them are the lines of energy currents that act as the pulse of the living earth. At the time of this writing, an example to be used is the New Madrid fault line, in the southeastern part of North America. It builds and circulates a current from the north to the south. Other lines include the grand lines of the Pyramids and other points of power, along with minor lines that are subtle and have nearly been forgotten.

Breathe life into them, if they are dying. Focus them with circles and stones, and there is always the ability to redirect the currents and remake the patterns in the earth, so long as the type of current is balanced in its new form. Channeling this power through an object can be a very good way to secure a power base, such as a staff and circle.

Causing destabilization in the flow can disrupt the physical elemental properties of the region on which you are working. Again, at the time of this writing, gates have been noted within the southern regions, branching new lines, and opening to the Fae realms. These gates, on a side note, relate with the foundations of numerical meaning, four, seven, ten, and so on. They are field tested and examples of how to manipulate to the currents of the earth.

Non-sentient created elementals can also be grafted to the points, to create a viable node with which you can use to control, so long as you control the entity's essence. It will develop an individuality if not maintained, and will begin to exhibit signs of the type of current. The use of the created elementals can be supplied as the batteries to these places, interlacing their created essences within the currents of the natural surrounding and your energy will be able to be worked with and harnessed from these regions, as well. All who spend time of the temple will be required to be able to identify lines of power on the earth, and the location of every nexus point for part of their study to add and keep up with the records already in the archives.

Nodes of power that are linked to either a location or an object require the use of a map where the lines are marked where the energy points manifest from natural emanations of the elements. Forks in mountain ranges and splits in streams or creek beds. Mineral deposits, crystals or metals. Cemeteries. Most churches and religious places are aligned on such lines of power. Once the Line has been found, then it can thus be manipulated.

Scribe onto paper or wood the Circle of Creation, as it is designed to focus all parts of the 8 rays to a single central point, focusing the power of the worlds into that very spot. Everywhere that circle is marked upon flesh, paper, metal, or stone is a place where the energies shall flow into the body upon which it rests. Now the circle upon the paper must then be aligned to the greater lines which are flowing through a region. Position the vertical lines of the circle when it is drawn to the direction of the flow of the energy point. When this is done, travel to the points where you seek to adjust the line's flow and implant a quartz into the ground. Subsequently place the remaining 6 crystals in the 6 points around the place in the earth, and call upon the the power of the earth, pulling it up or down from the glyph into the area where you would have it. The stones can be removed or left.

A focus of raw energy into the space should then have been achieved, but make sure the inflow of energy is stable and non-corruptible. If it becomes unstable, ground the energies out into the surrounding environment. Of course, these go hand in hand with the created realms being able to be grafted to the raw currents of the earth through the solidifying of ley lines and other naturally magnetized regions which yield the most possible energy, so that the energy of the mage flows within his will and the environment so they become as one unified force. It must be remembered that when you are making use of another Node or Nexus which doesn't carry your signature then you will have to adapt your energy to its alignments before use.

From a Person

Set the circle with the Gate of the Inner World. Use a black sphere or some point of calling. Have the personal effect burned to ash, and mixed into the ink used to draw the circle. There should be a mixture of herbs for drawing spirits. Write your conjuration that the demonic/angelic force rise from the host. From this, be set to task for either assistance or for the destruction of the host, or those around the host. To be fed from the subconscious mind that exists for the host.

From oneself

Ideally, one would not use this to evoke one's own personal demons, but the angelic forces to help one maintain a logical view, through what otherwise would be inert emotions or feelings. This will allow you to draw up the current from your mind and giving it purpose and direction. Use the seal of the Gate of the Inner World. Mix your blood into the ink that you draw the circle with. Use the black orb to pull the force out of yourself. Name it, give it purpose. Can also be used on power ascribed to the fictional characters created for imaginary realities, such as role playing games, novels, etc.

From a grouping of people

Use the seal of their collective worship, burned to ash mixed with the ink. The demonic force or angelic force should be given name, purpose, and set to task upon those who carry the mark. The cold and logical force that will destroy those not of this order, or the Demonic force that will cause them to self-destruct or burn from their own emotional instability.

From the Singular Collective

To create elemental forces that effect the natural world. Angelic forces and Demons drawn from the sources of creation must be contained in a secondary array just to be on the safe side. So make use of the Gate of the Inner World as the inner array and the Barrier Array or the Terrestrial array. It does not hurt to set up that extra stability. From here, use herbs mixed with the ink for conjuration, as the herbs form the extension of the living world.

Draw it from the collective mind. Pull your force up out of the aether through your own conjuration. Set it up that the force is given name, purpose, intent, and a place to reside instead of being drawn back into the primal currents, as that will erase programmings.

From the Human Unconscious Collective

Creation of the god-forms of the collective mind of humanity. For when you would influence humanity on the mass scale, use blood from a body that is not your own. Use the secondary protective array as well. Draw the force out of the collective unconscious mind of man. Use what ever archetype you would that you can form the god-force that you would set upon the whole of humanity.

Create the purpose, bind the intent to any who would use the archetype. Such a mandala is needed to store this force. Use a conjuration or such to draw it out when not in use. Such creations will create deified manifestations.

Conjuration of the Familiar Creatures

Take the effects of the animals that you would have become your spiritual medium and anoint them with blood. Animate the spirit to reform itself in the spiritual presence via a resurrection current for animal spirits. Cast into the fire a list of your desires, written in ink mixed with your blood corresponding to the nature of the intent you would have manifest in this spiritual creature.

I call upon the creation of the fires
Let now my servants form
Be brought before me
I that make this spirit my servant
By the dark fire
This spirit (x)
Shall serve me in the ways that I require
Be brought forth
Resurrected by this fire.

To Call the Red Dragon

I call upon the lightness of the day;
I call upon the darkness of the night;
I call upon the color of blood on which thou art to devour.
I call thee forth, Red Dragon, to feast upon this offering.

Calling of the Black Dragon

I call forth by the corrupted blood of mortality
I call forth by dead souls within flesh
Come, be called here forth to feast upon this my offering
Consume the corruption, Black Dragons come forth!

Dragon of the Ages

By the stars above,
By roots below;
I call forth the Dragon of the Ages,
Let the essence be consumed.
I call thee forth to feast upon my offering.

Conjuration of the Hounds of Hell

I call upon the ancient guards to the realm of the dead
You hunters who retrieve the lost souls,
Companions to the Ancient Gods.
I draw forth the hounds of the hunt
Take (x) back to the deepest pit.
By ancient laws of Justice
I call thee forth.
By the ancient covenant of the Underworld realms,
Come forth.
Seek out my request and take them back to the shadow lands of the abyss.

Creation of the Archetype

Since we ourselves come from the Singular Collective (SC), we understand that there are no gods for us, save for those we make. The difference, however, is that when we say "we call upon the god of (x)" for whatever task, it is that we are tapping into the idea to use the collective mind as the medium between the duties for which are attributed to that god-force, ourselves and the SC. So by following the same methods of the creation of a servitor, we can then put into form an idea that will take on the "divine" attributes of the archetypes.

We are all the power we need as we house the direct connection to the SC, so from this we can freely create the face to which will suit our purpose. When we evoke, summon, invoke the name of a god, we are assuming the mantle attributed to that face of the singularity, so as to have our will manifest through the power of the name of that being. We become that god, demon, monster of legend in order to use all the energy associated with it. We can create the familiar and have that spread its name, its seal, its powers that we give it license to achieve. When others call its name, in vain or in jest, so long as it's on their mind it lends the power to the construct, which fuels the archetype. However, we are through these means able to freely manipulate their works, as if they were extensions of our being, much like a secondary skin, or an external mind/perception source. So pick your favorite god, declare that as your patron and become the extension of it. So the same shall follow with any summons of anything in this text. We create the power behind the general name attributed for it, through the power the collective memory that has been ascribed to it. It does itself not exist in a way that is other than a description of how others have used those powers, deeds, and other such things that history has given us.

Going from this, we shall use the Christ as an example of how to create a godhead. They give an idea, they give it a shape, they give it symbols, rituals, power behind it. They get people to believe in this idea, and it is from this belief in it, that it is given reign to work on the world as though one would have a familiar do. However, instead of being controlled by the singular Warlock, it's controlled by the will of the people. Yet through the will of the people, there exists the distinction of the people and their gods; one is unlike the other. However, if you make manifest within your self/deeds/actions, that gap diminishes, allowing one to thus recognize the similarity in their own nature. Through this union of their nature, they can assume the head form of any god they would require. So if you want to assume the head of Hecate, of Themis, or any number of infinite faces. You must awaken these aspects in your own self, declare yourself as you are. There is no god we recognize above us, however they are open for us to grab as though it were a closet of different costumes we can don when the need arises.

When creating an archetype for general magicks, it becomes useful for one to be able to create their own gods for those duties which require it to be self sustaining. For example; if you create a realm and you need to have forces govern the time structure, and hourly duties of the energy, they then act as regulators for the general power as it flows from the sources. By giving them tasks, the archetypes become the frequencies of those tasks, as created from the source. To show this point, let us take Cronus, titan of time. We know the titans represent primordial forces of named and unnamed capacity, they were second created after the sources they were created from. So when we want to do something to effectively manipulate time, and regulate the power of what the effect is, we can use the Cronus archetype to become the link to the source of time, which is but one of the faces of the Singularity. This method is useful for entering into union with the sources, and the SC.

Creation of Realms

A vessel needs to be prepared. It should contain drawings and notes on the way the realm is supposed to be. It is to have a list of elements that are to be included. Elementals should be forged to become the foundation of the realm. These elements are to be woven together to form the realm out of the raw material. With what has been given above, into the mix should be all or as many united components as can be thought of. It is to be forged and bound, and united and set within the cosmos. A horizon of the soul, where the desires are made manifest.

What then needs to be forged, is a link between this realm and the realm to be created, so there is a path for the soul to travel. This realm needs to be cemented into the fabric of the universe so that it will be stable, and not collapse upon your vacancy.

Though temporary dimensions will be what the heart desires, to forge the realm the elemental must be created to sustain it. They must draw their energy from a source. The link must draw upon the lines of power within the earth, and be made be made stable by them. Any celestial influence should allow for the passage to and from this realm. All forms of creation must be used and focused into the link with the purpose of creating permanence within the realm.

With the creation of the realm you must also use correspondences that will allow you to access this world to the next. You must divide the materia of the of that which has already been created. From here you will be able to have a place where created beings can exist without the need for having objects crafted.

There needs to exist a set of laws which will allow for the easy transition of the elementary souls from the plane of creation to transition easily to the plane of desire. Such laws would be fundamental guidelines on the creation, incarnation, and gate mechanics. With the sympathetic elemental attributes which fire behaves the same on the plane of creation as it does where you would have the spirit come out on.

From here you can create your own heavenly planes, demonic planes, and other such places and pockets within the multiverse, which can act as safe grounds or staging areas for various works. As well as charges, and channeling directly from prima materia from this plane to use it as a filter to other currents which the body would otherwise be unable to handle.

The plane can be set up like a digestive system, where forces placed in one plane are broken down and fed into other planes and refined and purified, and then raised to higher levels and so on. This can be used for once born souls to modify them into multiple life forms.

Application

Any plane of existence becomes fair game for the conjuration of the power forth from it, if you have a solid foundation of view/correspondence.

Places that can be used from historical lore:

> The 9 Worlds of the Norse
> The 10 hells in the 7 Places
> The Spheres of the Cabala
> The Taoist Star Gates.
> The Shamanic Planes of the Spirit

This also opens up the conjuration of places, with the proper mindset and power given to any fantastical realm of thought or imagination. Such as the places of the dark like Lovecraft's' R'lyeh, and the phantasmagorical "world" in any fantasy series, created with enough detail that you can discern the order of how the world works, where it can be found, what point in the verse/dimension it exists in.

Exploring and exploiting these contact points between fantasy and reality pushes at the boundary of what is possible. It uses the connective power of a singular thought implanted in the heads of the many to give birth to a place of conjuration. To give birth to a world of potential manifestation where in these critters can exist, do exist, and can be manipulated by the will of the one who has created them.

Much in the way that the Judaic point of view would have us as figments and aspects of the mind of a much larger creation. We to can achieve this level of creation with the power of our minds, put to focus, though ritualized actions to make manifest the intents we would cause to be.

On Conjurations

When you are going to apply the created construct of reality, you must find the means by which they arrive, through the use of a corresponding medium. How do they appear? What herbs correspond to them to give them the incense that will be used to create their gaseous body?

Divisions of Creation

There are, according the Hermetic viewpoints, divisions of creation, as well as the mind of the all. These divisions are as follows for our purposes. We must create a world view, for orders of how things exist to give point of reference for their conjurations. In this we will examine planes of being, the divisions of the mind, and spiritual correspondences which will allow the Warlock to put themselves into the hierarchy as the direct extension of the Singular Collective as the thing which can command any force in creation. So long as one recognizes some pattern or hierarchy, then one can either choose to supplicate, or command the force according to the power and the connection of their spirit/the singularity/and the force of creation that exists within those divisions. As with anything, the power of the Warlock is reliant upon their understanding of the way the universe works. Yes, we are extensions of the singularity, we are the physical hands upon this spinning ball of dirt. However, there are other forces, entities that exist within creation, and it is our job to be able to deal with them in any form they might take to further our own ends as is required.

The Supernal Realms

The highest point attainable where the division of the archetypes of the gods, titans, and other myths exist. Here is where those forces reach their perfections. The Taoist Immortals, the perfected gurus, and the most advanced mages in recorded, and not recorded history. This is where the ideals are taken to their heights, and is the extreme of all things which embrace logic, justice, truth, war, chaos, madness, death. The highest attributed sources of creation. Where the mind rules above all else.

The Bestial Realms

These are the places where the animal instinct dwells. Where the shamans can tap into the great bear spirits, great wolf spirits, and other natural primal forces. Ideas and logic of the rationality in the Western mind is given way to the freedom of instinct, awareness. Logic in the traditional sense is out the window, and through these forces that exist within the bestial realm you have the dark gods of the Lovecraft myths, the gods of Egypt who combine the supernal ideal and the instinct to operate on mechanics different from human rationalization processes. Or, at least in the manner that the West views instinct, rationality, and otherwise animistic traits of character, mind, and behaviors.

The Celestial Realms

Planetary bodies, stellar bodies, that are made of gasses that are not locally found, or not in such abundance such as Saturn and its methane. Places that exist as burning gas balls in our night sky house spirits, entities and other such vibratory entities such to the like that they exist in some form of molecule. We might not classify life, consciousness or mind to these molecular structures, but they provide building blocks of energy which we can use to some degree from afar to bounce interstellar magicks off of. Opening the gates and other such energetic activities, or if we can make use of debris from space, can yield surprising results when our attentions are paid to them. Each place becomes housing for elemental spirits, and things which can exist just fine there as the physical building blocks of the worlds they need to create. We might see gas bubbles and clouds, storms and such, but in their own way each have attributed characters much like behavior patterns found in animals, and beasts on our own world. Storms have a habit of carrying some kind of personalities within the way the winds blow, the lightning strikes and so forth. It is the same on the other gas balloons that we find in our solar system.

The Infernal Realms

Places of the emotional, irrational, and extreme. Much the opposite of the attributes found in nature, principals that act as the categories for our gods. Hatred, Wrath, Love, Passion, Inspiration, and other such raw characteristics that embrace what it is to be an emotional body can be found within the many different places that these exist. The knowledge ridden realms of the Qlipoth, the dark forgotten shadows of the void-space. These places where the light of rationality is found but in such a way as that the heart rules the action. Mind and Instinct are to follow the emotions. If you find a demon or do something with the polar opposite to knowledge, then you do so based on impulse, knee-jerk reactions to situations that would otherwise be explainable from any point of logical thinking.

The Elemental Realms

The elemental bodies that exist in all forms of light, shadow, waves of energy, heat, and other collections of natural occurrences. These bodies exist in their states as the building blocks of the physical matter in creation. Djinn, Elementals, Golems, homunculi and such exist on the elemental level. Made of gasses, steams, odors, humors, plants, trees, stones, and other such physical vibrations. Through the elemental worlds you come into a more physical understanding of the operations of the world. So if you want to affect the physical world, you look to its elemental attribute. If it operates on the physical, it must have some elemental properties. It might be based originally from the planes of ideas, and instinctual behavior of the supernal, bestial, celestial, infernal realm, but if it is to act, then it must originate in some form of an elemental compound to give it a body to interact outside of its plane of origin.

Recreating a Living Mind

Get from the person as many emanations of their soul, body and essence that you can. Drawings, pictures they draw are expressions of their soul; stories they write, poems are expressions of the link they have between their mind and soul; blood is the link between the soul and the body; hair, flesh, is the link to physical; sexual fluids are the tie to the essence of creation, and their physical forms. Put all of this together you have their soul, their mind, how their mind interacts with the soul, how the body interacts with the source, and how the soul affects the body. Now that you have these links to who and what they are, you have the means of operation.

With these links, examine how they interact with the world, every facet of how their energy coils about them from their auric field to the greater environment, take what you find and make notes on how it could achieve what you want it to. Describe then, a purpose you would "implant" upon the soul of the target. Write in your blood upon a piece of parchment, your intent on what you would have their essence accomplish for you over their lifetime(s). This is how you would have their energy programmed; it needs to be as specific as possible. The energy they generate in their lifetime that they may or may not be aware of is going to be directed; one task, one specific goal per person is all this will affect as it will be done over their entire life. You charge their aura with intent by taking all that you have acquired from them and burning it to ash, and making the parchment on which you transcribe what you would have done. You then bind to them this task by removing their soul when they are sleeping and casting it into the fires of creation, or some purging force of creation and rework it become a living spell. In this, you must rename their soul, and give it a glyph or sigil, that when they see it, identifies the purpose.

This last part is to be done while they sleep. Transcribe then your intent in your blood upon this paper and give life to your creature on the level, that its current life is yours to shape and you shape it in the image of your intent, that without their awareness they have become your intent, in a manner so subtle they think it is the natural progression of their soul, and graft the image of the programmed sigil into their essence. While they are in their dream state, with the paper made of ash with the intent transcribed in blood burn this again to ash, and recharge the ashes to the intent and then get the target to consume the ashes in some manner; food, drink, etc. Over a period of three days, seven days, or thirteen days, they are to be programmed by the ashes in their food, with the intent focused into the food, or inspire them to become tattooed.

Greater Modifying of the Living Mind

Aspects of the personalities must be mapped out before you begin the modification process. As much of a profile as you can generate, the more accurately you can work the body. Gain from them aspects of each of the 12 emotions. Such as emotional states:

Love/Lust	Empathy
Fear	Curiosity
Rage	Despair
Jealousy	Frustration
Guilt	Grief
Hope	Awe
Shame	Hysteria
Contempt	Angst
Surprise	Annoyance
Disgust	Pity
Euphoria	Remorse

From this point you will need to identify 4 aspects of their life from the mind, body, spirit. Choose from the list, or something not said. Find what riles them the most, find what makes their hearts flutter, find whatever you can about them. Attribute, through the rite of naming and creation, the spirits that will be the manifestation of these actions within the body. Use the formation of the gate of the inner mind to construct you spiritual servitors. The reason for these servitors is to act as the anchors to the emotion of the one you would open up.

After the servitors are created, draw out the seal of the gate, and use an ink made from personal effects, the more personal the better, from the body of the one you're going to modify. Blood, hair burned to ash, teeth, flesh fresh or dried, whatever the case may be, sexual fluids, menstrual fluids.

Continue with preparations for creating the servitors of the 8 aspects of life. The Life itself; death it will have; the mind it generates; light of the self; darkness of the self; spirit; Chaos that it generates; the time which it was born. This being said, mark them out as the outer seals on the circle. Name them, give them all a personal summons.

Do this on the dark moon, when the dark gates are open. There should be one large white candle on the right. One large black candle on the right. Carved with the name of the individual. Upon the circle there should be a mirror, or sphere, or some point where the spirit shall be pulled up from the aether itself.

You are using the middle pillar to open directly to the source of this soul. Name the spiral in the center to be of the pure unconscious mind of the one you're going to modify. Work your conjuration in your own system, in your own symbolism. Make sure that it encompasses the following:

The 8 source currents that give to the life and existence of the one you are modifying.

The 12 emotions that make up the majority of the individual.

With this you should have the 8 and 12 come forth from the point of conjuration. Draw these aspects of the personality out and have them consumed by the influences you will have them undertake. Set the servitors with intent, activate them, give them life unto your purpose, call them by name, and command them to remake the individual from the inside of their deepest mind. Awaken the spirit through these servitors to take effect upon their union back into the mind you are modifying.

Demonic Creation from a Person

When you would create a demon like those of the old grimoires, you need to select the type of creation you're making. As has been said before on how to create demons and other such critters, you will need a symbol that you create specifically for this archetype. From there, you need the physical link to the person you are drawing this energy from. With the link, and the sigil, as well as the other materials you will need for creating and housing this creature, set your array with the candle of intent upon its center. Bleed upon the candle for the living catalyst. Create it out of the material, draw its symbol, create its name, and then when you are ready, animate it, and conjure it for the first time.

From self I divide from self
I set apart and create the rift of the void between
(X)
and the emotional nature
I divide forth from the will of (x)
The body of (x)
The essence of (x)
Be subservient unto my commands
From now until the ending of all things
As I command the seal to form on the spirit
By the seal you will be ordered
In the seal you will be stored
By the seal you will be bound
It shall be marked upon your essence
For now through all time
You are branded
This is bonded
You are created from the creation
You are named (Name the spirit)
Hence and forever you shall be (Name)
Servant unto my command
By this seal and your name (Name of spirit)
Come as I command it
Formed of the prima materia
Animated by the Living fire
Achieve the tasks set before you
I forge you in the eternal fires
Achieve all that I require!

When you have achieved a manifestation of the entity. Command it thus as its first task.

Enter forth into this sigil,
Find your refuge here
By this eternal bond of this mark
Be bound within
I set you to the task that I require.

When it has entered into the seal and has been fully bound by it, command it as you would any other demon or spirit. Draw the seal in blooded ink, fresh for every use. Keep a master copy in with your personal works so as to maintain it in a stable environment. As it was first in flesh and animated, so too should it be on leather in blooded ink. Your will can never falter when commanding spirits.

Nesting Consciousness

The Concept:

The united mind of a created core which links to the minds of those within the territory grid. This will allow for instant knowledge of the aetheric displacement zone, assimilation of energy currents through the conduit and node points that are present within the region. This will allow for greater defense capabilities if the region is aware of itself, and has influence over the people within its region. This is in such a way as one would connect to the network server. One can also insert this into a living body. Doing so will root the intent or programming into the individual and in their environment for your purposes.

Environmental Effects:

When not anchored into the earth current, or node point, it will speed up rates of decay and draw from the surrounding energy to sustain itself. All work from those that it is connected to will use it to sustain itself. When it becomes self-aware is when it becomes the parasitic influence and will cause decay and deterioration to everything from the people, the environment.

Energetic Demand:

This energy tax does so at low rates for whatever energy is expended, both naturally and from conscious workings. In this work, it must be sustained by both terrestrial current and by the energy of the living mind. The core links to the subconscious mind and drains from dreams, sleep patterns, spell work, and other emanations of current from the body. This further roots the consciousness into the hosts and environment. Set the tax rate low enough to not be noticed when you are programming the core.

The Core:

The center node of the array. Centered on an altar, the crystalline points shall be large surrounded by 8 smaller points in the 8 directions. The center of the nesting mind. Build the array like a servitor, link it to your energy in order to maintain control over the flow of the conduit. Animate it, give it a name, and breathe life into it. Then draw up the current from the earth to sustain it. Anchoring the current into the node will limit the deterioration that occurs from the high level of current that is absorbed.

Tethers:

With the array network, there needs to be the anchor points to make use of this core. To remotely access the central "brain" current of the array use a crystalline necklace made of the same material as the core array. From this, all involved in the use of the network should have something they craft with the stones. This will be the link from the core to the host(s).

Remote Anchors:

Use the crystals of the similar material placed at points around the region your are going to do primary operations. Shadow tendrils can be anchored outwards to and from these points, as well as energy conduits to build large scale arrays. Use of the remote anchors for various effects are possible.

Activation:

To awaken the array, one should use their blood upon all the anchors, tethers, and the core at the same time. This is done in order to align the awakening and spirit that is named as the consciousness; its anchor becomes the housing for the mind. Can be implanted within bodies.

Creation of the Homunculus

The human body is made up of 8 major energy centers, and those are broken up into the major Chakra points. Correspondingly, any creation is made as such with 8 major centers where exterior energies are balanced out and filtered through the system. Basic servitor constructions are with a single thought construct. It is outwards from this that such things are developed into greater forms of creation. The next ones being Elementals and then Demon/Angelic servitors.

A quick overview:

> *Elementals* - energies with an elemental based system wherein it takes account of the 7 elements which are earth, air, fire, water, wood, metal, and electricity. Through which the material and the construct become a manifestation of.
>
> *Demons* - emotional constructs with more or less control based on the balance of the emotional thoughts within the created body, with energy centers set in place to maintain controllable restraints over the construction.

Putting an emotional construct within an elemental construct, and blending them into a unified "body" will give it a form of humanness. Giving it a sound body, and a sound mind. The soul which is generated then is the reaction between the interactions of the mind and body. Thus to have a created soul within a construct will then be able to act and function spiritually as a uniform spiritual body. Angelic hosts, demonic hosts, and elemental forces; each of these have different manifestation on a physical level. The angelic/demonic construct can be given a form in a particular degree in the wind shift, or in the shape of a cloud, or wisp of smoke, the manifestation of both an object, or the shadow from an object. Blending the highest aspects of the body, with the primal self motivating currents will create different effects on such constructs.

Humans can be implanted with these "forces" upon birth, or traumatic event in which case the body opens up to such outside influences. If possession is deemed possible, then it will occur based on the application of the laws of incarnation and possession. The animating force, this case being the created construct, will be birthed into an empty human vessel. The active, passive, and neutral qualities within the mind are what will allow its interactions to exist on a personal level.

Humanoid qualities

To create the proper blend of humanness within a physical elemental body, blend the 3 aspects of each of the animated currents into a single body. What results will be the spiritual equivalent of a human spirit. Such constructs can open their currents to the external world and develop along paths which are available for any spirit. Such as when they are created with the tree within them, they can upon animation have a drive to seek out their place on it. Be in the highest form or the lowest form. Some would consider this form of creation a forbidden thing, as it's the construction of a soul-body that will have both elemental and emotional qualities, the Anima behind a Homunculus or any other living and dying thing.

Elementals are made from such as:
>A Spirit of Fire with a body of fire,
>A spirit of Water with the Body of fire,
>Spirit of Earth with the body of fire and so on.

The more the development, the less one needs to rely on the physical elemental influence, and can deal better with the frequencies of the current finding the best ones on which one can operate. This method can be used to create the souls one offers up as offerings for pacts, or creates essences from which to feed. Or to implant into a human animal to culture spirits. If it looks like a rose, tastes like a rose, and smells like a rose, then it must be a rose. So, to make use of this method is to completely build the construct of the spiritual body, with every single point that mimics the bodies of the human.

Spatial Distortion

To begin, we find ourselves looking at what the potential of the world is. If we see the world as a series of events that lead one moment to the next, or perhaps it is the imprint of the perceptions of others upon the things we experience which give us the base for our reality? This is where our understanding of the world outside of our perceptions is called into question. The reason we must question how we view reality; is because if we see it in a specific way, where the energies and the fixed energy of a space can lend itself to opening up the free energy for manipulation.

When you begin with illusory changes upon your environment, you have at hand an idea of what you would like to see occur. If you can see the imprint of the image in your conscious mind, you can begin to focus your Chi into this, and from there you have the ideas of where you stand in relation to that object. From calling these illusions into existence on the physical plane where you can interact with it as though it was real, requires more than this discussion. In this case, our focus is the imprint on the worlds of creation. There is a division of consciousness when the spirit and the conscious mind interact independently from the physical. It is this place which is commonly considered the astral plane.

As you focus on one type of energy, it can manifest itself to that plane of desire. You will then be able to cause that to manifest around you, in your own radius of energy. As you will this to come to "earth-side," or the physical world, very subtle changes in the nature of the environment can occur. It is this radius of distorted space which you can then conjure, what mental imagery exists when you are working spells/technique and discharge methods. From this distortion we have a focus for where the energy comes from. Like working in the ritual circle or the ritual space. When you use methods of occult principals to "cast a circle" or some such, what you are doing is creating a focus for a ritualized/repeated distortion. It is in this place that energetic works, magicks, communions, summonings, conjurations occur. These places act as pockets of the world, wherein your rules are the ones that matter. If you worship a god-archetype then it is their rules, etc. Whoever sits at the top of your cosmological construct, is the order of what can occur within your ritual space. The ability to pull this to the outside world in proper focus can have a projection upon the physical world where you can decide the boundary for your working, without the need of prop.

The best method of using this technique is when you are doing any works with the 36 gates. The reason for doing so is that what would otherwise be limited by what the physical world can produce. This then allows for the full range of external celestial powers, temporal forces, and elemental forces which are otherwise too unstable or raw for the natural world to be able to properly manifest. It also allows for points of desire like gates, to open up and the raw energy to have a source of origin that exists in an untainted environment.

Remote Spatial Distortion

The use of this method is to be best applied when you are working at a distance to cause a distortion in the mind's eye. If you project your mind there, using something tangible as a base, be it some object you left behind or have set in place as an anchor point, you can project to this place. From this projection, you can, as you are on the mental plane, pull the formative astral plane around the imprint of that environment. Like you're standing in a construct of the environment as though there was a blanket of energy that is modifiable to your will. Like in the construction of a place where you are thoroughly in control of, like a ritual space that is with your physical body, it is your mind which creates this place, wherever it is you happen to project to.

Through this method, you can then pull or summon other things/people/spirits/energies into these spaces in which to work, causing whatever spell you have set into motion. In this manner, when you are working remotely, your mind builds the world, interacts with the world, and can on the mental planes create what you want to have occur. If say you wanted to have your designated target, you can cause it to be surrounded by darkness. In that darkness, you can put in the flames, the divisions of the heavens and the earth, what sorts of minds they will have, and how they interact with their environment. In this way you make nightmares more real, and affect the body of the spirit/mind of your target. Works of healing which are limited to spiritual/mental damages can be worked on. Communions with the spirits that work in the space which you need to remove. Working in places which would otherwise make it impossible to get there physically, to bridge distances, can be used in the distortion. You can fold different spaces into this construction, allowing for all the desired energetic elements, to act in a way that you designate by your will.

Reality blending

Like with the spatial distortion, you become the master of your world. When you are in your ritual space or working space, and you have the need to make some force or another manifest, have the idea at the forefront of your mind, and bring it forth. With the remote spatial distortion, that should be mostly mental with little to no spoken word, as it is meant to affect regions from afar. In this method, you are affecting the direct correlation of how energy flows in the space to how you want it to flow in the space. Temporarily replacing that natural current with one you command.

Use of a vocal evocation to the place of desire. To pull that up upon the plane of origin, in our case here the terrestrial physical plane.

Something barbaric perhaps:
Vi ego anima conjuro tu inferna, anima tartari mutare terra

Its translation thanks to Google. Something in English, perhaps:
By virtue of the soul, I conjure you the hells, the soul of hell to change the land.

In this method we have the foundation for our ritual grounds. When using this work to transform the entire environment, it allows for standing upon the type of energy that would best be suited for your kinds of working. These planes can be celestial, infernal, angelic, supernal, infernal. It matters not, so long as you can feel what it is within the words you use to pull that place to the physical, and over-ride the earth current of the area you're in. This work will be temporary unless you use some sort of natural anchor. It should be when the energy of the spell that is tied to the plane of conjuration is discharged that the environment returns, keeping the area from going into a major displacement zone.

Like filling a human body with energy for the ridding of a spiritual influence, you do the same method to the earth. From this method you then burn it off the imprint of the earth by discharging the spell/rite/ritual within that place. When the primary spell is released, so too should this in unison. If it's lingering, use another spoken invocation to turn it back to normal. Incenses and perfumes can help to augment these methods, to pull allusions to the spaces you are attempting to manipulate. This can of course be achieved on any plane, or place you can link with. If you happen to have a stone, or object that ties to that location, or concept to further enhance the property of this projection.

Conjure of Linking

To create a ritual circle regardless of distance between mages. Light two candles at the same time in all the locations to be used, however there needs to be 2 crystals facing center at the base of each candle, with one pointing to you in the center. For all the people using it, light the candles all at the same time say:

Cogo Vos Mutare Terra

Of the Internal View

Inside the body there exists currents of energy made up both of cellular and atomic structures, as well as spiritual points of current known as Chakras. We have covered these in other places. However, what is to be the topic of discussion here, is that what we perceive as the internal flow of energy extends to and from the vessel. Until now we have addressed the forces inside the body as they flow and manifest through elemental and planetary mediums in the internal correlations to the external forces. Let us now examine the body when the auric field becomes a single column of currents and the internal world becomes open.

The experiment is to take a slinky and make it into a circle. Let us say then that the the slinky represents in this doughnut-like shape the world of man as it interacts with the currents of the outer world. The internal energies, meeting with the outer worlds. The outer ring of this doughnut is what would be the auric field. Examine now this doughnut slinky on its side. Look through the rings of the metal or plastic, and see them not as bands making up a whole, but as separate currents which are flowing into and out of a singularity. It is in this where we move to a new level in our cosmological structure.

If we hold that there exists within creation a current which is known in circles as Zero point energy, we will say for our purposes this Zero point current, will be our concept of Soul. That in our doughnuts of current there exists a center hole where seemingly nothing passes through. However, it is exactly in this state that Zero point energy manifests, all and nothing at the same time. Its current's a part of the very fabric of all creation, at the same time because the interactions of the elements with its nature it develops individuality in its manifestation; thus no two things are created the same, unless of course things happen like, twins. However we will ignore for the time the mention of chaotic intervention until the idea is established.

While we have our doughnuts, and at the very center of this exercise, with each currents flowing into and away from what is its center. We take then that the soul which exists as neither of the body, or wholly without form, and mutable. It is our will, desires, actions which comes as stated from the perceptions of the events, the mental observations of them, the actions related to following through with the intent. However, it is from this central node, which manifests the "True Will" of the individual that the energy comes. Gnostic practitioners since the dawn of conscious thought have sought to get into this "no- mind" state, in which they become co-operators with god. It is while in this state that all the limits become removed, and the capacity of the individual to make manifest their will becomes possible.

Some might call this "soul" this Zero point channel, the manifestation of god. Our personalities only aspects of a greater mind. On some level this is correct, but there is also higher level to completing this notion. One that states if there is a connection to a higher mind through the internal quantum core of the body, then there is also the manifestation of the individual for the possibility of godhood. Meaning that if the personality manifests because of the relationship of a particular current of Zero point energy with the elemental and planetary currents, then that individual has the capacity to establish the personality within the current, and work as one of the elder gods as discussed above, or even one of the ancients if they would go so far as to align their will, and work upwards through the pillars, and pathways. What the Kabalists call the spheres are also home to their opposites; these they call the shells. This is the map of creation.

To connect through some spiritual journey, is to connect through meditation to the degree of enlightenment, or on a quantum level to the source of all creation. It remains and shall forever remain, as different roads one can use to connect to their inner self, and truest nature. Through their working with the paths, or the shells, whatever the journey, the end of the journey is the same.

Divisions of the Mind

The Singular Consciousness is the mind of the Singular Collective from which we all stem. It is our union and connection with the Singularity that allows us understanding and development, as well as fuels the inexorable power we have within us. Whether it is based on our silver charging, free energy manipulation, general common magicks, or other intuitive based ability, we have within us the same mental patterns as the realms in which the entities exist that are non-humanoid. In creation there exists animals, minerals, elements, insects, and other critters we just have to classify by attribute, property, purpose and general correspondence.

We are the ones who create the whole of our understanding using classifications to act as the points of reference for what the things are that we find. We are own gods, our own demons, and our own angels. But there are things which exist which are not from our own bodies. Such as your pet, his personality, and his nature. Or the wild animal that exists in the woods in some far off place. It has a life of its own. However, we can recognize the living natures, the personalities, and the essences of those things because of our awareness of the divisions of those things within our own psyche.

In this work, the definitions of those are :

Supernal Mind- gives rise to our archetypes, our supreme ideas, and it is the mode by which we operate, judge, and determine any other course of action. If it falls in line with how we view ourselves, then this mind represents our nature.

Super Consciousness- gives rise to the ego, and the ideal; what it is we see ourselves doing, our aims, our goals. How these goals fit with the supernal mind which represents the pinnacles of our development.

Subconscious Mind- unknown to us, but the manifestation of our supernal and super-conscious; the unseen, unknown drive we find ourselves possessing as we journey the paths of our nature and desires.

Physical Mind- that which allows us to embrace the physical world around us, to see what we want and where we want to go. To make our world fall into place with any of the ephemeral concepts of idealism, desire, and goals.

Infernal Mind- is the mind that will find the path of least resistance; the paths we walk and force upon ourselves for the development of the union between the physical mind, the supernal mind, the super-conscious, the bestial mind. We walk all paths as one path when embracing this ideal; all roads lead to our goals.

Bestial Mind- is the root of instinct, feeling, emotion. Raw potential that shows itself at the edges of one's personality.

For a more complex structure of the world and the emotional states, do research into the Jungian archetypal minds, the Egyptian and the hermetic mind and its divisions. Judaic sources and the Asian sources also have their divisions of the mind/body. Develop your own thought construct. From this you will be able to work better with your art, and any of the material contained herein.

Developing the Core

Sit cross legged in a space where you are comfortable. Breathe in deeply. Allow your mind to wander for a few minutes, till it becomes silent. Close your eyes, and fall into the black.

When you have done this, see yourself in your mind's eye in outline; just your silhouette. After you have this image in your mind, see your core. It should be small and glowing whitish. Condense it down with your mind's eye to about 3 inches in diameter. This should cause your stomach to tense as the energy follows suit. Breathe deeply and slowly. As you inhale the core condenses. As you exhale, the core will relax a little, and impurities off of the core will be expelled then through this breath.

As you are breathing and the core is small and glowing, exhale and relax yourself. Do not over exert yourself in the beginning. Repeat this as necessary to solidify the core and find your center.

Working with this energy as you exhale, the current should naturally flow upwards through your body and down your dominant hand.

Form an orb in the center of this space as it then flows upwards into your recessive hand, and downwards into the core. This will form a perpetual loop that occurs while you breathe.

Daily Exercise

As you have developed the core to be able to flow in accordance with your will, reverse the flow. On a soft exhale bring the energy up your recessive arm, down through the palm Chakra into a one inch sphere between your palms. Upwards on your dominant arm and then down into your core. This circuit will flow against your nature, but you must be able to do this before you progress.

When you have achieved the dual directions, it is time to unify the current. One current up the dominant side down through the sphere between the palms and up the recessive arm into the core. The recessive hand should have energy from the core up it as well and down through the same sphere between the palms, upwards through the dominant arm and back into the core. This will be a dual Yang circuit.

The Spoken Word

When it comes to most of the arts described in this work, there will be passages that are spoken. This is done to give a medium of focus for the body and command the energy towards its objective. It in this manner is done that one can release the energy contained within their speech.

In dealing with the spoken word, one deals with the cognitive spirit of the thing. "To know the name of a thing is to have power over it," has been a popular saying in a lot of references from Hollywood. However, this is a true passage to understand the meaning, the history, and the essence of the thing and command its physical energy towards your desire, and is what spoken word magick represents.

There are words that command, words that heal, names of spirits, and the "true" angelic and demonic names found within the works of literature. However, it is in our use of these terms we connect with the consciousness in those names, words, and descriptions that gives us the power over them. How well you can extend out your will to those words, phrases, and descriptions to pull the very spirit behind them, demanding, asking, and compelling their manifestation before you.

Instantaneous manifestation rarely occurs, as it takes a period of generation with this sort of magick. However, it is possible to obtain such results if you have previous experience with the working through your spoken craft.

There is a popularity of barbaric names, and conjurations in languages long lost, and obscure for pronunciation. However this can be a good thing for some kinds because you are looking to pull the spirit of the word from your words, as the bridge the void from the inner world and the outer world. Barbaric word are best pronounced as they are spelled, but if you are working with old dead languages, make sure you are using the vocabulary charts they give for pronouncing. Practice first softly before you start using such words.

Thoughts are directed through the energy of word vibration and is sent outwards to develop in that direction. There are words that can negate the effects of other words. You would have to know the meaning and exact intent if you wish to do such thing. There is no counter curse, there is no "deafness" that the cosmos can grant for certain words. Some are permanent and can carve into the very fabric of creation. It is these words we must seek to master.

The Unspoken Word

The root of the word is the spirit of it, all the things which that vibration has come to represent in the mind of all those who hear it. The imagery, emotions, meanings, reactions, memories, which such words can conjure. Yet when one uses unspoken words it is only speaking the root of the word on this plane. The best description of this would be bands of frequencies that flow around the body like the electrons around the nucleus of the atom. When they combine to produce the vibrations we hear as words, syllables and phrasing it it is like unto the roots of the trigrams; when they combine they form the I-Ching. When the hexagrams of the I-Ching combine, they form the 10,000 things from which all creation extends.

When using this image structure, draw yourself a map; of how your energy flows, where the roots would meet, what lines on the body they would manifest. If you're right handed then your active roots would exist on the right side of your body. The recessive hand would control all of the passive roots. Your mid-section would create the division between the elemental world and the abyssal world. Beneath your feet would be the infernal worlds. Above the head would be the roots of the words of the celestial.

As soon as you have a map of where beginning terminology would extend from, use your fingers, charged with energy. Pull the root syllables together; feel their differences, where you can sense which energy lays within the roots to create the unpronounceable formula that recreate the material world using the words of the spirit.

When you grasp the roots with charged hands, use your own energy to keep them stable. Speak the root of the word with your voice, while saying the words in your mind. Use the gesture of the pulling to come forth to some form of direction, blending them in your palms like with the daily core exercises. Form the words and release the words towards your intent with as much power as you can pull from yourself, the environment, and the unspoken spiritual word behind it. The spirits of the words respond when you shout the words with your mind and speak aloud the root, the louder you speak the root is the stronger, faster and harder that the results will come forth.

The results from this can be instantaneous. There is also a tax that doing such things takes out on the body. Generally there is some form of union from the inner world to the outer world. One does this through the use of blood, saliva, or some other vital fluid dependent upon what one is doing.

Conjuration Quick Reference

Passive Manifestation

Want – something that one would like to have but does not need for their daily survival.

Desire – The drive that refuses to be satisfied; wants that move towards becoming need.

Dreams – Desire of the subconscious mind

Need – the driving focus that sets one out to seek methods of manifestation to achieve their goal.

Neutral Manifestation

Prayer – The desire which has become through dream, and want a need that is willed into manifestation.

Active Manifestation

Petition – Directing of desire through a physical medium such as papers, carving into candles, or involving some non-verbal action of setting something into motion.

Spell – The means by which an operation is preformed for a single desire that encompasses a petition and verbal direction of
energetic/ethereal mediums.

Ritual – The means by which invocation, conjuration, or some action of spell craft is repeated to add power to spell craft.

Rite – The operation which is to be singular in nature that encompasses both spell work and ritual, for a single use.

Types of manifestation

When comprising a ceremony from the basic to the advanced, it is always good to remember the nature of these sorts of levels of manifestations, as it will serve as a guide to make the most out of the results.

The breakdown of a prayer which is common to all paths of practice where religion is involved is best summed up by the references in the Cabala of the Golden Dawn.

From the Sphere of Objective Consciousness,

1) We feel we need something to happen, so we want it to occur. We feel we want love/happiness/wealth/power/gain/peace.
2) We realize that things might not be what they seem when it comes to having what we want. To think about what we would pray for if we wanted it bad enough, or the rationalization as to how it would come into our lives.
3) For us to know that it can happen in a logical way is how we know that our work manifests according to the divine plans of whatever force we are petitioning to.
4) If we cannot rationalize with ourselves that our belief in the power that we are praying to is going to help bring the needed elements towards manifestation through the proper channels of cause and effect, then we have no foundation of belief. We cannot rely on higher powers whose whims are so 'vague' that they would leave us in our moments of need.
5) When we cannot maintain the focus of our connection to the "power" we are praying towards, then we cannot have the faith that our desire will manifest. We cannot give over to blind faith, but we cannot give over to the impossibility of the possibilities that our desires can manifest.
6) When we have rectified our connections to the nature of the power we are drawing from, to come and influence the working we are then given over to the manifestation of the prayer we have set into motion.

When we have the focus of our wants, desires and dreams we can pray to the higher powers or we can craft spells, rites, and rituals. All of them can include any forms of ceremony, any of them can omit any form of ceremony depending on how soon one needs the work to manifest for them. It doesn't take anything but a focused mind to make the manifestation occur.

So to give us the anatomy of spell craft we have the following formula:

$$I + W(D) + DR = X$$

Intending the Will, combined with (Desire), in addition to (Direction) and (Release), makes the intent manifest. This model gives you a working formula of how the spell operates. What you bring as your intent, the reason for the spell/prayer/ritual carries with it the will and the desire for manifestation upon its application. So when you are actually performing the ceremony/speaking any verse, you are fusing the idea of the intent with the will and desire of manifestation. You are then directing the currents and energies through the ceremony, spell, gestures, thought, and releasing it towards the intended goals. When you apply this you have (X) the manifestation of the spell.

Omitting the above mechanical breakdowns of prayers where you have to constantly reaffirm your faith/belief in a higher power; this model gives a way we can take our ceremonies, and workings towards manifestation through the will of the self. When you rely on your own will/ intent, regardless of the forces you invoke, evoke, conjure and draw, the influences of the manifestation will differ from that greatly in the successful outcome if you can focus on this model.

The Application of this model of manifestation is that spells when repeated will give us rituals. Those rituals combined with a spell of for a singular purpose gives us a rite. Something that only needs to occur once in order for the manifestation to change the nature of the world. Through the remainder of this course remember this model when working on the assignments.

Here is an example of how one would break down a spell into its various parts, and understand the mechanical nature behind it, to add in the aspects that are missing from it.

Intent and Will, combined with Desire, with Direction and Release, gives you a working model of how the spell operates. You can apply it in such ways as: If the intent is to cause the love of someone then I intend to find that in them which is what is loved, and bring about the change in them, and in the one who wants them to love back, and it is that desire for the emotion which will fuel the direction to achieve the proper intent. Releasing it in act where it will bring about the desired changes in the outer world. Bridging the external microcosmic and macrocosmic together in the form of the desire, and the will of both parties to mutually agreeable terms. By the desires and till in the inner world, and the tides and currents of the outer world. Which will achieve a logical progression of them mating.

The solution will then be a resultant possibility of choices. In that party A, and Party B have in their capacities a desire towards being together, or potential of being together. Meaning that if say Bill loved Joan who was not in love with Bill. Bill then decides to work magick to make Joan love him. What then occurs is a number of potential outcomes.

A) Joan will love him back, and it will be all together fine and dandy. This situation is what can be hoped for but rarely occurs.

B) Joan is married to someone, and has kids and a life of her own, and it is only a mild infatuation that allowed her even to express some interest in Bill, and Bill correspondingly is only suffering from lust and a wanting desire to have said lust fulfilled. Thus creating a messy situation which will require that the husband and children become questionable collateral damage in the desire of Bill to fulfill his lust. Through him seeking damaging ways for said lust to be fulfilled.

C) Bill who is in love with Joan, but unable to act upon it because of his wife, kids, family, and mortgage payments, and it's Bill who is doing work on Joan to get her to open up to love in her life, and find someone who would be a better match then a man who would have a ruined life on his hands because he extended his emotional base too far from the center.

D) Bill who is doing a working on Joan, because they are married and Bill is trying to kindle the spark back of what was there. Allowing for the manifestation to occur in a subtle ways, where he can stimulate the feelings of his wife.

E) Bill is trying to get Joan away from her girlfriend, Jill, while Fredrick is working spells to get Bill to be his lover.

There are possibilities that will range and include someone's death through a car accident; someone's pain and suffering with abuse to make the situations unstable and fall towards their centers, and thus allow for things like a new relationship with Joan, and Bill, while their respective lives fall apart. And any obligations they may have agreed to, go unfulfilled because of the nature of the currents which they invited into their lives. So when you deal with cosmological construction you have to determine which scenario you want to have take place.

You need then to be able to recognize the influence of the currents of the macrocosm and their relationship to the inner world. Be it through a Venation love, or a lunar influence where the tides are stimulated to be able to focus down and choose the current which you can make manifest.

Situation A will almost never happen. This is due to the other energies of life. If it will ,however, occur in a dream type of state where the individuals will find some form of love, and be happy with the idea. B-D occur quite frequently, and have the capacity for being influenced by working with the high Art. If you have the means to cause something, there will be an effect.

So the same occurs as true for working with the Art on a mechanical structure. So you cause those currents to occur in the lives of both individuals, then you will have a subtle guide to the progression of the relationship to its most likely outcome. The ideal scenario is one where both individuals experience the love that is shared which will stimulate both of them towards a better end. Situation E happens often enough to have it addressed. Like elements, the emotions have the same desire to flow through the course of least resistance. The course of least resistance is found through your model, if this current does Y, then it can be included to achieve X.

Example of exact spell breakdown mechanics:

Restoration of the Soul

I call forth from the Mountains of the East , Ao, of the Cleansing Waters;
Come forth and cleanse the body which is before you.
I call forth Erh-Lang, Goddess of Restoration;
Restore the Spirit which is before you.
I call forth Aset that raised Asar to life;
Return the Power of the Spirit to that which is before you.

In this the intent is simply stated within the Title of the Spell. It takes no tools to preform when you understand the mechanisms, which are:

The **Intent** is stated as cleansing, and restoration.
The **Will** is what does the calling.
The **Direction** is to the body that lays before the power of the Forces evoked.
The **Release** is the conclusion of the Passage.

The action of speaking it aloud affirms the Desired will of the intent.

The Calling is the medium of manifestation, to call is to evoke the forces.

The active nature of this spell to cause change is attributed to the Yang nature, or active, changing nature. To preform this spell it requires the will to cause direct change within the body that needs to be affected for restoration, by stimulating the internal currents of the body with the external forces of Ao, Erh-Lang, and Aset through the medium of water.

So this is also a water cast spell, in that it calls upon the watery nature of restoration.

Ascension Magick

Ascension of the Body

The Energy body of the human body allows for the source currents to flow through each of the gates of Chakra points. This is why we open the gates to make ready the body to be able to handle the conditions of the higher arts that are contained here. The reason we have the gate in the earth is to represent each of our connections to the elements.

The Summoning circles in the palm and feet Chakras represent the points where energy is drawn in via the Yin Chi and Yang Chi currents that flow through the body up the Prana tube. The Kundalini current is the serpentine force that is the double helix structure that flows and unites each of the 7 gates. Each of the planets have their gate correspondences, and it is in this manner that we convert the energy pockets inside the microcosm and open them up to the macrocosm.

We do this to body to open the conduits to all; for the free flowing currents of the sources to flow through us, to create that which we will. The soul being the medium between this plane and others, will have the ability to come and go as well as develop a body that can pass through all fields of energy. The body of the spirit and the body of the flesh can be both integrated to awaken the spirit within. This allows one actions, as one would see in an independent body; however, both the flesh and the spirit can move as one.

When the body and the spirit move as one, regardless of dependency on need for flesh, the Chi currents that one has flowing through them will allow them to tap into the roots of all the formative powers present upon the plane of their operations.

This work can be achieved through direct connection with something that is one with the source directly. As one develops in one's art, there are many ways to achieve this state of being. Some call it enlightenment or the ultimate aim, after this point all else is meaningless, etc. Not for the works contained herein. It is a mandatory state of being to awaken and ascend to have the body be able to withstand the direct raw source current.

When this is achieved, the further works of the spirit can be achieved with greater ease. The power of the sources can be directly felt as the animation current and living breath principal that animates the body. This is when the macrocosm and microcosm blend, and things like unspoken word magick, and the consequent manipulation of the free energy that is present within any plane of creation. The desired current can then flow through these points more freely and in balance with the other energy currents that go into sustaining the body.

It becomes necessary for constant work with the energy of the body, shadow, and spirit to maintain the conduits and prevent blow-outs or backups of the current. This then becomes the foundation for the Tower of Art which is created when the gate of the earth and the gate of the heaven become aligned within the body; when the Warlock becomes the union point of creation, a pillar of the world sphere that connects to the source of all things, and to the physical plane.

"Awakening"

It is, in the course of our discussion, necessary to suspend possible disbelief. The things we explore do not need to be accepted as truth, but there is some truth to the acceptance of certain concepts. Such is the case of celestial rank, position in hierarchies, and initiations into astral orders. In these orders, etc., as we are only on this earth for so long, we tend to carry over attributes from the spirit world. This is not always true, it is not always untrue. It is a rare enough occurrence that most books that discuss other-world critters such as fairies, vampires, etc., do so from a perspective that they are born that way and you can't really "be made" into one. This is true to an extent. It's got to be who you are when you're incarnated into this world. We come from somewhere; we are an aspect of the Singular Collective. We have duties, jobs to do, and lessons to learn that we might do them better. Some are not aware of this growth; some never will be aware of it. Each life they live will be like it's the first one. Others of us are aware of what goes on between incarnations, and what has gone on during past incarnations. It in this is what most people call the "awakening" when it comes to one's "Other" status.

A lot of my findings over the years have been that people who claim this path, do so from a point of madness, and inability to process the nature of "being" that makes up the whole of who they are. They try and categorize themselves into such a structure that many attributes of their living body go neglected, and they degenerate into madness, chaos and death. It might not even be physical death, but it is a death; a stagnation of the soul on the path, which unless the stagnation is realized, then it's not going to change. There is a point to this, for the developing mage; and that is to understand there is a nature to your energy. Once you have this, you can progress and really get into it using what you find about yourself. To get the most out of the following sections, you have to walk the line of madness.

Acknowledging your nature, as celestial, infernal, elemental etc, is the first step towards moving down the road of how things progress. You have to then be able to make the clear distinction between the soul that is you, as this critter with the mind that animates your meat. Your essence, who and what you are, is an incarnated spirit in meat. The human body is a shape, a host. The mind that animates before this "awakening" process occurs is generally at odds with what comes. Your acceptance of who you are, what you are, at the core of your being. It is this acceptance of who you are, that allows you to move onto your next phase of development.

You have to take everything with a grain of salt, and understand that something about it will help you learn more about what it is you're able to do, or the "flavor" in which you do it. It helps you in becoming an extension of magick, not just working with it, like your witch or wizard would. Like a Warlock, who embraces that they are an extension of the Singular collective, so too are they also something else. It is this something which separates us, and yet unites us, a familiarity beyond flesh, distance, and time. So from this awakening of your true self, you are able to proceed to what comes next. Many people get lost on this part of the path; they go off and join cults, and revel in the madness never progressing past this stage. It is fine for them, but our purpose is on mastering magicks, at least what we can of ourselves, given what we have experienced thus far.

From here, you have a difficult journey because you will have read my work, hopefully, or at least followed this text along to a point where you're interested and seek out the other stuff. I hope for your sake, my dear reader, that it is still in print. As from this point the work becomes highly speculative and only comparisons can be drawn with examples I can give which you can reference other works. Case in point, Crowley. He was the Great Beast. That was his contribution, and he opened it up to a discussion on such things, from which very few of his works make sense; unless, of course, he was some off-world critter wrapped up in meat, and put to task of bringing occultism into the modern world. Just as my aim is to contribute a body of work which will help the next generations of thinkers.

The Hierarchies

In the realm of creation, we have the division from the source; it's an explanation that you can either believe what you want about what happened after the big bang, or you can do much meditating and seeking out where your place is in creation. Which creation do you come from, which source do you most closely identify with? When you have reached a plateau of practice where you need to pick up another book, or pick up an old work of things you either haven't covered, or you missed out on, and found a new direction in which to head. You come to a point when you question yourself; you put to test all the things which you have been working on. In my case, when I do this, it is the periods of time when I write one of these books, or a few of them. Giving me a chance to reflect on all the things that I worked on over the last year, or two years, or even a decade or more.

When you find yourself confronted with this challenge of the what, why and purpose, then it is time for you to go back to your beginning. Find which things made you question, what things do you want to experience more of. As you become more stable in where your soul's place is in the grand scheme of things, the greater focus you will have on this plane as well. The reason for this, according to my findings, is that the universe is mental; it is the great mind of a larger, far wiser thing than any meat. However, we have our places in the world of flesh, and in the world of spirit. We are spirit that affects the physical world because we are flesh. So we are, by nature, ranking members of various celestial hierarchies. There are a far fewer of us out there who are aware of their position in the hierarchies of the celestial orders due to the number of people that fall off of the direction. It is this fall from the direction which keeps it out of publication, makes us lose so many potential new directions; we can head from the inter connected world of the macrocosm.

So when considering the functions of a hierarchy, it is much like say, a retail sales clerk, a bartender, a writer, a buyer of products for retail establishments, a priest, an exorcist, an alchemist. These are just titles, which describe some of who we are, and what we do. I am all of these things, and much more. Titles and descriptions of caste only glimpse at part of the picture. It is damn near impossible to have a single term which can define a body/soul/mind more completely then a clear will to attempt to put together the great mystery that is why we are the way we are. How we are, who and what we are, becomes irrelevant. We are. Any one is a lifetime pursuit till mastery. It is all these facets like a fine cut gem stone which shape who we are, how we interact with the world around us. However, what is presented is my understanding at this point in my life, and the lives of those who I have watched for years on their own journeys.

I find there are 3 principal ways that one becomes an extension of the hierarchies. The first is to be chosen, by the divine spirits which select their followers, based on whatever resonates most with the one being chosen. These can be good things, or they can be painful things which unite those forces. More often than not, it will come at the result of some painful lesson . A way out of the pain by being able to see around the edges a bit easier. The second method of becoming of the hierarchies is to ritually devour someone who is part of the hierarchies and assume the mantle of their position. Yes, this a violent way to do it. And last, that becomes relevant to our case study here, is that one can make an agreement for it. There is an exchange in this last one. Services rendered, or that shall be rendered in order to be accepted as an extension of what it is you are making this pact with.

The first grade is something will be acquired from dedication, the second from greed, the third from desperation. Those who make it to this step on the path can fail if they do not see that the only way to progress is to be selected by archetypal forces which view you, or your deeds as the extension of their own natures, and the sources which they serve as the guardian forces for.

What I mentioned holds true when it comes to celestial rank. Generally, these things are achieved via some gnosis, or meditative experience. Like the duplication of the hierarchies of the churches, covens, and guilds and the oldest of empires; kings, lords, priests, knights, etc. ad nauseum. These ranks do exist likewise in the spirit world. However, what humanity conceives of as a Lord, just gives for a terminology to define an area of dominion, with subjects, spirits, and critters, as well as work that is motivated by the Lords work with their Archetypal Source, and its perspective on creation.

The Singular Collective – is the progenitor of all things

The sources of creation – Divide to attributes the physical world to its base components

The Archetypal Forces of Perception – Light, Dark, Shadow

The Elemental Forces of Perception – the Earthy, the Airy, the Fiery, the Watery

The Five Fold Division of the Physical Elements – the wood, the metal, the fire, the thunder, the aether/space/void

etc...

The list is to show that there is an order to the way this system of obscure magicks operates. Basing it upon the foundations of an acceptable numerology, and to give a point of reference for building one's own mental construct of creation. When it becomes a united view to the structure of creation, you can then do path working techniques like the rite of transformation, and a bunch of other various ascendancy meditations/rites. Those ascendance ceremonies deepen the inner well that the mage has the ability to work with. From there, they allow the mage to develop a sense of understanding about the purpose and the order to which the universe operates. Regardless of what one god-force says in the head of one devotee.

When you become one of the celestial order, it doesn't matter which side of the perception you're on; each source has those 3 faces, and the 8 sources have 24 divisions. So, you have as an example:

From the source of Light, and its Light side, the dark side of the Light, and the shadowy side of the Light. You also have then, the Earthy Light, the Watery Light, the Airy Light, The Woody Light, the Fiery Light, the Thundering Light, and the Aetheric Light.

Each of the sources can be divided again and again by what is contained with their own natures. So much so, that every division will allow for the inclusion of the other 7 sources within the source being examined. From this event, what I call the "Source" current has aspects of the other, which when all aspects cease to be divided from each other to create a working model of relationships, they in their combined state make up the Singular Collective. The great mind of the all and nothing, is what guides what occurs, yet at the same time, there is an element of free will. We are Hands of the Singular Collective but we can work freely with any station in creation according to what it is we need on the path.

So you can seek out the angels, demons, gods, daemons, djinn, elementals, etc. for each of the corresponding divisions of the Singular Collective, and you can work with them accordingly. Yet they all come from the human mind to give them shape, to give them form beyond just their invisible vibrational influences. Not alive in the conventional living sense, but still in existence to interact depending on what lens one needs in order work with the Singular Collective.

The Oath of Service

There is a time in our practice when we must dedicate ourselves, to ourselves. This is our oath, a declaration of our path, that we will walk the road of the arts for the rest of our days. The vow of service is much like a path of a priest; it is not something that you should do without having spent at least a few years contemplating your next step. When you have determined the course of action you would take, the method of swearing such an Oath, Vow or Pact is up to you.

Those who would dedicate themselves to a god-force would do best with a vow of service, or an oath of service in exchange for services. Those who beseech the demons and angels would do best with a pact of service.

When man enters into a bond of service this bond becomes a pact. This is the most common form of bonding. There are also bonds known as Oaths or Contracts; these are temporary and are contractual only for the duration of their agreement. Whereas when one gives spoken bond when the conditions meet the following is regarded by the cosmic law as a pact.

- The service to be rendered.
- The service to be returned or goods to be exchanged.
- The time frame for when the services are to be rendered for either party.
- The acts which constitute violation of the bond.
- The consequences of violation of the bond.

When such bonds are made, and have been made under willing agreement, then there is no reason which should prevent the bond from being fulfilled. So when you as the mage enter into bargain with a lesser man, in this case one man or woman who hold their words like a sieve holds water, and they as their nature dictates do not hold to their end of the bond; you have every recourse through both legal means where applicable, and through the art, to the conditions of the consequences. When dealing with people, their nature is to worm their way out of bonds which they set into place. It is common, and it has lead to many unfortunate ends to souls who would have just held up their end of the bargains they agree to. Take payment first.

Payment for contractual should always be taken first, in form of goods, or monetary repayment for services. There is to be an exchange equal to the services rendered. Nothing is done for nothing, do not get screwed by your own hopes in the better nature of the human animal. However, in the cases of service for service bonds, then begin with service that you can go without repayment of. Ensuring that they must in good time return their service. When this is done, then you can progress with the services which you exchange. Where enforceable, contact local authorities for the violation and theft of goods or services when one backs out of, or denies a signed agreement, or written contractual bond for lost materials should they back out.

As the living human is an animal much like a worm, you will have to hold them to their bonds; where as any other bond you make, you will be held to yours, as you are also human. To be a mage is to have a word which is never thought to be any less than what you say. If you say you are going to do something, then do it. Whether or not that will end badly for you, if you agree to it willingly, then you must hold to it. Likewise the people that come to you, or associate with you, should be held to like standards. However, this is rarely the case when they willingly fulfill the nature of the bond.

So most cases result in the one bonded being held as an oath breaker, and everything they have forfeit unto the nature of the bond, and the consequences accepted by willing mark, or statement. When you have a soul who has broken their word, and violated the nature of the agreement, then you have a responsibility to weigh their deeds upon the scales, and do work calling in the forces which you are aligned with, in order to cause the scales to balance for services rendered. This never ends well. If the bond is broken by the other party, if an agreement was not kept which was a signed agreement in front of a medium of some form, or mediated between two opposing parties. Then all their actions will be laid bare, and they will have no recourse. If they are workers of the art, who do work against their word, then they will find that they lose the capacity to work in any area of the art. To be of the caste, is to hold the Word as god.

If you cannot hold your word as the most sacred thing about you, all that you truly possess, then you are deserving of a worse fate then any can be described. Betrayers, treacherous souls all of them who break their bonds, and break their service without proper method, will have all their deeds laid bare by the ones who hold to their bonds. When they are forced to break bond, when circumstances beyond normal day to day occur, then they are laid bare, and the consequences of the conditions are brought to bare upon them. So it has always been.

Pacts of the Divine

Common bonds and contractual oaths between the living constitute a living pact. Whereas the bond between the spirits of men and the greater forces and powers such as their patrons shall be held with more weight then with a bond between the living, or with spirits. A note for the one undertaking these bonds; should you be held in violation of your bond to the greater force/power, then your capacity to form bond again will be removed as that force sees fit, in any capacity it has to silence the treacherous soul. All greater forces have a mode of operating when they silence those who break bond with them without proper method.

When bonding with the spirits of the Divine, herein all greater forces of the celestial or infernal realms; you take upon yourself the fate of that force. You take upon yourself the weight of all the energy of those who have perished in service to that force, and you also gain from them the power which is reserved only to those who bond with such forces. Common reasons why such pacts are struck are: to get out of a bond with a lesser spirit; power; influence of lesser forces,;or something which cannot be achieve through normal means within the capacity of the mage. Whereas the common reasons why the bonds are made from non-practicing people with the greater forces are protection, love, desires of the flesh, or guidance along a path which seems fitting for their nature and needs. Which for their having wanted, found in exchange of service the guidance they seek.

The violation of such bonds usually ends when the spirit becomes forcibly arranged into servitude, and if they are not doing their agreed actions, they will have as stated above, those capacities removed from them in any form that deity wishes. The manner in which such bonds are made is up to the nature of the Deity to which the bond would be made. You will know what form is acceptable to the force you are working with, because bonds with deity are not undertaken lightly. Power gained from such bonds always serves the ends of the god-force from which it comes, regardless of the wants and whims of the one who is bonded to that current.

Pacts of Spirits

When forging a bond between a spirit lesser than a god-force, it becomes imperative that you understand not only the nature of the spirit to which you bind yourself. You must know what the alignments of the spirit are in the elemental capacities, as well as any higher forces to which they are bonded, and the reasons they would go through the efforts of creating such bonds. It is to your doom if you are a foolish soul and willingly become bonded by a spirit offering a temporal gain, for something a bit more then what it's worth.

Elementals, Daemons, Demons, Spirits, Angels, Nature Spirits and so on are on this list of lesser spirits, as they are lesser than the god-force which created them. They all have purpose, goals; they are powers unto themselves, to serve their purpose for the elements which spawned them.

Common reasons for such pacts being created are that you would be gaining power, you would be gaining alliance which otherwise would not be possible. Such to the like that is found in Goethe's *Faust*. There is many a station which you can achieve, by aligning with, and bonding with elementals, or with lesser spirits in a plane to gain favor of the intelligences in the powers which you work with. The intelligences being the greater forces in command of the spirit you would work for, but still less than the deity which those forces serve.

Bonds of this nature usually require not just deeds and service in exchange, but also include a regular offering, or act of submission unto the spirit in recognition of the bond. That you must do for them, before they do for you. Nothing is gained without equivalent exchange for service. The true bonds of the spirits between the races of men cannot be annulled unless you complete the terms of the arrangement, or you seek out that force which is the greater force and can transfer your bond. Transfer of bonds in exchange of greater power, or different service is entirely permissible, and often times is done, as it gains power. Especially if you can get one bonded to you, then you transfer their bond as offering to a greater force in exchange for something in return for the service offered by the bonded.

Pacts of the Elements

When you bond with the elements you not only take them into you, but you extend and become part of them. Their fate is yours; you must be in control of the balance between the elements within your body. If you become unbalanced in your bond, then your own nature and your own elements will consume you. When you have, however, balanced out the bond you have with the element, in any one of its emanations, you have gained. Nothing is a greater bond than that between the mage and the elements of creation to which he has aligned himself. His word is bonded by the element, his body forged of the element, and his will becomes strengthened by the element.

When you have bonded in a true form to the primal source currents, there is no capacity for violation other than that of ceasing your journey; to which the elements will arrange themselves in a way which will cause you to continue against your will or not, because as one of the elements, you are guided by nature. You embrace your part in nature and you accept the duties of nature when you take into yourself any one of the elements. It is not for the careless to take into these bonds, because you will be held to your path, and you will be forced to follow the course of nature, in exchange for capacity within all of nature.

It is your connection to the elements which determines what capacity you are bonded, as it is your will which is made part of nature. The greater your will is, the stronger your connection is, the more resolved and aligned your spirit is, the more you have in your capacity. This is the aim of the mage; to be able to be one of nature, to be a creator instead of just passive creation. It is through the connection to the elements and to their patron which forges their own strength, to endure and survive what occurs. Yet when one bonds with the elements, one becomes a co-operator with their patron, being able to shape with an even hand the actions which are required. As the patron no longer is just a teacher, an employer of means and ends, but a true patron. One with whom you work, as your ends are the same, you desire what they desire, and they are indistinguishable from your will, and works.

This only occurs once in a lifetime when you have found what element you are comfortable working with, and which one you have the most natural alignments to. You prepare your space and clean everything. You make sure you are clean. Everything must be set in the prime hour for your bond. It will do that you should at each hour of the dawn twilight, the noon hour, the evening twilight, and the midnight hour. You bleed into a vessel of the element.

> I forge by the traditions of the past
> I that forge by the rites of living blood
> Do bond hence to this elemental source
> Let my will be manifest as it is bound
> By this pact I forge that we shall be as one
> It shall be of me,
> I shall be for it.
> Our will one.
> I make this covenant with this my element.
> I make this at the twilight of the dawn, at noon, at the setting sun,
> The midnight hour, that in this and every hour
> This covenant shall be a bond eternal.

Pacts with Places

In dealing with places of power, when you form bonds which strengthen what you're doing, then you can forge pacts with the places where you hold to be your center. The nodes, which can be described as the living forces which stimulate growth; plant life, animals, and even the people which live in the place. You can forge a pact with the spirit which protects, enlivens and also destroys the things those which go contrary to its flow. As said in *Advancing the Concepts*, you must maintain your domain, your region, and any territory which you live and work in. This is because the eventual step is that you forge a blood pact with the land. That your life becomes tied with the region; if the region successfully thrives under your watch, then you will be rewarded with riches. If you allow your region to fall into decay, then you will suffer for it.

Every place holds a memory, as people come and go. Places age, and their capacities change for what they are designed for, and remade into. These forces can be contracted like the elemental forces. Though these are forces which verge, and in some cases have a will and spirit of their own, becoming powers you can enlist the aid of. Binding yourself to a sacred location which you use to connect to the higher forces as well as the lower forces, establishes a connection to the earth as a living force, a power which lasts through the countless eons. It is in the best interests of those who forge such pacts and bonds never to speak of these. Keeping these as one of the most private bonds, which need not be spoken but it should be clear to anyone who reads these words, that through dedication to a space, through the maintenance of what it can yield and offer, is sign enough of such a significant force within a mage's life. As it becomes an extension of the power; tapping directly into the nodes, into the living currents of the region, the territory in which they live, as well as the domain which they swear blood oath to be bound to. Such bonds can never be broken, and there will always need to be a reminder of some bond such as this, the maintaining of soil from these sacred sites if one moves or leaves it. That they become bound to the fate of the region which gives them power, and strength to do as they need.

Awakening of the Spirit

On the evening of a new moon, or the full moon depending on your path. In the time when the influence of Mercury and the Moon are aligned; either in the day of Mercury in the hour of the Moon, or in the day of the Moon in the hour of Mercury. With Gemini to draw out and bring into reconciliation the two bodies. Light a white candle and carve the name of the soul whom you wish to awaken upon it in script. As you light it, meditate on their third eye opening and them being able to see all of that which can be seen by the fully opened third eye. Let thus the third eye be glowing blue.

> Fire of the second sight
> Lift the veil make darkness Light
> Clear vision for (x) to see
> Sight be granted to the eyes to thine eyes by me

For use on yourself:

> Fire of the second sight
> Lift the veil make darkness light
> Clear my vision to see
> Sight be granted now to me

Invocation of Power Of Consciousness

On a day when the time is peak for your own connections. The incense should be mellow and earthy, and you should be in a meditative state to connect your essence with the way that the mind works. Your mind should be able to expand out of your own consciousness, and embrace the cosmic mind. If you require it, speak the following or come up with your own mantra, and just give into the feeling of your higher mind uniting with the cosmic mind.

> I call forth the essence of all mankind,
> I call forth the power to unify the essence with my desires.
> I summon forth the power of all humanity throughout the ages.
> I call forth this most ancient power to enter into my vessel.
> I call this forth to become one with my soul.
> I call this forth to have the strength
> To work the magicks that will make me whole.

To Align to the Darkness of the Soul

    Cleanse a space of every object that does not get incorporated with this work. Set the altar with two green candles on the top left and right corner. In the center place the skull of the art. Position an altar seal with points of two pointing to the corners of the altar. Place then candles around the circle where this is to take place – a candle of green in the north, a candle of purple in the east, red in the south, and blue in the west.

    Upon the center of the pentagram, place a chalice of red wine which has been blessed to be a catalyst of change for your body and soul. Allow then a few drops of blood to be mixed therein from your dominant hand. Start then an hour glass flowing, when it is half spent tip it on its side. When this is completed the following is to be done.

    Light the candles starting in the east, drawing in the elements with a charge similar to thus:

> From the east (south, west, north)
> Elemental forces I call you here to attend my working

    When the candles of five then are lit, and then light the two green ones upon the altar. Draw in all the energy you can as you lift the chalice and raise it to the direction of your working, speaking a charge of or like the following:

> Asar, Aset, Hecate, Ea charge this vessel,
> Mutate my essence forever more.
> This I ask from great ones before,
> What I take in of blood and wine,
> Crosses all boundary and planes of time;
> I ask for the darkness as I consume
> So my essence can walk a thousand lifetimes or more
> To serve the forces of the night
> So my essence will be balanced by dark and light
> I drink of this wine and take into me the darkness
> As is consumed but let me not be consumed.

Rite of Transformation

When you must, as a mage, set out from the ordinary paths of the self and religious order. To seek the things which only the few embrace. There is this method of the building of the celestial body. In order to pass through to worlds beyond this one, ancient thought has been that one must awaken within their own natures similar currents as those found in the great spheres of the 7 planets. This is an initiation ritual of sorts, whereby one can leave the need for pathworking and embrace the path to the Singular Collective as a whole being.

Begin by inscribing 7 black candles with the gates of the 7 and seals of their planets. Make by mixing flour with herbs that are of the influence by the 7 planets enough to ring the base of the candle that corresponds its herb. Your blood should be mixed with the flour/herb mix, as well as the Tea of Transformation.

Brew then a tea of the 7 herbs in equal parts, noting your allergy and their properties. It should be sitting upon the heat for 3 hours. After 7 days of its fermentation, speak the charge of becoming and it shall be consumed upon the final sounds of the invocation of the becoming. The timing of this work should be on a period of celestial transformation. The new moon in October is a good time, so would be Walpurgisnacht, or any other solstice or high equinox. You should have a circle with the the 7 pointed enneagram ringed with the characters representing the Yin and Yang, I-Ching; the abyssal hexagram should be in the center.

Pour a circle of white flour around the area you are going to be working. Place then the 7 candles as they correspond to the planetary symbols within the enneagram. These candles should be then ringed with the flour/herb mixture around their base so they are within their own circles within the greater circle. You should then take sea salt and form a secondary circle outside this flour ring.

The space before you begin set up should consist of smudging the area of some form. Separate off the circled area, and lock the door to the ritual chamber. There should be no music unless you feel it will aid. The only one you should do this work with would be one who balances out your astrological sign. If you are Mars, then they should be a Venus, and so on.

When it is time to begin, pour the Tea of Transformation into a chalice half filled with wine or water so it becomes 1 to 1. Place this chalice upon the center circle. Light a white candle so that you may see your work as you enter forth from the world of light, into the world of darkness and magick. Recite the 7 charges of the spheres. In order of the candles as they go clockwise around the circle. Alternating between you and the secondary if you have one. When the circle of candles are lit. Extinguish with your fingers the white candle with this charge :

> Be called forth by the unspoken words
> By the power of the damned on earth
> In the shadow
> I seek shelter
> By the Black Sun in the midnight hour
> I seek to be hidden
> Let nothing of the works within be seen
> By the mind's eye of others
> Let the words go unheard
> By the ears of kine
> This circle shall stand outside of Time!

When you have extinguished the candle begin the Invocation of the Becoming. If there are two people working this rite, they should speak it in unison.

Invocation of Becoming

As one of darkness forth from light
Hear me, spirits called of time Before
Hear me by the blood of the forsaken
Hear me by the ancient forces
Of the black forest at midnight
By time forgotten
Those that were
By the unborn souls
The never born fallen
Hear me in the time of the lost
Hear now my summons
By the blood of the forsaken
Open forth the first Gate
From which all comes forth as the seed
The base of the true will
I call forth by those that
Are never named
Those which are of the ones of power
By the shadows made flesh
Hear me And be opened!

Hear me, spirits called of time Before
Hear me by the blood of the forsaken
Hear me by the ancient forces
Of the black forest at midnight
By time forgotten and those that were
By the unborn souls and
The never born fallen
Hear me in the time of the lost
Hear now my summons
By the things to come
Open forth the gates!

Hear me by the middle pillar
Hear me by the shadows in heaven
Hear me, my demon fallen kin
Hear me by the Forgotten waters of power
Hear now this summons
By the time of the lost
By the blood of the forsaken
Hear me in this time outside of time
In this place beyond all places

Hear me, spirits
Called of time Before
Hear me by the blood of the forsaken
Hear me by the ancient forces
Of the black forest at midnight
By time forgotten

Those that were
By the unborn souls
The never born fallen
Hear me in the time of the lost
Hear now my summons
By the will made flesh
Let the second gate be opened
Open forth this passage of balance
In this time that is not a time
In the place that is not a place
At the meeting of the worlds

By the time of the lost
By the blood of the forsaken
Hear me by the middle pillar
Hear me by the shadows in heaven
Hear me, my demon fallen kin
Hear me by the Forgotten waters of power
Hear now this summons
By the time of the lost
By the blood of the forsaken
Hear me in this time outside of time
In this place beyond all places

Hear me, spirits called of time Before
Hear me by the blood of the forsaken
Hear me by the ancient forces
Of the black forest at midnight
By time forgotten
Those that were
By the unborn souls
The never born fallen
Hear me in the time of the lost
Hear now my summons
By the blood offered forth
To the Eternal Darkness
I evoke here of the realms of
Shadows in my soul
That which is of the third gate
from the flames, the power of the Aeons
Hear me and be opened

By the time of the lost
By the blood of the forsaken
Hear me, spirits called of time Before
Hear me by the blood of the forsaken
Hear me by the ancient forces
Of the black forest at midnight
By time forgotten
Those that were
By the unborn souls

The never born fallen
Hear me by the middle pillar
Hear me by the shadows in heaven
Hear me, my demon fallen kin
Hear me by the Forgotten waters of power
Hear now this summons
By the time of the lost
By the blood of the forsaken
Hear me in this time outside of time
In this place beyond all places
Hear me in the time of the lost
Hear now my summons
Open forth these gates
Open Now the fourth gate
From which stems the power of the
Will, Flesh, Shadow, Life
These forces which play upon
The eternal wheel of Fate
Opened now shall be this gate
Hear me and be not abstinent
Hear me and be brought forth
Hear me and come forth as my
Will is made flesh

Hear me by the middle pillar
Hear me by the shadows in heaven
Hear me my demon fallen kin
Hear me by the Forgotten waters of power
Hear now t,his summons
By the time of the lost
By the blood of the forsaken
Hear me in this time outside of time
In this place beyond all places

Hear me by the blood of the forsaken
Hear me by the ancient forces
Of the black forest at midnight
Those that were
By the unborn souls
The never born fallen
Hear me in the time of the lost
Hear now my summons
Open forth the fifth gate
From which flows the word
That which is of power
To mold the darkness
As a sculptor his clay
Hear me by the middle pillar
Hear me by the shadows in heaven
Hear me, my demon fallen kin

Hear me by the Forgotten waters of power
Hear now this summons
By the time of the lost
By the blood of the forsaken
Hear me in this time outside of time
In this place beyond all places

Hear me, spirits
Called of time Before
Hear me by the blood of the forsaken
Hear me by the ancient forces
Of the black forest at midnight
By time forgotten
Those that were
By the unborn souls
The never born fallen
Hear me in the time of the lost
Hear now my summons
Open forth this sixth Gate
Let its power be evoked in this
Place beyond all places

By the unborn souls and
The never born fallen
Hear me in the time of the lost
Hear now my summons
By that which shapes the
Worlds of light and dark
Shaping them anew in this
The time of change and death
Hear now these words
That issue forth the words of power
Of those who have come before
Hear me by the middle pillar
Hear me by the shadows in heaven
Hear me, my demon fallen kin
Hear me by the Forgotten waters of power
Hear now this summons
By the time of the lost
By the blood of the forsaken
Hear me in this time outside of time
In this place beyond all places

That this thing shall pass
Let now the seventh gate be thrust open
That which brings sight of the words of power
That cause the world to bend when uttered
That these things made by the unspoken now spoken
Bring forth the gate of the sight
Let now this be evoked from primal chaos
Let this now be opened

Hear me, spirits
Called of time Before
Hear me by the blood of the forsaken
Hear me by the ancient forces
Of the black forest at midnight
By time forgotten
Those that were
By the unborn souls
The never born fallen
Hear me in the time of the lost
Hear now my summons
Out of the void of creation
I come as keeper of the keys
As the gate-keeper of the way
The eighth gate,
The crown of my becoming
Shall be opened now
By The will made flesh
By the flesh made shadow
By the words now spoken
By their power seen
By the Transformation to the Akhaharu
Hear me by these forces open now the
Eighth gate of transformation
Let the pure darkness eternal
Wash over me so I am worthy
That this is made so by logos

By those of the first time
By becoming one of the Akhaharu
By this the transformation
To become by blood, Akhaharu
I enter forth this realm beyond
The veil of life and death
Let the chains of my mortality
Fall free as they be set upon the followers of Yahweh

Hear me, forces here evoked
From the deepest space and darkest realm
This is the time of the lost
My blood is blood of the forsaken
I am made worthy
To enter hence the house
To become as the timeless
Now I call forth to the open gates of power
In this the time of shadows

As I stand in the devil's light
As one of the Akhaharu
Hear me, spirits called of time Before

Hear me by the blood of the forsaken
Hear me by the ancient forces
Of the black forest at midnight
By time forgotten
Those that were
By the unborn souls
The never born fallen
Hear me in the time of the lost
Hear now my summons
Open now these Eight gates
So that within me they are open
As those we seek as was in time before

When desire ruled
Dream was king
When mythos and nightmare
Walked in the open
When havoc and pain
Crossed the land as wind in the trees

Nothing shall stand of the times before
As we enter the realm of change
As we become as the lost
We are made as the forsaken
We enter and call forth
The pact of the timeless
Which brought mortality
To the flesh of the kine
We enter and become
We consume of ourselves
Yet not ourselves consumed
We are made hence

Like those that shall never die
We become as the first to be of the timeless
I am the gate keeper
Without me the gate is shut
I am the keeper of the way
Without me the way is barred
Let the gate be opened as
I tread the way of the Akhaharu

Drink the wine, and draw in the energy to your core. This rite should not be attempted by those under the influence of alcohol or some other chemical alterations.

Summons of the Draconian Spirit

After you have delved into the shadows of the celestial bodies. There are similarities between the ageless spirits/entities that exist in their places to which we are originally of. These long forgotten forces are those primordial spirits which existed as the first breed of creation, the children of the Singularity. There are those perfected things, and those things which are less then perfection. Embracing the nature of that origin will help in connecting one to the Singularity. This is just a communion of the souls, as it were, to help solidify one's mental understanding of the planes, and their natures.

By Connecting the Summoner with the underworld of the gods, it allows one to anchor one's consciousness closer to the source. Primarily, the draconian forces of creation after the one began its division. Write the following in accordance with what you have developed for yourself on your path. Mold into a ritual if you feel the desire.

I stand at the crux of the world,
Having passed the gates of creation
To stand as one of those of the first time,

I swear and call
By blood the dark eternal fire
Come forth,
Forge this bond
To the plane of souls.

I am he who walks as the timeless,
I am as I am,
My being destroyed as a creation
To be forged as my own creation.

I walk forth
From this place
Creator,
I became through becoming

I am he
Who has crossed the gates
Entered the world of the dead,

I command, Satan,
Destroy my form where i am a creation,
Forth from this place into the graveyard of the gods,

I command Moloch
Open the gates to the world
I am creator,
I am lord of the land of shadows,
High Priest of the Temple of Black Fire
Master of the gates of the Way
Keeper of the keys of creation.
Guardian of the Frozen Sun
Open now the pathway

To the first creation
By the blood of the third creation
I command it.

Khepr ank set ka
Khepr ank setka shu

The blood of fire
Burning in my soul,
Floating in the abyss of inner space
The fire eternal,
Frozen sun of the ancient world
That calls to the souls of the lost.

In a time without time,
In a space separated from any place,
I draw that I summon,
I ask and come
In supplication of
The fire of the frozen sun
That burns in my core.

Forth from me this world is open,
Forth from you the ancient world is open,
I stand now
As a medium of creation
Let us walk together
The path of transformation.

That which has barred
The ageless ones,
The undying ones
In the lands beyond
Beneath the ageless seas
That which has been buried
In the flow of time
Those forgotten
The never-born fallen
Into the shadows
Into the void
By the will of blood
The bond between us,
Open the gates
To the ancient ones
I conjure these forces
From the deepest depths
Within me,
Stand strong as the bars
Which hold them back.
By the blood of my flesh,
The sound of my spirit,

The word of my mind
Let us walk together
We cross now the ancient gates
Bring forth
Those of the first time.
I am the lord of transformation
I am he who has crossed all boundary of space and time
It is in this place is where I stand
Where I conjure the cross of the worlds
I stand at the angle of the heaven, earth, void, and endless space
I have come here by the blood
I have come here by the word
By will, and deed I have come
By the flesh, and mind I have been brought

In this place, in this time
In this hour and my rhyme
I set the bonds of heaven loose
I unbind the bonds which have been set
I unchain the doors which have stood fast
I am he who commands the seas to part
Come forth that which of the first time

Brought forth ancient ones
Brought forth undying ones
Brought forth androgynous ones
Brought forth, the mother of all
Brought forth, the father of all
Brought forth unto me

Come unto me
Receive my words,
Accept my offering
Of blood
Of word
Of deed
Of becoming
Join with me
Unite with my essence
That we may walk together
In the ways of power
Open now the way!

Ceremony of Removal

This is a good example of declarations of the Luciferian ideals that some might hold. To break the mental bonds of the gods, the ties and tethers they hold in their spirit. So using what we know of ourselves, we must ritually remove ourselves from any structure or schema that would bind our own spirits.

It is in this world view through Thaumiel that Satan is the destroyer of the world where the adept is the creation. So we will use the Arts of Destruction to remove the world that the adept is a simple creation, to then be able to open up and enter the world where the Adept is creator. Draw an array which represents the world gate. Set your space with dark things, where the only light comes from a candle placed upon the array. Bleed onto the candle and extinguish its flame, that by your blood, you are free of the creation.

I am he that stands prostrate and ready upon the altar of creations crux
I am he that spreads wide in the mysteries and secrets of creation
I am he that gives birth through my thought will and deed
I am he that gives rise to worlds through my will and creation
Unto the ending of time
I am he that holds the key of creation
Burn now my name forth from the book of life
Inscribe me into the black book of death, as I become as death
I forsake life of the unknowing ones
I give up my comforts as I become
I consume now that which would make me the creator
I am free forth from the creation of the one god,
To enter into the union of the singularity
I am as an embodiment of the singularity
From dualist perspective, from singular will
I rise forth and proclaim myself
Thrust open the gate from this world
Into the world of my creation
I conjure forth that the horrors part and nightmares flee
I command that the World crack open upon my coming
Let this world pass before me as I leave as child, as son, and servant
I am become father, master, god
No force may stand before me as equal
No blood may stand as better then mine

I am he who crosses the abyss and has survived
I am he who commands the heaven and earth tremble; It obeys
I am he who wills the winds to stir and the tempest rise; It obeys
I am he who has become the lord of the shadows
Master in the abyss and the lands between
By my blood, I open now the way forth from the creation
I am the creator now, unto the ending of days as I so will it
No force in earth, on heaven or that stirs in the primordial abyss is my equal

I am forth from the collective consciousness
I am Master of the path that I walk,
I am keeper of the keys, I open the gate
I am the keeper of the gate, I open the way

I am the black lord of the ageless fire
As it is made so in blood,
On stone,
Through air,
And of water,
It shall be so,
Now and forever!

Ceremony of Return

Through the power of Thaumiel we can have Moloch open the universe where the adept is the creator. no longer the creation. So, the rites of Moloch are what we are going to be focusing on in the development of the adept on this stage. Upon an array that is designed to become the foundation of your arts as master of the world view and direct link from the source of creation to this world. You need a single candle that you will make your conjuration to and extinguish in your blood.

I am he who stands upon nothingness and all,
I am one who has come forth as the black endless void.
Here before me stands the gateway of all of creation!
I stand before the great gate of the construct,
I open the way as the master of keys,
I open the gate as the keeper the of the way,
Forth from this world to any other.
It is open now before me,
I am father of creation,
I am the master of creation.
I am progenitor of all things under will,
Here in this hour I enter birthed my art.
I am born of myself,
I am given myself to myself.
I am created of my blood, bone, flesh and will.
I am eternal an extension of the collective.
Here before the world I have been outside,
Here before the world I have created,
Here before the world I have observed,
Here before the world I enter,
No longer a creation, but creator.
Forged in the very source fires of the universes,
I am one who walks between the stars.
Between the earth and sky at will,
I am here before this gate of my own creation,
I open it unto the world where I create!

"So how far down does the rabbit hole go?"

Dearest reader,

By this point in the discussion of the above topics, you may finding yourself scratching your head. Do not worry, this is common. A friend of mine once took a White Out pen and scrawled across my backpack in band class, in the nasty white paint the words; "Don't Panic". So do yourself a favor, and get used to the ideas that you might not under the right influence; understand all the things that have been discussed, will be discussed, and possibly be discussed. (The verdict is still out on a few things, reference the disclaimer in the beginning if you have any question on the completion of this stuff.)

All things in time. Back to the point as has been stated here. We are getting into the second section of works designed to raise the bar for the pagan who would have their will a bit more Johnny-on-the-spot when it comes to manifestations.

Please know, dear reader, that we do not care if you set your cat on fire, or murder it, or put it in a bag and throw into on-coming traffic. If it is that you blame the author or anyone else for your behavior, or anyone involved in the production or sales of this work has anything to do with any of your psychopathic tendencies; you will be laughed at, mocked and otherwise referred to your local padded party room "with the nice young men in the clean white coats." Hee hee...ha ha..

So do try and enjoy. Stay tuned for the next installment of my commentary under "Where is the rabbit, and why am I in this hole?" By the time the middle of the book comes out if you haven't muddled your brain, then under, "I think I am in a hole, was there even a rabbit?"

Yours infernally,
Infernal Warlock

Elemental Magick

Union of the Elementals

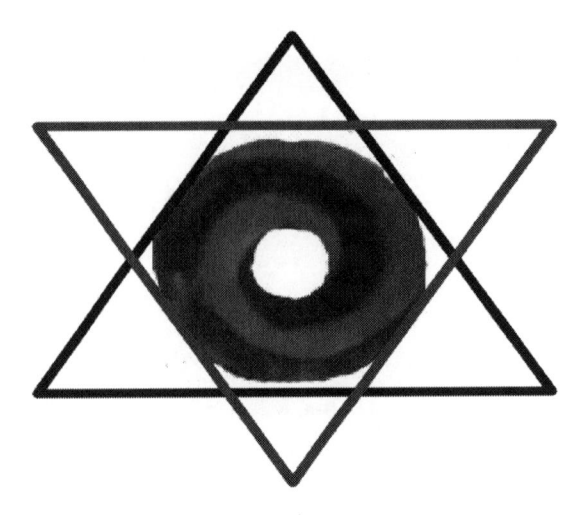

This is the great work of blending the primal Chi into a usable construct.

Allowing for the blending to occur in the body requires the balancing of the Chi currents for the Yin and Yang to blend within the core of the being.

The blending of the currents that occurs outside of the body is not as stable as internal blending, however, more current can be channeled for a greater force than the system of the body can maintain for too long internally, unless the individual has done work to expand the core accordingly.

The construct is to be used with a dual gate conjuration. One from above, one from below, to exist between the heaven sphere, and earth sphere, or whatever is the requirement of this work.

It is usually a dual current that is exactly opposite that works best with this method.

Water – Earth	Fire - Water
Water – Air	Fire – Earth
Water – Fire	Fire - Air

Air – Fire	Earth – Air
Air – Water	Earth – Water
Air – Earth	Earth - Fire

Come forth;

Exist between,

Heaven and Earth.

Come forth;

Exist between,

Earth and Heaven

Earth

It begins with sitting beneath the oldest tree in your region. Feel the flow of the earth's core. The breaths of the world becoming your breath. Your Prana going deep into the core of the earth, flowing back upwards into you.

From this point, you solidify this connection within your body. Push your core from your body and down into the earth's core. So that as the earth spins, rotates, breathes the life of all things, that the roots of the earth flow into your being. This to become the very bones and flesh that make up your body. Work this until you can walk with one of the earth and by the earth.

Beneath, within, around; this is the element that entwines with everything on this plane. Sit beneath a great tree by a stream where you won't be disturbed. Feel the pulse of the earth, feel your energy as it reacts with the earth as the other elements react to each other. As it flows and pulses to your energy, flowing up into you naturally. Draw this strength into your core, pull this in and become an extension of the earth, as you have already become an extension of the other elements.

Water

  Begin by sitting in the shallow end of a pool, or at in waves on the beach. Stand outside on a rainy day. Feel the flow of the water, notice its behaviors. Find its natures, feel them, find how they respond with your own. As you did with the earth, find out what similarity you have to the water, as you did with the earth, and will do with the air and fire.

  Feel the core of your element outside and vast, flowing to the pulse and tide of creation. Feel how your own core moves in response to this force. Feel the connection between the element and the body, then pull the core of the element into the core of the body, uniting them as one force.

Air

  Stand out in the wind. Feel the flow of it upon your body. As you breathe in and exhale, notice the connection between the body, the breath, and the act of motion in space through its connection to the elemental foundation of the air.

  Feel the core as it exists externally from the world, how it it moves and breathes as one breath from all of creation. Feel how your core responds. Pull it into yourself. Become one with the air current. Your breath should be the worlds breath. Feel it, and your body movement should cause the very air to stir at will.

Fire

  The heat of a roaring fire, blazing in a pit before you, is the best way. Stand or sit feeling this current and its overwhelming flow. As it moves through your body, feel the heart of the flame, feel the white hot core that burns just by those things which come into its presence. Not the flame, but of generation of that heat. The spirit behind the flames which compels them to consume all the world in flame.

  Feel this core, and feel your body's response. Feel the nature of your spirit in relation to the spirit of the fire you notice before you. Pull the core into yours. Feel its nature, and how it responds with your own emotions, causes your spirit to move. The body of your spirit as the heat that causes the world to rise to flame around you, if that is your will.

Elemental Forces

The elements of this world are simple yet complex. Their origin is from a celestial equivalent to their source, that which spawned them in the beginning. Some have to rely on certain conditions more than others, but regardless, they, in essence, are all elements which we can subject to our processes and make our will manifest.

What is the source of everything? Since there are so many ways to classify it, here are the simplest and most generally complex terms:

Chi- the universal mind, of all things stems as the union of the others, the raw power of the body. As located in the center of the body, midway between the navel and the groin, halfway between the front of the body and the back of the body. This is the best location to put as the body center, for our reference. It is where we must meditate on bringing our energy in alignment with the Chakras and the elemental energy of the macrocosm (outer world).

Yin- Passive, Feminine, Dark. The Void. In all things there is gender, and this is engendered by the recessive traits in all things, the way of least resistance, the yielding of the spirit. The passive, receptive, the constant. This energy is male or female aligned depending on the stricture of the doctrine you make use of in your cosmological structure. It doesn't matter so long as you understand all aspects to this are very simple. It is what is, because it is that way and will always be that way. It is dark, it doesn't need anything to sustain it, not good, not evil, just dark: it is the space waiting to be filled. This is feminine, this can be masculine as the force waiting to be moved by the active feminine.

Yang- Active, Masculine, Light. This would be chaos. That which causes action, the fiery nature of the sun. This is the active current, the creative current. The spark of the light, which manifests by taking on and willing the Yin into form. This, as been said by others, would be male, or female depending on your traditions. It is creation, it is the actions that cause creation. The female that gives birth, or it can be man that plants the seed.

Earth, Air, Fire & Water- These are the formative elements, arising from the composition (the alchemical union) of both genders of the source. They bring the foundations to form worlds, and destroy them with their currents. From these come forth the life and death of all things.

Life and Death- As all things have a life, so all things have death. These elements occur when all things come together to form the body. From the void, the masculine and feminine, the elemental body, the element of life animates it, and when it loses the flow of the energy and drains like a battery, death comes for it. However, there are some examples of death not being the ultimate end, contributing to the animating current that gives us the spiritual element. What can be described as that which gives the animated body a drive to move along the path it is best suited for as an emanation of the elements which forged it. Giving power to the final element, the breath, the sound.

The Focus of the breath, the giving things names, calling them, recognizing their power, and yielding to it, creating by it. It is by the union of these that the true source can be called upon. Breath, soul, life, death, earth, air, fire, water, light, dark, all unified by that which was first, that which is, and shall always be. The singularity. The ten ray star, each point emanating one of the elements, unifying above, and below, all coming out of the center, the source. The collective Consciousness.

Now comes the work with the life and death current. You have elemental energies; you may prefer some over others. However, you should be aware that even the raging fires die down to ashes. You must be aware of how the ashes feel energetically. You must know how the calm wind feels after a storm, you must send your energy and work the above meditations through everything both living and dead. You will need to visit a cemetery and simply lay hands upon a grave sending your energy down through the earth, through the body which lies beneath, up through your respective arm. You must be able to do this with one hand, a finger if you have to. You need to learn how to read these currents. You will notice the elemental flow between recently dead things, and long dead things. Realizations like this come when you must also balance out the death current if you will, the stagnant decaying energy which is beneath you. You must do this with plants that are alive, and those that have died. To fallen trees. If you can go hunting, bring down an animal: feel the energy with your own as you have with nature. Feel the life as your will has drained it. Learn this energy, learn to recognize this energy, to work with it in time. You will need to know its nature, what does it have a propensity for? Like Chi is manifested with the Tao, it has a tendency to go its easiest route. You have caused the microcosm to become one with the macrocosm, so will its body, spirit, essence return to the macrocosm to be part of the greater wheel. It is not good, or bad, as those are points of view. You must know life and you must know death. You must know the light side of seeing something sick and passing, and the violent death taken of something before its time. Do keep in mind if you take this to any extreme, you are exercising folly, and deserve what you would have done to you as a result. Learn small, work your way up. If you can, you can learn this exercise with a goldfish you forget to feed. Murder is an energy you should like not to experience. So if you go off and commit crimes, then that is on your own hands, not mine or the publishers as has been stated; do this work at your own risk. So then that being said again, and out of the way, moving on. The essence of a thing, its spirit. It is the thing that connects it to the Singular collective.

    A simple exercise in the nature of things at this point. When you have been able to identify that all things extend from the source, when you have then been able to break your own energy into its active and passive currents, then you have subjected the elements of creation to your inquiry to get your body to know the energy, to know what current is what, and to be able to sustain a charge through these currents. You then must go back to the very beginning. You must start again with your meditations on the elements, on yourself and on nature. You must be able to reach out with your mind and feel with your own will the spirit of the thing which is what the active and passive properties have joined to create.

    You should see the spirit in your mind's eye as everything about that object. From the subatomic structure to what it is before you; what its uses are, and what its uses are going to be; the existence that it has, and has had. You must be able to, with your energy, feel out its nature. You must be able to then recognize the nature of the thing, and energetically charge this to your intents. Your Spirit should be aware of itself and how it relates with other spirits of the elements. You should move beyond basic energy work and into an awareness of the spirit of the energy you are working with. The charge for the current you are communing with.

    For example: A spirit of wind would be jittery, unable to calm, and manic – this would be what you focus on if you sought to manifest such things as a breeze on an otherwise hot day. A spirit of lightning is sharp, to the point, and destructive but it unifies both the heavens and the earth so it balances, feeling this within yourself and then willing such things to manifestation is what will bring you your lightning bolt. However, keep in mind all things have the tendencies towards the easiest path. Your will has to subject them to a state outside of what they are predisposed for doing. So wind that is windy will remain windy because it is the nature of the spirit to be so. Fire that is raging will rage because it has the nature to do so. The rising flood waters have a tendency to swell and rush to their lowest point, the earth has tendencies towards subtle motion. You should be aware of the spirits of both the elements and the tools which you would make use of as your focus.

    When you can feel out the spirit of a thing in your area, to know what elements form it, to know by its energy the intent of the spirit behind, you can begin to exercise control over it. Thus having all the things at your disposal to form the proper connections between your energy and it, in order to generate the proper circuit which acts as your "spell" to affect the intent. As you have noticed no doubt already that words have the power to stir the spirit. Have the power to move people towards peace or anger. Actions speak louder then words, but words are what guide the concepts of our actions.

    Agrippa holds that there are two types of words, the spoken word and the thought. It is when you make the internal world one with the external world that change begins. That the forces of Yin and Yang are stirred and their union is then caused which is seen as chaos to the unobservant in the dance between them. It is this energy which has the power to level mountains, to kill, or heal, or protect and love. Giving up all pretense to dispositions of light and fluffy, High Magick is about the manifestation of the will as directed by intent, willed to its desire and released to allow the currents to manifest the greater thing upon the will. You can use high magick in ceremonial form by conjurations to demons and forgotten things. Shouting barbaric things written by men to undersexed and over worked to forces inside you and outside you which manifest as the perception of the entity. It is no secret among the intellectual mage who has researched the lesser key that the demons therein are the internal workings of the mind. That the 72 spirits correspondence to the human mind to those effects are possible by meditations. They are aspects of the microcosm, and as such they are the "demon" which causes them to manifest in the life of the mage.

It is true vibrations cause the stimuli to enter into the proper mindset. As such the sound, the uttered word, must bring to the mind the world as it is perceived and the charges so spoken should further actualize all of the work with the previous elemental currents to get you to a point where when you want to "cast your spell;" all you have to do is is feel out its energy, the energy you want to manifest, and then will it to be. However, this is what takes training under all the aforementioned meditations, and as such, you must be able, as an individual, to charge your words with their proper tone in order to reach the efficacy of what you would have.

The human mind is a remarkable machine. Dr Emoto has been doing fabulous work with words, and their power the symbols themselves, reflected in the spirit of the thing he manipulates. This has been known to any mage worth their salt since the dawn of the spoken word. It was a mage who uttered the first grunt, it was a mage who turned that grunt into a word, a mage who turned it into writing, who gave it its name, and called it what it was. Giving it form and substance in his mind. It is the word of the thing, the spirit of its elemental balance and manifestations that determine how the thing can be used or manipulated. This is where people get pretentious; do not fall into this trap of ego. To declare oneself as a god-force, one does two things. One sets himself at the top of his cosmological scale. He puts all things under his will that he observes and how he relates to everything and everything relates under him. The second thing is to cause conflict within all things that exist that are not of the self. It puts him at odds with the aspects himself he doesn't yet know or understand. It doesn't do him a damn bit of good to allow his ego to run rampant when he is working his art. However, it does come in handy because one must have the will of the gods in order to cause such changes as can be he declared, Thaumaturge.

It is a state of mind one must embrace when working his craft, but also keep in check that there are a great many things in the wide open world which would no sooner see him dead as anything else. It is not a matter of having pretension, but knowing one's capacity to learn the true natures of good and evil, to know light, and dark, and to maintain balance. However, one may say that there is interplay between the nature of the Yin and Yang currents in the elemental nature of things – they are always striving for a balance. The balance will happen naturally and not declare itself balance, for doing so is to negate any system of balance on may have temporarily achieved. Your focus must be on your words so that your will is manifested in accordance with the nature of yourself acting on the environment.

Elements hold power over us in so many ways. The first and most logical way is that we are formed of them. The body and organs, the water we drink which becomes our blood and fluids, the air we breathe which becomes the vital breath for our chemical substance. The fires of our spirits and wills which make us formidable in our own rights. After that, we move on to the elemental correspondences of how we behave. What aspect of ourselves are more watery, fiery, airy or earthy. Every student of the occult should have this at one time or another. Listing everything, from the good sides to the character flaws that make up one's nature. This list is private and should always remain so. When one studies this list they will see what parts of their personality connect them to that aspect of the element. If they are more loud or outspoken, they could be more fiery perhaps, and have better luck working with the fire elementals and things relating to that aspect in them. Where as it would take them a while to learn to work with watery type elements if they are less inclined to pay attention to what is going on and blunder through their studies. At this point, however, you should all begin to get these aspects of yourself in check. To be the proper gentlemen and ladies that will be held with honor and esteem in any setting you may find yourself in. After this step has been achieved, you should now know which element stirs what in you. You should make another list, this one comparing yourself to the variations within that element. If you are more easily agitated like a storm, or emotionally calm, like a cool day. You should be able to see where this takes you. It should be an ongoing list that you save throughout your studies in order to gain a better understanding of yourself and the elements.

    Upon the successful starting of these lists, you will also need to become aware of your geography, and the regions in which you travel. Going back to your domain, your territory and your region. These spheres of rotation all encompassing aspects of every human, animal, plant, mineral, and spirit that exists above and below the surface of the region. You should also be very aware that these things change and no two regions are the same, for any amount of time.

    Time shifts everything from our moments of recognizing the planetary and astrological influences as best aligned to our desires to the elements themselves and the conditions which they exist under.

    Every place has a different natural energy. Hillsides vary depending on which side of the hill you are on, their relative position from the other elements, as well as their positioning from the celestial perspectives. A grassy field has a more calming earthy energy, whereas a desert has a more fire based earth feeling to it. Elevation plays a key role as well. As magick is a current, it exists under different structures and becomes more condensed at the higher elevations, so it takes less power to work, whereas coastal areas need more power to be drawn in, as the natural current takes them to higher points. There are valleys which act as reservoirs for these currents, there are mountains which store these energies. What connects them, like the D.N.A. that forms the body, are the lines of power running through the earth. These frequency lines are called ley lines, dragon tracks, or spiritual channels. Commonly found at places where these points intersect are called nodes, or nexus'. It is this current which also affects the type of energy work being used in the region. Some nodes are small and barely noticeable even to the trained eye, while others are rippling with chaotic current. These forces cause the balance of energy between regions on the map. Commonly, fault lines run either parallel to the lines, or perpendicular to nodes depending on the region.

    These can be manipulated with practice, but you must first learn the elemental connection between you and nature. What do you feel when you think of a tree, a rock, a precious stone, or gem, an herb and so forth. You must be able to look at your lists which you have been working on. You need to be able feel for yourself the connections you have made from Volume 2 and now. When you have felt these connections you must then be able to see them in your mind. When you want an elemental current to manifest for you, you must take the raw energy within you that connects you to that link of the element you would work with. You then must pull this element out of you, by immersing yourself in the feeling of that emotion while maintaining an exterior calm. Your mind and spirit must be frenzied, yet your body must look calm and centered.

    You will get the hang of this with practice. Do this with every element. If you notice you have an electrical personality or a fiery one, then work with that energy becoming aware of that current, and what it does. How it responds to nature and to your will. Study it. Study them all so that you have those connections when the time comes to make them manifest as the elements in your spell craft. As such with these elements form them into the constructs of your mind, form them between your palms as though you hold them in your hand. Feel how they respond. Charge your ritual tools as receptacles for these currents. All you need at this point is your will to do this. Work on this till your muscles feel like they are going to burn. Make sure you stay hydrated and fed while working on this energy work.

    Getting attuned to the elements, taking advanced steps in knowing their procedures, their behaviors, their spirits, how the elements respond to each other. What happens when an energy orb based on the water current mixes with a fiery current, or an earthy current. What you feel like inside when that happens. At what point does the water become an acidic energy when it mixes with more fire, or more earth, or a combination? These are things which should be basic to you. The forming of the elements, what causes what when put together. How does having fire, air. water and earth turn into a hurricane? How does having water, air and earth turn into a typhoon? It is these mechanics that you must understand. You must answer these questions for yourself before you move on. You should make a list of what makes what along with the other lists you are already sustaining as you see more of yourself reflected back when you are working with the mediums and tools of the art. When working with these forms, you should be aware that timing them becomes increasingly difficult the more specific you wish to be; however, there is give and take when it comes to time.

Creation is the greatest act that any creature can achieve. It is all by means a union of the spirit, of the elements. As an embodiment of the source, it is possible to give, and create anything that the awakened animated soul wishes, so long as they have drawn into themselves all elements, all energy being able to expand their spirit out, and contract it to a singular focus.

The forces of the earth give for a solid chance to learn and experience. The planes of the other elements are where one learns their true nature. Anything that walks on the earth, that which exists on the physical, is subject to the elemental force of earth. By this you can use the world to solidify a realm that you have created' by harnessing its physical qualities, you establish the link between this world and the one of desire. From which you can store egregores, and other created beings until such time as you need or require them.

The idea behind high magick is not that you have all the pretty trappings and the piles of tools, but that you know how to apply all of the elements with surgical precision to effectively work with or without tools as the situation dictates. Your magick comes from you, and your connection to the elemental forces or the sources of creation, which will be approached in another course. Your use of tools should be that it doesn't make the magick for you, but if you apply tools in your art they should be the physical manifestations of your will, unifying the above and the below, inner with the outer, into one force to focus the intent.

The elements are very special in working with Ceremonial High Magick (CMH). It is here the mastery comes out, as you will be working with the elemental meditations to get a feel for their personality, for their energy, and for how you yourself relate to them. It is a process which should take the dedicated student years to fully realize the potential of. Together they balance. Both the Yin current, and Yang current are present in everything.

Everything is shaped by virtue of the these two. Everything extends forth from their unions. As concepts, they can be researched to the end of the world, but as creative forces you must realize what they mean to you, by the nature of their correspondences. It is through these two that you can create and bring life to things, you can bring passion and reconciliation. Above all, you can create, shape, and reshape things.

The planetary forces that you're going to be evoking have different properties depending on the sources which you work with. Either from the left or right hand path perspectives the personification of these energies are: justice, war, love, magick, transformation, death, light. As far as celestial bodies go, even the stars have significance. As has been stated previously, there are entire dissertations written on these, and you should have already come across some in your quest to compile a volume one.

You can find the tables of correspondences listed in every single pagan book ever printed – except for this one. They are useful and they are great sales tools for you to do what you want with them. However there is a lack of material that requires their knowledge from the onset. This, then, is such a work.

All planets have their conjunctions, their peak periods and their astrological as well as astronomical points. Each of these has meaning. To get a ritual timed just right; you have to have the the time when these celestial bodies are at their peak in the zodiac sign, their relative positioning to where you're located on the planet so you can be facing the right way when you start your conjurations. You also have to have the hour of the day when they are to be at utmost efficacy. The planets shift every *two hours* per zodiac sign in the Eastern arts; each house has a two hour time period in the day, whereas they shift every *hour* in Western calenders. I would also venture to remind you all of the procession that earth enjoys which gives us our climates. Keep this wobbling in mind when you calculate your hours, zodiac and associated charts. It would be nice to have all of these factors listed, but frankly so much work is required for one ritualized example, that it really does get confusing if you don't already know what you're supposed to be doing. But for those of you who insist on such things, here is an example of properly setting up a time table when to do a rite of destruction. Remember there is no Karma; there is balance. If it is deserved, it will benefit you, if it's justified, then you have done nothing for which you should expect to pay more then you already have.

The Rite of Destruction

I require that it be with the Saturnine energy to be in alignment with Jupiter energy to bring forth proper justice, as I fancy nocturnal energy on the day I intend to blow the target apart. For example: The day would be Thursday. The hour of the night would be 2:00 or 9:00. This would be if I was going by Western calculations, in order to achieve a working with more efficacy towards Judgment of death. If I was working under an Eastern system: The day would still be Thursday. The hour however would be from 8-12 pm. In this 4 hour period, there are two zodiac signs which need to be taken into account: the dog and the boar. Since one is Capricorn and the other Aquarius a choice needs to be made as to the proper timing under which of these signs to bring about the desired result.

- Boar/Aquarius having natural tendencies to bad luck with electricity.
- Dog/Capricorn tends to bring on willed change in motion.

Let us then say that my want for destruction brings me to a more blood thirsty work, and it is going to be far more efficient if I decide that this work will take place on a day where Saturn has most sway, and since I still demand justice for what has been done to me, I would that it would fall on the times such as :

- Saturday, at night, at 4 pm or 11 pm if I was still after Vengeance to be the hand by which justice is served.
- Saturday would remain in Eastern timing. But it would be under the hours 6 pm if I wanted greater influences from the Rooster or Sagittarius. Or, if I wanted the Rat or Pisces at 12 midnight Saturday morning.

Supposing I decided to toss out justice all together and just wanted them to suffer horribly, I would use unifying Saturn energy. If I want more fun, I will add the energy of Mars to have this be achieved. If I am particularly feeling a touch of scorn, I would make use of the Star energy which fell under the zodiac house.

It's Saturday, at 11 pm and I am after the energies of Jupiter by means of Sagittarius with the star Aculeus, which is 25 degrees in Sagittarius. So at 11:25 on Saturday I will be making my charge. Especially if this falls under the sun sign of Sagittarius, with the star Aculeus at 25 degrees, which can be found out through proper research in stellar journals, or you can calculate these times yourself if you can find the proper astronomy programs for your computer, or old fashioned celestial observation. It doesn't matter much how you come to do this, so long as you have all of these things set up properly.

So for this particular rite of destruction ,which is to be performed on the day in November or December, which is going to be the day where the sun sign is in proper alignments – according to the chart of procession it may not fall in November or December depending on what year it is. The proper way to figure out procession is every 70.5 years the astrological year shifts by one day. Currently making it that April 15 is the last day of Pisces. If you are not confused enough, you also have to take into account the phases of the moon. Is the moon waning or waxing, is it new or full; it is also these factors which will help you determine the opportune time for this working. So, you have the day of the year all picked out, you have the hour of the day when you're supposed to do your working. You have it timed by the stars, the planets, and the moons. But you also have to have all of your tools charged by their own celestial observances, lest it all be for naught.

Exercises of Elemental Magick

Write out a paragraph describing the results of each of the meditations in relationship to the element you have noticed, as well as connection to the Yin and Yang nature of that element.

Create your own elemental mediation that will help connect your energy center to the elemental current.

Work on your elemental meditations, and divide them into their Yin and Yang attributes.

Create from them the listing of roots that go into the formation of the words used to represent earth, and position them in proper space on a map of your body.

Use this map to create the movements, and gestures which can pull power from those roots, and tap into the collective power of the will of the elements.

Time

The easiest way to get your head all muddled up with useless garbage is to take into account time. Time is an odd thing in and of itself. However there is a saying: "A place for everything and everything in its place". The same goes for rituals, rites, spells, and petitions. All of them have their proper time. When you can understand this and work within these times effectively, then you have the leg up on a lot of the pagans who simply disregard all of this and hope that something responds.

There is a lot to be said for Chaos mages and their way of working, but let's face it, no one always likes to roll the dice, so here is High Magick. The most retentive art on the face of the earth because of time, right?

Wrong. In the end, it comes down to the need for things to be correctly timed so as to bring them into utmost efficacy. There is a lot to be said for someone catching the bus when the bus is scheduled. It is convenient to have these things to where we can time them to catch the celestial trains to bring out the proper manifestations of our desires.

When timing your rituals, it is important to understand the implications behind the working. If you are working to summon up a dead god, then the timing has to be right; if you are working to heal your loved ones, or seek communion with something that is not here, then you must be aware of the times in which such things are possible. Far too many people are a few seconds later than they mean to be, there are too many "oops, I was 5 minutes late."

In Ceremonial High Magick, you must be precisely on time. Your work must end, or begin, or be in the middle of the conjurations exactly when you need them to be. Not one second more, not one second less. If you are late, then your work will fail. Perhaps not utterly, but they will not be what you have worked for. Now, most of the time, the above statement is false; you can do a work when you want to work you simply may. There are some magicks which are tedious, and time require this precision, but most of the things you will find in this text that are not so ... well, anal. This measure of working acquaints the student of the occult with the methods that are found in the old grimoires of the ancients. In those, you miss a day, you have to wait at least a year to begin again. However, there are always substitutions you can attempt to make, without diminishing the integrity of the work.

The Elemental Divisions

In our study of the 4 elements, we now know that there is elemental current flowing within us, and around us in our environments. Sometimes it becomes necessary to understand the divisions between the elements within themselves, as we observe them and seek to command the spirits that exist within those energies. We start off with the division of the "selves" of the elements.

Elemental Divisions:

The Supernal – The highest point of the element closest to the source of the element; the "pure fire", "pure water", "pure earth," or "pure air". This is the element without any influence of the other elements. These are the celestial elements uncorrupted by material forms, but that have given the material forms the energy which sustains them. Here is where one would find the "god-forces" of the elements.

The Bestial – These are what would be considered the animated forms of the elements; when they have an animal style of body such as a dragon, or a mermaid, or some body created from another form of the element giving to its form, nature, and power.

The Physical – The world of the elements we have already acquainted ourselves with in earlier lessons, where we have united the body of the external elements (macrocosm) with the inner body (microcosm). These we know as the earth, air, fire, water.

The Light – The Yang active masculine and feminine currents. That which is creative, generative, and motion. This could be said to be the active side of evolution.

The Dark – The passive side of evolution, the Yin current, where generation occurs within itself. inner transformation, manifestations through the will as opposed to through outside forces. There exists a dark side element association with every elemental.

The Celestial – These would be the angelic elemental forces from the source of light, that have inter-mixed with the physical worlds in order to give them bodies. Angels, and such to the like which are bound to the will of the source that created it. As in the Hermetic thought there is references to the cosmic mind, this mind has a will; some might call it destiny, others fate. The manifestations from this division are the servants of this will, and have no free will of their own. There can be Dark Celestial Elementals as well. To be the celestial is to be bound to the will of the element.

The Infernal – These would be the divisions of the Yin current who are created to serve the darker elemental will, the generation through the self, and prompt the changes that occur in evolution. These forces give to the elemental thought. These forces give to the freedom of the element and exist independently from their source, being able to interact with whatever form they choose. This would be the "spirit" of the elementals that exist by their own will after the sources of their creation came into being.

The Primal – This is the chaotic nature; where it is the primordial without form, without function, there is a will but it operates like the cosmic mind, on its own momentum. It is what we think of in regards to the first fire, or the first air, or the first waters, it is as close to the source of the element that you get when dealing with the manifestations of the source. Here would be found things like monsters, titans, and other "lawless creatures".

It is through these divisions that we begin to see the nature of the "source of the element," this is the point of generation (point where the essence of the element can be found that created all from itself). We build ceremonial consciousness though meditation to the physical elements, but we can also journey the roads of the divisions of the elements, as they created the foundation of what we understand as the physical world, the universe, the microcosmic structure and the microcosmic view of the world. There are correspondences that tie in each of the organs; in Eastern thought there are meridians, points of energy in the body which flow according to their elemental significance.

Here in the context of learning we must observe the mapping out of how these elements interact with each other. How they come to balance themselves and how manifestations occur from the points of origin where we can connect to the "source of the element" through a ritual ceremony.

> Earth is Black
> Air is Green
> Water is Blue
> Fire is Red

In this, you will begin to notice that all of the divisions of the elements connect through the identical nature of the square with the diamond. In the center point we have the 8 ray star. The division of the wheel of the year, the 8 directions, the means by which we can find any direction within three dimensional space.

It comes as no surprise that we have the 8 points listed, one for each of the 8 divisions of the element; however, if you look closely, we have 10 points. The center point which represents the inner world of the self aware, the Chakra systems of the body, and the outer circle which balances all things in what could be considered to be the macrocosm. Through this union of the 10 points, we have the balance of the Yin current, and the Yang current when the energy flowing upwards and the energy flowing downwards is balanced.

Through this we have a three dimensional model of what comes from where, and how we understand what comes from each source. With the working models of creation in this manner, we can plot out the means of what is required to make our will manifest.

Exercises on Correspondences

For each of the 4 Western elements, create a table of correspondences that will tell you the element, its 8 attributes, and the name of one creature that can be attributed to the attribute. Create a chart that includes the Eastern elements. If you're particularly masochistic, develop a chart using Middle Eastern elementals.

Elemental Seals

Structure of the Seals

The seals themselves are three dimensional representations of the cosmos in smaller form. Where the manifestation of the currents arises from the influences of the presence of one of these seals, or more of these seals compounded in a way which causes the creation of various planes, to shift. On the standpoint of examination for the foundation of our work, the 8 point will be used. Much like the circles of the arts are three dimensional, so too are the seals.

The Seal is self sustaining by the primal energies contained within, assuming the elemental gate successfully opens in the center.

Dimensional Seals of the Elements

The circle around the 8 points acts as the catalyst of currents to keep the forces self sustaining upon themselves. The three dimensional rotation of the seals mentioned before are the forces which cause the opening and operations of the array in which they are applied. They need not have a physical medium of conjuration, but are drawn forth by the will of the mage who conjures them forth. However, it is prudent to have on hand in one's ritual space the drawn and painted seals to act as the lubricant between the powers, so that they can operate with independent power sources to the mage as an extension of the will, through the mixing of the blood with the paints.

The central point of union, where the above meets the below in the middle of the sphere, is the point of generation from where the seal exists. It becomes a three dimensional field of influences above it and below it, much in the same way the auric field does around the body.

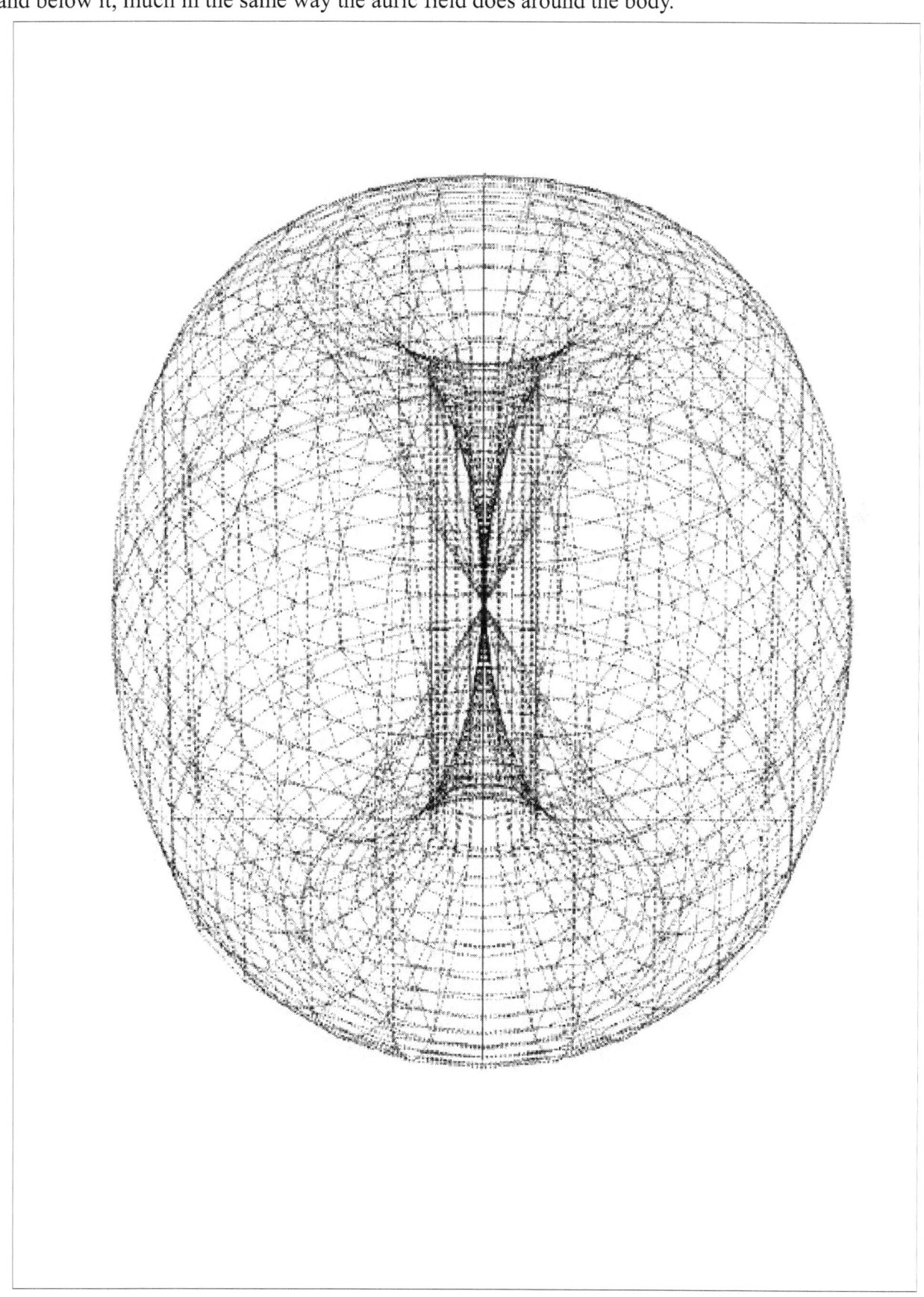

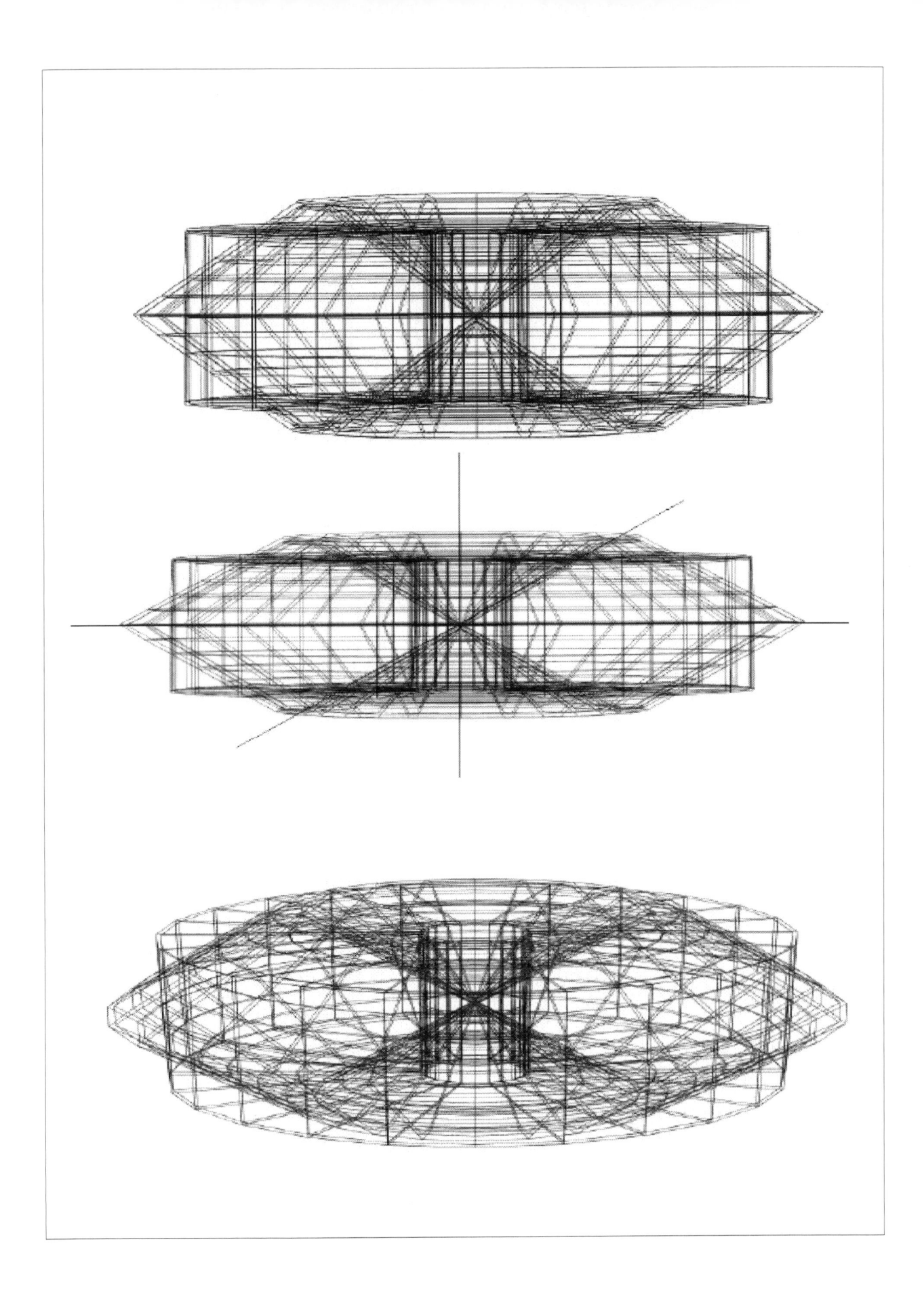

Elemental Seal Design

Seal of the Earth

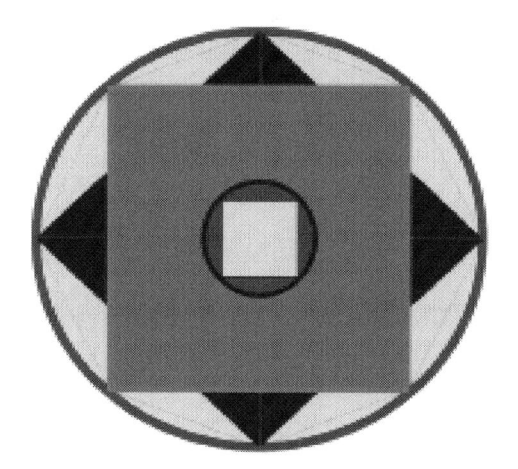

Seal of the Air

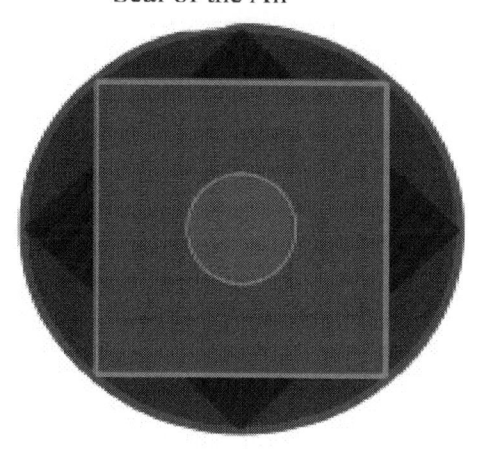

I summon forth the primal force,
By the covenant of blood,
Come forth through this Seal.

Seal of the Water

Seal of the Fire

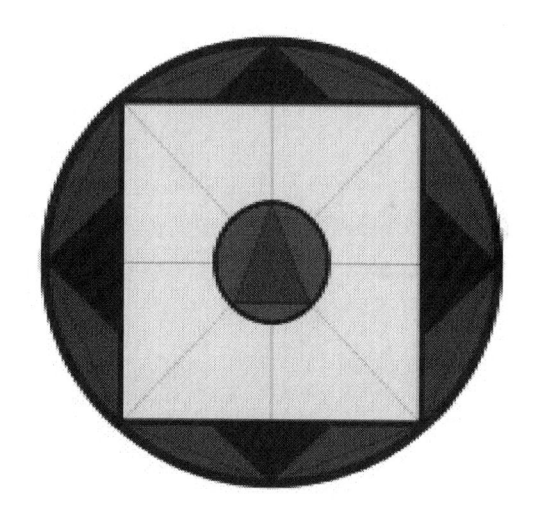

Seals of the Elements

When we begin to understand the correspondences of the elements, we notice that there is a symmetry to the balance. There is pull and a push; there is also the influences of the other elements. So if you want to make it rain in an area that needs it, you must find a way to balance the air, earth, fire, and water when you are making your ceremony. If you do not do this, then something will cause extra damage and if you wanted a simple summer shower, then you might get a mudslide, or lightning storm that causes fire to rage against the land, or a flood. The best way to balance is to make use of the Elemental forces in a way that will call upon all of them to aid you in your task.

The traditional elemental directions are:

Earth is the North
Air is the East
Water is the West
Fire is the South

For our southern Hemisphere friends:

Earth is South
Air is West
Water is East
Fire is North

If, for example, you were to call upon a force of the element, you would be able to use the 8 point array in a manner that will unify the forces of the element and create a "seal" of the element which represent all sides of the element and a channel directly to the source. Those can be found in the array section earlier in this work.

It is that these use the balance of the 8 natures of the element, with the Hindu Tattwah (gate of the element); there are many combinations of these forms, but they all represent the connection from the physical world to the spiritual world. The task is to understand the things that occur in the natural world and be able to work with an even hand in the balance.

Understanding that these elements can act as the "gatekeepers" or "Watchtowers" that have their forces watch over your ceremony and provide balance to it, as well as protecting you from outside influences of the world. However, that is in reference to the elemental spirits that come from the sources of the elements. When you use the seal, you draw the raw elemental force, not a spirit, that comes from it. So, in the beginning we have the seal as a tool that aids in the manifestations of those elements. It gives a more stable energy to those spiritual currents we call upon during ceremony.

Exercises on Seal Creation

Create a seal for each of the 4 elements, with the a description of why you chose to add the things you did, how you would make the seal as a tool, how you would charge the seal, and a spell on opening it. Create a seal for the Eastern elements as well, with the description of how you make it, why you chose those attributes or symbols, how to make it, how you charge it, how you open it.

Elemental Energy: Defensive Techniques

Basic Shielding

Form a bubble inside your core, and then force it outwards repelling all forces from your aura/space. Conversely, you can use this technique to draw forces into your core and consume them.

Elemental wards

Use the elemental conjuration for the protective purposes.

Auric Hardening

See your aura in your mind's eye; focus on this force as you would any other, as an extension of your own will. Solidify this space to be as "titanium" or some other great force of strength that none may penetrate.

Auric Mirrors

See yourself in your mind's eye within your aura; use a spoken or mental charge to transform your aura to a mirror, and reflect all the energy that is sent your way.

Geometric Shield

The shapes of the platonic solids can be constructed around you, using your personal energy, the energy of the infernal/celestial/elemental forces that can be bent through the utterance of your will.
Square becomes the cube
- Circle shield becomes the sphere
- Pentagram becomes the pentagon
- Hexagram becomes the 'Merkabah'
- Heptagram becomes the heptagon
- Octagram becomes the octagon
- Decagram becomes the decagon

With the center of these 'solid' shapes layering the space where your aura meets the environments.

Cross Shield

Draw energy from above down, and from the right left to form a banishing shield. Draw energy from the down to above, and from the left to right, forming the infernal summoning shield.

The Spiral Shield

Focus energy from the dominant hand in a spiral pattern solidifying to form around your aura, flowing outwards and away from your center. Can be bolstered by the use of your other elemental alignments. Focus energy from you recessive hand flowing around your aura, drawing the energy into your core for their destruction and thus consumption into your essence.

Braided Elemental Shield

Drawing up the elemental current from the earth interlacing it with another elemental, so as to surround the aura in a pattern similar to the double helix; can draw in as well as force outwards. The drawing upon the celestial forces for the similar ends; can achieve better results for things which the elemental forces are not suitable for combat.

Singular Elemental Shield

Draw energy into the palm Chakra and spin the current into a form, either the Melchizedek Merkabah or some other force, but focus on the singular elemental, celestial/infernal force assuming the constructed form. Can repel or draw forces into your core for further manipulation or greater banishment/destruction.

Multiplied Elemental Shield

Draw the energy into layers with the top current flowing in one direction, and the subsequent inner layers flowing in opposite directions, and different angles to assume a shape similar to a gyro pattern.

Greater Auric Mirror

Transform your aura into an elemental layered shield by placing the water current as the outer layer, and then layer within these currents different shadow flows on consecutive inner layers to deflect all incoming environmental or other currents. Conversely can be used to draw energy in and nullify any intent behind this current that you can focus it into your core and feed from this.

Charge of the Waters

Take a bowl of water, and place a white or blue candle inside it. Bleed into the water. Light the candle, clearing your mind of all thoughts, and will your mind into repetition of a single mantra of protection.

Waters of the deepest sea
Be called to spin about me
Waters of the ancient sea
I call you forth to protect me

Charge of the Fires for Protection

Take your incense burner, or your cauldron wherein you contain ritual fires. Build within it the herbs of protection or the woods of protection. Place a Red candle within the this vessel. Bleed onto the herbs to tie your will and life force to the element. Light the fire, as it burns clear your mind.

Fires of the hottest sun
Around me here be spun
Fires of the darkest night
Protect me in my fight

The Twin Pentagrams

Generating the twin pentagrams for protection can be achieved through the manifestation of the forces of earth and air. By a crystalline structure in a tree, and the same in the earth. One can call forth the power of both the air and earth, to form a protection boundary around the property.

I call thee by the pact of the seal of air
I call thee by the pact of the seal of earth
By the breath of the eternal life
By the eternal repose of the living dead
I call forth this space
Be set within the boundary
Of the art, by the art.
Through the rites of blood and pact
Through the contract of the covenant
I set this ward upon this space.

To Protect A Space

Recite this mantra while seeing your area glowing with your energy, expanded out as an extension of your aura. You can use this in tandem with the tools required for the Mirrored Aura. Wherein you place a candle in a box, or bleed into a box, and project your will into it so that it becomes the walls that surround you and your space.

What these walls surround
Protection is now cast around
So only I may walk or see
What in this space I cause to be

To Protect A Fixed Loci

The same as the above. Only this one calls upon the earth, so form a covenant with the elements of earth to become a manifestation of your being.

Gaia I ask raise your arms,
Raise the wall
Protect me from harm.
Circling arms arise and shield me;
Bar this place from all entry!
Let this barrier rise from the ground,
Now as protection is cast around

The Dream Catcher

This should be spoken as you weave the thread, or gut, clockwise around the woven willow ring. The thread should be the intestinal gut that the native tribes make use of. A stone should be suspended from the center of the knot. This to ensnare spiritual forces permanently or until further study can be completed.

These knots I weave
All horrors to bind
To snare the fears
That grip the mind

Crystal Barrier

Hold a crystal in the palm of your dominant hand. Project energy into it, so that the energy is magnified by the structures within the crystal, so you become encased with in a bubble. Within your mind's eye hold this image of yourself. As your will holds, so will the barrier. This one you can carry with you while you need to get to a protected space, or to cease a psychic attack.

With these words my foe disarm,
Energy surround protect me from harm.
Broken space, protected space
Opposing forces now displace.

Mirrored Aura

To prevent to a psychic attack, or to force an ongoing one to a halt. Light a white candle, and hold a mirror with the non-reflective surface facing you on the other side of the candle, so you are the candle, and your aura the mirror. You can create a box of mirrors of this arrangement, and have perpetual candles burning if you wish. In repetition, speak a mantra that focuses your intent.

I see my mirror self reflecting me,
Turn my aura,
A mirror reflecting negativity
With words now wrought
Weaved by me
I am protected as I will to be

Ex Nul

Bringing Down the Barrier of Gaia

Release the visualization, and extinguish any fire or elemental intermediary.

Bring down your arms
Gone is danger, and all form of harm
Gaia please withdraw from this place
So it may return to a neutral space

To Dissolve Spiritual Walls

In rhyme I forge my spell as it is spoken,
Obliterate all trace of the veil!
Let its existence fade,
Its hold be broken as my spell is made.

To Dissolve Spiritual Shields

When it comes that a space which is protected and has thus been a hindrance to your work. Focus with your mind's eye on the target ward. See then that the fires within are made manifest, and draw forth these words with all the might you have, to enter where others cannot.

That which protects and defends
The power that sustains it,
Is brought to end
So my target standing strong and well
The wards dissolved
By that which created
Both the heaven and the hell!

Removing Power from Exorcisms

In a place where the exorcism has been performed, or where one has been performed. The following is an example to be performed on a grave where exorcisms of the god of slaves have been performed. In a cemetery, or other place of death, on the night of the full moon, this rite is to be performed as the clock strikes midnight on the day when the veil is thinnest. Burn in a fire these items:

A rosary blessed by a Catholic priest
A Bible or book of Psalms
A white cloth soaked in holy water
A wooden cross

The circle is to be set up with 13 black candles around a center fire. In this fire, the rosary is to be in the east, the Bible in the north, the water or cloth in the west, and the cross in the south. At midnight begin the fire. As the fire is to burn down the barrier, blood from the dominant hand of all present is to be upon the center of the fire. Place 6 cleansed crystals around the fire in the shape of a hexagram.

These are the tools that built the walls
By our blood that will make them fall
The astral barriers broken
Fire hotter than the pits of hell
Consumes these tokens
Sealed by ash and fire,
Blood and stone
What once barred now is free
Obey thy command given hence,
Harm not those who have summoned thee!

The fire is to be left to burn down, and the crystals are to be taken and place upon a grave of one who died at the hands of the clergy. Again position them in the shape of a hexagram and with the knife that drew the blood, pierce the center of the grave and call forth all that was banished by the priest castes, summon them up to become your army. They are bound by the laws of this summoning.

Offensive Elemental Techniques

Offensive Mirror Shield

See the aura in your mind's eye; feel it as an extension of yourself, that the dark side of the mirror becomes your strength, and that all that come in contact are forced to see their own negative reflections, forcing them to become as the forsaken by their own doing. That they become the target of their own negativity, protecting you from their attacks while turning their own works against themselves.

Greater Mirror

See the aura of the target, turned inward to contain all of the reflections of negativity. All that needs be done is but a thought towards this intent. Every manifestation of the force that stands against you be consumed by their own weaknesses and downfall.

Destruction of the Greater Mirror

Find a strength within yourself, and then conjure up the force that is the source of this strength to open the path before you. That no matter the "shield" that has been placed upon your soul, that you can force by the greater source the way to be opened again to you. The "mirror" will be shattered by the Source, which you have bonded with.

The Perpetual Energy Construct

Draw masculine energy upwards from your core through your dominant hand, and the feminine passive current up your recessive hand. Form these as you would the platonic solids shield, and force by the conjuration an elemental/celestial/infernal force within the center to become your means of manifestation, that when it interacts with the target it shall rend all protections of the target by focusing the energy inwards to the core "source" of this construct, and then upon impact with the source of the construct, with the source of the thing you attack, it explodes outwards upon impact. Conversely, this can be done with the opposite effect; that it shall consume the force that it impacts upon and use the energy for a number of scenarios, some of them being:

Situation A: the energy is consumed to form a bigger "blast" zone, or area of effect around the targeted environment

Situation B: the energy consumes the force that has aligned with it, as a sacrifice for something greater to be brought forth through the assimilation of currents

Situation C: through the impact the space becomes nullified by the forces interacting, and the local shall be stricken of all but similar types of forces to those that caused this "dead space".

Situation D: the pattern can be forced upon the center source, like a vacuum or black hole construct, and consume all energy of the environment/target leaving it much emptied of all current.

Ovum Udinbak

This is a chaos egg. As a medium for life, the egg is the perfect form. Take one and dry it out from all the fluid that may have been inside. It must remain whole. You then fill the vessel, with herbs, and stone powders, according to what purpose you would have it work. Take this creation and write upon it in the Ouranian Script or some barbaric or celestial tongue that which you would have manifest.

Fill this with the condensers, and charge your will accordingly. Hurl this egg at the target, or bury it to make its effect grow forth from the earth. Or keep it on your altar to bring to you what you desire, to act as a magnet for life. You can scribe onto it the sigils of the Saints, or the veve of the Loa, or the sigils of demons, and gods better left in history. You can do these things, and you bleed into it. You give it charge to exist by your life blood, and vital spirit. It exists because of your desire to bring into your life, or keep from you, that what you will.

Nightmares of the Soul

Light 13 black candles carved with the name of whom you would give this punishment. You should repeat this, every night for as long as it takes for the candles to burn themselves down. When this has happened, you should have written out the nightmare you would will upon this soul, you then burn these with the remaining wax, and solidify your conjuration by summoning up your deepest power, and projection of your will into their dreaming state so their nightmares become real.

By these words I call;
By your thoughts within;
I bring to life your sins.
What within,
Is bound in flesh and bone,
The horrors in your mind ,
To you I cause now be shown.
Bring to life your nightmares here,
What within the horrors of your mind.
A living nightmare to you I bind!

To Magnify Discord

Take the crest or coat of arms of the order which opposes you and place it in the flames of a fire which has become the base for the fires of hell. Channel then all your rage, anger, hate, and any other dark desires that you can focus on this group to be consumed by all that you send at them. When all is ash, scatter to the 4 winds. The timing should be when War is most manifested, and Justice had influence, while the moon watches on with her face diminishing.

What evils in the world you wreak
This punishment to you I seek
All who bear this token
All who wear this crest
Anger rise,
Bring hatred and unrest
Brother against brother,
This group I rend asunder
Fires from the inferno grow
Black lightning in the void now flow
Nameless spirits in the darkest night
Against these my enemies set to fight

Chains Of Eternity

Bleed upon dirt taken from the graveyard, in which a black candle has been placed, as well as the personal effect or sigil of the spirit against whom you are working.

By blood be called forth,
From Sheol come forth,
Aretz, dry and crumbling earth
Bind now my target
Trap, ensnare and cage my desire.
Dry crumbling earth become
A bond immovable
By my sacrifice come forth
Darkest earth of the Abyss
Obey this covenant

Rite of Decimation

Tools:
- Dark rum for Ogun – 151 if you have it
- Walking stick for Legba
- Tobacco for Baron
- 8 candles
- Knife
- a photograph with the crimes listed on the face,
- - the full name on the back.
- a dish that contains fire in the center

Remove everything not a part of this from the room, and clear the floor. Clean it, and wash it with a cleansing blend of herbs, if you can make sure nothing contaminates the workspace. Burn sage and sweet grass beforehand. Place an elemental representation of earth in the north, air in the east, fire in the south, and water to the west Outside the boundaries of the star.

Engrave each of the 7 candles with the seal of the 7 planets, and the gate that corresponds to it. The order shall be;

Moon, Mercury, Venus, Sun, Mars, Jupiter, Saturn.

As you light the candles, begin with the candle of the moon. Say the charge of the gate and light the flame. Do this for each of the candles clockwise around the circle. The center candle is to be engraved with the 8 pointed star of Algol, this is then to be placed in the dish. When all boundary candles have been lit, call forth the God of fire to become as the flame as the candle in the dish. Light the center candle now. Bang the staff on the ground 7 times and say each time saying the evocations for each of the Loa

Evocations of the Loa:

Evocation of Legba

Papa Legba, Open the gates
Open them as your child calls to you
Please stand firm
In this working
Open the gates Papa,
Let my work pass through
Open the gate Legba,
Let this art flow.

Light the tobacco and exhale the smoke and say the evocation of the Baron.

Evocation of the Baron

Between the land of the living and dead,
Baron Samedi come thou forth
Accept this my offering unto you
Come forth unto this my circle of the arts
Come thou forth you who walks between the worlds

Pour the rum around the candle in the vessel and drink from the bottle after there is a small bit in the bowl.

Evocation of Ogun

Ogun God of war
HEAR ME,
By this rum on my breath
Fire in my spirit
I call upon thee,
Please accept this offering.
Attend now this working
See justice is brought forth

Stand center over and face the direction of the north east south and west, as you make following call.

Evocation of the Forces

ELEMENTAL FOCES
HEAR MY CRY,
COME AND ATTEND
TO ME THIS NIGHT
SPIRITUAL FORCES
FROM BEYOND THE VOID,
COME AND STAND
BEFORE ME THIS NIGHT
I CALL FORTH THAT WHICH IS
THAT WHICH HAS BEEN,
THAT WHICH SHALL BE,
THAT WHICH IS FORGOTTEN
I CALL TO THE FORSAKEN
I CALL TO THE NEVERBORN
I CALL TO THE ESSENCE OF CORRUPTION
THE DEMON FALLEN KIN
OF THE ANCIENT FORCES
KIN OF MY KIN ATTEND TO ME
IN THIS MY WORKING
STAND BEFORE ME
HEAR MY CHARGE
STAND BEFORE MY WORKING
BARE WITNESS UNTO THIS

Place the the images over the flame and as the fire begins to consume them speak the charges against the soul. Then call forth the law as such:

I call forth the law
I call forth the covenant sworn
Of the law of the arts
This soul that is in these flames before you
Has violated this law
That at all times one of power shall speak
Not against others in betrayal

Lest they be betrayers
Powers in attendance
Hear me,
Acknowledge this betrayal
Let nothing stand before you
As is in accordance with the
Ancient laws of justice and balance
Let nothing cause cease unto the call
For his life to be taken
I call forth that this betrayer shall be burned
By the most sacred fires of all the realms.
By the 12 dancing gods in their places,
By the 12 stars in their heavens,
By the living and dead gods
By the works of darkness
By the word of darkness
By the word of true will
Be brought forth this Night

Drop the flaming photo into the rum as the entire fire burns recite the following if you can from memory then the better.

I PLEDGE MYSELF
TO DARKNESS
THE DARKNESS
BEYOND TWILIGHT
DARKER THAN
THE DARKEST NIGHT
BLACKER THAN
THE BLACKEST PITCH
ETERNAL DARK FIRE
GUIDE MY WAY
I CONJURE THE
DARKEST SHELLS
I CONJURE FORTH
THE DEEPEST HELLS
PAIN BEYOND REASON
TORMENT BEYOND TORTURE
NIGHTMARE OF
THE FIRST NIGHTMARE
COME THOU FORTH
ACCEPT THIS OFFERING.

Project all of your hate into the fire, every last bit that you can muster, and then only after the fire is out do you dismiss your guardians, and backwards release the gates by snuffing the candles with your fingers not your breath. Lastly you should thank Baron, Ogun, and Legba.

"Where is the Rabbit...?"

Dearest Reader,

If you have made it this far on your journey – congratulations. You have now stumbled deep into the hole. Hopefully you have managed to stay out of jail, or some insane asylum. With any luck you have kept your mouth shut and avoided falling into the crowd of those who seek to dress oddly, and have no flair for actual development.

This work, regardless if you have decided to embark experimentation, will help you become a better person, more aware of your surroundings. If not it sure makes it easy to keep the stupid away. As we have no time to waste in our lives, for they are all increasingly short. With the political climate what it is, there may or not be a world for us to carve out for ourselves. We dedicated souls on the path of the arts do seek to have the means available. To rediscover and make a return on that discovery contributing to the advancement of the world people as a whole. Bridging the two fields of science and magick. Where they become unified once again under the term Art. We learn the ways of nature, our quest does not stop there; however, what we must also learn is enough to save ourselves if we grow in the ways that will benefit our lives. It is not one man or woman, it is One World. And that world should be prepared.

Power to the people, power as the gods would have to the people who would become as god. No longer seeking in vain for those forgotten things to return and redeem our salvation. But we, as men and women of the world, have the right, ability, and with the strength of will to grow to be as the Gods. Seek us in earnest, if you would advance not just yourself, but the entire race of the humanity. Or those you deem worthy enough.

Keep up the good effort! Next is an interesting section; at least, I find it interesting, 'cause it's all the magicks, ceremonies, and fun stuff that can get you into some neat shit of trouble when you're not careful! So here ya go kiddie, you get a pack of matches and a barrel of gasoline...Again, it's on your own head if you fuck up and go to jail. Not my fault.

Yours Infernally,

Infernal Warlock

Alchemical Arrays

On Creation

If all things in creation extend from the source, then why cannot the source extend from the works of properly motivated mage since the essence of creation rests in all things?

    The tree of life provides a foundation for the soul to work and create worlds governed by the will of the practitioner. In providing the mage with an even ground on which to work, I provide this circle as an example of the type of glyphs necessary to establish a foundation to summon up the essences to create said worlds.

    The only thing required of this circle to finish its energy resonance between the word of "He Who Creates", and its connection to the elements of creation, are the elemental figures on the vertical and horizontal lines of this circle. Along with any symbolism placed on appropriate lines governing the power which you would use to create. Around the ring of the circle is space for a script to encircle the foundation, as it were, further stating the intent of what you would have occur. Either creating a cairn of power in your workspace, or focusing on the essence of creation to manufacture spirits for your own purposes.

    The uses of this circle extend, but are not limited to, tapping into and forming a nexus between tracks, creating and grounding souls and other forms of spiritual/elementary creation.

    On the nature of the forces, this circle has the ability to focus; be certain that you are stable spiritually, physically, and in your intent. The forces of creation, though beautifully potent, can also be destructive if one were to so put such intent behind it, adding to its axis the correspondences of lower realms. However, this is specifically designed to give the skilled practitioner a focus on which to further enhance the works they create out of the raw essence provided above and below on a level playing field, so to speak.

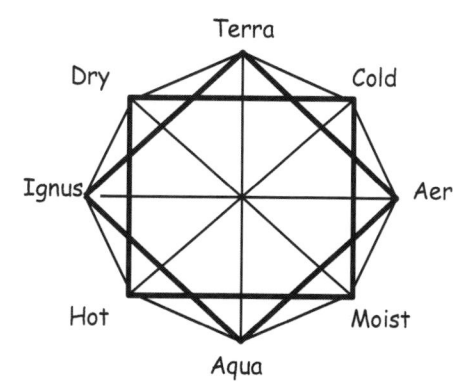

The basic form to alchemy is that there is a sulfurous nature, a salty nature, and mercurial nature to all things. What has been covered at length has been the spirit, the energy that makes up its body for the purpose to which it can be used. All the meditations and such to current focus on this point. The forging of objects using the principles of nature. The principle composition of these elements cause the desired and applied changes to nature and how it is perceived.

Mercury – Mind – Active – Gold
Sulfur – Body – Passive – Silver
Salt – Blood – Vital Spirit – Blood

The active and passive in all things, and the salt that transforms the spirit. Chemically the salts are as acid, breaking down and establishing a new form through the destruction, rebirth, and creation. What this can then be taken as in a spiritual format is that the mind, body, and spirit as they are contained in the whole vessel will constantly be in cycle to change their states to find an acceptable form of balance between them.

We know they then produce what is termed magick. For there is no other way to describe accurately the uses of these elemental forces, as they have no true description other than loose concepts and fragmented ideas. The blood is the link to the flesh, mind and spirit that the vessel contains. When the blood is shed in a ritual context that has been conditioned by the mage, as it is his own blood the level of efficacy increases to a level not otherwise attainable. The mind being so focused, the body working in harmony with the mind, then the act of its release allows the blood to assume the nature of mercury, of transformation. Each work becomes a living experiment of the "Grand Arcanum." Chemically, spiritually, and physically, each work that unifies the body, mind and soul as a single catalyst for change to occur.

There is a sulfur aspect to all things physical, because all things physical have a body. There is a mercuric aspect to all things, a mind of some form; having their dislikes and likes, their mated and resultant currents. The salt represents the spirit. All things have their spiritual alliances, as they cannot exist within the physical world without a spiritual substance to them. Here is where the microcosm and the macrocosm become as one. Both must be part of the thing to constitute it. When you subjectively break down a current of energy and build it back up, reworking what it is to become, then you have created a work of alchemy.

When your spirit blends with science to create something which having physically manifested something as a result of a spiritual quest to make it better, you have achieved a level of understanding about this world. As you will have not only changed yourself into an idea of what you want to be, but also physically the materials what you are working with, so they become a refined product of your experience. With this form of science you must read and study, learn from nature, observe how nature handles most of her transformations. Vibrations, Sounds, Waves, Particles. All these bits are what make up the order to the elemental world we see, feel, touch, taste, perceive. As this is just the basic overview of what is to come in later volumes, what you should understand now is that all things have their conditions and their cycles.

Materials

Leather has many attributes; it can act as a lightweight body armor, it can look stylish, or it can be used as part of the ritual wear of the individual. To start with a simple pair of leather gloves, we look at these as we understand their potential to be something which will allow for us keep our hands warm. As this is for metaphysical discourse, we will then use these gloves in our rituals. We will use them not only for their utilitarian purpose to hold hot things, to have our hands reflect the station of office, but also to help us channel our power.

As with all things living, they take on the attributes not only that they held in life, but also what they are used as channels for. As with herbs, stones, woods that we make use of in magick and rituals, leather and cloth act as the same as well. So for a pair of leather gloves where one has them on and directs currents through them to act as a second skin, the gloves will become more prone to that current. As the living tissue of the mage is such that it can channel all the energy though learned repetitions and muscle memory, the resonant current within a pair of leather gloves will allow for that memory to imprint itself upon those items. As such, the more times they are used will adjust and work with the energy of the mage who owns and wears them, acting as a medium or intermediary for that current to which the mage can assume, much like if one were to wear a mask or ceremonial hood. Each of these taking on that current of energy in the working.

Should one wish to have more dramatic rituals, one would adorn themselves in masks of woods, cloths, stones, leathers. All of these become charged with the repetitions on intent, becoming more and more in sync with the work. These will only aid the experienced mage in that he will be able to reserve more energy to focus deeper into the intent, as the gloves or the items themselves become vessels of reserved energy and power. So anything that was once alive and such can be used in rites and rituals to lend not only their attributes and spirit, but also that attribute and spirit can become aligned with the working of the particular current of energy needed for that specific spell, rite or ritual.

So, sticking with gloves only as our example, currently we have a second skin applied to the hands. This skin has a memory not just of life but of energy as well, and can and will be imprinted with the currents. Thus it aids the experienced Magus, allowing him to focus surgically those currents of energy to which he has aligned himself with. If such a man had red leather gloves which he wears during rites of warfare, then those gloves will be prone to doing acts of war by virtue of the energy used in the ceremonies. If he has gloves of white leather that are made use of during healing ceremonies and death rites, then they will become prone to doing such as well. If such a man also had green or brown leather gloves for his work with the natural elements, and nature, as all things on this earth are emanations from predominant earth currents, he will be able to manipulate the physical with such items. Should he require a general purpose glove, as all mages should start their training with a pair of black gloves. These become aligned like the skin and muscles to the energy of the mage and will grow in power with the mage, through his training.

With this, we then apply this same level of attributes for the storage capacity for such an item. We must then consider how this is achieved. All of creation existing and non-existing can be drawn out from a single particle. So thus a glove becomes the storage of an infinite space within the physical. Inside of it the mage can open up portals, consume energy, and conjure up his devils and demons to do his bidding. As the ritual circle is the world that the mage will change, so too are the gloves the means by which he can do the changing. A puppeteer guiding his marionette. The strings of his magick flowing through the infinite medium, affecting the real world as well as the spiritual at the same time. The means by which the will can be made flesh. All of this increases the direct arts of the sorcerer, all of this creates the connections for the mage to begin to get a handle on his magick in a physical sense.

Moving on to other objects beyond the gauntlet. There is the arm bracer, which allows for strength of the wrist and arms to channel that current down into the hand. The arm band, to circle the energy down the arm giving a motion to the magick. Boots, which draw up the current from the earth. As one stands within infinite space, one begins to understand the connections through the recognition of nature within themselves, pulling up those roots they have already acknowledged through their earlier meditations. The pants, which like the arm band and wrist brace channel that energy up their body, through the spheres. The belt doing the same, adding the control of the current to spin that energy within the body and the auric field. The vest or shirt containing that current stimulating the proper drive for such energy as needed for their working. The coat, jacket or robe of their station drawing up the power not only in the efficacy but treating the entire wardrobe of the mage as something which empowers them. Everything about the appearance of the mage becomes paramount in the control, observation and manipulation of the energy to which he will be working with. This extends to the undergarments one wears, as well. All of it goes to enhance one's energy, or generally stimulating currents to the mage. The clothes make the man, as it were, but also the man makes the clothes specific to his intent. Dressing to impress. All of it will enhance your working if you take care to pay attention to how you dress, what you wear, how you wear it. For its utilitarian needs and for its style which further enhances the effects you wish to achieve. Dressing for success, and power suits are good real world examples of this. The same holds true with the mage and his wardrobe. Everything should stimulate an energy not only within him, but also the world at large.

As such our topic here is leather, as the best skin to clothe not only oneself in is that of something once alive such as cottons, silks, leathers. All of them retain the energetic capacity. Wool more than standard cotton; velvet as refined cotton has more than wool; silk more than velvet. At the top of the list sits leather. As it was animal, most like unto the human body as it is also an animal. The connections remain on many levels to which there is no point going into now as they should be obvious by the previous parts of this work. As animal, anything that relates to the animal or physical world should contain some form of a living catalyst or form of leather. The reason is to connect the spiritual world to the physical world, which causes greater effects and more specific effects that can be brought about through the application of the systems of causation.

So we have our spells. We have our notes, and references those loose papers we scribe out the observations we make regarding the worlds. Well written on vellum or leather, these will not only give an impressive product for style, but it will also give a greater retention of energy. These pages then bound by leather, accented with metal, will also form a body of work. Both spiritually and physically, this work will contain the energy from the words, acting as a receptacle for power, but also as a living entity as it is never truly finished, there can never be an end, so the capacity it has will always be growing. The same work could take lifetimes to finish. This should be the goal of every Magus; to expand upon their body of work so that there is always learning, always growing. That their flesh never stops learning, that the muscles are always fit for working and they are ready and able to perform the magicks that will makes manifest in the physical.

We have then the sacred swords, knives, and other blades of the art. These will contain in their construction some wood, and are wrapped in a leather, or something relating to the item. Be it the scabbard made of leather to hold the blade of a ritual knife, or a sword sheathed in leather for storage and safety. The blade acts like the soul of the mage. It responds to the energy which surrounds it. So if you take a blade to perform a sacrifice with, that blade will remember the taste of that sacrifice, becoming attuned for it, and aligned for that current. Wrapping such a thing in a piece of leather will bring about the resonance of that intent within the leather as well, acting as the catalyst to keep such currents active within the blade.

You have now an idea where this study should be headed. As leather is the best way to connect energy to a physical object, by the virtue of animal sympathy, you can achieve not only the means to adorn yourself in finery but also to work your art effectively through the items that you wear, the objects that you hold and keep close to you. They act as storage for your energy. Your energy becomes infused in very physical ways into these tools which you make your own, which you train with and grow with. These become extensions of your will. As such, they should always remain extensions, lest you fall prey to the traps which relying on such items bring. They become your master instead of you mastering them.

Summoning up these combined concepts into the last part of this discussion, the sword of the art. This should be a weapon that you are comfortable with using. As such there will most likely be leather or animal sympathy found within its construction, be it bone or leather. But for this we will use the example of the Katana. It has cotton cording, bronze, the metal, and the ray skin. The proper student knows these by their function. But spiritually speaking, the way one can align a sword to their spirit, having it become more than just an emanation of their body but by the virtue of the animal sympathy the body channels energy through the cording which is wrapped around the leather which is wrapped around the wood which is wrapped around the blade which is accented by the bronze pieces. This becomes the total emanation, a second hand, like the glove. Which can and will take on the aspects of not only the magick, but also the soul of the owner. The finer the sword, and the more skilled the mage, then they will be as one.

It is through the virtue of animal sympathy that leather brings the greatest connection not only to life, to muscle, to flesh of another living thing, but also to the spirit to which that connects. Leather bridges the gap of the living and the dead. It provides in the space between the living tissue and the dead tissue, the corresponding counter currents to be able to shield and defend oneself from incoming currents, acting as spiritually defensive clothing and items as well. If the living mage writes in his leather tome on their vellum pages with the sacred metal as its bones, then the spirit of that mage is the only one who can ever fully make use of all the virtues and subtlety to that art which he develops. Should his gloves, coat, boots and so on adorn someone else, they will have the power left behind, but the control will not be there. They will not be able to master the subtleties of such items. Should the sword come into ownership of one who does not have the soul which is like unto the sword, then that person must respect the tool and never make use of it until the proper soul comes to reclaim what was.

These items of power have natural sympathy to the spirits which claim, which make them theirs and work with them. Training not only their living flesh, but aligning the dead flesh. Encompassing the life and death states which are only aspects to the greater balance. Everything having its cycles, everything making its due turn upon such rotations. The mage who sets out to experience all things must in his term experience his own death. He must know what it is to die, and he must return to the world of the spirit, then he will in his cycle return to the world of the living. Life, death and rebirth are cycles that the spirit will never escape. The bonds will never be broken, and escape can never be had. The reason is because of the sympathy. So long as there is life there will be death and rebirth, because that is the way of nature. So your tools that you will craft with such care, will in their time pass from your possession upon your death; they will pass hands again making the journey, if they survive, back to your soul when you cause your reincarnation. Just because everything dies in its own time, does not mean a mage who has mastered the higher levels of his art cannot in his own time return to flesh to continue the work he has embarked upon by the nature of his spiritual attributes. The leathers that he made use of in life, will remember the touch of their owner's soul. The blades which were used in life, will retain a piece of who the owner was, to allow them to remember. Should these items be in their course lost or destroyed they will become nothing more than empty vessels. Anyone trying to make use of such things without the proper training, will become lost and unable to be guided by what is stored within. Everyone must have their own. As there is individual spirit and purpose, so must there be individual tools and materials, so that all can properly work their arts with the utmost efficacy.

Circles of the Art

In our studies we have come to understand the nature of the elements, the divisions of the spirits, as well as created a comprehensive table of correspondences. The servitor creation method is a good way to practice evocations in a "safe" environment, as these are forces that extend from your own mind. However, when dealing with the forces found in nature, it is not always "safe." Many things can occur, many things can go wrong.

Studying the warnings of the grimoires, reading on how things can or cannot be banished is all a matter of what school of thought you apply, and what the sources of power are that you draw from. But it comes down to the circle which you focus as the "space" in which your will takes shape and the means through which the manifestation is generated by the frequency. If you form the proper barriers of space/time, then you will have no problems doing whatever you need to accomplish if you have the right circle for the right job.

A simple circle is just a single line of salt, or chalk, or rope, or a few candles engraved with symbols. These are good when you only need to balance one or more currents; but, like the seals, the ceremonial wizard is at their best when using things in relation to the sources of the creation to generate the needed currents in a stable way.

Traditions vary on what you would include in some circles; names of power being those of Gods, Angels or Demons. Runic scripts warding off anything to cross, and conjurations of pantheons to protect the space. It is a matter of how you make use of the charts of correspondences that you have created which will give you a list of things that help when creating these circles.

If you want to get a good idea of some of the historical uses of circles, then here is an example of the circle of Solomon. The image has the 72 names of the Shahemphorash, the 4 pentagrams of protection, and the triangle of summoning with 3 sacred names and a circle to contain the manifestation. If you don't want to go through this much elaboration when it comes to the creation of circle, there are a few ideas. This one has the 8 points surrounding the center, and then it also has positions for the 12 symbols of the zodiac.

This one is useful when you are needing to balance out the worlds with the spheres; it gives 4 points where each space has elemental influence, as well as is balanced out by the currents flowing in and around the circle, allowing for an open window into the sources.

The circle can be as elaborate as you want, it can be as simple as you want. But it should be the center point of the opening aspects of the ceremony. You want to establish the barrier and boundaries of the space as quickly as possible before you begin working with the energies contained within this space. If you are unable to give the circle its full marking upon the floor or the altar you are employing, then you can draw it upon a piece of paper in ink, or paint. Then have candles at a farther distance accordingly aligned to the major lines of the circle. So if you are using the 8 point style array, then one candle represents each point. If it is a pentagram array, then one candle for each of the 5 points.

There are also different ways to use the circles, and that is to have it as a point which you are standing outside of it, and the energies you are calling down are contained within it. Or that you are standing inside it, and the energies you are drawing are brought into a different part of the circle. Farther still that you call them to a space outside of the circle. Each of these scenarios are for a different type of ceremony. If it is a ceremony of creation, then entering the circle may or may not be needed to form the energies into the construct.

If it is a conjuration of some power or force that is not a spiritual intelligence, then it can be done within the circle. If you are going to be working with any kind of raw force of the element, then it is best done with you outside the circle.

Exercises of Circle Construction

Create a circle which will allow you to channel elemental energies with you inside of it.

Create a circle that will act as a barrier to both things that are contained within it.

Create a circle that will act as barrier to the things outside of it.

Write up a written explanation all references to angles, colors, names of power, etc.

Create a circle that will be able to be used for something summoned within it, or outside of it, or allow for the generation of the natural forces within it. Explain all aspects of it, and how you would apply it, for your references later. Then create the full ceremony to go with it.

Array Mechanics

The most common thing to use is a single band of energy that acts as the division between this world from the plane of ritual/works. The technical aspect of how this is achieved is in similar fashion to the study of Geburah. Where the all had to pull back from itself, and divide a space where it was not, in order to create actively. So the use of a circle is more than just a division from this place to the void/astral plane. It becomes a universe of manifestation, fit for those works which create from the raw material of creation. Angles represent the current that flows from the points. Geometric shapes correspond to planar spheres and star systems which have resonant energy for use in the works undertaken. Any names inscribed in the circle, or seals and sigils are the points where those energies are drawn from in order to achieve the greatest potential manifestation.

On a standard array the horizon point, where the world's current and the plane of the art meet, is equal to the angles that meet at the central origin, upwards. When you use a single band of current, say 9 feet, the horizon point would be about 4.5 feet above the ground. The larger the circle, the higher the horizon point. When you conjure, summon, or otherwise draw forces, around the waist line is a good place that way you can pull things up and maintain your control over the energies. The more complex the circle, the higher the horizon point. When this column is achieved, where it stretches above your own height, it acts as the door from this plane to the next. This greater column will allow alignment of the points in the circle to those points which are represented in the angles of the celestial bodies.

The power of the circle's natural resonance depends on what it is that you construct the primary array out of. These materials should be prime currents that are common in your body, and the work itself, so that you can draw out the maximum potential energy. Materials such as carbon, sulfur, nickle, gold, silver, sodium/salts, magnesium and so on should be a composite array, or use of things that will stand up to the use of your introduction of blood into the array will give the angles your DNA imprint, and allow you to spread your will easily through the construct. It would be most beneficial to use silver as its capacity to store, refine, and direct the brain waves to the desired current so the most desirable manifestation is achieved. If you are using a central array of silver for this process, then you would need to have something that will work for all of your arts, for every purpose, so you must design one and have it constructed accordingly to your needs; that way you can also add in what other materials or symbols you have that will be needed in any possible working that you find yourself faced with.

When building your circles, you need to keep in mind what it is you're going to achieve through the application of the angles, symbols, and shapes. If you are building a barrier circle to contain currents, then you want the most solidified defenses possible, and so bands of double circles work the best. If you are going to summon, conjure, or create from the energies, then symbols that extend past the barrier circle in angles with the diamond patterns and so on, you can use those spots to contain the desired currents, and filter them through the bands into a unified current for use in the central array. The greater the division from the outer world, such as double and triple bands, the more energy that the array will take to activate its deepest potentials, as well as the more stable that it will be when using the celestial energies in such a way that it will balance into a singular current, which is the aim of the circle. To balance creation to create directly the vibrations of the macrocosm in such a way that the manifestation is achieved in the best possible way.

Terrestrial Array Foundation

Purpose

To unify the current of an established object to its 8 respective parts, to work directly with the elements. This acts as a point of creation or genesis for whatever is placed inside the inner ring.

Mechanics

The outer ring stabilizes the current within the 10 point array of all aspects of the 4 elements and the 4 states of being. The inner band stabilizes the celestial field of the post-natal Chi or prenatal Chi, as it flows within this space; in other instances can be used with the 8 source seals. What then occurs in each of the 8 points is a form of balance brought on by each of the 8 sources not represented. Then we have the center sphere of generation. Any array can be placed within the center seal, to be remade, or broken down accordingly.

Sacrificial Array

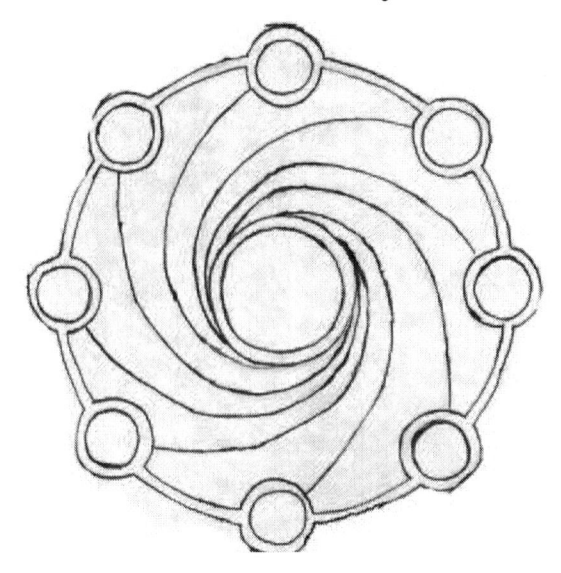

Purpose

To tear an object apart through the essence, allowing for a total recreation of the inner Chi into the separate fields of holding. So that each energy point can be modified one at a time. Such an array would be good for reprogramming spirits, demons, familiars, etc.

The establishment of an 8 point array through the use of the principal Chi current found within the center point of origin. This array can pull separate intents based upon the addition of various symbols, seals, and compounds upon the micro gates, or in the center.

Mechanics

This array is designed to draw the 8 points of Chi away from the core through use of the post natal hexagrams. Where the flow is counter clockwise, to the Chi that exists within the core. This has the dual effect of both taking the inner current and pulling it to the outer band to sustain the 8 arrays with equal current. Or, it has the effect of tearing an object apart and using the 8 points as a storage space until such time as the current is returned to the unified state in the center.

Generation

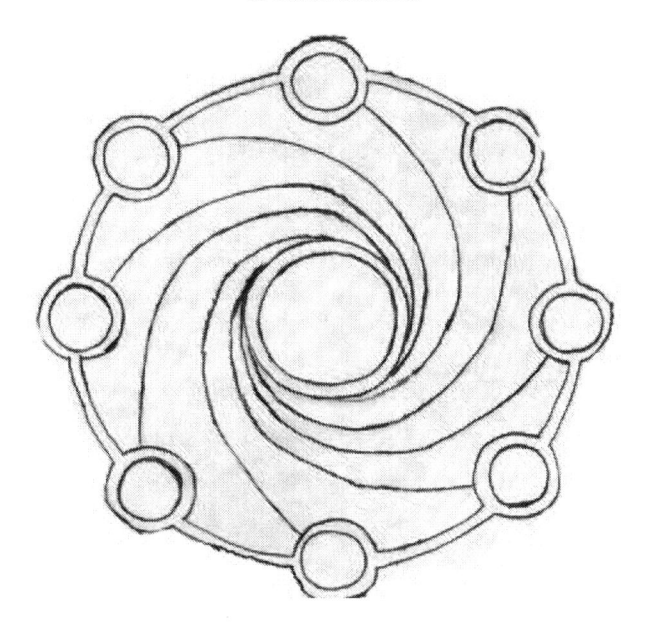

Purpose

To build things from 8 separate currents within the center point of origin. The prenatal hexagrams in the 8 points will draw the boundless creation of the clockwise pattern of the principal materia from the void space where the primordial Chi originates.

As well as the establishment of an 8 point array through the use of the principal Chi current found within the center point of origin. This array can pull for separate source based upon the addition of various symbols, seals, and compounds upon the micro gates, for use in the construction of a portal/gate/vortex in its center.

Mechanics

This array is designed to draw the 8 points of Chi into the core through use of the prenatal hexagrams. Where the flow is clockwise, to the Chi that exists within the core. This has the dual effect of both taking the outer current and pushing it to the inner band to sustain the center point with the 8 points of origin with equal current. Or it has the effect of bringing an object together through using the 8 source points for a specific origin, until such time as the current is returned to the unified state in the center.

Barrier

Purpose

Used for the development of protection rites, defensive spells, and shield techniques. The 8 seals can be used around the center circle. The elemental seals will anchor it to the terrestrial plane. The space in the center is both point of generation and the thing protected. Used to anchor with four currents.

Mechanics

The circles in the points anchor the elements to the array. The space around the central circle can be used for the I-Ching, or the 8 seals of the planets, or the sources. The circles are used set up a castle style defense where the outer squares, inner squares, and circles, represent the unbroken currents of generation and protections. The outer lines must be connected to stabilize the full current. In this pattern however, motion is given unto the central wheel, and it will spin with the current breaking it apart and storing it, and locking it into the base four points.

Gate of the Inner World

Purpose

To open the pathway to the inner spirit within flesh. Allowing for the inner consciousness to be made manifest for various intent. Some intents will allow for the reconstruction of the self through creation of a new persona using the eight by twelve aspects of the body. The implanting of direction into the subconscious of the body. The evocations of specific current, emotion, behaviors from the deepest and most private places of the spirit in flesh. This can also be used to open a gate to the inner worlds of the singular collectives unconscious mind.

Mechanics

Using sigil of spirits that have no name, attribute to the 8 of the outer band to be spirits of the 8 aspects of the body of the source. The 12 nameless spirits within should be the 12 principals of the humors of the body. The unintelligible script within the 4 bands, separates the mind of the body and the mind of the spirit. Opening the inner band which goes directly into the subconscious spirit within the body.

Celestial and Abyssal Seal

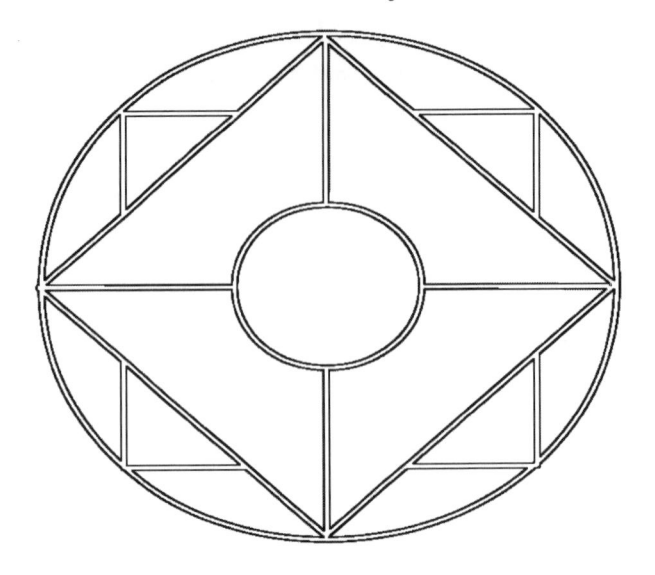

Purpose

To use either the celestial aspects or the abyssal aspects of the thing being summoned. In the case of the Elemental colors will overlap in different ways. But it must be used in conjunction with the color for some symbol of the element, or the sigil of the elemental from the central point. In order to open a stable channel from a plane of origin, or from the current directly in order to generate the the creation of the spirit desired. Such creations of Angels, Demons, Stellar, and Planetary forces given the support of the heavens. Any primordial creative power that can be drawn through aspect can be used with this seal.

Mechanics

From the description of use, it works in the similar way. It isolates a pocket of the creation where the influence of elements are not. As such, it finds the bones or the support of the desired current through the exact opposite current that balances this force out, creating a stable medium of conjurations. In this manner does this seal act as the point of generation for thought forms, spirits, angelic, demonic, or other deified manifestations of the forces that are balanced through this seal for your needs.

Active and Passive Seal

Purpose

To use either the active aspects or the passive aspects of the thing being summoned. In the case of the Elemental colors will overlap in different ways. But it must be used in conjunction with the color for some symbol of the element or the sigil of the elemental from the central point. In order to open a stable channel from a plane of origin, or from the current directly in order to generate the the creation of the spirit desired. Giving this a point of manifestation for the creation of natural spirits, and other primal currents that could other wise only come from the foundation of the world instead of the currents the flow as the archetypes of the mind.

Mechanics

From the description of use, it works in the similar way. It isolates a pocket of the creation where the influence of elements are not. As such it finds the bones or the support of the desired current through the exact opposite current that balances this force out, creating a stable medium of conjurations. In this manner does this seal act as the point of generation for thought forms, spirits, angelic, demonic, or other deified manifestations of the forces that are balanced through this seal for your needs.

Array of the Doppelganger

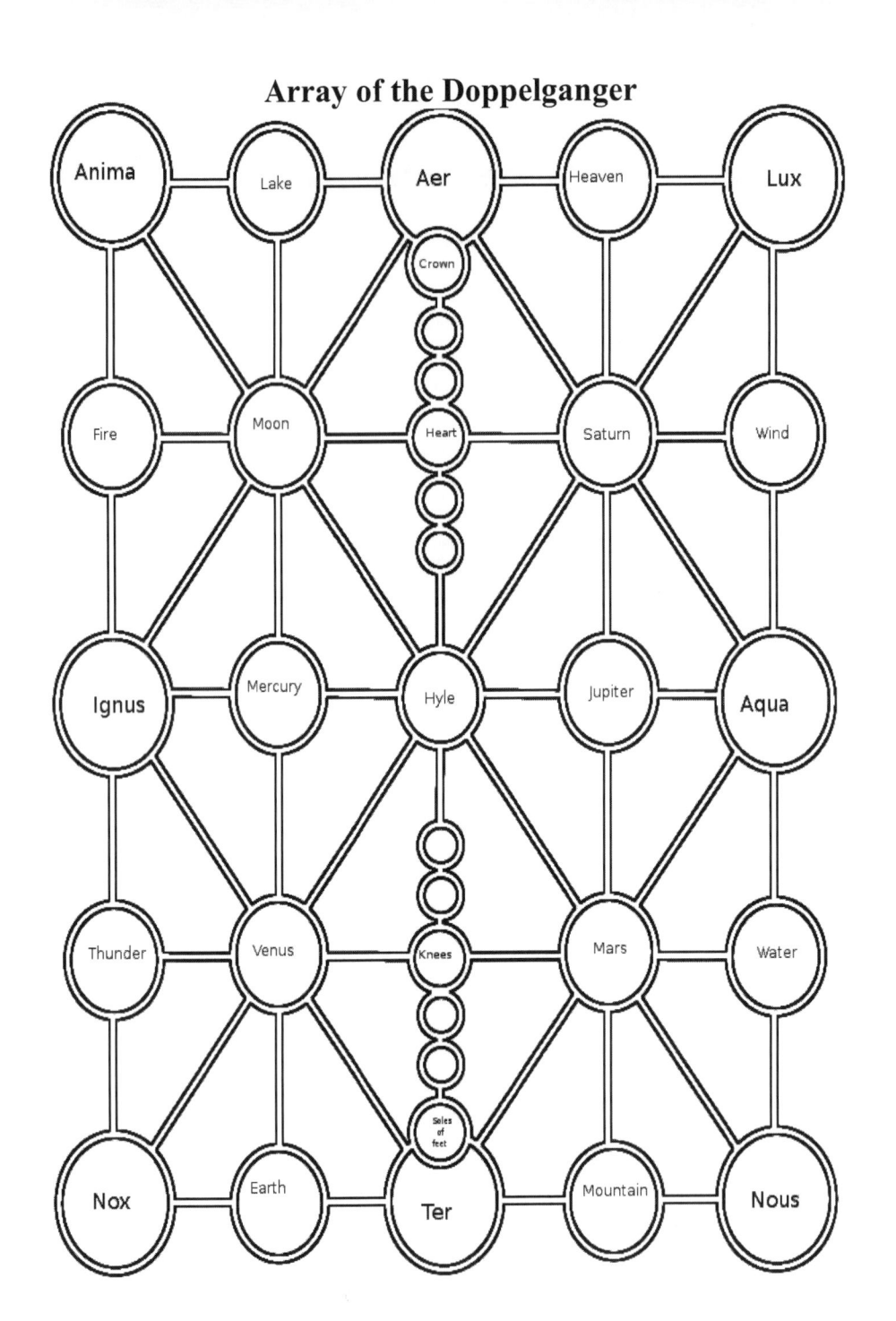

Purpose:
The array design is to duplicate the currents of the human body. In this manner, we are able to copy the flow of a body externally from that body with only personal effects. From this, we can use it for any number of purposes, such as inserting cloned cores and reconstructed body patterns for any number of healing or harmful works, depending on the needs at the time of use.

Mechanics:
Use blood, or a blood condenser to draw.
Latin elements should be the symbols that represent the Hindu Tattwah.
Square for Ter
Triangle pointed towards Hyle for Ignus
Crescent with points towards Hyle for Aqua
Double banded circle is fine for Aer
The planets should be their alchemical symbols in the west.
The I-ching characters or trigrams should be written in their trigrams or in their character in the small circles between the hermetic anchors: Heaven, wind, water, mountain, earth, thunder, fire, lake.
The anchors for the spirit - Anima, light - Lux, dark - Nox, and mind, should be present as the seal of that source to flow freely through the celestial gates into the energy body. The reason the other 4 are omitted is that time is when you work on this body, life and death is the blood field that unites these disparate elements.
From what we need then is the personal anchors from the original body to the clone. Such as blood or personal effects to duplicate the flow of the living current within the body, and allow for external modification. In this way the human form is open to us, as we can access the inner world directly and without harm to the host body, or the interference of its condition.

Sahasrara – Crown
Anja – Third eye
Vishyddha – Throat
Anahata – Heart
Manupura – Solar Plexus
Svadisthana – Navel
Mudlahara – Root – Hyle

Atala – Hips
Vitala – Thighs
Sutala – Knees
Talatala – Calve
Rastala – Ankles
Mahatala – Feet
Patala – Soles of the feet

Blood Circle of Summons

Infernal   Celestial

Purpose

This circle is designed to draw things up from the infernal planes, and focus it in an array that surrounds the core. As such, one would use this to, say, call something up from the infernal planes and surround with the cold, frozen power of the purgatory. That way the spirit can function and have a reprieve from the current of their origin. The kinder way to summon things from above or below, and subject them to differences in the current depending on the purpose of such a work.

Mechanics

There should be scripts, seals, and other things placed within to set the link from the plane of the origin, to this plane. The inner circle should be made with a condenser designed to summon the force you're dealing with. The outer barrier should be a condenser made of an opposing elemental force; that way it acts as the buffer, and neutralizes the inner current. Both of these should have the blood, or blood substitute used to establish will over both the currents to control their flow.

Blood Circle of Binding

Celestial Binding

Infernal Binding

Purpose

This circle is designed to draw things up from a celestial origin or from the infernal planes. To focus an array that surrounds the core. As such, one would use this to call something from the celestial planes, and surround it with current that will allow it to be constrained to one place. That way the spirit can be compelled within a location much as a demon would, so the angelic hosts can be subjugated by much of the same methods. For anchoring them to a place where they are not able to access celestial power.

Mechanics

There should be scripts, seals, and other things placed within to set the link from the plane of the origin, to this plane. The inner circle should be made with a condenser designed to summon the force you're dealing with. The outer barrier should be a condenser made of an opposing elemental force; that way it acts as the buffer, and neutralizes the inner current. Both of these should have the blood, or blood substitute used to establish will over both the currents to control their flow.

Blood Gates

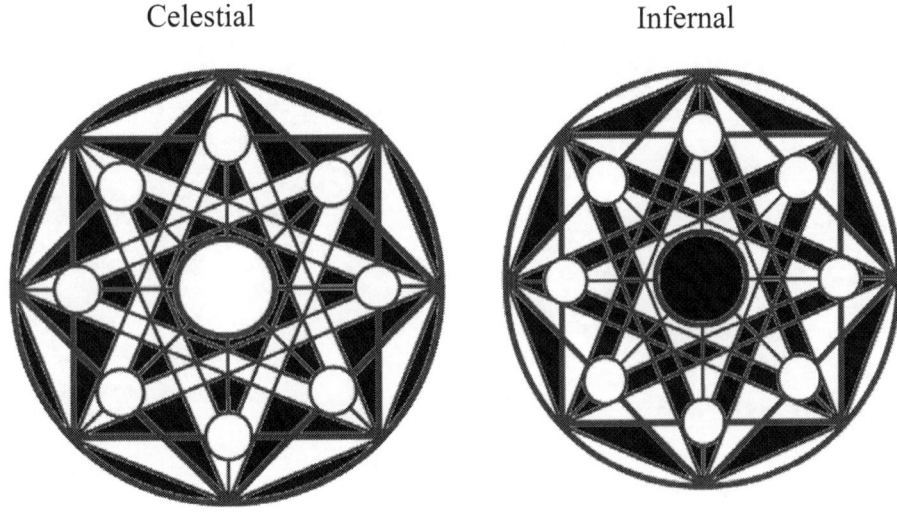

Celestial　　　　　　　　　　　Infernal

Purpose

Using the power of the blood, one can access the celestial gates, or the infernal gates resident within the body of the one whose blood is used. This can get right to the core of the power in their body and open it up for the manipulations. Much as the sacrificial circle tears energy from nature apart, this can be used to tear the energy of the body apart.

Mechanics

With blood or a substitute, the array can penetrate through defenses of the body to open up the direct current for modifications. The Celestial array would deal with the "Logical" aspects of the body. The Infernal array would deal with the "Emotional." There needs to be the effect of the person in the center. This will allow for the modification of the source currents as they interact with the body. This technique can be built upon by the other arrays, and other processes to build a better body. There is also the ability to modify the nine aspects of the self based on the Egyptian bodies. From there you will be able to properly modify the body in anyway you choose all at a single time.

Dream Array

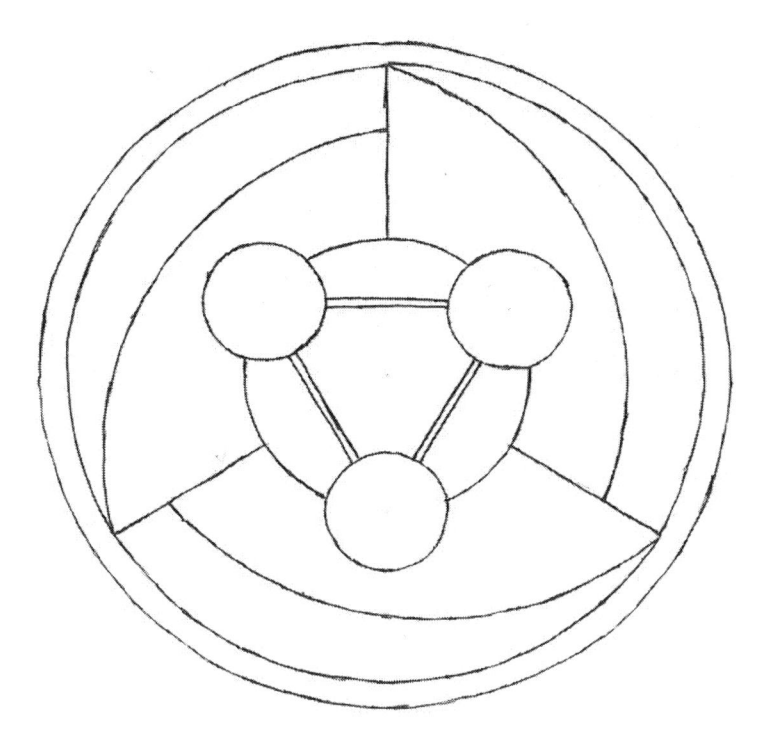

Purpose

When using things like the subconscious mind of others, it is sometimes necessary to start with the observation of the subject. This circle with candles, placed within the 3 circles. An effect or some marker to the host in the center. To unite open the channel between the waking mind, the subconscious and the super-conscious mind. To use to modify the individual through their dreams.

Mechanics

Using the power of the blood one can access the dream gates of the target. Ideally, one works with the source of the mind when using this array, and the central tertiary points become the anchor for the opening. The blades become the thing which forces the channel open, and the flow of the inner mind unites with the entire mind, to thrust open the conduit in the mind.

Elemental Gate

Purpose

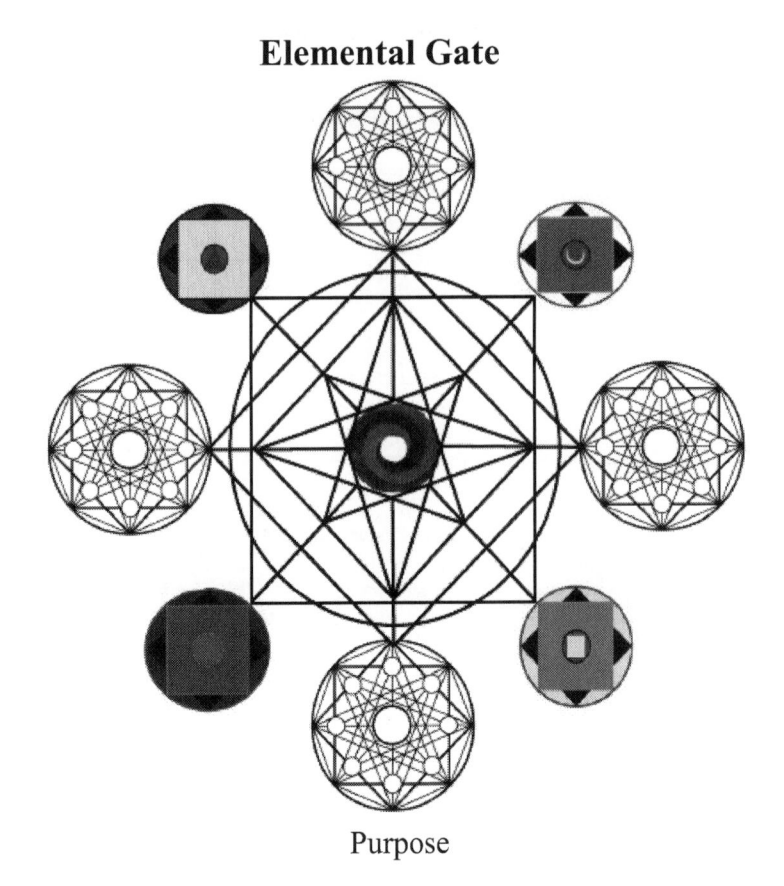

This is to use the ceremony of the union with the gates of the sources, along with the elemental power to create a space of unity where one can redesign their stellar body, or shift the planes ones consciousness resides on. Higher workings are also done through the uses of this technique.

Mechanics

The elemental seals form the anchors to this plane. The sources used with the other 4 gates represent the 4 major planes in creation. For our purposes, we will use Hell, Shadow Planes, Heaven, Spirit Planes. The inner squares anchor the foundations of the new plane together, in the creation of a pocket plane. Or the creation of a sub-plane of one of the 4. It is through this that one can forge their own realms for a variety of purpose.

Integration Array

Purpose

The 3 act as the points of insertion in otherwise stable current. This can cause rifts, portals, and help establish gates. Like the Dream Array, this can be used to insert or integrate other forces into established forces. To peel back layers, create openings through established materia.

Mechanics

Where one can rend something apart by the integration of energy which cause the break down of the initial current, or can augment the established current. The trick is to insert stable current or unstable current, slowly and without notice to the natural current. Small pockets such as this can be as small as the atoms that are spinning, or can be as large as territories.

Elemental Stasis

Purpose

The outer circle represents the division of the space where the stasis field occurs. The square represents the foundational elements in their 4 states of being; dry, wet, hot, cold. The central cross that is behind the disk represents the point of interaction, where creation occurs. Tattwahs for the creative elements. The layer of the cross over it represents the same states of conditions in the elemental forms. Binds the current through each of its states. The central ring represents the field of binding where the force is contained.

Mechanics

This shows creation as it exists in the elemental world. From this point, we have a point that we can use as a focus to isolate and contain a plane within a field which duplicates the one that is used to establish the Binah/Geburah current. Like when the Ain Soph was divided to remove itself from itself, so that it could create within the space that is no longer itself, a world of its very own. At best this array becomes a planar tether, where it can create and hold worlds within itself.

Opening Seal

Purpose

The outer circle represents the division of the space when the field becomes unified current that blends the individual currents of the 8 into one. Seals of spirits, sources, or planets should be put into the circles to get them to flow in unison. Crystals then placed atop the circles to bring the array upwards to a point to direct the current to a focus. This will allow for seals to open up and currents be generated through the central current.

Mechanics

Using the 8 points, one blends the individual currents into a single force of interaction. Like vessels that empty into a center chamber these unify the singular currents into one unified current. Forcing a union of all 8 aspects of the element, the airy, the watery, the fiery, the earthy, the dry, wet, cold, and hot. All elements hold to these states of being, so it forces their manifestation within the central current as you pull the energy out from the seal or sigil in the center.

Storage Array

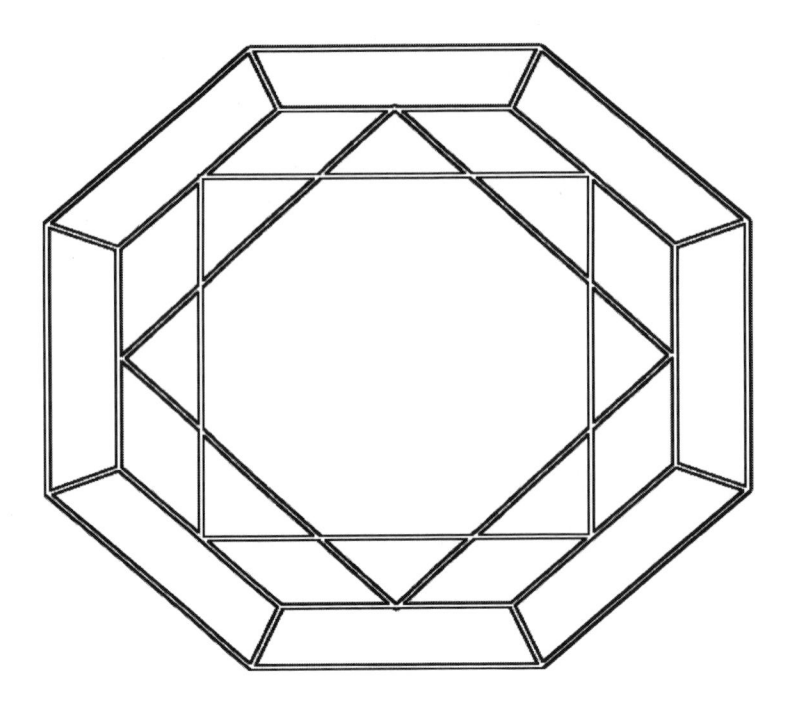

Use of the above array would be a good pattern for storage of 25 different aspects that could be compressed from a singular source. An array like this would be most useful for a singular body that you could pull apart and form each one of the sources, elements, emotional sources, from their mind. Doing it this way will allow for one body to create 25 different spiritual entities. When commanded, you could pull that power out independently from the array and set it loose. Such things like this could be applied to personal application of hollowing out bodies and replacing them with "created" aspects, so that way for the duration of the process, they would only be that which you have pulled to choose what is dominant in their nature, while suppressing the rest. This can be then applied to marking the body, tattoo magicks, and other blood magicks.

Gate Magick

The Nature of Gates

To properly understand the notion of gates, you must already be aware of what significance the 7 spheres had to the ancients. Both the people and alchemists of cultures long since turned to dust knew that there were currents which came "through" these gates. Each of the 7 major planets, and similarly every planet found in our solar system has correspondences to some form of the primal currents. However, the Ancient Sumerian belief was that if you opened the gates, you would develop a body capable of traversing the other world, those places which exist outside the gates. It is only through the passage of these gates that one develops the spiritual body. Open the gates, and you gain a way to travel outside of creation into the planes as kept and watched over by the other elder gods. Those forces from everything from the first creation up to the present created realms of the spiritual.

Things which do not resonate with anything, which can be "channeled" by all the psychics, seers, and meditation circles on this sphere who connect with the galaxy of whatever. When you open these, you become yourself changed for the going; it is not a thing you wake up from one day, and you're done with it. You open yourself to it, and it becomes a part of your nature, your make up, and your day to day life. If you open the gates of the 7, then you develop a spiritual body which is more advanced than run of the mill astral projection. In order to successfully be able to establish one's will as independent within the view of creation, one's cosmological perspective must be able to encompass such viewpoints, if not then madness and/or death can occur.

The 7 gates of the planets open and the body is then altered. There is a rite in this work which opens the 7 gates and the 7 Chakra and aligns them together, for the purpose of bridging the body with the outer world and inner worlds. Reflections of the microcosmic and macrocosm at this point are good in gaining the overall perspective of what is occurring in the worlds. However, it is when the inner will of the individual meets with the greater forces outside the body, that magick occurs.

There are many forms of lower magick, but the High Art, specifically the Arts as developed herein, is focused on those currents which exist at the limits of perceptions and awareness, always seeking to expand and grow out to gain better understanding of the individual and their relationship to it. Magick is about bringing out the inner will, the true will, and making it manifest within the creative world, and forming it into the material. This is done through laws of sympathy and antipathy because it is a safe way to do it.

Dealing with god-force spirits and assorted guardians to keep the individual safe from the damaging primal currents. However, whom do we rely upon for the fact that the currents are damaging? Religious men with agendas, assorted one way viewpoints all trying to take power of the individual. If the individual can hold their own way to the other world, what need do they have of priests with their bondage of religion? So, now it's time for the individual to declare their independence, and work with the gates, and learn that the world is not a nice place: that things which lurk in nature, lurk everywhere. Open the gates, and find it for yourself. From doing this you have the ability to know what your inner nature is - but you have to face it. There are traps and pitfalls when dealing with gates, and the trials which you will find. When you understand and take unto yourself this responsibility, then you will be able to progress with your development. With this, you will be able to open the gates in your own inner world, and align them with the outer world. There are a number of different ones which can be opened - it is your choice, your own development. Along with the opening of the gates, you also gain traits from doing so. Howe these traits manifest which fits into the view of your cosmological viewpoints.

When you set on these paths to yourself, and you do so in a way which puts you at odds to the "main-stream" life, you will be forced to stand on your own. You will know what you can survive, and you will know if you can endure what roads your life takes you down. Through gates we connect ourselves to the Singular Conscious, in this we can open up the different layers of our own being, and embrace who we are fully capable of being.

In order to create a gate to another plane or another location, so that it will be stable for astral passage, what is required is to have an entity that you have created to become the base on the other side of the portal. As soon as the portal is created into the other world, the puppet entities must be sent through with a mental link or connection to you so that you can operate with the necessary precision in establishing another node of power on the opposite side, becoming the link from the node to the open portal, and causing the influx of power to create the link back to the plane of origin.

Needless to say, this becomes difficult; when you are working to access another plane of existence, you must have the elemental properties in sync with those you have on your plane of origin. So you need to have a base circle set with the elemental energies being projected through the open portal. There is a mathematical correlation to the plane of destination and the plane of origin. You find the links that will become the foundation by remotely locating those points and elements where the nodes are strongest. Base 4 with the 4 elements. Base 7 with the planetary spheres to act as a launching point. Base 12 for the cycles and rotation of time.

You combine these so that your overall output projection relates to the time, location and elements to the position of the opening of the portal. When you have these energies projected onto the plane of desire, you must have control over the entities that have been sent through to perform the needed energy dispersal to create the node and link the elements in upon the moment of entry, because the portals will only last so long. If, however, you are trying to link to a plane similar to this one, then you will have problems.

Portals

When working with gates, you have the plane of origin and the plane of desire. What comes form here is the plane of origin. What originates in front of you, is what you must use to send it to the other space as a tether to hold the two places together. From this tether you anchor the current of the plane of origin to the plane of desire. Portals are one way tunnels that originate for the purpose of anchoring it to another place.

These are one way tethers which must have a return current from the plane of desire allowing the energy of that environment to stabilize with the plane of origin. To do this, you must open the portal and then pull from the essence of the environment energy to open it up. Keep in mind that whatever sent through the vortex is on a one way trip. You have to have the ability to have the current merge with the landscape, and then have the energy to reabsorb it go through the vortex back to the plane of origin.

To Open Portals

Place 3 white candles in a triangle, and in the center a candle carved with the plane of destination, in the color corresponding to the plane as well. Light the center candle last.

We are three, We are three
In the past to the future forever to be
We are three, We are three
We the neutral, We the light, We the dark.
I conjure and open that which is sought to be
Open what is required
As the fires burn for what is desired.

You should, at this point, know exactly what plane of origin you are on, with the corresponding glyphs, as well as the sigil to the plane of desire. You will be able to use the mathematical correspondences tied to the astrological correspondences to make the most of out of these forms of openings.

Vortexes

These are the methods of travel that exist as one way tunnels from the planes of desire as we could call them on this plane. Or they would be on the exit side of the plane of origin. When you make a portal, the other side cannot enter through unless its energy is already intermixed and unified with the current. If this occurs, then you will have corruptions in your signatures when entering this place, if there is no unified balance between point A and B. When we come across these, they are generally on ley lines, or other places of natural/unnatural energy that has collected enough for there to be a gap between one world and the others.

A quick note on the other planes/voids/spaces that exist in the universe. They exist in different forms, each body has its appropriate world, or dimensional origin when it is attributed form and function on this plane. Generally, that is because it follows through what must happen when it comes here, and needs some sort of definition. Such as a class ranking, a caste ranking, and elemental ranking.

With that being said, the things which find their way through are not usually whole critters, and so with vortexes you have to have an ability to project some form of energy through from the portal side of it in order to unite the 2 sides in balance. A little from plane A, and a little from plane B. What can go through a vortex is only base energies; nothing will retain its form, body, or nature without getting torn apart and into the current that sustains the portal. Spirits, generally Djinn, Fae, and other such natural elementals, will use these as their exits into this world from the other world. If you happen to find a vortex occurring in your region, then experiment with it, figure out what energies make it up, and then see if you can stabilize it.

From here, if you can, experiment on it, you can the manipulate its point of origin, and turn the vortex into a two-way portal or gate.

The Opening of the Way

The gates, being the forces that contain energy within this world, are what keep this world in accordance with the elemental formation. The Buddhist monks develop the Mandala by creating a drawing in which they then ceremonially evoke their pantheon of gods. The doorway to whatever world is then opened by the formation of the diagram. To expand upon this, and in combination with the Circles of the Arts, the following is made possible that there is a direct channel to the other world from a localized point. Using the planar creation methods from earlier parts of this work, it becomes needed to build a symbol set for the usage of applications for this work. For our purpose, the Gate of the Elemental Union.

The center of the diagram is left open, and unmarked because it's through the seal for the plane you would open the gate to. Either one of your own construction, one of the heavenly realms, or one of the infernal realms. This way can be opened unto any plane for any length of time, assuming that the influx of the power is a stable one. All that this achieves is the foundation of a gate.

Using the portal mechanics where you must have an elemental link found within the planes of creation that connects the 2 planes through which a gate shall be forged. Use of the 8 forces needs to be balanced by the elemental currents to achieve a stable opening. Carving the seals onto the bottom of crystalline objects that have received a proper charge in a condenser will align the power of your own body, and the gates to affect the opening. Placing structures atop the seals of the Eight will give an extra tie to the opening of the Outer Gate.

Conjuration of the Elemental Seals

My will forges this bond
Between the earth and heaven
By my blood and eternal fire
From these raw forces I create the gate between the worlds,
Forth from this gate I now create
By the sacred, and infernal
United within thought.

Conjuration of the Gate

Manifest unseen beyond the reach of time
This place of mind and shade
I throw wide the gates
Open now unto the darkest planes
By thought, will, blood, becoming
I summon forth the fires within my body
I evoke the eternal fire
Open now this gate before me
By the blood of Power
By the Thought made Word
This is the gate of the Way between the Worlds
This gate opens
By the power of this soul offered
It is become my key to open the Way
I hold the key to beyond the veils
I am the Gatekeeper,
I open Now this Gate!
I am the keeper of the Keys,
I open Now the Way!

Conjuration of Celestial Gates

This gate design is omitted, as anything can be placed here. It is used to be the foundational point for where we draw our conjurations of the 8 gates from. This is the central point of neutral manifestation when dealing directly with the 8 planets and their powers. When you are ready to begin the work, use this to open the point of desire after the ritual disks are put into place.

The following order is put down in the initiation sequence for the cult of Mithra. Aside from the lunar gate which is out of place. So do enjoy, and walk each of these in stride.

The Lunar Gate

Ate me Peta Babka
(Gatekeeper, open the gate to me)

Ana harrani Sa Alaktasa la Tarat
(the road whose course does not turn back)

Petu Babkama Laruba Anaku
(Open the gate so I may enter here)

Ina Kadinger Semu ina Mamitu
(the Gateway of the Gods, obey the Oath)

Peta ina kunuk babu ina Nanna
(Open for me the seal of the Gate of Moon)

Zi dinger Kia Kanpa
(Spirit god of the earth remember)

Zi Dinger Kibrat Erbettim Kanpa
(Spirit gods from the regions of the four, remember)

Gate of Mercury

Color: Yellow
Source: Spirit

Conjuration of The Mercurial Gate

Ate me Peta Babka
Ana harrani Sa Alaktasa la Tarat
Petu Babkama Laruba Anaku
Ina Kadinger Semu ina Mamitu
Peta ina kunuk ina babu Nebo
Zi dinger Kia Kanpa
Zi Dinger Kibrat Erbettim Kanpa

Gate of Venus

Color: Green
Source: Life

Conjuration of the Gate of Venus

Ate me Peta Babka
Ana harrani Sa Alaktasa la Tarat
Petu Babkama Laruba Anaku
Ina Kadinger Semu ina Mamitu
Peta ina kunuk ina babu Ishtar
Zi dinger Kia Kanpa
Zi Dinger Kibrat Erbettim Kanpa

Gate of Mars

Color: Red
Source: Mind

Conjuration of the Gate of Mars

Ate me Peta Babka
Ana harrani Sa Alaktasa la Tarat
Petu Babkama Laruba Anaku
Ina Kadinger Semu ina Mamitu
Peta ina kunuk ina babu Nergal
Zi dinger Kia Kanpa
Zi Dinger Kibrat Erbettim Kanpa

Gate of Jupiter

Color: Purple
Source: Time

Conjuration of the Gate of Jupiter

Ate me Peta Babka
Ana harrani Sa Alaktasa la Tarat
Petu Babkama Laruba Anaku
Ina Kadinger Semu ina Mamitu
Peta ina kunuk ina babu Marduk
Zi dinger Kia Kanpa
Zi Dinger Kibrat Erbettim Kanpa

Gate of the Sun

Color: Orange
Source: Light

Conjuration of the Solar Gate

Ate me Peta Babka
Ana harrani Sa Alaktasa la Tarat
Petu Babkama Laruba Anaku
Ina Kadinger Semu ina Mamitu
Peta ina kunuk babu ina Shammash
Zi dinger Kia Kanpa
Zi Dinger Kibrat Erbettim Kanpa

Gate of Saturn

Color: Black
Source: Death

Conjuration of the Gate of Saturn

Ate me Peta Babka
Ana harrani Sa Alaktasa la Tarat
Petu Babkama Laruba Anaku
Ina Kadinger Semu ina Mamitu
Peta ina kunuk ina babu Ninib
Zi dinger Kia Kanpa
Zi Dinger Kibrat Erbettim Kanpa

Gate of Neptune

Color: Blue
Source: Darkness

Conjuration of the Gate of Neptune

Ate me Peta Babka
Ana harrani Sa Alaktasa la Tarat
Petu Babkama Laruba Anaku
Ina Kadinger Semu ina Mamitu
Peta ina kunuk ina babu Neptunus
Zi dinger Kia Kanpa
Zi Dinger Kibrat Erbettim Kanpa

Gate of Uranus

Color: Violet
Source: Chaos

Conjuration of the Gate of Uranus

Ate me Peta Babka
Ana harrani Sa Alaktasa la Tarat
Petu Babkama Laruba Anaku
Ina Kadinger Semu ina Mamitu
Peta ina kunuk ina babu Ouranos
Zi dinger Kia Kanpa
Zi Dinger Kibrat Erbettim Kanpa

Conjuration of the 72

I am the one that was first

I am the one that became the two
That by the thirty six become the seventy-two
I am the one that became the three that by the twenty-four become the seventy-two
I am the one which became four
That the by the eighteen becomes the seventy-two
I am the one which became the six
That by the twelve becomes the seventy-two

I call that the will becomes word
The word that becomes flesh
The flesh that becomes manifest

The one of the source
The origin of all things
That becomes in all times and hours
The hours of the light
The hours of the dark
That which is the twelve of the day
That which is the twelve of the night
That which is the zone of the sky
That which is the division of the heaven
That which is the division of the hells

I am the one who calls the divide
I am the one who commands the gate

I am the one who summons the will
I am the one who becomes two
I am the two which becomes three
I am the three which becomes the four
I am the two by six
I am the four by three
I am the twelve by six
I am the twenty-four by three
I am the seventy-two
I am the twelve of the zones of heaven
I am the twelve by the angels of the heaven
I am the twelve by the demon of the night
I am the one which became the twelve
I am the will that stirs creation
I am the creation that is divided
I am the divide which is the reflection of the one
I am that which is above and below
I am the earth, the sky and the heavens source
I am these things in the zones of the twelve by six
I am the word
The word which divided and created worlds
I am the one

The one which divided to create the two
I am the keeper of the keys of creation
I open forth the seventy-two fold lock
I stand here as the one who charges the gate

The gate shall be opened forth
The one that is two
The two that Is four
The four that is the world by three
The twelve which becomes the zones of the heaven
The twelve which has become the hours of the day
The twelve which has become the hours of the night
The twelve which rule the earth
The twelve which rule the heaven
The twelve which rule the stars
The twelve which have shaped creation

By the sixfold twelve
The seventy-two gates are open
Conjuration is set in blood
The way is open by blood
The word has been spoken of creation

That which is and has been
That which is to be and the possibility
Is conjured by the seventy-two fold
The spaces in creation for the worlds to open
I call forth the seventy-two
The seventy-two that becomes by twelve
The twelve that becomes six
The six which becomes one
The one which commands the all
Open forth to the world

Conjuration of the 1728 Gates

I am the one, that was first
I am the one that became the two
That by the thirty-six become the seventy-two
I am the one that became the three that by the twenty-four become the seventy-two
I am the one which became four
That the by the eighteen becomes the seventy-two
I am the one which became the six
That by the twelve becomes the seventy-two

I call that the will becomes word
The word that becomes flesh
The flesh that becomes manifest

The one of the source
The origin of all things
That becomes in all times and hours
The hours of the light
The hours of the dark
That which is the twelve of the day
That which is the twelve of the night
That which is the zone of the sky
That which is the division of the heaven
That which is the division of the hells

I am the one who calls the divide
I am the one who commands the gate

I am the one who summons the will
I am the one who becomes two
I am the two which becomes three
I am the three which becomes the four
I am the two by six
I am the four by three
I am the twelve by six
I am the twenty four by three
I am the seventy-two

I am the twelve of the zones of heaven
I am the twelve by the angels of the heaven
I am the twelve by the demon of the night

I am the one which became the twelve
I am the will that stirs creation
I am the creation that is divided

I am the divide which is the reflection of the one
I am that which is above and below
I am the earth, the sky and the heavens source

I am these things in the zones of the twelve by six

I am the word
The word which divided and created worlds
I am the one
The one which divided to create the two
I am the keeper of the keys of creation
I open forth the seventy-two fold lock
I stand here as the one who charges the gate
The gate shall be opened forth
The one that is two
The two that is four
The four that is the world by three
The twelve which becomes the zones of the heaven
The twelve which has become the hours of the day
The twelve which has become the hours of the night
The twelve which rule the earth
The twelve which rule the heaven
The twelve which rule the stars
The twelve which have shaped creation
By the sixfold twelve
The seventy-two gates are open
Conjuration is set in blood
The way is open by blood
The word has been spoken of creation

That which is and has been
That which is to be and the possibility
Is conjured by the seventy-two fold
The spaces in creation for the worlds to open
I call forth the seventy-two
The seventy-two that becomes by twelve
The twelve that becomes six
The six which becomes one
The one which commands the all
Open forth to the world

The road whose course does not lead back
Gatekeeper open the gate to me
Obey the oath and open the gate of the
Seal of the earth

Open now this gate
Spirit gods of the heavens, remember
Spirit gods from the regions of the four, remember

I am the one, that was first
I am the one that became the two
That by the thirty-six become the seventy-two
I am the one that became the three that by the twenty-four become the seventy-two
I am the one which became four
That the by the eighteen becomes the seventy-two
I am the one which became the six
That by the twelve becomes the seventy-two

I call that the will becomes word
The word that becomes flesh
The flesh that becomes manifest

The one of the source
The origin of all things
That becomes in all times and hours
The hours of the light
The hours of the dark
That which is the twelve of the day
That which is the twelve of the night
That which is the zone of the sky
That which is the division of the heaven
That which is the division of the hells

I am the one who calls the divide
I am the one who commands the gate

I am the one who summons the will
I am the one who becomes two
I am the two which becomes three
I am the three which becomes the four
I am the two by six
I am the four by three
I am the twelve by six
I am the twenty-four by three
I am the seventy-two

I am the twelve of the zones of heaven
I am the twelve by the angels of the heaven
I am the twelve by the demons of the night

I am the one which became the twelve
I am the will that stirs creation
I am the creation that is divided

I am the divide which is the reflection of the one
I am that which is above and below
I am the earth, the sky and the heavens source
I am these things in the zones of the twelve by six

I am the word
The word which divided and created worlds
I am the one
The one which divided to create the two
I am the keeper of the keys of creation
I open forth the seventy-two fold lock
I stand here as the one who charges the gate
The gate shall be opened forth
The one that is two
The two that is four
The four that is the world by three
The twelve which becomes the zones of the heaven
The twelve which has become the hours of the day
The twelve which has become the hours of the night
The twelve which rule the earth
The twelve which rule the heaven
The twelve which rule the stars
The twelve which have shaped creation
By the sixfold twelve
The seventy-two gates are open
Conjuration is set in blood
The way is open by blood
The word has been spoken of creation

That which is and has been
That which is to be and the possibility
Is conjured by the seventy-two fold
The spaces in creation for the worlds to open
I call forth the seventy-two
The seventy-two that becomes by twelve
The twelve that becomes six
The six which becomes one
The one which commands the all
Open forth to the world

The road whose course does not lead back
Gatekeeper open the gate to me
Obey the oath and open the gate of the
Seal of the water

Open now this gate
Spirit gods of the heavens, remember
Spirit gods from the regions of the four, remember

I am the one, that was first
I am the one that became the two
That by the thirty-six become the seventy-two
I am the one that became the three that by the twenty-four become the seventy-two
I am the one which became four
That the by the eighteen becomes the seventy-two
I am the one which became the six
That by the twelve becomes the seventy-two

I call that the will becomes word
The word that becomes flesh
The flesh that becomes manifest

The one of the source
The origin of all things
That becomes in all times and hours
The hours of the light
The hours of the dark
That which is the twelve of the day
That which is the twelve of the night
That which is the zone of the sky
That which is the division of the heaven
That which is the division of the hells

I am the one who calls the divide
I am the one who commands the gate

I am the one who summons the will
I am the one who becomes two
I am the two which becomes three
I am the three which becomes the four
I am the two by six
I am the four by three
I am the twelve by six
I am the twenty-four by three
I am the seventy-two

I am the twelve of the zones of heaven
I am the twelve by the angels of the heaven
I am the twelve by the demon of the night

I am the one which became the twelve
I am the will that stirs creation
I am the creation that is divided

I am the divide which is the reflection of the one
I am that which is above and below
I am the earth, the sky and the heavens source
I am these things in the zones of the twelve by six

I am the word
The word which divided and created worlds
I am the one
The one which divided to create the two
I am the keeper of the keys of creation
I open forth the seventy-two fold lock
I stand here as the one who charges the gate
The gate shall be opened forth
The one that is two
The two that is four
The four that is the world by three
The twelve which becomes the zones of the heaven
The twelve which has become the hours of the day
The twelve which has become the hours of the night
The twelve which rule the earth
The twelve which rule the heaven
The twelve which rule the stars
The twelve which have shaped creation
By the sixfold twelve
The seventy-two gates are open
Conjuration is set in blood
The way is open by blood
The word has been spoken of creation

That which is and has been
That which is to be and the possibility
Is conjured by the seventy-two fold
The spaces in creation for the worlds to open
I call forth the seventy-two
The seventy-two that becomes by twelve
The twelve that becomes six
The six which becomes one
The one which commands the all
Open forth to the world

The road whose course does not lead back
Gatekeeper open the gate to me
Obey the oath and open the gate of the
Seal of the fire

Open now this gate
Spirit gods of the heavens, remember
Spirit gods from the regions of the four, remember

I am the one, that was first
I am the one that became the two
That by the thirty-six become the seventy-two
I am the one that became the three that by the twenty-four become the seventy-two
I am the one which became four
That the by the eighteen becomes the seventy-two
I am the one which became the six
That by the twelve becomes the seventy-two

I call that the will becomes word
The word that becomes flesh
The flesh that becomes manifest

The one of the source
The origin of all things
That becomes in all times and hours
The hours of the light
The hours of the dark
That which is the twelve of the day
That which is the twelve of the night
That which is the zone of the sky
That which is the division of the heaven
That which is the division of the hells

I am the one who calls the divide
I am the one who commands the gate

I am the one who summons the will
I am the one who becomes two
I am the two which becomes three
I am the three which becomes the four
I am the two by six
I am the four by three
I am the twelve by six
I am the twenty-four by three
I am the seventy-two

I am the twelve of the zones of heaven
I am the twelve by the angels of the heaven
I am the twelve by the demon of the night

I am the one which became the twelve
I am the will that stirs creation
I am the creation that is divided

I am the divide which is the reflection of the one
I am that which is above and below
I am the earth, the sky and the heavens source
I am these things in the zones of the twelve by six

I am the word
The word which divided and created worlds
I am the one
The one which divided to create the two
I am the keeper of the keys of creation
I open forth the seventy-two fold lock
I stand here as the one who charges the gate
The gate shall be opened forth
The one that is two
The two that is four
The four that is the world by three
The twelve which becomes the zones of the heaven
The twelve which has become the hours of the day
The twelve which has become the hours of the night
The twelve which rule the earth
The twelve which rule the heaven
The twelve which rule the stars
The twelve which have shaped creation
By the sixfold twelve
The seventy-two gates are open
Conjuration is set in blood
The way is open by blood
The word has been spoken of creation

That which is and has been
That which is to be and the possibility
Is conjured by the seventy-two fold
The spaces in creation for the worlds to open
I call forth the seventy-two
The seventy-two that becomes by twelve
The twelve that becomes six
The six which becomes one
The one which commands the all
Open forth to the world

The road whose course does not lead back
Gatekeeper open the gate to me
Obey the oath and open the gate of the
Seal of the air

Open now this gate
Spirit gods of the heavens, remember
Spirit gods from the regions of the four, remember

I am the one, that was first
I am the one that became the two
That by the thirty-six become the seventy-two
I am the one that became the three that by the twenty-four become the seventy-two
I am the one which became four
That the by the eighteen becomes the seventy-two
I am the one which became the six
That by the twelve becomes the seventy-two

I call that the will becomes word
The word that becomes flesh
The flesh that becomes manifest

The one of the source
The origin of all things
That becomes in all times and hours
The hours of the light
The hours of the dark
That which is the twelve of the day
That which is the twelve of the night
That which is the zone of the sky
That which is the division of the heaven
That which is the division of the hells

I am the one who calls the divide
I am the one who commands the gate

I am the one who summons the will
I am the one who becomes two
I am the two which becomes three
I am the three which becomes the four
I am the two by six
I am the four by three
I am the twelve by six
I am the twenty four by three
I am the seventy-two

I am the twelve of the zones of heaven
I am the twelve by the angels of the heaven
I am the twelve by the demon of the night

I am the one which became the twelve
I am the will that stirs creation
I am the creation that is divided

I am the divide which is the reflection of the one
I am that which is above and below
I am the earth, the sky and the heavens source
I am these things in the zones of the twelve by six

I am the word
The word which divided and created worlds
I am the one
The one which divided to create the two
I am the keeper of the keys of creation
I open forth the seventy-two fold lock
I stand here as the one who charges the gate
The gate shall be opened forth
The one that is two
The two that is four
The four that is the world by three
The twelve which becomes the zones of the heaven
The twelve which has become the hours of the day
The twelve which has become the hours of the night
The twelve which rule the earth
The twelve which rule the heaven
The twelve which rule the stars
The twelve which have shaped creation
By the sixfold twelve
The seventy-two gates are open
Conjuration is set in blood
The way is open by blood
The word has been spoken of creation

That which is and has been
That which is to be and the possibility
Is conjured by the seventy-two fold
The spaces in creation for the worlds to open
I call forth the seventy-two
The seventy-two that becomes by twelve
The twelve that becomes six
The six which becomes one
The one which commands the all
Open forth to the world

The road whose course does not lead back
Gatekeeper open the gate to me
Obey the oath and open the gate of the sphere of the moon
Open now this gate
Spirit gods of the heavens, remember
Spirit gods from the regions of the four, remember

I am the one, that was first
I am the one that became the two
That by the thirty-six become the seventy-two
I am the one that became the three that by the twenty-four become the seventy-two
I am the one which became four
That the by the eighteen becomes the seventy-two
I am the one which became the six
That by the twelve becomes the seventy-two

I call that the will becomes word
The word that becomes flesh
The flesh that becomes manifest

The one of the source
The origin of all things
That becomes in all times and hours
The hours of the light
The hours of the dark
That which is the twelve of the day
That which is the twelve of the night
That which is the zone of the sky
That which is the division of the heaven
That which is the division of the hells

I am the one who calls the divide
I am the one who commands the gate

I am the one who summons the will
I am the one who becomes two
I am the two which becomes three
I am the three which becomes the four
I am the two by six
I am the four by three
I am the twelve by six
I am the twenty four by three
I am the seventy-two

I am the twelve of the zones of heaven
I am the twelve by the angels of the heaven
I am the twelve by the demon of the night

I am the one which became the twelve
I am the will that stirs creation
I am the creation that is divided

I am the divide which is the reflection of the one
I am that which is above and below
I am the earth, the sky and the heavens source
I am these things in the zones of the twelve by six

I am the word
The word which divided and created worlds
I am the one
The one which divided to create the two
I am the keeper of the keys of creation
I open forth the seventy-two fold lock
I stand here as the one who charges the gate
The gate shall be opened forth
The one that is two
The two that is four
The four that is the world by three
The twelve which becomes the zones of the heaven
The twelve which has become the hours of the day
The twelve which has become the hours of the night
The twelve which rule the earth
The twelve which rule the heaven
The twelve which rule the stars
The twelve which have shaped creation
By the sixfold twelve
The seventy-two gates are open
Conjuration is set in blood
The way is open by blood
The word has been spoken of creation

That which is and has been
That which is to be and the possibility
Is conjured by the seventy-two fold
The spaces in creation for the worlds to open
I call forth the seventy-two
The seventy-two that becomes by twelve
The twelve that becomes six
The six which becomes one
The one which commands the all
Open forth to the world

The road whose course does not lead back
Gatekeeper open the gate to me
Obey the oath and open the gate of the sphere of Mars
Open now this gate
Spirit gods of the heavens, remember
Spirit gods from the regions of the four, remember

I am the one, that was first
I am the one that became the two
That by the thirty-six become the seventy-two
I am the one that became the three that by the twenty-four become the seventy-two
I am the one which became four
That the by the eighteen becomes the seventy-two
I am the one which became the six
That by the twelve becomes the seventy-two

I call that the will becomes word
The word that becomes flesh
The flesh that becomes manifest

The one of the source
The origin of all things
That becomes in all times and hours
The hours of the light
The hours of the dark
That which is the twelve of the day
That which is the twelve of the night
That which is the zone of the sky
That which is the division of the heaven
That which is the division of the hells

I am the one who calls the divide
I am the one who commands the gate

I am the one who summons the will
I am the one who becomes two
I am the two which becomes three
I am the three which becomes the four
I am the two by six
I am the four by three
I am the twelve by six
I am the twenty four by three
I am the seventy-two

I am the twelve of the zones of heaven
I am the twelve by the angels of the heaven
I am the twelve by the demon of the night

I am the one which became the twelve
I am the will that stirs creation
I am the creation that is divided

I am the divide which is the reflection of the one
I am that which is above and below
I am the earth, the sky and the heavens source
I am these things in the zones of the twelve by six

I am the word
The word which divided and created worlds
I am the one
The one which divided to create the two
I am the keeper of the keys of creation
I open forth the seventy-two fold lock
I stand here as the one who charges the gate
The gate shall be opened forth
The one that is two
The two that is four
The four that is the world by three
The twelve which becomes the zones of the heaven
The twelve which has become the hours of the day
The twelve which has become the hours of the night
The twelve which rule the earth
The twelve which rule the heaven
The twelve which rule the stars
The twelve which have shaped creation
By the sixfold twelve
The seventy-two gates are open
Conjuration is set in blood
The way is open by blood
The word has been spoken of creation

That which is and has been
That which is to be and the possibility
Is conjured by the seventy-two fold
The spaces in creation for the worlds to open
I call forth the seventy-two
The seventy-two that becomes by twelve
The twelve that becomes six
The six which becomes one
The one which commands the all
Open forth to the world

The road whose course does not lead back
Gatekeeper open the gate to me
Obey the oath and open the gate of the sphere of Venus
Open now this gate
Spirit gods of the heavens, remember
Spirit gods from the regions of the four, remember

I am the one, that was first
I am the one that became the two
That by the thirty-six become the seventy-two
I am the one that became the three that by the twenty-four become the seventy-two
I am the one which became four
That the by the eighteen becomes the seventy-two
I am the one which became the six
That by the twelve becomes the seventy-two

I call that the will becomes word
The word that becomes flesh
The flesh that becomes manifest

The one of the source
The origin of all things
That becomes in all times and hours
The hours of the light
The hours of the dark
That which is the twelve of the day
That which is the twelve of the night
That which is the zone of the sky
That which is the division of the heaven
That which is the division of the hells

I am the one who calls the divide
I am the one who commands the gate

I am the one who summons the will
I am the one who becomes two
I am the two which becomes three
I am the three which becomes the four
I am the two by six
I am the four by three
I am the twelve by six
I am the twenty-four by three
I am the seventy-two

I am the twelve of the zones of heaven
I am the twelve by the angels of the heaven
I am the twelve by the demon of the night

I am the one which became the twelve
I am the will that stirs creation
I am the creation that is divided

I am the divide which is the reflection of the one
I am that which is above and below
I am the earth, the sky and the heavens source
I am these things in the zones of the twelve by six

I am the word
The word which divided and created worlds
I am the one
The one which divided to create the two
I am the keeper of the keys of creation
I open forth the seventy-two fold lock
I stand here as the one who charges the gate
The gate shall be opened forth
The one that is two
The two that is four
The four that is the world by three
The twelve which becomes the zones of the heaven
The twelve which has become the hours of the day
The twelve which has become the hours of the night
The twelve which rule the earth
The twelve which rule the heaven
The twelve which rule the stars
The twelve which have shaped creation
By the sixfold twelve
The seventy-two gates are open
Conjuration is set in blood
The way is open by blood
The word has been spoken of creation

That which is and has been
That which is to be and the possibility
Is conjured by the seventy-two fold
The spaces in creation for the worlds to open
I call forth the seventy-two
The seventy-two that becomes by twelve
The twelve that becomes six
The six which becomes one
The one which commands the all
Open forth to the world

The road whose course does not lead back
Gatekeeper open the gate to me
Obey the oath and open the gate of the sphere of
Mercury
Open now this gate
Spirit gods of the heavens, remember
Spirit gods from the regions of the four, remember

I am the one, that was first
I am the one that became the two
That by the thirty-six become the seventy-two
I am the one that became the three that by the twenty-four become the seventy-two
I am the one which became four
That the by the eighteen becomes the seventy-two
I am the one which became the six
That by the twelve becomes the seventy-two

I call that the will becomes word
The word that becomes flesh
The flesh that becomes manifest

The one of the source
The origin of all things
That becomes in all times and hours
The hours of the light
The hours of the dark
That which is the twelve of the day
That which is the twelve of the night
That which is the zone of the sky
That which is the division of the heaven
That which is the division of the hells

I am the one who calls the divide
I am the one who commands the gate

I am the one who summons the will
I am the one who becomes two
I am the two which becomes three
I am the three which becomes the four
I am the two by six
I am the four by three
I am the twelve by six
I am the twenty-four by three
I am the seventy-two

I am the twelve of the zones of heaven
I am the twelve by the angels of the heaven
I am the twelve by the demon of the night

I am the one which became the twelve
I am the will that stirs creation
I am the creation that is divided

I am the divide which is the reflection of the one
I am that which is above and below
I am the earth, the sky and the heavens source
I am these things in the zones of the twelve by six

I am the word
The word which divided and created worlds
I am the one
The one which divided to create the two
I am the keeper of the keys of creation
I open forth the seventy-two fold lock
I stand here as the one who charges the gate
The gate shall be opened forth
The one that is two
The two that is four
The four that is the world by three
The twelve which becomes the zones of the heaven
The twelve which has become the hours of the day
The twelve which has become the hours of the night
The twelve which rule the earth
The twelve which rule the heaven
The twelve which rule the stars
The twelve which have shaped creation
By the sixfold twelve
The seventy-two gates are open
Conjuration is set in blood
The way is open by blood
The word has been spoken of creation

That which is and has been
That which is to be and the possibility
Is conjured by the seventy-two fold
The spaces in creation for the worlds to open
I call forth the seventy-two
The seventy-two that becomes by twelve
The twelve that becomes six
The six which becomes one
The one which commands the all
Open forth to the world

The road whose course does not lead back
Gatekeeper open the gate to me
Obey the oath and open the gate of the sphere of the Sun
Open now this gate
Spirit gods of the heavens, remember
Spirit gods from the regions of the four, remember

I am the one, that was first
I am the one that became the two
That by the thirty-six become the seventy-two
I am the one that became the three that by the twenty-four become the seventy-two
I am the one which became four
That the by the eighteen becomes the seventy-two
I am the one which became the six
That by the twelve becomes the seventy-two

I call that the will becomes word
The word that becomes flesh
The flesh that becomes manifest

The one of the source
The origin of all things
That becomes in all times and hours
The hours of the light
The hours of the dark
That which is the twelve of the day
That which is the twelve of the night
That which is the zone of the sky
That which is the division of the heaven
That which is the division of the hells

I am the one who calls the divide
I am the one who commands the gate

I am the one who summons the will
I am the one who becomes two
I am the two which becomes three
I am the three which becomes the four
I am the two by six
I am the four by three
I am the twelve by six
I am the twenty-four by three
I am the seventy-two

I am the twelve of the zones of heaven
I am the twelve by the angels of the heaven
I am the twelve by the demon of the night

I am the one which became the twelve
I am the will that stirs creation
I am the creation that is divided

I am the divide which is the reflection of the one
I am that which is above and below
I am the earth, the sky and the heavens source
I am these things in the zones of the twelve by six

I am the word
The word which divided and created worlds
I am the one
The one which divided to create the two
I am the keeper of the keys of creation
I open forth the seventy-two fold lock
I stand here as the one who charges the gate
The gate shall be opened forth
The one that is two
The two that is four
The four that is the world by three
The twelve which becomes the zones of the heaven
The twelve which has become the hours of the day
The twelve which has become the hours of the night
The twelve which rule the earth
The twelve which rule the heaven
The twelve which rule the stars
The twelve which have shaped creation
By the sixfold twelve
The seventy-two gates are open
Conjuration is set in blood
The way is open by blood
The word has been spoken of creation

That which is and has been
That which is to be and the possibility
Is conjured by the seventy-two fold
The spaces in creation for the worlds to open
I call forth the seventy-two
The seventy-two that becomes by twelve
The twelve that becomes six
The six which becomes one
The one which commands the all
Open forth to the world

The road whose course does not lead back
Gatekeeper open the gate to me
Obey the oath and open the gate of the sphere of
Jupiter
Open now this gate
Spirit gods of the heavens, remember
Spirit gods from the regions of the four, remember

I am the one, that was first
I am the one that became the two
That by the thirty-six become the seventy-two
I am the one that became the three that by the twenty-four become the seventy-two
I am the one which became four
That the by the eighteen becomes the seventy-two
I am the one which became the six
That by the twelve becomes the seventy-two

I call that the will becomes word
The word that becomes flesh
The flesh that becomes manifest

The one of the source
The origin of all things
That becomes in all times and hours
The hours of the light
The hours of the dark
That which is the twelve of the day
That which is the twelve of the night
That which is the zone of the sky
That which is the division of the heaven
That which is the division of the hells

I am the one who calls the divide
I am the one who commands the gate

I am the one who summons the will
I am the one who becomes two
I am the two which becomes three
I am the three which becomes the four
I am the two by six
I am the four by three
I am the twelve by six
I am the twenty-four by three
I am the seventy-two

I am the twelve of the zones of heaven
I am the twelve by the angels of the heaven
I am the twelve by the demon of the night

I am the one which became the twelve
I am the will that stirs creation
I am the creation that is divided

I am the divide which is the reflection of the one
I am that which is above and below
I am the earth, the sky and the heavens source
I am these things in the zones of the twelve by six

I am the word
The word which divided and created worlds
I am the one
The one which divided to create the two
I am the keeper of the keys of creation
I open forth the seventy-two fold lock
I stand here as the one who charges the gate
The gate shall be opened forth
The one that is two
The two that is four
The four that is the world by three
The twelve which becomes the zones of the heaven
The twelve which has become the hours of the day
The twelve which has become the hours of the night
The twelve which rule the earth
The twelve which rule the heaven
The twelve which rule the stars
The twelve which have shaped creation
By the sixfold twelve
The seventy two gates are open
Conjuration is set in blood
The way is open by blood
The word has been spoken of creation

That which is and has been
That which is to be and the possibility
Is conjured by the seventy-two fold
The spaces in creation for the worlds to open
I call forth the seventy-two
The seventy two that becomes by twelve
The twelve that becomes six
The six which becomes one
The one which commands the all
Open forth to the world

The road whose course does not lead back
Gatekeeper open the gate to me
Obey the oath and open the gate of the sphere of Jupiter
Open now this gate
Spirit gods of the heavens, remember
Spirit gods from the regions of the four, remember

I am the one, that was first
I am the one that became the two
That by the thirty-six become the seventy-two
I am the one that became the three that by the twenty-four become the seventy-two
I am the one which became four
That the by the eighteen becomes the seventy-two
I am the one which became the six
That by the twelve becomes the seventy-two

I call that the will becomes word
The word that becomes flesh
The flesh that becomes manifest

The one of the source
The origin of all things
That becomes in all times and hours
The hours of the light
The hours of the dark
That which is the twelve of the day
That which is the twelve of the night
That which is the zone of the sky
That which is the division of the heaven
That which is the division of the hells

I am the one who calls the divide
I am the one who commands the gate

I am the one who summons the will
I am the one who becomes two
I am the two which becomes three
I am the three which becomes the four
I am the two by six
I am the four by three
I am the twelve by six
I am the twenty-four by three
I am the seventy-two

I am the twelve of the zones of heaven
I am the twelve by the angels of the heaven
I am the twelve by the demon of the night

I am the one which became the twelve
I am the will that stirs creation
I am the creation that is divided

I am the divide which is the reflection of the one
I am that which is above and below
I am the earth, the sky and the heavens source
I am these things in the zones of the twelve by six

I am the word
The word which divided and created worlds
I am the one
The one which divided to create the two
I am the keeper of the keys of creation
I open forth the seventy-two fold lock
I stand here as the one who charges the gate
The gate shall be opened forth
The one that is two
The two that is four
The four that is the world by three
The twelve which becomes the zones of the heaven
The twelve which has become the hours of the day
The twelve which has become the hours of the night
The twelve which rule the earth
The twelve which rule the heaven
The twelve which rule the stars
The twelve which have shaped creation
By the sixfold twelve
The seventy-two gates are open
Conjuration is set in blood
The way is open by blood
The word has been spoken of creation

That which is and has been
That which is to be and the possibility
Is conjured by the seventy-two fold
The spaces in creation for the worlds to open
I call forth the seventy-two
The seventy-two that becomes by twelve
The twelve that becomes six
The six which becomes one
The one which commands the all
Open forth to the world

The road whose course does not lead back
Gatekeeper open the gate to me
Obey the oath and open the gate of the sphere of the Saturn
Open now this gate
Spirit gods of the heavens, remember
Spirit gods from the regions of the four, remember

I am the one, that was first
I am the one that became the two
That by the thirty-six become the seventy-two
I am the one that became the three that by the twenty-four become the seventy-two
I am the one which became four
That the by the eighteen becomes the seventy-two
I am the one which became the six
That by the twelve becomes the seventy-two

I call that the will becomes word
The word that becomes flesh
The flesh that becomes manifest

The one of the source
The origin of all things
That becomes in all times and hours
The hours of the light
The hours of the dark
That which is the twelve of the day
That which is the twelve of the night
That which is the zone of the sky
That which is the division of the heaven
That which is the division of the hells

I am the one who calls the divide
I am the one who commands the gate

I am the one who summons the will
I am the one who becomes two
I am the two which becomes three
I am the three which becomes the four
I am the two by six
I am the four by three
I am the twelve by six
I am the twenty-four by three
I am the seventy-two

I am the twelve of the zones of heaven
I am the twelve by the angels of the heaven
I am the twelve by the demon of the night

I am the one which became the twelve
I am the will that stirs creation
I am the creation that is divided

I am the divide which is the reflection of the one
I am that which is above and below
I am the earth, the sky and the heavens source
I am these things in the zones of the twelve by six

I am the word
The word which divided and created worlds
I am the one
The one which divided to create the two
I am the keeper of the keys of creation
I open forth the seventy-two fold lock
I stand here as the one who charges the gate
The gate shall be opened forth
The one that is two
The two that is four
The four that is the world by three
The twelve which becomes the zones of the heaven
The twelve which has become the hours of the day
The twelve which has become the hours of the night
The twelve which rule the earth
The twelve which rule the heaven
The twelve which rule the stars
The twelve which have shaped creation
By the sixfold twelve
The seventy-two gates are open
Conjuration is set in blood
The way is open by blood
The word has been spoken of creation

That which is and has been
That which is to be and the possibility
Is conjured by the seventy-two fold
The spaces in creation for the worlds to open
I call forth the seventy-two
The seventy-two that becomes by twelve
The twelve that becomes six
The six which becomes one
The one which commands the all
Open forth to the world

The road whose course does not lead back
Gatekeeper open the gate to me
Obey the oath and open the gate of the
Zone of Aries
Open now this gate
Spirit gods of the heavens, remember
Spirit gods from the regions of the four, remember

I am the one, that was first
I am the one that became the two
That by the thirty-six become the seventy-two
I am the one that became the three that by the twenty-four become the seventy-two
I am the one which became four
That the by the eighteen becomes the seventy-two
I am the one which became the six
That by the twelve becomes the seventy-two

I call that the will becomes word
The word that becomes flesh
The flesh that becomes manifest

The one of the source
The origin of all things
That becomes in all times and hours
The hours of the light
The hours of the dark
That which is the twelve of the day
That which is the twelve of the night
That which is the zone of the sky
That which is the division of the heaven
That which is the division of the hells

I am the one who calls the divide
I am the one who commands the gate

I am the one who summons the will
I am the one who becomes two
I am the two which becomes three
I am the three which becomes the four
I am the two by six
I am the four by three
I am the twelve by six
I am the twenty-four by three
I am the seventy-two

I am the twelve of the zones of heaven
I am the twelve by the angels of the heaven
I am the twelve by the demon of the night

I am the one which became the twelve
I am the will that stirs creation
I am the creation that is divided

I am the divide which is the reflection of the one
I am that which is above and below
I am the earth, the sky and the heavens source
I am these things in the zones of the twelve by six

I am the word
The word which divided and created worlds
I am the one
The one which divided to create the two
I am the keeper of the keys of creation
I open forth the seventy-two fold lock
I stand here as the one who charges the gate
The gate shall be opened forth
The one that is two
The two that is four
The four that is the world by three
The twelve which becomes the zones of the heaven
The twelve which has become the hours of the day
The twelve which has become the hours of the night
The twelve which rule the earth
The twelve which rule the heaven
The twelve which rule the stars
The twelve which have shaped creation
By the sixfold twelve
The seventy-two gates are open
Conjuration is set in blood
The way is open by blood
The word has been spoken of creation

That which is and has been
That which is to be and the possibility
Is conjured by the seventy-two fold
The spaces in creation for the worlds to open
I call forth the seventy-two
The seventy-two that becomes by twelve
The twelve that becomes six
The six which becomes one
The one which commands the all
Open forth to the world

The road whose course does not lead back
Gatekeeper open the gate to me
Obey the oath and open the gate of the
Zone of Taurus

Open now this gate
Spirit gods of the heavens, remember
Spirit gods from the regions of the four, remember

I am the one, that was first
I am the one that became the two
That by the thirty-six become the seventy-two
I am the one that became the three that by the twenty-four become the seventy-two
I am the one which became four
That the by the eighteen becomes the seventy-two
I am the one which became the six
That by the twelve becomes the seventy-two

I call that the will becomes word
The word that becomes flesh
The flesh that becomes manifest

The one of the source
The origin of all things
That becomes in all times and hours
The hours of the light
The hours of the dark
That which is the twelve of the day
That which is the twelve of the night
That which is the zone of the sky
That which is the division of the heaven
That which is the division of the hells

I am the one who calls the divide
I am the one who commands the gate

I am the one who summons the will
I am the one who becomes two
I am the two which becomes three
I am the three which becomes the four
I am the two by six
I am the four by three
I am the twelve by six
I am the twenty-four by three
I am the seventy-two

I am the twelve of the zones of heaven
I am the twelve by the angels of the heaven
I am the twelve by the demon of the night

I am the one which became the twelve
I am the will that stirs creation
I am the creation that is divided

I am the divide which is the reflection of the one
I am that which is above and below
I am the earth, the sky and the heavens source
I am these things in the zones of the twelve by six

I am the word
The word which divided and created worlds
I am the one
The one which divided to create the two
I am the keeper of the keys of creation
I open forth the seventy-two fold lock
I stand here as the one who charges the gate
The gate shall be opened forth
The one that is two
The two that is four
The four that is the world by three
The twelve which becomes the zones of the heaven
The twelve which has become the hours of the day
The twelve which has become the hours of the night
The twelve which rule the earth
The twelve which rule the heaven
The twelve which rule the stars
The twelve which have shaped creation
By the sixfold twelve
The seventy-two gates are open
Conjuration is set in blood
The way is open by blood
The word has been spoken of creation

That which is and has been
That which is to be and the possibility
Is conjured by the seventy-two fold
The spaces in creation for the worlds to open
I call forth the seventy-two
The seventy-two that becomes by twelve
The twelve that becomes six
The six which becomes one
The one which commands the all
Open forth to the world

The road whose course does not lead back
Gatekeeper open the gate to me
Obey the oath and open the gate of the
Zone of Gemini

Open now this gate
Spirit gods of the heavens, remember
Spirit gods from the regions of the four, remember

I am the one, that was first
I am the one that became the two
That by the thirty-six become the seventy-two
I am the one that became the three that by the twenty-four become the seventy-two
I am the one which became four
That the by the eighteen becomes the seventy-two
I am the one which became the six
That by the twelve becomes the seventy-two

I call that the will becomes word
The word that becomes flesh
The flesh that becomes manifest

The one of the source
The origin of all things
That becomes in all times and hours
The hours of the light
The hours of the dark
That which is the twelve of the day
That which is the twelve of the night
That which is the zone of the sky
That which is the division of the heaven
That which is the division of the hells

I am the one who calls the divide
I am the one who commands the gate

I am the one who summons the will
I am the one who becomes two
I am the two which becomes three
I am the three which becomes the four
I am the two by six
I am the four by three
I am the twelve by six
I am the twenty-four by three
I am the seventy-two

I am the twelve of the zones of heaven
I am the twelve by the angels of the heaven
I am the twelve by the demon of the night

I am the one which became the twelve
I am the will that stirs creation
I am the creation that is divided

I am the divide which is the reflection of the one
I am that which is above and below
I am the earth, the sky and the heavens source
I am these things in the zones of the twelve by six

I am the word
The word which divided and created worlds
I am the one
The one which divided to create the two
I am the keeper of the keys of creation
I open forth the seventy-two fold lock
I stand here as the one who charges the gate
The gate shall be opened forth
The one that is two
The two that is four
The four that is the world by three
The twelve which becomes the zones of the heaven
The twelve which has become the hours of the day
The twelve which has become the hours of the night
The twelve which rule the earth
The twelve which rule the heaven
The twelve which rule the stars
The twelve which have shaped creation
By the sixfold twelve
The seventy-two gates are open
Conjuration is set in blood
The way is open by blood
The word has been spoken of creation

That which is and has been
That which is to be and the possibility
Is conjured by the seventy-two fold
The spaces in creation for the worlds to open
I call forth the seventy-two
The seventy-two that becomes by twelve
The twelve that becomes six
The six which becomes one
The one which commands the all
Open forth to the world

The road whose course does not lead back
Gatekeeper open the gate to me
Obey the oath and open the gate of the
Zone of Cancer

Open now this gate
Spirit gods of the heavens, remember
Spirit gods from the regions of the four, remember

I am the one, that was first
I am the one that became the two
That by the thirty-six become the seventy-two
I am the one that became the three that by the twenty-four become the seventy-two
I am the one which became four
That the by the eighteen becomes the seventy-two
I am the one which became the six
That by the twelve becomes the seventy-two

I call that the will becomes word
The word that becomes flesh
The flesh that becomes manifest

The one of the source
The origin of all things
That becomes in all times and hours
The hours of the light
The hours of the dark
That which is the twelve of the day
That which is the twelve of the night
That which is the zone of the sky
That which is the division of the heaven
That which is the division of the hells

I am the one who calls the divide
I am the one who commands the gate

I am the one who summons the will
I am the one who becomes two
I am the two which becomes three
I am the three which becomes the four
I am the two by six
I am the four by three
I am the twelve by six
I am the twenty-four by three
I am the seventy-two

I am the twelve of the zones of heaven
I am the twelve by the angels of the heaven
I am the twelve by the demon of the night

I am the one which became the twelve
I am the will that stirs creation
I am the creation that is divided

I am the divide which is the reflection of the one
I am that which is above and below
I am the earth, the sky and the heavens source
I am these things in the zones of the twelve by six

I am the word
The word which divided and created worlds
I am the one
The one which divided to create the two
I am the keeper of the keys of creation
I open forth the seventy-two fold lock
I stand here as the one who charges the gate
The gate shall be opened forth
The one that is two
The two that is four
The four that is the world by three
The twelve which becomes the zones of the heaven
The twelve which has become the hours of the day
The twelve which has become the hours of the night
The twelve which rule the earth
The twelve which rule the heaven
The twelve which rule the stars
The twelve which have shaped creation
By the sixfold twelve
The seventy-two gates are open
Conjuration is set in blood
The way is open by blood
The word has been spoken of creation

That which is and has been
That which is to be and the possibility
Is conjured by the seventy-two fold
The spaces in creation for the worlds to open
I call forth the seventy-two
The seventy-two that becomes by twelve
The twelve that becomes six
The six which becomes one
The one which commands the all
Open forth to the world

The road whose course does not lead back
Gatekeeper open the gate to me
Obey the oath and open the gate of the
Zone of Leo

Open now this gate
Spirit gods of the heavens, remember
Spirit gods from the regions of the four, remember

I am the one, that was first
I am the one that became the two
That by the thirty-six become the seventy-two
I am the one that became the three that by the twenty-four become the seventy-two
I am the one which became four
That the by the eighteen becomes the seventy-two
I am the one which became the six
That by the twelve becomes the seventy-two

I call that the will becomes word
The word that becomes flesh
The flesh that becomes manifest

The one of the source
The origin of all things
That becomes in all times and hours
The hours of the light
The hours of the dark
That which is the twelve of the day
That which is the twelve of the night
That which is the zone of the sky
That which is the division of the heaven
That which is the division of the hells

I am the one who calls the divide
I am the one who commands the gate

I am the one who summons the will
I am the one who becomes two
I am the two which becomes three
I am the three which becomes the four
I am the two by six
I am the four by three
I am the twelve by six
I am the twenty-four by three
I am the seventy-two

I am the twelve of the zones of heaven
I am the twelve by the angels of the heaven
I am the twelve by the demon of the night

I am the one which became the twelve
I am the will that stirs creation
I am the creation that is divided

I am the divide which is the reflection of the one
I am that which is above and below
I am the earth, the sky and the heavens source
I am these things in the zones of the twelve by six

I am the word
The word which divided and created worlds
I am the one
The one which divided to create the two
I am the keeper of the keys of creation
I open forth the seventy-two fold lock
I stand here as the one who charges the gate
The gate shall be opened forth
The one that is two
The two that is four
The four that is the world by three
The twelve which becomes the zones of the heaven
The twelve which has become the hours of the day
The twelve which has become the hours of the night
The twelve which rule the earth
The twelve which rule the heaven
The twelve which rule the stars
The twelve which have shaped creation
By the sixfold twelve
The seventy-two gates are open
Conjuration is set in blood
The way is open by blood
The word has been spoken of creation

That which is and has been
That which is to be and the possibility
Is conjured by the seventy-two fold
The spaces in creation for the worlds to open
I call forth the seventy-two
The seventy-two that becomes by twelve
The twelve that becomes six
The six which becomes one
The one which commands the all
Open forth to the world

The road whose course does not lead back
Gatekeeper open the gate to me
Obey the oath and open the gate of the
Zone of Virgo

Open now this gate
Spirit gods of the heavens, remember
Spirit gods from the regions of the four, remember

I am the one, that was first
I am the one that became the two
That by the thirty-six become the seventy-two
I am the one that became the three that by the twenty-four become the seventy-two
I am the one which became four
That the by the eighteen becomes the seventy-two
I am the one which became the six
That by the twelve becomes the seventy-two

I call that the will becomes word
The word that becomes flesh
The flesh that becomes manifest

The one of the source
The origin of all things
That becomes in all times and hours
The hours of the light
The hours of the dark
That which is the twelve of the day
That which is the twelve of the night
That which is the zone of the sky
That which is the division of the heaven
That which is the division of the hells

I am the one who calls the divide
I am the one who commands the gate

I am the one who summons the will
I am the one who becomes two
I am the two which becomes three
I am the three which becomes the four
I am the two by six
I am the four by three
I am the twelve by six
I am the twenty four by three
I am the seventy-two

I am the twelve of the zones of heaven
I am the twelve by the angels of the heaven
I am the twelve by the demon of the night

I am the one which became the twelve
I am the will that stirs creation
I am the creation that is divided

I am the divide which is the reflection of the one
I am that which is above and below
I am the earth, the sky and the heavens source
I am these things in the zones of the twelve by six

I am the word
The word which divided and created worlds
I am the one
The one which divided to create the two
I am the keeper of the keys of creation
I open forth the seventy-two fold lock
I stand here as the one who charges the gate
The gate shall be opened forth
The one that is two
The two that is four
The four that is the world by three
The twelve which becomes the zones of the heaven
The twelve which has become the hours of the day
The twelve which has become the hours of the night
The twelve which rule the earth
The twelve which rule the heaven
The twelve which rule the stars
The twelve which have shaped creation
By the sixfold twelve
The seventy-two gates are open
Conjuration is set in blood
The way is open by blood
The word has been spoken of creation

That which is and has been
That which is to be and the possibility
Is conjured by the seventy-two fold
The spaces in creation for the worlds to open
I call forth the seventy-two
The seventy-two that becomes by twelve
The twelve that becomes six
The six which becomes one
The one which commands the all
Open forth to the world

The road whose course does not lead back
Gatekeeper open the gate to me
Obey the oath and open the gate of the
Zone of Libra

Open now this gate
Spirit gods of the heavens, remember
Spirit gods from the regions of the four, remember

I am the one, that was first
I am the one that became the two
That by the thirty-six become the seventy-two
I am the one that became the three that by the twenty-four become the seventy-two
I am the one which became four
That the by the eighteen becomes the seventy-two
I am the one which became the six
That by the twelve becomes the seventy-two

I call that the will becomes word
The word that becomes flesh
The flesh that becomes manifest

The one of the source
The origin of all things
That becomes in all times and hours
The hours of the light
The hours of the dark
That which is the twelve of the day
That which is the twelve of the night
That which is the zone of the sky
That which is the division of the heaven
That which is the division of the hells

I am the one who calls the divide
I am the one who commands the gate

I am the one who summons the will
I am the one who becomes two
I am the two which becomes three
I am the three which becomes the four
I am the two by six
I am the four by three
I am the twelve by six
I am the twenty four by three
I am the seventy-two

I am the twelve of the zones of heaven
I am the twelve by the angels of the heaven
I am the twelve by the demon of the night

I am the one which became the twelve
I am the will that stirs creation
I am the creation that is divided

I am the divide which is the reflection of the one
I am that which is above and below
I am the earth, the sky and the heavens source
I am these things in the zones of the twelve by six

I am the word
The word which divided and created worlds
I am the one
The one which divided to create the two
I am the keeper of the keys of creation
I open forth the seventy-two fold lock
I stand here as the one who charges the gate
The gate shall be opened forth
The one that is two
The two that is four
The four that is the world by three
The twelve which becomes the zones of the heaven
The twelve which has become the hours of the day
The twelve which has become the hours of the night
The twelve which rule the earth
The twelve which rule the heaven
The twelve which rule the stars
The twelve which have shaped creation
By the sixfold twelve
The seventy-two gates are open
Conjuration is set in blood
The way is open by blood
The word has been spoken of creation

That which is and has been
That which is to be and the possibility
Is conjured by the seventy-two fold
The spaces in creation for the worlds to open
I call forth the seventy-two
The seventy-two that becomes by twelve
The twelve that becomes six
The six which becomes one
The one which commands the all
Open forth to the world

The road whose course does not lead back
Gatekeeper open the gate to me
Obey the oath and open the gate of the
Zone of Scorpio

Open now this gate
Spirit gods of the heavens, remember
Spirit gods from the regions of the four, remember

I am the one, that was first
I am the one that became the two
That by the thirty-six become the seventy-two
I am the one that became the three that by the twenty-four become the seventy-two
I am the one which became four
That the by the eighteen becomes the seventy-two
I am the one which became the six
That by the twelve becomes the seventy-two

I call that the will becomes word
The word that becomes flesh
The flesh that becomes manifest

The one of the source
The origin of all things
That becomes in all times and hours
The hours of the light
The hours of the dark
That which is the twelve of the day
That which is the twelve of the night
That which is the zone of the sky
That which is the division of the heaven
That which is the division of the hells

I am the one who calls the divide
I am the one who commands the gate

I am the one who summons the will
I am the one who becomes two
I am the two which becomes three
I am the three which becomes the four
I am the two by six
I am the four by three
I am the twelve by six
I am the twenty-four by three
I am the seventy-two

I am the twelve of the zones of heaven
I am the twelve by the angels of the heaven
I am the twelve by the demon of the night

I am the one which became the twelve
I am the will that stirs creation
I am the creation that is divided

I am the divide which is the reflection of the one
I am that which is above and below
I am the earth, the sky and the heavens source
I am these things in the zones of the twelve by six

I am the word
The word which divided and created worlds
I am the one
The one which divided to create the two
I am the keeper of the keys of creation
I open forth the seventy-two fold lock
I stand here as the one who charges the gate
The gate shall be opened forth
The one that is two
The two that is four
The four that is the world by three
The twelve which becomes the zones of the heaven
The twelve which has become the hours of the day
The twelve which has become the hours of the night
The twelve which rule the earth
The twelve which rule the heaven
The twelve which rule the stars
The twelve which have shaped creation
By the sixfold twelve
The seventy-two gates are open
Conjuration is set in blood
The way is open by blood
The word has been spoken of creation

That which is and has been
That which is to be and the possibility
Is conjured by the seventy-two fold
The spaces in creation for the worlds to open
I call forth the seventy-two
The seventy-two that becomes by twelve
The twelve that becomes six
The six which becomes one
The one which commands the all
Open forth to the world

The road whose course does not lead back
Gatekeeper open the gate to me
Obey the oath and open the gate of the
Zone of Sagittarius

Open now this gate
Spirit gods of the heavens, remember
Spirit gods from the regions of the four, remember

I am the one, that was first
I am the one that became the two
That by the thirty-six become the seventy-two
I am the one that became the three that by the twenty-four become the seventy-two
I am the one which became four
That the by the eighteen becomes the seventy-two
I am the one which became the six
That by the twelve becomes the seventy-two

I call that the will becomes word
The word that becomes flesh
The flesh that becomes manifest

The one of the source
The origin of all things
That becomes in all times and hours
The hours of the light
The hours of the dark
That which is the twelve of the day
That which is the twelve of the night
That which is the zone of the sky
That which is the division of the heaven
That which is the division of the hells

I am the one who calls the divide
I am the one who commands the gate

I am the one who summons the will
I am the one who becomes two
I am the two which becomes three
I am the three which becomes the four
I am the two by six
I am the four by three
I am the twelve by six
I am the twenty-four by three
I am the seventy-two

I am the twelve of the zones of heaven
I am the twelve by the angels of the heaven
I am the twelve by the demon of the night

I am the one which became the twelve
I am the will that stirs creation
I am the creation that is divided

I am the divide which is the reflection of the one
I am that which is above and below
I am the earth, the sky and the heavens source
I am these things in the zones of the twelve by six

I am the word
The word which divided and created worlds
I am the one
The one which divided to create the two
I am the keeper of the keys of creation
I open forth the seventy-two fold lock
I stand here as the one who charges the gate
The gate shall be opened forth
The one that is two
The two that is four
The four that is the world by three
The twelve which becomes the zones of the heaven
The twelve which has become the hours of the day
The twelve which has become the hours of the night
The twelve which rule the earth
The twelve which rule the heaven
The twelve which rule the stars
The twelve which have shaped creation
By the sixfold twelve
The seventy-two gates are open
Conjuration is set in blood
The way is open by blood
The word has been spoken of creation

That which is and has been
That which is to be and the possibility
Is conjured by the seventy-two fold
The spaces in creation for the worlds to open
I call forth the seventy-two
The seventy-two that becomes by twelve
The twelve that becomes six
The six which becomes one
The one which commands the all
Open forth to the world

The road whose course does not lead back
Gatekeeper open the gate to me
Obey the oath and open the gate of the
Zone of Capricorn

Open now this gate
Spirit gods of the heavens, remember
Spirit gods from the regions of the four, remember

I am the one, that was first
I am the one that became the two
That by the thirty-six become the seventy-two
I am the one that became the three that by the twenty-four become the seventy-two
I am the one which became four
That the by the eighteen becomes the seventy-two
I am the one which became the six
That by the twelve becomes the seventy-two

I call that the will becomes word
The word that becomes flesh
The flesh that becomes manifest

The one of the source
The origin of all things
That becomes in all times and hours
The hours of the light
The hours of the dark
That which is the twelve of the day
That which is the twelve of the night
That which is the zone of the sky
That which is the division of the heaven
That which is the division of the hells

I am the one who calls the divide
I am the one who commands the gate

I am the one who summons the will
I am the one who becomes two
I am the two which becomes three
I am the three which becomes the four
I am the two by six
I am the four by three
I am the twelve by six
I am the twenty-four by three
I am the seventy-two

I am the twelve of the zones of heaven
I am the twelve by the angels of the heaven
I am the twelve by the demon of the night

I am the one which became the twelve
I am the will that stirs creation
I am the creation that is divided

I am the divide which is the reflection of the one
I am that which is above and below
I am the earth, the sky and the heavens source
I am these things in the zones of the twelve by six

I am the word
The word which divided and created worlds
I am the one
The one which divided to create the two
I am the keeper of the keys of creation
I open forth the seventy-two fold lock
I stand here as the one who charges the gate
The gate shall be opened forth
The one that is two
The two that is four
The four that is the world by three
The twelve which becomes the zones of the heaven
The twelve which has become the hours of the day
The twelve which has become the hours of the night
The twelve which rule the earth
The twelve which rule the heaven
The twelve which rule the stars
The twelve which have shaped creation
By the sixfold twelve
The seventy-two gates are open
Conjuration is set in blood
The way is open by blood
The word has been spoken of creation

That which is and has been
That which is to be and the possibility
Is conjured by the seventy-two fold
The spaces in creation for the worlds to open
I call forth the seventy-two
The seventy-two that becomes by twelve
The twelve that becomes six
The six which becomes one
The one which commands the all
Open forth to the world

The road whose course does not lead back
Gatekeeper open the gate to me
Obey the oath and open the gate of the
Zone of Aquarius

Open now this gate
Spirit gods of the heavens, remember
Spirit gods from the regions of the four, remember

I am the one, that was first
I am the one that became the two
That by the thirty-six become the seventy-two
I am the one that became the three that by the twenty-four become the seventy-two
I am the one which became four
That the by the eighteen becomes the seventy-two
I am the one which became the six
That by the twelve becomes the seventy-two

I call that the will becomes word
The word that becomes flesh
The flesh that becomes manifest

The one of the source
The origin of all things
That becomes in all times and hours
The hours of the light
The hours of the dark
That which is the twelve of the day
That which is the twelve of the night
That which is the zone of the sky
That which is the division of the heaven
That which is the division of the hells

I am the one who calls the divide
I am the one who commands the gate

I am the one who summons the will
I am the one who becomes two
I am the two which becomes three
I am the three which becomes the four
I am the two by six
I am the four by three
I am the twelve by six
I am the twenty-four by three
I am the seventy-two

I am the twelve of the zones of heaven
I am the twelve by the angels of the heaven
I am the twelve by the demon of the night

I am the one which became the twelve
I am the will that stirs creation
I am the creation that is divided

I am the divide which is the reflection of the one
I am that which is above and below
I am the earth, the sky and the heavens source
I am these things in the zones of the twelve by six

I am the word
The word which divided and created worlds
I am the one
The one which divided to create the two
I am the keeper of the keys of creation
I open forth the seventy-two fold lock
I stand here as the one who charges the gate
The gate shall be opened forth
The one that is two
The two that is four
The four that is the world by three
The twelve which becomes the zones of the heaven
The twelve which has become the hours of the day
The twelve which has become the hours of the night
The twelve which rule the earth
The twelve which rule the heaven
The twelve which rule the stars
The twelve which have shaped creation
By the sixfold twelve
The seventy-two gates are open
Conjuration is set in blood
The way is open by blood
The word has been spoken of creation

That which is and has been
That which is to be and the possibility
Is conjured by the seventy-two fold
The spaces in creation for the worlds to open
I call forth the seventy-two
The seventy-two that becomes by twelve
The twelve that becomes six
The six which becomes one
The one which commands the all
Open forth to the world

The road whose course does not lead back
Gatekeeper open the gate to me
Obey the oath and open the gate of the
Zone of Pisces

Open now this gate
Spirit gods of the heavens, remember
Spirit gods from the regions of the four, remember

Blood Magick

Of Blood

Like words, blood is the bridge of the inner world and outer world. Blood becomes a medium, or catalyst, as it causes some form of change. It is a sensory experience as well, because the pain imprints the memory; it gives the rise to the emotional flow that directs and anchors those intents. It is the highest price one pays in their working. It is not a beginner who would bleed for their work, to solidify their connection to the intent, but one who understands that what they do, how they mark upon their body, mind, emotion, and spirit the intent they would cause to manifest in the world. So to create inks that are blooded, and paints that are blooded, herbal formulas that have blood mixed in, is a way we can harness the full power of what is resident within the body/mind/spirit to get the full connection. We shed our own blood for our magicks, and it is that magicks we will command to manifest.

However, in most arts, we need only load with intent our words and thought, needing not to bleed like pigs to the slaughter. It is some work that can only be brought about by implanting flesh, blood into the process to cause the manifestation of our intent upon the world. Those who would kill, or feed upon the blood of others, draw out the Prana current, draw out the living Chi, and it is that Chi, which can augment the ability otherwise lacking in the mage. If you would feed upon the living blood of the willing, you will be able to connect with them on a different emotional level. You will be able to stimulate parts of yourself that are otherwise dormant. Taking upon yourself the vampirism of their Chi, your work will increase its potency. However, only temporarily until their blood is out of your system.

The concentration of this potency is highest in those who culture their bodies, who do works that blend the world of their waking mind, sleeping mind and their body. To find a donor of blood, who works the magicks, and builds their own Prana is a great treat, as their blood is already familiar with the imprints of the frequencies that you would seek to generate. Always be cautious in the work of consumption of blood. Devouring the Prana and integrating it into yourself, building the extra pathways, is a way to increase your control as well. The more in depth the persons connection to their blood, and the power you would manipulate, the greater the effect on your own output potential.

Willing donors are the only way you should consume the blood of others. Do not seek to harm your donors, as the more freely they give the current, the more power you can gain from it, the deeper you can pull in their essence to ride with yours. Only in sexual blood magicks will you gain a current deeper then this when you feed upon that Chi. Blending with your being, their being, sexually, emotionally, and mentally, reaching a point of ecstasy that gives way to gnosis, and other forms of trance. The aim however is to no longer need to use these aids to power in order to achieve physical manifestation. To use these arts in combination with work of the singularity is to link the collective powers so as to channel the highest possible reserves of power from the source.

Bloodless Sacrifice

In our work we have a need for collected power. In the original days of the Judaic era, there was a time when the creation of the mind was offered up towards greater purpose. There will be the requirement of future works to offer up such creations for rites and ceremony that take months and years of construction. As such is the great arts of blending the worlds can achieve.

In the setting up of the sacrifice, the tools should be prepared, the words of the conjuration memorized so that nothing shall interrupt the will on its path. There should be the circle into which the force will be transformed.

It is in this manner the array is crafted to generate the needed force, but to draw in the forces which will be sacrificed unto it that anew form will rise from this manner of art. No blood will be used in the sacrifice, as there is already blood as has been given to the servitor during its construction.

These sacrifices can open the way from this plane to different worlds. Given the means to do so, they will make the work entirely personal, and only the ones who craft the tools will be able to use the tools. Such is the needed loss of energy used to fill a void, give it up, and something will be gained. Offer up word, thought, deed, and you will gain in balance.

In doing this, you become like the Rabbi of the ancient world, in that you become the creator of the new through the sacrifice of old. It in this manner what separates the sacrificed and the sacrificing of the living blood the union of the different Chi patterns to recreate.

When the Rabbi creates, he does so in offering to the power of his gods through the sacred names and 72 emanations of that holy name. Conversely the sorcerers of the ancient world have the 72 demonic names of the primal demons and their servants. We know both of these as the divisions of the nine-fold divisions. There are also the nine-fold elemental creations.

We can use the rites and processes of creation to form our own versions from the source currents. Even if the current is pulled from a name of a god, demon, elemental, or some other primordial force. We can create directly draw that power down from the collective consciousness into that which we would sacrifice in the works of creation.

If one does not stand firm in their will when working the sacrifice, then part of themselves, if not all of themselves, will be forfeit unto the rite.

Awakening the Inanimate

Working with the inanimate objects that we are presented with for our art, one needs to become familiar with the ability to give them a life of their own to be able to with stand the currents we force through them.

In our discourse, we charge objects to become our vessels at such a time as they would be pressed into the services we require. Begin by holding the object in your hand. Feel the charge already present within the object; there should be a pushing sensation and a pulling sensation as the energy is looped in the flow of the object. Integrate your energy into the motion.

From this you should be able to determine the active energy and passive energy within it. Mentally extend the energy upwards, that it can flow in spherical pattern. From this pattern you should be able to feel its rotation as it becomes like the ball in the image, flowing around the object as the spirit of it. Bleed upon the object a bit to give it life and mind to obey. From here feel the flow within the life of the object. Look again for the Yin and Yang currents within your mind's eye, and extend them out like the coil on the sphere. From the core of this object, stretch it to heart of the sun, and to the core of the earth. This should create a solidified channel where it becomes a perpetual motion conduit of flow between the above and the below.

Such an object is necessary when you are working on projects that require an external source current other than the body one inhabits. At the same time such objects will, if made properly, become cores that with further modifications can be unified to the source current.

Modifications to an object that would normally just receive a standard charge of intent, can be used for much larger and long term projects. Uses include such things as; anchor points for gates, portals, and other such points where things would need to have an energy that can span creation itself. Other uses might include, but are not limited to, using the construct to be the core of a created elemental, familiar or some other construction-based project where self-generating currents are needed.

Objects of this caliber should be and remain few and far between. They will only respond respectively to those that share blood, as it becomes an extension of the source, and consequently that connection will go towards the ascension of the body to remain as the master to such a key to the source of creation. Without having to go through the painstaking rituals and other such meditations that getting unified with the source normally requires.

Over time, these currents will spread beyond just the scope of a singular item and link with others of similar natures. These can be used to power perennial magicks that would have a shelf life of no less then 100 years without needed upkeep. The more pure the metal for the core is, the longer and more stable the core remains. If you could get it 99% to 100% pure materia then you would have something that will last eons without needed maintenance. Of course, for every generation such objects are passed down if not blended into some other form, or sacrificed for a greater power/purpose. Then the inheritor is to be the one to give up the life blood unto the object.

Marking the Blood

The Rite of the Marking

Take a sample of the blood, or some other marker, to prove the anchor for the effect. Mix this into clay which has otherwise been unused. Light the candles to represent the Eight. Use the array of the inner world to call upon the 12 aspects of the body, and the 8 aspects of life, that the gateway to the blood be opened as you take a knife or some implement of carving that has been marked with your blood, and that you bind the seal directly to the intended. From this, you weave the spell of binding that through the generations of the blood those of this line will be marked..

Here remember that the spell should be researched and worked out that no other symbol should be used to mark one. As the mark is forged in your blood, those with the stronger influence will win out. So generally the will must be maintained. This spell is then augmented if there is a tattoo of such a mark or a scarification process. The idea is to carve it directly into the body, which is then transferred over into all the blood that flows through it, anchoring your mark within the living essence.

From here you have the influences of a tether that will allow you to communicate via links such as mental and emotional bonds. You will be able to draw power from the one who you place the mark upon. Such a use for this process would be ideal in setting up a sect of warlocks bound by blood. This will ensure that there is a level of union between them as they can act and function as a collective, despite whatever distance they might find themselves. Even after the body has died, the power of the spirit can be called upon as the blood once connected to it is not cleansed easily.

Rite of the Unmarked

Form the ceremony like the rite of the marking. Have the clay mixed with the blood or the seal which has been carved into the body, or blood. When the seal is cut from the flesh, or is to be cleansed from the blood, pour upon the marked sigil some acid to remove the seal from existence. While it is bubbling or otherwise being dissolved, make a conjuration to the 8 aspects of life, and 12 aspects of the personality. Open the gate to the body, and purge it by the Rite of Restoration.

Command the cleansing forces to be restorative in the body, blood, and spirit, that no force will remain within the body undisturbed, and that all traces of this deed are removed from the flesh. Call upon the celestial fires to burn from their essence the corruption that has followed from such a mark.

The mark itself is viewed as an attacking parasite, that is anchored to the blood directly. So when removing it, it must be burned out from the inside. Any link or tendril that is connected to the link must be removed and burned away as well because if it is to stick around, it might re-anchor itself into the blood. So you have to change the blood after you have it opened and purged to make it a different signature than the mark was placed into.

Doing this requires a ceremony of rebirth, that the link is passed off to the earth in a funerary rite. Where the body is then interned and the link is transferred to the earth and then buried and sent to Du-at to allow the gods of death to lay claim to the living mark. From here there should be a birthing ceremony to change the essence that it comes from the earth as new current.

Blood Substitute Condenser

Table of Condensers

Chakra	Planetary	Sephirot	Herb	Metal
Crown	Sun	Tiphareth	Angelica	Gold
Third Eye	Moon	Yesod	Star Anise	Silver
Throat	Mercury	Hod	Mandrake	Mercury
Heart	Venus	Netzach	Burdock	Copper
Solar Plexus	Jupiter	Chesed	Sage	Tin
Navel	Mars	Geburah	Tobacco	Iron
Root	Saturn	Binah	Wolfs Bane	Lead
	Neptune	Chokhmah	Mugwort	
	Pluto	Kether	Damiana	
	Uranus	Da'ath	Mandrake	

Elements of Malkuth

Earth – Mugwort
Fire – Tobacco
Air – Star Anise
Water – Wolfs Bane

How to Mix:
Simmer rain water that has been gathered and stored in glass with the herbs listed above in equal portion. Let simmer together until the liquid is reduced to a thick paste of the herbs.

Water- Base Version:
Simmer, without breaking a boil in a non-metallic pot. When you have united these herbs, strain and keep stored in a glass jar. Add a personal effect of the individual into the concentration. Let stand as long as possible to absorb the energy of the body that will be duplicated by the condensers. Keep in a dark space.

Tincture Version:
Grind to a powder, and add the alcohol or oil just above the herb line in an air tight container. Let steep for the night to absorb all of the virtues of the herbs. Then let the effect soak in this mixture. It takes on the color of plasma. Blood red and bright yellow.

How to Use:
Use wherever any construction would otherwise have blood as a requirement. It in this matter can be used to anyone's personal effect into the link of their blood.

After you have constructed the Doppelganger Array, you will then cover all lines and the symbols with this mixture. It is this which duplicates the effects of the ink being mixed with the blood if the blood is not available.

Mechanics:
We duplicate the effects of the divisions of the source currents into their "tree" or DNA strand, effects on the body and we can duplicate all things within the body. In this we apply the principals that all things alike, will respond in kind to that which like unto itself. In this manner we duplicate the blood.

Clone Generation

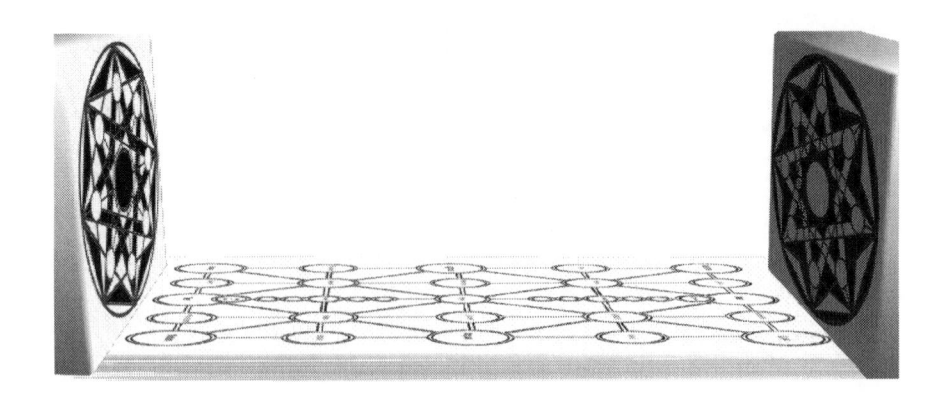

General Mechanics:

With the dual array pattern set up here atop the array of the doppelganger, in the center point should be the effect to give a point of generations. You have the elemental flow going from the source currents, from the core current of the body, through the Gate of the Infernal World, and the array of the Gate of the Celestial World. Everything that is drawn within this array should be mixed with the blood or the substitute of the individual for whom this work is being done.

Practice with a ceremony like this will allow one the ability to just grasp the object and project from it an array design like this without the need for blood or blood substitute. For exercise, practice in development of other techniques this work is done with the arrays.

In this array the energy can be separated from the source but still be able to be studied. Introduce the source current in the array and you will have a stable field of study. From here you can have this become a base to modify for creation, stabilization, transformation, and other various states of being for whatever can be achieved through the modification of body.

Advanced Uses:

This array set-up is designed to make a clone from the blood, or a blood substitute, using a personal effect, or sigil. In this manner all things can be given a body, or a form. In such cases as archetypes can be modified in the capacity as well, as they have their spiritual bodies. This can be used to create an energy source that duplicates normal body currents in the forging of constructs.

Upon the reintegrated current entering the host body, there must be a period of introduction or diffusion from the modified current into the host. A double array such as this above should be created around the host, so as to switch the current, or modify the current directly.

If you can impregnate an object with the power of its god, giving it any one of the 9 bodies, then it becomes a viable tool for the modification of its essence. Either directly or into something else entirely. The larger the object is to modify, the more subtle the integration must be. Like the modification of the mind, the body energy can be unstable and the "will" to survive can override the capacity to modify. Be aware of your subjects energy make up, as well as currents in the environment during transference.

Conjuration of The Beast Bird of Paradise

Kindle the fire of oak or a sacred wood. Bleed into the flames or onto the wood before you set the fire. Call forth the pact of the fire, that it shall be manifest as the dark fire of creation. That your will shall be manifest through this fire.

What shall be created hence shall be of me,
The dark fire of eternity
Now is kindled to serve

Into the fire cast feathers of a crow or some great black bird anointed with your blood.

Accept this sacrifice
Give unto the spirit of the raven
In these flames
Manifest my desires.
By the dark fire
Spirit of the raven
Become my servant.

Drop into the fire herbs of passion, love, lust, fire and air.

I give of these herbs unto
The fires so their energies
Now aid in the manifestation of my intent.

A map marked with a circle of conjuration over the area where you wish to effect should then be dropped into the fire.

I give of this earth
Let the souls within
Know the fear of passions,
Know the tragedy of lust
By their own emotions and their sins consumed now
By these herbs, by feathers and blood
I conjure forth the spirit bird of paradise
Let your black wings stir the currents
Within the region overwhelmed in destructive passions
Send forth a current of self-destruction
By this black fire burning here
As living fire
By the blood oath,
The covenant of the elemental bonds
Come forth
Bring the horror
Draw forth their inner sins
To the light of day.
Consume them as they are consumed,
Destroy them as they destroy
All within this territory

Immolated in black fire
Are forfeit unto their deepest desire.
By the fire of the Black Sun at midnight
Break forth through the gates
Within their hearts and souls
Come forth Beast of Paradise
Fly this night,
You demon shade
By darkness spawned
I send you out to greet the dawn!

Mounting of the Familiar's Spirit

This is achieved by summoning your familiar spirit into your Auric body. Taking on its nature, its power, becoming one with its essence. Its purpose is to give you an expanded reach in your workings, so it is possible for you to invoke the spirit of your familiar. Cautiously proceed with training under this form, as what you will come to find is that you crave this state of union. As you work more and more with this level of control with the energy, will and mindset of your familiar, you will become more accustomed to falling into those mental patterns; until that what is of you, originates from it. All this union actually does is form the link within your own mind to your subconscious and your own power.

Possession can occur, where you lose yourself to the bestial and lesser mind of your servitor, or higher mind; depending on what the task at hand becomes. To release yourself from this, your will should be resolute and you speak aloud a word for "release." Every time you would dislodge your conjoined union, you must speak this vocalization of your intent, to force your familiar to withdraw from you. Familiars themselves being servitors created to serve any need or desire that you direct them to fulfill, have no existence beyond this state. If you do not give them a task, they will fade. Without purpose or the charged command to serve you in your desires they will not be controlled.

A reminder that care should be taken that the method of the invocation matters only to your connection to your own spiritual familiar. If you have to appease the link with blood, then through blood will it respond. Should you be unable to unmount this secondary thing from your consciousness, then you must work through the spheres and shells, becoming as one with your own nature as how they relate to you. Finding yourself, your own source of power, beyond that which you have created to serve you.

DO NOT let yourself be lead to believe that it is your destiny to be controlled by the very things you create in order to make your life easier.

Shadow Magick

Basic Technique

When you are standing in the shadows of some lit place walking down the road at night, stop for a few minutes and observe the world around you. From this observation, find the line which you draw for yourself, a line that you would not cross unless given a life or death situation. Find what would propel you into the very void to get through unscathed. If you cannot do this then do not continue.

Hold your dominant hand out before, you palm down over your shadow. Feel yourself, and your current that extends from it, link that current with your own. From this, develop the body via the core exercise found in the reference section.

When you can do this with the core exercise held out in front of you where the energy comes from the shadow half way between your out stretched hands. Then apply this method to the elemental alignment methods. With this you have developed your awareness of the shadow currents and the underside current of the world.

To draw forth the shadow current is to blend both sides of your body with the energy that flows between the planes. Not astrally/aetherically based nor is it bio-kinetically based. This is the current that unites both of these planes. Working within the shadow current is a way to override common natural limitations that would otherwise be the case with certain arts.

Advanced Manipulation

The complex conjuration of the body would be to duplicate the conjurations to the "physical world," the "elemental world," the "Infernal World," and the "Physical world of blood" to work within the shadow with the same energy and ease that you do within the other earthbound and celestial currents.

To further advance this technique, pull forth all the shadow elements in union with the light side elements to create a charge that represents both the Yin-Yang properties of the force to be conjured. The Tangible and the Shadow. When these two create the entire construct, you will gain more a stable energy construction.

Send the core of your body into the shadow to integrate both sides of your body into one. This allows you to pass through places with all of your being where only shadows may pass. At the same time, if you need to be stealthy and hide your signature, you can hide your presence in your shadows. You can also absorb current through the shadow particles.

Draw up the shadow body to envelope the flesh. Doing this technique will assist in channeling large amounts of energy and currents through the shadow body into your own body. As energy does not disperse shadows but condenses them, it acts as the perfect media for conditions that require a thick skin.

Extensions of the shadow body in both the physical world and the plane of shadows such as tendrils that can attack, defend, absorb energy, and assorted other abilities must be worked on. It is the focus that controls the speed, width, length, density, and amount of these which you can produce. At the height of this art one can alter their forms with their own shade.

Basic Tendrils

Pull the shade up around your body, and feel its pulsations; feel the energy and the cool current that blends with the flesh. Focus on the shade body and will then a tendril into creation. Focus on one in the palm of your hand. As wide as about three inches, about 12 inches long to start with. Practice work with density and length, as you use the tendril like you would an arm. Flex it, curl it. Work your single tendril until you can extend it out at least six feet. You should be able to control motion, speed, density, thickness, and length. You should be able to maintain this for no less than 1 hour.

Complex Tendrils

Pull the shade up and expand the tendril to three feet. Feel the current flowing inside this tendril. There should be a singular core to each tendril. Find this core and wrap it with similar energy. Blend it like ribbon up a pole. From this, unbind it and pull the shade current apart. You should end up with three tendrils about one to three feet long, probably one inch thick and not very dense. Practice until all three become independent in motion, varying density, speed of motion and length. You should be able to control all three with your will. Do not progress until you have been able to do this successfully for no less than one hour.

Terrestrial Tendrils

Use the above techniques using the shadow body as it exists upon the earth. Pull out the shade with the elemental force.

Shifting shades

When you have extra workings with the elements and notice the different shifts that can be achieved through saturation of environmental foundations, you can alter the space in which you would intend to work. Pull the shade current around your body, as you would when you are wrapping flesh in it, but pull everything into the largest body of shadows around. From here you can absorb, transfer, and work with any energy that would other wise disrupt the natural flow to the environment in which you exist. You should be able to maintain this field of manipulated space for as long as a day before you progress further.

Remote Tendril

Reach out with your mind's eye to where you can feel the other energy, Send out a tendril through the shadow planes to connect with that point of the physical plane. If you have someone in a remote location, have them help ground you with telling you when you have arrived. Practice till you can maintain three tendrils at the location for no less than an hour per tendril.

Spelled Tendrils

When you have the tendril as described in the first form of the shadow manipulation, focus on one of the more basic spells and have it manifest from the core of the tendril. Practice till you can draw energy into the shadow core, cast spells with them, or deliver spell/ritual quality intent to a target with an extension of the will that travels faster then through void-space.

Basic Shadow Servitors

Creating from the source current directly requires the concentration, familiarity and constant flow of current directed in a focused manner. If it's not the entity won't be crafted like one would have made from the recipes in the references.

These are the custom molded guards of the shadow planes, bound to serve for lifetimes, as they follow the power that creates them. These are like other shadow arts, the more they absorb in energy, the denser they become.

The more power you have behind their creation, and the more they are infused with the ability to craft spells of their own, to be able to fulfill commands through the power they can generate, all is required is the initial crafting and birthing process. These are forces that at the highest level become the duplicates for the soul which has created them, a created army, of limitless potential.

Create a shadow space to work in.

Mold a tendril 6 feet by 4 feet. This will be the raw materia from which you craft the servitor.

Form it into any shape you desire to mimic something living. Humanoid works best, as they will be able to grasp and move through things that would be able to interact with a humanoid form.

Then follow the rest of the directions on the crafting of a servitor. Do not use any physical elements in the creation of this force, as it is to be made out of the shade current alone.

If you develop this tool start with one. Do not over exert your resources in creation of multiple servitors.

Advanced Shade Servitors

Use the basic method of creation. From here, use a conjuration of the the gates of one or more of the aspects of the sources of creation. Pull from one or more of these gates the threads to bind with the core of the tendril, forming it into a singular body.

The resulting creation will be able to use the art and respond unto the orders as one would expect from a servitor. However, it in this form is given unto the servitor to be granted the powers of the god-head.

Delay of using this technique is good until you successfully have created your own servitors out of the shade current. Make them only as strong as you require them to be. Anything more than what you are able to handle, and you will have something that will break off and form its own independence.

To maintain the construct longer then necessary is a dangerous occupation, as the longer the things like this exist, the more power they gather and can make use of. The use of a standing army in peace time is unnecessary.

However, storage of such servitors can be kept in alternate pockets. Use in the beginning a seal to represent the place of storage, until you are able to call them forth with will alone. Do not give them name, do not give them limitations. Allow them the ability to grow as you grow, and they will stay loyally to the power that created them. From this you will not suffer the independence that you would have from other constructs not properly given direction.

"Was there even a rabbit?"

Dear Reader,

    By now you have a more in depth knowledge of what can be considered the applications of High Arts. For those of you who have read this far, and have made it a part of your workings, good for you. Assuming you're not being stalked by the demon chicken. Even if you are, it's all part of the growing process. Get used to it. With the facets and layers of this work, each spell or ritual can stand on its own, yet can be blended into larger more complex attributes that will allow you to develop the works, which are more than just the singular elements of a complete ceremony. What we will cover next is given its own course of study. The work provided here is an introduction to the rites and ceremonies that I am continuously developing. That is why these texts are written as a Text Book type format. Everything builds upon itself, much like the knowledge gained from study does.

    These works are not taught to those students seeking ordination into our orders, but it does remain that it is always nice to see into the world of another when it comes to their practices, without much anecdotal commentary. These works exist for the students of any path to be aware of the things which operate outside of the mainstream "pop-cultural denominational explosion of the pagan paths." Warlocks are outside of these paths. However the arts contained herein are a part of them. So do your best to enjoy, and if you do find yourself wanting to explore deeper things.

    "Always question, always explore. When we do not grow we cease to be alive"

                                                      Yours infernally

                                                      Infernal.

Daemonic Magick

Of Archetypes

There are the intellectual forces of the cosmological structures created by humanity since the dawn of time. This with the source creating all things, and all things coming from that source. Well, this is true, in a sense. As far as can be said or should even be discussed, it will have to be put off for a later discussion. What is a God force? It is the mind behind all conceptions of a single idea. It is the spirit of that idea as created by the virtue of the word which is used to conceive of it, becoming both the speaker, and the thing spoken.

To make it as simple as possible, a God is the spirit behind the idea, as the idea is formed in the hearts and minds of all things as it relates to the force at hand. We will have to look at this through an example if you would try and understand it properly. Let us use Themis. She is a Titan from the ancient world, who is also attributed to being Gaia. We can say that her properties are birth, sacrifice, law, morality, divination, assembly, vengeance, wise council, and salvation. As the earth she is all elements: the earth, air, fire, water, aether (the stuff of stars). She is what created every physical body; all things which have mass, she created and is responsible for. We can say she doesn't exist, that all these things are just concepts and so on. But in so saying we only get to our end point by a fraction. She, as a being in and over herself, is pictured as a woman holding a sword, and scales, with or without a blindfold. As justice is not blind, we will hold that from here out. She may not exist in that form. Her attributed abilities to overseeing law, birth, etc. are conceptions of language which mean something higher. You cannot touch, taste, see, smell, or eat law; but you can perceive it. So in its perception you have acknowledged it exists. So thus it exists within you, and is reflected in nature. Courtrooms are not nature, they are machinations of the human corruption which would make more laws than nature provided us with in the beginning. You feel these forces. You can feel within yourself what is law, sacrifice, birth, vengeance. You can see how they relate to the world at large. You then can say, that yes, in these acts where that takes place, there is a spirit about them, by the virtue of the acts a spirit is created. That spirit is part of the greater conception of the idea of what is attributed to that deity. Man and god are not separated forces. They are one and the same. You work with a deity like you work with the demons. You take of your mind, and you connect to the greater attainable attribute which is represented by that which is the name of that godhead. If you can get a grasp on this concept you're doing well. A God force is the doing and the done, by all parties involved in the perception and experiences of the single act. What you do not only affects you, but the world at large. Not only does this affect the world at large but it also affects in very personal ways everyone and everything for the rest of time.

You can take a rock and throw it into a pond, the water will ripple and go back to calm. However that rock will always remain in the pond. The entire body will be different for the rest of time. Your will must be as the rock, your deeds must become the throwing of your will, and you must have your intent willed to manifest in nature and the world at large for your work to reach any point of success. When you can understand that the gods are a part of you, when you can understand that they are your actions, the lesser spirits and demons who are responsible for your perception of those actions are all aspects as what is brought about by the mind and the soul of the living thing which is perceiving of that event, then you are on your way to becoming a mage.

What happens in the world at large is the same as what happens to you in the moment of your doing. If you walked into a store and something you wanted you could not get because you didn't have the means to pay for it, that want becomes a spirit of lust. If you then get into a foul mood, that is a demon of greed; if you then cut someone off in the parking lot because you were annoyed, then you become as a god-force of vengeance. You cutting them off will have effect on their life for the moment, there will be decisions they have to make to perpetuate that cycle, and so on. They could get into a car wreck or cause one for someone else. The point is to not try and not step on anyone's toes or give in all the time, but to understand this balance, so that your life is better for it.

Of Demons

What is described as a demon is dependent on which faith you follow as your own. What should have been determined by those who follow this work so far, is that faith has not been discussed. We haven't gotten involved with the mention of dedications and such to the celestial mind as found in so many paths of the modern day. That will come later. But what can be said about these forces is very concrete. What you would call a demon is a mindset beyond what normally is made use of. Using the Grimoire of Solomon, or any of those spiritual conjurations with sigils and what not. It all corresponds to the parts of the human brain which give function over to those abilities. There are some great examinations done on this system by some very well written authorities. Go seek them out. Part of being able to work with this series is that it requires you to go out and do the leg work yourself. .

When the spirit corresponds to the part of mind, that part of yourself which you would come to face to get something done, you call upon your subconscious to bring out that aspect of you as a "genius" or "mind" which interacts with yours. This isn't to say that you should be happy if someone calls you a schizophrenic when your perceptions on these forces will manifest differently for each of the things you would make use of. But you will come to smell, taste, see, feel, and know these things as what they are. An extension of you in some form or another, some part of you which you need to reconcile and take in and make a part of you in order to become the complete mage. It is not something that needs to be undertaken at a moment's notice, not something that one can do on a whim.

To face down and recognize those parts of you which are found as intellectually separate from your own nature must be consumed by your consciousness as you work down the tree of death. You must face the tests of the demons of your own mental spheres. You must embrace those forces which you would have under your command should you need them. To be complete upon the path you must have this balance. You must seek those for yourself to study with this.

The Source

When you have mastered yourself to the point where you can have recognition in yourself and others, you can elevate your awareness to what it is you embody. You then, being aware of your natural perceptions on the world, being aware of the spirits in others and how they relate with you, to how your mind and its aspects work, causing your actions to reflect the Godhead of that idea, will relate it back to the elemental nature of what it is.

In the beginning there was the single Chi, which split and created everything. When it split itself, not only did it separate into light and dark aspects of everything, with the neutral being the work to sustain both sides evenly, but it did so with the primal elements – those forces which are in everything. The fiery, the watery, the earthy, the airy, the active, the passive: these 7 conceptions of what comprise the nature and spirit of everything. You must dissect your views on your deity to your own personal nature, and your own elemental alignments. You must become aware of what element you embody. You from this point will not be subject directly to your patron, but you will work with that guiding energy as an artist their tools. Because if it is based on your perceptions, your thoughts, your deeds, your will, then your will is the source of your being. It is not something you can do without, it must be lasting. Everything you do you must intend.

Upon reaching this point, working through the paths that others have laid, through your own meditating and your own ritual work, it is all well and good to follow someone else and their ritualized conceptions of the world. But, everyone who seeks themselves for who they are can be perceived of as an emanation of the source, with their own patrons as to who and what they are. Becoming an aspect, where all the worlds and creation become the clay in the potter's hands. You must know these connections, you must be able to seek them out where they lie. You will come to understand that recognition of this power and this connection is something entirely different from being able to actually do anything about it. So you must then start to apply this level of control and creation through your art.

Invocations of Elemental Forces

We call into ourselves those forces we invoke. The forces of the elements are the foundation for any working, that they are present to lend their aide within the body of the mage, so that the mage can be the channel for those currents which is required. It is when one has or is working on connection to an element that one can invoke that force into their body to strengthen their own will, and the spiritual reserves which they use to power the rites they embark upon. It is also dependent on what mindset that the mage is in, resulting in the type of power invoked. Because when you invoke a force, you become a channel for it. You become the medium, the intermediary of that element. You become the element you invoke, you become the god which you take into yourself, and assume the will of.

Elemental force has nature, has passions and likes and dislikes, it has the sympathy and antipathy of its being. It has its own mind, though it might not have will outside the natural states of its nature. So study and meditation on the element, and you will understand this, as has been said over and over again, in the corresponding works; you must know yourself through elemental correlations, you must know the element, you must know the things which the element is present in, and all the manifestations possible for that element when you decide to work with it, and you must be aware of all the ways that element interacts and grows, and shifts, changing with its interaction between the other elements.

You must know these things, and you must know them in yourself that way when you have opened yourself up as the channel for these forces you are not over whelmed with the connections you have to those things which are the emanations of that element. You will have successfully invoked and developed a personal relationship you do your workings with before you forge pact with them, to serve as your bonded forces which will be with you into your next lives. When you forge pact with a force, and you hold your end of the bargain then you can assimilate that force into yourself and invoke the strength to your work.

Invocations of Planetary Forces

Like the elemental forces which you have a familiarity working with by this time, you should also be grasping and working with the planetary currents. Every planet influences the mind and body in some capacity. You have the ability to draw down these forces into you, in an invocation of that current. This then can be applied or channeled into spells and things at the time when you do this, within the confines of your ritual setting. Ritual now should mean to you, all the things which safe guard and prepare your working environment so that you are at ease when you enter into the circle and get into the proper mindset in order to invoke the forces with which you are building relationships with, so that you will as you progress need less ceremony, and can call them forth as you will it, when you need to with a shift into the proper mind which should eventually become a fluid ability, that you can slide through each of your states of consciousness.

The planetary forces are very mental, they are very aligned to the currents which have been attributed to them throughout the ages. So you will have to know yourself and your relation to the planet in each of your mental states. You will need to know the supernal aspects of each planet, you will need to know the infernal and the physical aspects of that current. You will need to know what part of your body that this force relates to, and your reactions to this current, gained through working with it, you will need to know the symbols used to channel the forces of these planets as well as the timing when you can work with the energy as it changes from house to house in the zodiac, as well as the relations between those planets when you, say, invoke Jupiter during the Astrological phase of Aries when the Sun is in conjunction. You will need to know these things, and you will have to study and prepare how they react with your working as well as the element which they are associated with, and the relationship of that element within the mind of that element through which you are working and how they relate to you, and your intent. Only practice, and study can assist you on proper invocation, which is more then just reading or speaking aloud "I invoke you: X". To invoke it is to know it.

Invocations of Deities

When you connect yourself to a deity, and you draw the persona and aspects of them into yourself, your life, and your art. Then you will be aware of how magnificent any deity really is. It is the unidentifiable force which causes the change that you want. Calling it by a name gives it understanding in your own mind, how it relates to you in ceremony. But to really invoke deity, occurs on every level of your life. A god force is action, immortal in that action, it is in the case of Themis, Natural law, Sacrifice, Birth, Foresight. In these actions in any capacity of these actions she is present. She because she is the embodiment of the earth, air, water, fire, and the "aether, the stuff of stars"; it is these that she is corresponding to the physical plane of earth; she can also be considered to be a manifestation through the sphere of Jupiter. So thus any time which is particularly usefully in her invocation would be through the day of Jupiter, or any hours of Jupiter. However since she is manifest in all elements, then she can be drawn from any time, under any condition because all the elements balance out. If there is time, if there is something you can work with Themis through it.

When you know that your forces are the roots of how you view your world, you will see then how you live and breath these roots. Sometimes harsher than others, and sometimes in ways that you never expected to experience. But when you call forth deity into your life, every aspect of your life will change. When you leave the circle, you are connected to that deity, maybe not as actively as in the ceremony, but with you, where ever you go, what ever you're doing, your patron is with you. Manifesting in your life, as you live the work you do in ceremony. Your word holding your bond strengthening what you do, and your connection to the currents. Others who work with their own patrons are not your enemy. Those who have power different from your own do not need to fear you. What needs to fear you is nothing, because there is no reason to fear it. You walk your own path, others walk their own paths. If you have a patron, and in your relationship you cross paths with something who is to caught up in their own little world, then you do what you have to, but try to refrain from battling mages, it's tacky.

Invocation of the Spirits of Places

When you make a summons of a spirit of a place, when you call the force of that spirit, or that place into you and your work, you are connecting it to everything that you are, so that it becomes a part of you. The best way to describe what occurs when you invoke a place, be it a plane of existence, or calling forth the energy of a scared place, or just pulling the power of space up into yourself, and drawing the current through your vessel as a channel; is that when you stare off the edge of the Grand Canyon, all the feelings that evokes within you, those changes which it brings out, are what you are bringing up in you when you invoke the place inside of you. As has been said, it is the changes which are internal in the microcosm of your body which cause the desired mindsets. So drawing up the lower realms of Gehenna, or one of the lower planes in the abyss into yourself, connects you to the bestial mindsets associated with these places.

Never is it wise to draw into yourself something which you are not familiar with. Such to the effect that when you work with elements and energies as singular forces, just like with invocations of Deity as the entire spectrum of emotions from that perspective so to is invoking a place; drawing everything about that place into your body, into your center, and out through your work. Study the corresponding links, their elements, their planets, and their references so that every effort can be made through what you are drawing into yourself will balance with your own energy as well as the purpose of the rite.

There is a meditation called the union, which is an invocation of a place to increase the potency of the work. Major planes such as supernal planes, or shade realms, or the entirety of the hell planes. How you do this is the one to preform the invocation, has a period of meditation, and focus on all aspects of this plane, every planet which feeds their current into it, every element which forms this, and recognition of these links within their bodies. Through spoken charges they can then manifest the invocation through their current to verbalize that meditation, in a balanced way.

Evocations of Elemental Forces

To call of the elemental forces to manifestation outside the living vessel, is to call it forth to achieve some physical result. This is done through the spoken, or mental calling of the essence. Reaching deep within yourself so that your elemental can do your will outside in the macrocosm. Thaumaturgy, in its simplest description, is the causation through physical changes, or some other miraculous means, with the aid of natural force to mimic the divine miracles of the Clerics of Theurgy. In being a mage, one must be able to invoke their forces to what ever ends they will. This can be through elemental manipulation such as changing weather patterns, natural disasters, or some other physical means of having the chosen element manifest as you desire it. This is said, that those who seek out to be Thaumaturges, working without the need or aid of a gods, seeking to become their own force, will find a higher force which they will serve without hesitation so long as it serves both their ends, and the will of that force. It is through this journey one becomes Warlock.

In speaking of the wills of higher forces, Fire seeks to consume those which are not a part of it so that it will burn hotter, it will consume without understanding the need for it to slowly consume so that it lasts, it will seek its chance to be the blaze it wants to be. So to is this true in the impetuous mage who seeks to command great tempestuous fires that annihilate life. This is not what working with fire is about, as the mage must learn to control their will, that their will for the time of the evocations becomes the will of the element. Water's elemental will is flow to its point of least resistance. So thus when dealing with an evocation of the forces of this element you will deal with things which will move from the highest points to the lowest point, the speed of this is dependent upon how much you can temper your will to make it manifest through this force. Air manifests like whims, the flighty nature of the manifesting currents can cause the creation of storms, or be used to stir other elemental forces or powers depending on what your evocation requires. Earth will be the foundation, anything which supports can be called forth through this element, the essence of everything is an embodiment of this.

Evocations of Elemental Powers

Like the Elemental Forces, the powers are the spirits which respond through actions to those who work with their element. 'Sylphs', 'Undines', 'Salamanders', and 'Gnomes'/'Goblins' (dark earth) are the elementals of the physical plane. It is through these creatures whose nature is determined by the spirits created, the life granted from the elemental forces, to balance out nature, to be the spirits of the Will of the Elemental. In modern texts and sources the elemental creatures are the best embodiments of the eternal and ageless elemental forces, immortal currents which operate as spirits only for the will of that element. When you call forth the spirit of the element, it is one of the elementals that responds.

The spirit which is made of the element, behave like the element; their nature is to destroy mostly, or create depending on the aspect and the attributes you are working with. However in dealing with the Elemental powers like the elemental forces, your working on a level of creation or destruction only, of the things you would have happen. You can evoke the fires of the inferno to stir the passions of a person towards or against you or another, the result is dependent upon which you call forth, the mindset you are in, and the capacities to which these elementals can manifest in their lives. How you go about determining which elemental you are going to be working with is through your own notes, charts and correspondences which you have spent your time in meditation on the connections of. It has been said many times that if you learn the spirit of a thing you have power over it. Well, when you have observed the nature of the spirit, you can recognize the manifestation of that spirit within nature, and within yourself, and thus making use of it for your own ends.

The bonds you forge with the elemental forces are what will give you command of the elemental powers; conversely, **it is not true** that a bond with elemental powers will give you full command of the elemental forces or even other powers. You become kin to the elementals when you forge bond with their source element, you become a manifestation of that elemental force, like them, so being flesh you will be responded to, as those in the world of flesh, draw from the world of the spirit.

Evocations of Planetary Forces

When performing an evocation of the planetary forces, you call forth that attributed to it, within something else, within the microcosm of the in which you would have the desired result manifest. As the elements function as the emotional passages for manifestation, the planetary passages, are the attributes of the thing on which you're working on. The form through which the elements are to manifest determined by the planetary body which corresponds to it. For example: Mr X wants Ms Y. So that Ms Y becomes more lovable by stimulating the Venetian aspect within her, he can call forth the fiery elements to cause her progression towards passion.

In the example it is because the person is point of fact, female, thus susceptible through the influences of Venus. You're calling upon the thing outside of herself, to open up the channel to that which is within her, through one of the Chakras or her overall nature, as it overlapping with the elements become mutable. If it can be taken care of through the essence of the thing, then do so before you work with the spirit of the thing. If you can through the nature of the thing, then use the essence to manipulate the spirit of it, then by all means do so if it serves to further your means along the path. It is not a safe world we live in, the high arts are filled with traps, and the 'transcendental authorities' responsible tend to forget this, when they write. So deal with the nature, deal with the essence, if you can avoid dealing with the spirit of it.

When dealing with the planetary currents, you draw out your manifestation through the gates which are responsible for the maintaining of the stability of that current or attribute in nature as a whole, or in the nature of something. If you have forged an elemental pact and you seek manifestation in something be or needs subtle manipulations then seek to evoke the changes through the channel of the planetary forces. If you have a pact with the planetary forces then you have bonded to the gate and the attribute, so you must invoke that you can evoke in something outside yourself to call upon the bond within to link your attributes with the attributed links within the target to be changed.

Evocation of Planetary Spirits

Not for the faint of heart when you call upon the spirit of an attribute that governs the nature of the thing. The planetary spirit is the power of the Spirit of the Planet, the attributed ways the will of the forces of the planet works, and comes about through the interaction with the other forces within both the microcosm and macrocosm to stimulate a balance through the elemental make up of things in creation. In history there are several references to the Planetary Spirits, and Powers, angels called by names from a-z with demons done the same. The planets are related to the Deities as they are the major means by which changes happen. This is so because they are the Attributes of the things which are manifest from the Will of the body of the Planet. The current/will of the abstract force which is the Mars current, or the Saturn current, is in its relationship to the spirit of it. The god-force one calls upon is the spirit of it which encompasses all aspect of that current. It's like calling everything which consists of having some water, all of the water contained within is the god force of the Planet, only by the attribute. Ex: Mars is warlike, masculine, strong, passionate, warm, rational, and so on. Its god-force spirit would be like Aries, who is all of these things.

The division of the spirit from the Planetary force, is that the god force is all of that force as one. Where the spirit, or lesser powers are the embodiments of the will of the lesser powers, rationality, war. These are what the old books consider the spirit of the planets, the starry bodies also are considered powers which can be evoked in similar manner. Pacts can be forged with any celestial power, or any spirit or force through which the mage would bind himself. In dealing with the attributed nature of a thing, and giving it independence from the natural mindless force, which only wills to perpetuate itself, you enter into territory which will leave you unbalanced and vulnerable if you are not careful. Deal with the spirits as the last resort, because if you can work with the nature of it, then you have access to its essence, and through its essence you can safely rework the nature and the spirit. It is when you know the nature of the thing, and the attributes by which it works that you can call it forth to manifestation.

Evocations of the Forces Within a Place

When you have a place which is your domain, and if you have a relationship with the forces of it, which is the self perpetuating will of it to sustain itself, then you have of course the force which the place grows to have. A church is a building of stone, glass, brick and steel, wood, and whatever else. Same with a place where anyone lives, or any place in nature which is just rock, and stone, water or fire. When you evoke the force of a place, you call upon the self perpetuating will of the place to work, or aid what you will.

When you build a node, or find a natural one, and make a nexus, or establish one. You then have the capacity to make use of the force of this place, to increase your working. You're calling on all the elements, all the spirits, all the planetary correspondences within this place as you evoke it as the force of that region. This becomes effective when you seek protection in an area, by calling upon the essence and the attributes within that region. As locations are both elemental and planetary, you can call forth the will of the place to exist to unite with yours. Such as protection rites; 'I call upon the roots of all, and stars above, hear my cry, protect me from all on earth and in the sky'. Forging bonds and binding your energies to a location increases the strength you have to your territory, to your domain, and the region in which things are located. You by doing so incorporate everything which you claim, as part of who you are and what you work for. That through the combinations of the essences of the planets, and elements in unison with your will what you desire shall be made manifest.

To be able to evoke a place, is to have the invocation already preformed that you know where you are going, or what you are calling on because of how it makes you feel. Your connection to that place through an invocation binds your mind and energies to that current, and through your work allows you to draw it forth to do what you have to do, as it corresponds to the intent behind what your working for. Know your places, and how they work in you. If you have within you what a desert feels like, what a hot scorched valley is, then you can call forth the dry desolate regions in the four directions, etc.

Evocations of the Spirits of Places

When you know the nature, and the attributed currents within a place, you can then see the attributed currents within it. The spirits that form each grain of sand if it's a desert, the spirits which are resonant within every molecule of trees, plants, etc. You call it forth by the spirits of the elementals within the regions of the 4, that it is made so by your will for them to be called forth. In so calling the spirit of the place you by your own will invoking within you the currents you would have manifest outside of you, so that you can align to them. Calling upon the spirit in a place is what gives the space its potential for manifestation. Example: When people invest a place such as a church with the notion that it is a holy site, it is sacred, the energy begins to resonate as such. When the people create with the power of their wills that there is a spirit within that place which manifests their desires, their band aid for their pain, or the means by which they can ascend to the heights. There becomes a spirit. The older the location, the greater the spirit. Every place has a spirit, a will which by its attributed force will seek manifestation in order to perpetuate the nature which sustains the spirit. It's a cycle of creation within a space. There exists like elementals and planetary spirits; a spirit which seeks to perpetuate the nature of the place.

So thus churches being sites of worship, and reverence will establish a spirit within that is for those who revere it, and worship it, lending to its power to expand out in their communities and protect them. It is through this, that the current expands out and a single church can influence the goings on in a region. If mages in a community go to war, the one with the bigger bonds and forces will over come the one with the weaker spirits. Those who form bonds within regions whose spirits are supported by more, have more available to them, then those who bond to regions, or deal in calling out the spirits kept private. So as mages you must, if you are dealing with a bonded place, or a spirit of a place to bond with it, or having bonded from it. Know the nature, and the attributed forces which caused the place to be the spirit which it is. Learn what powers are in a region, know the mechanics by which they exist.

Evocations of the Bestiaries

These are the animals, the spiritual powers resonant in life forms, you can call for the spirits of any animal, including humans, anything ever bound in flesh, or having a flesh, one time flesh, or structurally similar connection to creatures on earth. Every spirit has a form when it is manifesting as powers; these could be as the dragons which would be hills, valleys and so on which form their bodies, these could be the cats and dogs, or even humanoid in shape. But these are the Spiritual bestiaries which a mage has at their disposal to employ. When dealing with the animal nature, you deal with the infernal minds of it, when you deal with the primal urges of survival and sustaining, directing it to your will, you must maintain your focus. Because what you evoke and set to task, must have the capacity within its spirit to preform such a task.

You can make a physical mock up of the creature, giving it the correspondences and the nature, with the attributed will and spirit as you craft and unite it to the natural currents. Through this you can through drawing, or thoughts, or working off the spirits of things which already exist form your own spiritual bestiaries. You can work with spiritual animals and icons, or you can make new ones. It's up to you, but so long as you understand the underlying attributed forces which you are giving new form to, in order to achieve your will. You must keep these things in mind, and it is always best to keep record of the forces, and powers you deal with, so that you can continue to work with them as your studies increase. Like with the spirits of places, the more you work with the spirits of the bestiaries, the more potent they will become over time.

Animal servitors, and familiars as they have been called through history, can be made, or bound into service, or birthed from other ones. It matters not by what means they serve, or how they were acquired, but so long as they serve the will of the mage, nothing else will be able to sever the bond between the two, except for the master of the two. When you have a spiritual familiar which you are comfortable with you can also invoke it, but there will eventually be a union with each spirit into one.

Evocations of Deities

When you work or have a patron god force, you have within you the capacity for an understanding of the forces which you are connected to. As stated it is all the powers which that current has overall, overlapping and corresponding to the will of that current, it is the god-force of that current. To evoke the deity, is to evoke the forces which make up the deity, so every nature it encompasses, every elemental correspondence it is attributed to. Everything which makes up this force can be called forth to manifest through some action, through some means of manifestation.

This being an add on for all powers and forces so that in calling these spirits to manifestation outside of your body, in the microcosm of another, or in the macrocosm. You will have to know your consciousness in relationship to what you are willing to manifestation. It's between you and the embodiment of the things which work through you, the Deification of the attributed forces will manifest themselves like any spirit. Speaking and communing with you as extension of them. To come into contact with your patron on a one on one level is something which happens through your dedication and development. The more you work with forces, the more your nature comes into contact with the attributes of the eternal actions which are determined by the divisions in the macrocosm. You are recruited by the forces which are manifest in your nature. You become an extension for the Divine forces which are named by humanity. You become through your own becoming like unto the attributed will of the highest intelligences which are the eternal consciousnesses operating and willing through their existence the balance between all forces, and spirits. These forces are the blind, or mindless forces, given sight, given a mind, and thus making the spirit by which they encompass the will of the elemental sources. There are methods of evoking the god-force which you will need to learn through the communion with the spirits under their command. The specifics to their requirement of sacrifice, the medium of conjuration, and the places in which they prefer for their manifestations.

Living Evocations

When we have encountered this concept, we as readers of occult texts have poured over grimoires, or some obscure references to incenses, compounds, and other trance inducing mediums. As of yet, this author has not looked into the works of many "Modern" authors on the subject of Goetic conjurations of the spirit/non-tangible world. My focus is instead on using living bodies, things we know exist, and conjuring them.

Like forming an international network of mages, and so forth, one can effectively evoke them all into one place, at a time, by calling forth their position in the hierarchies much like was discussed in the *Principals of Manifestation* section. I would say that in this case, summoning a spirit of a living person to appear, or attend a ritual is the same idea that many would say try and use the spirit traps, or what have you. However the differences between summoning a soul to do works for or against, and to evoke them as one would evoke the god-forces are fundamentally different.

As with it being drawn from a living host, you have to have a time when the host is willing to let part of themselves be released by the nature of the construct. You as the person doing the evocation will be the one whom needs to be supplied with a conjuration of summons from the person to be summoned. When you do this there need to be arrangements and times agreed upon so one does not end up in a coma while doing something hazardous like driving, or cooking, or what have you. When the party is to be evoked from their body, to attend a ritual the purposes might vary. You can achieve a "Sabbat" and be summoned to the party by those who know your conjuration that you can attend in a spirit/mind form. Much like a spirit would be summoned for communion, as if raised from the dead.

In this matter your book of sigils, seals and conjurations take on the effect of a "phone directory" of living mages, whom you can summon and interact with. When necessary to augment the work that would be better done by using the power of a grouping of people. It is in this method that you must have first developed a position in the castes of the cosmos. By the creation of this hierarchy, you as the evoked In this way you can keep obscure who they are, if you know them by their sigil, or their place in the hierarchy. Much to function like living gods, whose work, can aid you. The requirements that I have observed in this are as follows:

1) Having a rank in the celestial orders – this establishes a position in the hierarchy, and lends itself for use on works outside personal advancement magicks. Such to the point that the invocation of the personal tower, can then be a means by which if turned into a summoning will be used as point of reference to call up the spirit.

2) Having gone through the Rite of Transformation – the reason for this is that the body which is tethered to meat, will not have the celestial current flowing through them which can sustain all their power for any extended session. If it was done without the rite of transformation it is more like an astral projection than a summoning.

The becoming of a member of the hierarchy is much the form of a commitment, it's a job one does while one studies. Generally service of a patron force. Such to the extent that the tides of life flow around the duty which you have aligned yourself. Much in the terms like a pact agreement, instead of being granted a horrible death where the soul is held as payment for services rendered and a free pass for 20 years, being of the hierarchies is a task that one undertakes, to give purpose to their power, to gain power, station from doing the job. Much like one who is in service to a particular god-force does the will of the god in all things, be it for or against the notion of what that god does. If you have sworn an oath of service to the gods, elements, or whatever else you have stumbled across in the odd journey through the gate. It is not a road you can return from. Being one of the hierarchy is to be one who devotes their life to the path, in a more intimate way than a priest of the same god would. To take rank as a dark knight of Hades, outranks the simple servant who worships him in the dark woods on the odd days of the week. The Knight has legions it can command, it has duty it must perform, and it has an oath of service, to abide. There are an infinite number of orders that one can fall under. A brief section where this would come in would be in your work with Calling of the Watchtowers.

With the call of the Watchtower, one has a working understanding of where they exist in creation, where they can meditate, and develop a certain skill set, by the nature of this bond of service. I will not discuss the results of pacts or bargains made for an exchange of connections such as the famous Faust. That is not my intent to encourage such works, when one can be a demon-god with more power than say Mephistopheles. Our intent in this section of the work, is to find for us a footing on which we can stand, that gives a job to do, sets our path in place. Something as simple as "I am a knight of (X), priest of (XX) and (YY)," It could be as complicated as "I am the keeper of the keys to all the worlds, nameless in my duty, gatekeeper of the gates to all the planes, and keeper of the way, Priest of (X), Lord of (YY) and so on..." it can sound ridiculously pompous when you write out the summoning for your essence. Yet it is here, you set yourself apart; it is here you divide the created world by the power you have, and the ability of another to seek out directly that power source as though they would from any god or demon.

The second reason, is to understand the Rite of Transformation. When you undertake the R.O.T., as I call it for short, there is a distinct advancement which occurs to the Chakras, and aetheric make up of the body. It in this manner is what sets people apart in the field of occultism, those who have gone through the gates, and those who have not. It does take some years to really understand what it is, that is so remarkable about this ceremony. It is designed that in a single hour long ceremony one opens the gates, and consumes an herbal/mineral/metallic mixture that functions as an internal catalyst of change. That way the currents which are summoned outside of the body, are then drawn into the body by the act of consumption. This spiritual devouring occurs, and is a permanent adjustment on where the currents come from, as the Chakra points as a single humans, independent structure is replaced with one sustained by the direct planetary currents, through the use of the 9 gates. This change of the body's structure allows for a deeper well of power to be able to be drawn from in working with the magicks. It is a personal advancement ceremony where one takes an active step in seeking the union with creation. To make the body connect to the Singular Collective in the same manner that the awakened mind will do so as well. The body will become reliant on the power of the solar system, and so long as these planetary bodies exist, or some aspect/long dead fragment of them exist, so too will the spiritual body/celestial body of the one who has done the undertaking.

With this being said that the undertaking of the Rite of Transformation is a major foundation to my work with obscure systems, and created systems. It is in combination of work with the Watchtower of the art, that you will begin to recognize where you set in the hierarchy. It sounds like madness, but when you are able to be evoked by another person thousands of miles from where your body is, that would be a confirmed success. There is also something to be said at this point about energy work. If you use this method, make sure the gates are open on the side of the evocation, that way the power can be pulled from the gates to maintain the evocation, instead of the one whose energy is summoning the living. In this method, the living mage who is evoked is to be one of the aids to the manifestation and is not a hindrance to it.

Greater Summons of the Living Spirit

Place the candle that correspond to the person in the center, Put 8 white candles in an array around the personal candle. Carve the colored candle with the name of the target, the 8 with each of the 9 names of the Egyptian bodies: ka, ba, kaibit, akh, sahu, sekhem, ab, ren. Put the candle on an array of the target to be summoned.

From here anoint the candles with a consecration blend. Light them in the order of the first through ninth.

From out the mortal vessel free,
The Souls and essence come forth to me!

Kaht be still, and release for me the souls that are contained within thee,

Ka, be released, unto this summons, beckoned to this place before me.

Ba, come thou forth,
Great bird that travels by night on the solar barque

Kaibit, the shadow of the man who is before me, be brought forth

Akh the immortal, be brought before me, as you are summoned here by this fire.

Sahu, the incorruptable, with all the traits of the living Kaht be brought forth to me

Sekhem, release from the Kaht, I call your life force before me!

Ab, the heart, the source of the good an evil within the Kaht, come before me!

Ren, the true name and vital part, be summoned here before me.

(Name of the target)
Thee I conjure

(Name of the target)
Thee I command

I evoke thee,
Come thou forth (name of the target)

Come thou forth
By will and word
By scourge and sword
By wand and blade
Come thou forth my charge is made

No chain hold
Nor bond be bound
From heaven loose

Be summoned here
Free from the bonds of flesh and blood
I conjure you: (name of target)

Through the time of times
Through the gate of gates
Be brought here by this plate
Be brought forth to me
I part the way
I rend creation
At this its cross be conjured
Where the creations meet in the timeless space
Be brought forth this instant to this place
So is my command!

Thee do I conjure, and thee do I command!
Forth the vessel of flesh be free
I command you to enter this space before me.

Essences

Essences are the integral part of things, making it what it is, and the soul is that part of the essence when combined with the other materials present in the material aspect, gives the essence distinction between other essences, separating it from other things. As all things contain inherently similar essences the soul is what distinguishes it from everything else. One can thereby create or recreate a soul already or not yet in existence to do the bidding of the one who would create it. As with the standard creation of beings discussed and expounded over in numerous volumes for the intermediate and advanced students, even some beginning volumes on this topic. What I present now is another method of doing such a task.

The ethereal realm is the realm of creation out of energy, the astral is the bridge between the physical and the realms of spirit, after the ethereal materials have gathered enough energy to become physical. Project your mind to the ethereal planes of creation, and find their center. Align your energy with it, becoming part of the plane, draw the plane's essence into yours. Merge with the essences of all the planes and realms, gaining attributes that will help get to your overall goal. Create the planes if you have to, they should be freely at your disposal.

After the elements and astral energies have settled in your core complete the following rites in order. The process of connecting with the elements can take anywhere from six months to a year for each element and plane. There are a select few essences that I will mention, as what lies beyond what is mentioned is for the seeker to find through their own experiences. You connect to these essences as you connected to the elements and planes, by drawing their center into yours.

Essence of Magick - the root of all, energy of creation, the singularity.
Primal Essence - the raw chaotic energies that lead to the evolution of the singular individual through its interactions with the sources.

Working and getting to know these forces, planes, and essences can take the better part of a few years for adjustment on how they function.

Of Souls

Souls form foundations, they form the base; like clay to be molded. You can use clay to form a body, but you can inject the clay with energy, and "create" a soul from it. The soul has to have a body to survive. Be it an astral form, or a condensed sphere, the soul has to be in a form on any plane, it cannot be its liquid state outside of a spiritual medium, such as the fires of the planes or the rivers of the souls, or the earth such as anything physical, or airy medium such as smoke.

The texture is like fine silk, the appearance is like unto mist, it is like unto lava flows in its natural movement, and power. Used as a form of spiritual currency on the planes, having souls to barter and trade comes in handy when dealing with the lower worlds, and as a toll cost to the other world. Use of souls in magicks can be to be as the battery for otherwise deadly rites. If they are of the once born souls then they return to the source from which they came. If they have developed an astral body, they go where they choose, or end up in purgatory realms if they have no conception of the planes. They can opt to become something greater on the evolutionary scale of the soul. If they have sworn allegiance to a source, then their soul returns to the source from which they bind themselves to in oath, and blood. If they have developed an astral body then it goes the plane in service of the force they have bound themselves to. The unawakened who believes in nothing, will go back to the source. Things that wonder as the lost, among the forsaken are merely outcasts from where they chose to be. They wander because it was their will to wander. They are lost because they choose to be lost. It is a choice of will. If they are of power, then they return to the source of power. If they are of power with a spiritual body, then they choose what they will. They can choose to exist on the planes growing until they choose to carry out a new cycle.

Spirits of the Departed

Spirits are so varied and the occurrences whereby they can be contacted are numerous and discussed at length in works by necromancers, spiritualists and anyone who has ever gotten that cold chill running up their spine. It's not as though that shiver is always a spirit of the dead, but it could be your own spirit when you charge your body energy to work the art. What needs to be kept in mind is that the dead have a very distinct way of doing things, there are laws relating to what spirits can and cannot do.

Nature has its tides, and because of the human world stepping in and the priesthood of the ages putting their form of magicks between this world and the other world, the spiritual barriers and assorted walls preventing their reentry to this plane are created to limit their perceptions by the layman. So you should be aware by now of spirits and how the dead feel with the currents when you are meditating with the dead, and on death. When you take that death into yourself and you feel all of your cells decaying as they do, you also need to get to the point where you can feel them being created within your body. As all things are contained within the outer world, so they are also contained within the inner world.

Soul Entrapment

In the journey of those who have experienced such actions that would cause your hand to be levied against them. There are such times when it becomes necessary that we don the mantle of those who fear us for the deeds we might do if we become pushed too far. We hold at our disposal with the text at hand, a means and a method of bringing about fitting punishments to those who would go off the deep end, or renegotiate contracts without actually expressing the wish to do so. Those in violation with such agreements are generally going to be held to a high standard of balance as it were.

This process, utilizes the separation of the mind from its spirit, in such a way as it opens the psyche and allows for the implanting suggestion using figments gathered from a mental bond with the subject. If you are not strong enough in your sense of self while you bond with the other, then you would be likely to have the same fates visited upon you. In such cases as we have to use this method, you must pick a location which befits the aim. What is it you are going to do? What is it you would like to have happen? How would you arrange it for the long duration and its effects on quality of life? How does it affect mood, and relationships, as the individual progresses in age?

When you have these questions answered you proceed. In the visual projections you would construct, you set the area up for your working. Adjust protective measures accordingly. Select your target, and range where the working will effect so as to gain the maximum working zone. Generally to property lines, will be enough space. If you are doing this from a distance, do what you can to have someone on the inside of the space telling you what they experience as you set about the work. After you have spoken the conjuration, project your mind to be as what would make them most at ease, use this point of composition with their psyche and the fears that you would conjure outside their body. Find the place where they are at their most calm, and then find your way into their subconscious. What it is they fear deep down. In this case we will be exploiting it, so as to cause the effect we are looking for. If you are doing this to legitimately aid someone's psyche and repair their world view.

This method must be written again as such to fit your needs. With this as we have it, the invocation. Unspoken mental magicks, while you read, and your thoughts project into the world around, creating the world the target fears, then implanting a point of calm within. Get the target calm, get them comfortable with the status of things, and from there you will be able to integrate into their open subconscious mind the suggestions, and ways of thought. It is in this point you must decide, or let flow how the situation ends.

Ex: If you're using a burned out old insane asylum. Then you would target the persons psyche to integrate with the spirits of those who suffered and got tortured in such a place. Then you would bind the madness to her, but in such a way that it came from a place of calm, and acceptance, that the world to fear was outside, and away. Imprinting on them that there is something horrible, and terrifying beyond the edges of their perception. That they would never be able to see it, taste it, experience it. However in their acceptance of it, they accept the lie they are being subjected to. In this lie, they become the mental patient having hallucinations about a world which does not exist. In the same time as their sanity is weakening on our side of things, due to the bleed that such a reality would hold. The idea then at this point is to manipulate the external forces of their reality as it is, not as the construction. So to accept the reality for reality sake, is to be forced to come to terms of there bring an undeniable lie. But since it is a lie that was in such a way that it made the logical conclusion.

So for the lie to be accepted, it has to originate from a source of truth, or fear. Then from this fear you can build the psyche around the individual. You do this mentally, psychically. You can speak the words to set about the gate, however, you must have a location selected. Create then your own conjunction according to your purpose.

Conjuration of Entrapment

Hail to the gates of the flesh, and blood,
Free from heavens bonds,
I construct the gates of the world

To the north I embody the death of all things,
Thrust open its pathways to the lands beyond

To the south and the regions of the damned
I call forth the pathway and thrust open the gate,

To the east of the rising sun
Where night mares and horrors swarm
In the twilight light hours,
I open the gate

I open the gate to the west
When the nightmares walk in the open

I open the gates in this place
I stand as the ground beneath me falls away
I stand upon the banks of the island of my dreams
In this place lacking flesh, lacking bone,
I draw upon the will of the earth
To return to me that which was forgotten,
Those souls named and unnamed
Those which lie in ruin on the banks of isle of death
I lay claim to those souls in the covenant for black fire,
I do bind them all by my will and the eternal fires
That in the fires they are purged of pain and torment,
Given refuge unto my bidding
Through the aid of the flames
Let all those who died and perished
Upon the bones of the ancestors rise
To the flames which they are bound,
Thus being bound
Drawn unto the pact of this age
In this palace of the elements,
Where in my will stands
At the crux of the world veil,
I summon those bound by blackened fire
In the shadows they are to come forth,
The gates of the north
Become the burning gates to the regions of the dead
Those of the south, west and east,
Shall too become my burning gates
Peel back the ranges of the dead
The damned those forgotten and the lost,
The tormented innocents that are buried

In the flows of time come forth
To my purpose inside the world of sleeping dreams,
Inside the mind the sleeper sleeps
Let the creeping darkness in.

I stand upon the crux of the world
Atop the burning island
I make now my stand
As the keeper of the way of the lost and forgotten
As the lord of the shadows,
Guardian of the 8 gates
Hear now the call of the mind
Be brought forth
I open the 8 gates of the celestial heavens
I open their contrary gates,
Into the realms of the dead beneath
I fill with these souls the black fire
The fuel for my desire
Inside the dreaming world,
The sleeper waits,
Inside the mind the sleeper walks,
Inside the room the darkness creeps
Into the mind it seeps
Flames of madness
Pry their mind
The sounds of chaos fill their ears
The claws of the damned tear at flesh
The evil that flows,
The darkness that grows
Into the place I set before thee
Into the room,
Into the mind,
Into the walls
Flood them for me
By the pact of the darkest fire
By which you souls were bound,
I command you tear their flesh
Rend the mind,
Raze the spirit and their peaceful slumber
Fill her with torments and the dead
This damned horror come for them,
Claim her make her your own
Devour what lay beneath their mind,
Fill them, tear at them,
Consume them!
Rouse Them from sleeps sweep grip,
Into nightmares jaws be flung
Peel it strip it, make it bare,
Upon their waking mind I set this fear

Bind the intended to what you would have, peel their mind and anchor this in their deepest world. Use their root of fear find the deepest connection to that fear you can, and anchor that to their mind. The process should be a psychic reaching, and influencing your target. If you have blood seals in the area use them as the means by which you can project. From this point, you will be able to affix their spirit to the dream time plane, which you can then set to become rejected by the environment. From this method you can force the environment to force the target inwards, becoming consumed by the madness. If you use the paradigm for the institution then they will bleed over into the waking mind. In this way they will be forced to take the medications. If done to such extent where the mind is then broken and unable to leave from this construct they should very well end up in the institution that you have thus bound them to in their mind. They will be trapped by fears, and so by giving into those fears be so bound by those who view them as a danger to themselves and others.

On Possession

No spirit shall enter into this world without taking on the form of one born of this world be it animal, or human. Any spirit or force originating off this world choosing to enter this world may do so by the following means:

A. Incarnating into mortal flesh.
B. Taking a host body.
C. Temporary possession may be granted in order to secure an establishment of a bloodline through which the spirit may choose to incarnate into at any time.

This world allows for spirits to take over, ride along with, or use humans or any animal they see fit and deem worthy of becoming their hand upon this plane. It is in so doing, that exorcisms are a violation of these laws. However there is time when one of the temple can lay claim to the soul of another who has been taken over by a spirit. It upon this occasion is the only time when one of the temple should require an oath of service be part required on the part of the afflicted as they are in the debt of whom uses this means of purging.

As I am a member of the Ancient Order, I lay claim on your soul, do you so swear service to what I would have of you in exchange for your release from the offending spirit?

They must be cognizant of this question. Proceeding then call upon the Ancient Covenant to purge the spirit and lay claim to the soul of the one afflicted to be oath bound to the covenant until payment is made upon this debt. There are to be no outrageous bonds of servitude, as the council will punish any who use its name to commit atrocities upon any world. The best means of payment is that they become your pupil, so they study, learn of the counsel, and serve the counsel for the service it provided to them in their moment of need.

When you are working on behalf of the Temple to extract a soul you will need to understand the agreements to which such things will be held, kept and bound. So we employ the Pact of Exorcism. It is a simple arrangement between the initiating priest and the possessed, which must be entered into before the spirit is removed, as it binds both spirits to service of the Temple. It binds the incoming spirit so that we may be able to find it a proper vessel to which it will be better suited in order to bring about its utmost efficacy, making it a guardian force or some such. Of course when one reaches a level in the Temple where they have a will which can rival the forces which they draw out, they can seek permission from the temple master to spiritually devour the entity in order to gain that power for themselves.

However if this permission is not granted and they do it anyway, as the spirit is a possession of the Temple, and the one who does the consuming of it without the backing of the temple is going to be consumed by that which they would have consumed for themselves. It is not a child's game of who gets to eat and devour what. But you take into yourself these attributes which would have benefit to you and what your ultimate aim to achieve is. If it is that you would become a dark thaumaturge then by all means seek out and study the infernal ways, and the ways of the demons, dark celestial forces, and dark deities. If you seek power of the light celestial forces then consume those angels and celestial beings which would be beneficial to your cause. If you would hold to balance in your soul which should be ultimately the aim of every member of the Temple, and anyone who walks, breathes, lives, dies and reads this work, then consume both.

On Spiritual Consumption

You lay claim to a soul it is yours. If the host vessel is animated by an unawakened spirit you lay claim and take responsibility of its actions and guide and punish it as you see fit. It's yours to devour, to feed from, or to spawn what you would have it. The unawakened are open to possession. Once possessed the laws of incarnation come to play, you can do what you will with the souls you have laid claim to. The awakened souls of the flesh bound spirit are subject to ownership and the rules governing their existence from their source. They have been claimed, and they are ruled by the will of their spiritual source.

The spiritual source energy of the souls under its dominion are forfeit to the will of the source energy. The source energy may be drawn off, but can never be consumed, subsumed or otherwise bound or destroyed. It can however be bound, chained and otherwise imprisoned so that the currents of the origin can be used to sustain the one who does the binding. However the binder cannot claim title over the bound through anything other than willing action of subservience, yielding them of all power unto the one who does the union: a kiss, sex, or some such willing bond.

If no union has been performed then the source remains the source, and nothing can it. Should it awake to its true nature then it remains unable to be bound for the term of its awakening until a transmigration occurs and the cycle begins again. If it wishes to transmigrate.

There are also spirits which you will find in nature, things that you bind, and you come across yourself, when out and about which are floating around and appear to be doing what they do. Be it for the service of something or not. You must be aware of the type of thing it is. But you can bind them by your art, and then consume them if you are of sufficient ability to take them into your core and have their attributes become yours. Upon doing this, you do a number of things which for the bettering or harming of your own nature become bound to the similar fate of what it is you eat. Say if you eat an imp you become responsible for completion of the work the imp was assigned before you walked by and ate it. If you have the will to devour demons of higher levels then you will be subjected to the potential of having their will manifest as yours, but opposite to what you want. So if you want magick, and have not yet figured out the purpose of the thing you consumed, and did not realize that within you, then you will be ineffective in your work. If you have at this time an understanding of what has been said then you may move on. But if you would tempt your fate by intermixing that which would have a path different from your own.

When you come up against a spirit in nature, which is made of the primal elemental forces, embodying a force, to take the core into yourself, to take its energy as your own, you become like unto it. An example;

When I was young, in a grove where I did a lot of work and practiced with my connections to the earth. I realized that there was a barrier. Something was being forced down and kept from returning to where it had once called home. So being young and impetuous I used my will and art and broke the natural barrier keeping it banished. All I could muster it was a hole at the time. But that hole was enough for it to start manifesting. With its manifestation into the grove, not only did the friend I was with and myself quickly climb out of the area, but we also managed to temporarily keep it stuffed in the grove. It was not entirely bound. It had these nasty little worm like critters; some with eyes, some could fly through the air or move the earth virtually unnoticed. Aside from them being the same energy manifestation of the thing bound in the grove. Time was short to make work of the spirit as it was a lunar shield we made use of which was going to collapse on the new moon. Going back into that place the entire area burned and glowed with the fighting between the trees and its will to consume the trees to gain a foothold in the physical. It was amazing to be around as you could feel the will of the trees, you could feel the power nature fighting it back. You could feel the power emanating from this grove. As well as the park this grove was in. Even the people who had no feeling for energy had a recognition that things were off about the entire park. The sum four miles square this place enveloped the grove itself was in the farthest corner, and emanated like a beacon trying to get a hold of something outside to get it out. It was an incredible month of perception and learning how these things work. How one spirit can call out by its power to something of like mind.

It was through this that I realized that to properly consume that which caused those problems would need to be summoned outside of the area which it was effecting so as to keep the energy focus and contained. So using a vase as an intermediary, we summoned it out of the natural area into the darkness of the space. My friend put her arm into the vase and willed that it be devoured by her power. She consumed it.

All of it, which in the end, wasn't much. However she does have in her disposal the little spirit fragments that can watch people, to know what they are up to, and whatever else that thing could do. But all and all it had a bigger bark than it did bite. She made quick work of the spirit. But the thing about spiritually consuming entities one must be aware that as the spirit fades within your core as you claim the power for yourself. Their power will also fade and merge into yours. So you will have the ability to do what they can do for a time, but you must figure out how to do that within yourself if you wish to properly duplicate the process later in your development. But you must be aware that if you go around summoning things up to consume them. Your energy will become tainted with their negative aspects as well as the positive ones, and they will manifest in you with your own flaws. This is not something one does without forethought to the considerable consequences that can result in madness or death.

I have since devoured many a spirit which I have come across for various reasons to deepen the internal well of power. It is a technique which comes in handy out in the field, when you need to quickly replenish reserves of energy. Particularly if what you're devouring was not summoned by you.

Devouring Spirits

It comes necessary at times to enter into combat with the spiritual forces. However there is a bit of a nuisance to have to banish said spirit all the time. There is no need to waste good materia, even if it is corrupted current. You can purge it and devour the essence. This is done using the shade tendrils.

When you have your spirit in the circle, bound or whatever the case may be. Send out spelled tendrils that represent the chains of the soul, as that will force the spirit to be bound unto your will. From here work the tendrils that they become sponges. From this have them assimilate and absorb all of the energy output from the source essence that forged the spirit. Everything should go into the shadow tendril. As it gets drawn into the shadow tendril, so you should have all of the currents getting drawn into the soul.

The feeding of your core the power, essence, and spirit of any spirit that originates externally from your consciousness is not easy. In practice you can assimilate any spirit. However in doing so you contend with the will to survive. That self sacrificing aspect goes out the window when one's life is about to be taken. It becomes an internal battle of will. However it happens that you utterly consume the spirit, you must not be consumed by it. To consume is to have the will of the devourer. Ethics aside, if you do not have the will to assimilate do not do it. As the spirit can hollow you out and ride you like a puppet till your vessel burns out. Apophis the devourer, or Ahriman, Set, and Ourbouros, all of these are the ancient devourers of the first time.

Greater Devouring

When you have mastered the basic techniques, you will then begin to notice not only energy is transferred. So is knowledge, skill and power over things which would otherwise be unavailable to you. To be able to achieve this. You must feel the power of the spirit through the tendrils as they are devouring. You must separate the spirit from the power, as you consume draw the core of its being into your own core, that you can sustain the type of power that the spirit had. As well as leave the threads of the power/specific currents intact as they are integrated into your core.

This again requires that you can strip an angel of the power that God itself gave to it, and consume it. Or that you can strip bare Lucifer himself of the vital essence that sustains him and take it for your own. However again it is not so much a warning as a fact. If you are going up against something bigger than yourself, you must have the will to consume.

You must be like unto the legendary void-space devourers in order to contain the power resident within the spirit that you are devouring. If you do not then they can override you, or lay dormant in your subconscious slowly consuming from the inside out.

Of Demons

What is described as a demon is dependent on which faith you follow as your own. What should have been determined by those who follow this work so far is that faith has not been discussed. We haven't gotten involved with the mention of dedications and such to the celestial mind as found in so many paths of the modern day. That will come later. But what can be said about these forces is very concrete. What you would call a demon is a mindset beyond what normally is made use of. Using the Grimoire of Solomon, or any of those spiritual conjurations with sigils and what not. It all corresponds to the parts of the human brain which give function over to those abilities. There are some great examinations done on this system by some very well written authorities. Go seek them out. Part of being able to work with this series is that it requires you to go out and do the leg work yourself. .

When the spirit corresponds to the part of mind, that part of yourself which you would come to face to get something done, you call upon your subconscious to bring out that aspect of you as a "genius" or "mind" which interacts with yours. This isn't to say that you should be happy if some one calls you a schizophrenic when your perceptions on these forces will manifest differently for each of the things you would make use of. But you will come to smell, taste, see, feel, and know these things as what they are. An extension of you in some form or another, some part of you which you need to reconcile and take in and make apart of you in order to become the complete mage. It is not something that needs to be undertaken at a moment's notice, not something that one can do on a whim.

To face down and recognize those parts of you which are found as intellectually separate from your own nature must be consumed by your consciousness as you work down the tree of death. You must face the tests of the demons of your own mental spheres. You must embrace those forces which you would have under your command should you need them. To be complete upon the path you must have this balance. You must seek those for yourself to study with this.

Summons of Demonic Forces

From the Goetia we have a very organized system of registry and cataloging of spirits and their legions. So we can take from this their seal, inscribe it into a candle that represents the color for which they are associated with. Generally overlaying an image onto the candle and using a sharp pencil can draw in the wax the symbol. Bleed upon the candle, and have some association of object with the spirit. As well as an established medium for it to embody. Incense clouds, water and herbs of the planet, skull with a crystal in its mouth. Something that will allow it to have a focus of energy that you can speak to and get information out of, or send after some task or another. This should be done in a place where your energy is matched to theirs on an even level. If they are pulled from hell, then you must become the master of hell to command them. If you are pulling an Angel of the fall out from the abyss then you must become the master of the abyss to properly and safely command these forces.

A common invocation of power before hand such as "It is not I, but the lord of magic, it is not I but Marduk that commands it" or something like that. If you are going to use a medium of focus to direct it and send it after a purpose, then a spoken conjuration of will, their summons should be made. In as clear a voice as you can command, while having made necessary preparation to set the space and get the needed environmental shift set. Light the candle, and while it burns the spirit should be under your sway. Snuff the candle when it reaches where you have enough left to bury, or light another candle. The demon candles should never be broken, or left to go out on their own. They should be kept safe from the influences of the elements. When the time comes they are no longer needed bury them, thank the spirit for their attendance and free them from the bonds of their mark in the candle. For to do otherwise is to cause pain to the spirit which you summon.

> I summon thee (name of the spirit)
> You who command (what their dominion is over)
> Whose master is (the lord/king/prince they serve)
> By the seal of blood, and the five elements of creation ...

The Summons of Djinn

This is the same sort of set up you have with the demonic force, and fallen angel. You need to have the seal of the spirit, you should have it engraved in the wax that while the candle burns the spirit should be set about its task. The family should be known, what king rules that family, what season the Djinn has power, what hour of the day it has power, what day of the week.

> I summon you (name of the spirit)
> Whose kingdom is of (name of the kingdom)
> Whose king is (name of the king)
> Whose queen is (name of the queen)
> By the seal of blood and the five elements of creation...

Complete the conjuration

> ...
> Come forth (name of the spirit)
> Obey the covenant
> Come forth (name of the spirit)
> My will is (name your purpose)
> Go forth in peace (name of the spirit)
> Go forth in haste to achieve what I require!

Of Archetypes

There are the intellectual forces of the cosmological structures created by humanity since the dawn of time. This with the source creating all things, and all things coming from that source. Well this is true in a sense. As far as can be said or should even be discussed it will have to be put off for a later discussion. What is a God force? It is the mind behind all conceptions of a single idea. It is the spirit of that idea as created by the virtue of the word which is used to conceive of it, becoming both the speaker, and the thing spoken.

To make it as simple as possible, a God is the spirit behind the idea, as the idea is formed in the hearts and minds of all things as it relates to the force at hand. We will have to look at this through an example if you would try and understand it properly. Let us use Themis. She is a Titan from the ancient world, who is also attributed to being Gaia. We can say that her properties are birth, sacrifice, law, morality, divination, assembly, vengeance, wise council, and salvation. As the earth she is all elements: the earth, air, fire, water, aether (the stuff of stars). She is what created every physical body; all things which have mass, she created and is responsible for. We can say she doesn't exist, that all these things are just concepts and so on. But in so saying we only get to our end point by a fraction. She, as a being in and over herself, is pictured as a woman holding a sword, and scales, with or without a blind fold. As justice is not blind, we will hold that from here out. She may not exist in that form. Her attributed abilities to overseeing law, birth, etc. are conceptions of language which mean something higher. You cannot touch, taste, see, smell, or eat law; but you can perceive it. So in its perception you have acknowledged it exists. So thus it exists within you, and is reflected in nature. Courtrooms are not nature, they are machinations of the human corruption which would make more laws than nature provided us with in the beginning. You feel these forces. You can feel within yourself what is law, sacrifice, birth, vengeance. You can see how they relate to the world at large. You then can say, that yes, in these acts where that takes place, there is a spirit about them, by the virtue of the acts a spirit is created. That spirit is part of the greater conception of the idea of what is attributed to that deity. Man and god are not separated forces. They are one and the same. You work with a deity like you work with the demons. You take of your mind, and you connect to the greater attainable attribute which is represented by that which is the name of that godhead. If you can get a grasp on this concept you're doing well. A God force is the doing and the done, by all parties involved in the perception and experiences of the single act. What you do not only affects you, but the world at large. Not only does this affect the world at large but it also affects in very personal ways everyone and everything for the rest of time.

You can take a rock and throw it into a pond, the water will ripple and go back to calm. However that rock will always remain in the pond. The entire body will be different for the rest of time. Your will must be as the rock, your deeds must become the throwing of your will, and you must have your intent willed to manifest in nature and the world at large for your work to reach any point of success. When you can understand that the gods are a part of you, when you can understand that they are your actions, the lesser spirits and demons who are responsible for your perception of those actions are all aspects as what is brought about by the mind and the soul of the living thing which is perceiving of that event, then you are on your way to becoming a mage.

What happens in the world at large is the same as what happens to you in the moment of your doing. If you walked into a store and something you wanted you could not get because you didn't have the means to pay for it, that want becomes a spirit of lust. If you then get into a foul mood, that is a demon of greed; if you then cut someone off in the parking lot because you were annoyed, then you become as a god-force of vengeance. You cutting them off will have effect on their life for the moment, there will be decisions they have to make to perpetuate that cycle and so on. They could get into a car wreck or cause one for someone else. The point is to not try and not step on anyone's toes or give in all the time, but to understand this balance, so that your life is better for it.

Patrons

So upon study of yourself as you relate to the elements, as you relate to the world of the living and the dead, and as you relate to you in all aspects of you mind and action, you will notice similarities in how you perceive things, how you think about things, and how you act. Upon beginning to see these parallels to the greater worlds, and yourself, you will come to find that your life has a flow to it. Your actions are aligned to a god-force. Your mind is a balance between the demonic and angelic aspects of your own nature, and your nature is as it is because of the relationship it has to the elements as they are manifest not only in the world at large but in your personality. Allowing you to take full charge of what it is that you would strive to become.

When you have connected these dots and put it together you will notice that your patron deity is the attributes in action in your life as they manifest themselves. Your deity and yourself go hand and together. Your faith, whatever it may be, falls bare to what is. You become your deity through your observations, thought and action. Your will becomes divine will. When you have reached this point then you are doing significantly better than most of the people that call themselves mages, witches, etc at the time of this writing. You are well on your way to embracing the whole of your nature. As you fit into nature, as you are of nature. It is this God Force which determines within your own life how you would lead.

You can be the embodiment of whatever force has been acknowledged as a god-head throughout the whole of human history. You will notice undeniable similarities in that force and you, without you even looking. Your goal from this point should shift from striving to be your own god, to becoming the best you that it is in you to be. That you will become what it is your power to become. Your daily life and your art should reflect what your patron force embodies in your own thought, deed, perceptions of the world as a whole. It must be stressed that you can from this point acknowledge your own power as a single power in the cosmological scheme of things but your journey is not over yet. You still have many years of self mastery. You must not only be aware, but live your life accordingly.

Source

When you have mastered yourself to the point where you can have recognition in yourself and others, you can elevate your awareness to what it is you embody. You then, being aware of your natural perceptions on the world, being aware of the spirits in others and how they relate with you, to how your mind and its aspects work, causing your actions to reflect the Godhead of that idea, will relate it back to the elemental nature of what it is.

In the beginning there was the single Chi, which split and created everything. When it split itself, not only did it separate into light and dark aspects of everything, with the neutral being the work to sustain both sides evenly, but it did so with the primal elements – those forces which are in everything. The fiery, the watery, the earthy, the airy, the active, the passive: these 7 conceptions of what comprise the nature and spirit of everything. You must dissect your views on your deity to your own personal nature, and your own elemental alignments You must become aware of what element you embody. You from this point will not be subject directly to your patron, but you will work with that guiding energy as an artist their tools. Because if it is based on your perceptions, your thoughts, your deeds, your will, then your will is the source of your being. It is not something you can do without, it must be lasting. Everything you do you must intend.

Upon reaching this point, working through the paths that others have laid, through your own meditating and your own ritual work, it is all well and good to follow someone else and their ritualized conceptions of the world. But, everyone who seeks themselves for who they are can be perceived of as an emanation of the source, with their own patrons as to who and what they are. Becoming an aspect, where all the worlds and creation become the clay in the potter's hands. You must know these connections, you must be able to seek them out where they lie. You will come to understand that recognition of this power and this connection is something entirely different from being able to actually do anything about it. So you must then start to apply this level of control and creation through your art.

Animation

The evocation of the living principal into your work. To give it the vital breaths, the quality of the living essence, or source.

I summon the forces that created this world
By the balance of all things
I summon within me the force of life that is inherent in all things
By the vital breaths
I give the vital breathes to thee
I draw in the consciousness of the source
I draw in the very life nature
I draw in the very essence of the source
I breathe upon thee the breath of consciousness
I breathe upon thee the breath of the life of nature
I breathe upon thee the vital breath
You are to be conscious of all things
In your need to fulfill this the task I give to you:
You are to be of the natural order of this world
Complete all tasks for which you are created:
You are given purpose and the mind for your task alone:
Rise now and be of the essence
Complete what I have set for you.

To Bring Life

A conjuration to bring forth the power of life, from the regions of the four elements, with the aid of the mother of life, and the spirit of life.

Zi ninti kanpa	Spirit Lady of Life, remember
Zi tiamat kanpa	Spirit Maiden of Life, Remember
Zi zikia kanpa	Spirit of the heavenly life, remember
Nisme annu sepsu sistu	Hear this powerful Summons
Ina kibrat erebitum	In the regions of the four
Ina sa belet	Through the rites
Ersetim ki'am parsusa	Of the mistress of the netherworld
Peta babkama laruba anaku	Open the gate So I may enter
Ina shuruppak	From the land of well-being
Ea, Enlil, Enki, Gibil,	Earth, Air, Water, Fire
Ina shiimti	From the house where the wind of life is breathed in
Nisme annu sisitu	Hear this summons
Alaka annu duggae	Come unto this lifeless mass of clay
Alme annu duggae tiit	Bestow upon this clay that which is life
Nadame annu duggae Ina shi	Give this clay the breath of life
Zi ninti kanpa	Spirit Lady of Life, remember
Zi tiamat kanpa	Spirit Maiden of Life, Remember
Zi zikia kanpa	Spirit of the heavenly life, Remember

To Take Life

To remove what was given as life, and take it to the place of death.

Ina qereb Emuq	In the midst of power
Adi la basi alaku	Bring to naught
Sa anna ina mitutu	Belong unto the dead ones
adi la basi alaku	Bring to naught
Tabalu Ina Gishtil	Take away the vehicle of life
Adi la basi alaku	Bring to naught
Tabalu ina ziana	Take away the heavenly life
Adi la basi alaku	Bring to naught
Tabalu ina shi	Take away the Soul
Adi la basi alaku	Bring to naught
Tabalu ina tiit	Take away Life
Adi la basi alaku	Bring to naught
Sa anna ina mitutu	Belong unto the dead ones
Adi la basi alaku	Bring to naught
Ina qereb emuq	In the midst of power
Adi la basi alaku	Bring to naught

Resurrection

    Resurrection is an advanced healing art that should take into account the amount of energy in the body. The amount needed to restore the Prana/Chi flows so as to restore the function of the spirit to which the anchor will be made. What resurrection accomplishes is an introduction to the dead a temporary stimuli. Like when a pond becomes stale, the resurrection would a stream finding its way to the pond so as to bring new life, and restore function. However the body and the mind of one who has returned to a decaying form will not entirely return to the form and functionality they had in life. Decomposition destroys the living functions and should not be attempted to be restored.

    The Journey will change them. Giving them feelings of rage, fear, unknown awareness. A sense of what's going on, where am I, why am I here, why can't I move! Is an over whelming sense. If they come back during mummification it would be they could feel the occurrence of organ removal. Even the Christian apocrypha make comment about how they will be different, their mind will function in different ways, as their souls have already reconnected with their other side. The text **Dispensational Truth** by Clarence Larkin from 1920 makes reference to this. The resurrection of Anu in the **Egyptian Book of the Dead**, also gives spells for returning the soul of the passed to the dead corpse as a way loved ones would be able to commune with the body.

    Some methods involve a living transfer of energy to the vital parts of the body. Much like a parasite the body will only respond when sufficient energy transfer is complete. In this method it is very much vampiric. As it will if done correctly be able to sustain itself off of such things such as vital Chi flows of others, from blood feeding, to consuming raw elemental catalysts. In this manner you can make a vampire. If you craft an egregore, you would be able to draw up a spirit to give it a host body, and you can then set it about feeding off of the territories that you would have it guard, protect, or influence.

    To heal the body when the spirit is broken, and make the spirit return to itself, after some form of trauma is also a type of resurrection. This method is done when you have the body, it is still alive, yet the mind has been over taken by some external force. Such as a possession. To clear out the corpse of all energy influence from the possessing spirit, you also strip away their energy. To return them to the empty shell, when this is done, is an act of restoration which requires a catalyst of their own will to return. They need something to anchor to.

    When you are going to work the ceremonial aspect of resurrecting an idea lost the river Lethe, you must understand what it was that surrounded the memory. So that your alignments are done in such a way as to balance the living energy and the dead. In this manner you would be able to return to a life, and time where you had those memories, learned those lessons, and based yourself off of some experience that lead to the doings. A resurrection of yourself through yourself, using your past incarnation as the body for which to learn such things. To travel backwards through the soul's memory and incarnation to reach the destination point, sought by undertaking such a work.

    When you would resurrect your memory of who you were, or gain a new lesson in some form of art, by passing into the body of that which you inhabited before your current time. Generally this is the only sure way to achieve a successful passage through time that has already occurred. You can see the memories pass of the life of the body your spirit inhabits for those moments, while the Prana runs dry in the body completely and living Prana from another mind will no longer satisfy its nature.

    If you are seeking to achieve this method to communicate with one who is in the past its a forceful sensation to pull your spirit into dead matter. To experience things like mummification is one of those special pleasures that will await those who want to see what life and magicks were like at the time of one's passing. You can choose to project your mind into the body of a dead person so as to see and observe from different anchor points in history. You can temporarily revive their Prana current with your own.

    This kind of focused restoration of the living essence is something that should be done when you feel a perspective shift is in order. Generally the freshness of the body is important. However with the right focus,you can achieve a sort of waking dream. On your waking moments just before sleep takes you project to the period in history where you would exist, and feel your memories. This should be instantaneous, so that you can experience what the feelings, smells are in the area around you.

You can choose what occurs at death as push the spirit out, and revive yourself as if it a were a coma, or some manner of recreation. This technique of passing into another body before the moments of death would theoretically allow a spirit the means by which they could choose the manner of their passing into the other world. In such a way you could feed off of the Chi, of those surrounding the body as to draw a length of stay.

When using the methods of returning life to the body. You are forcing the spirit to become affixed to the body for a temporary period. This work is neither beneficial for the spirit, nor is it something which is particularly pleasant. If you have someone who is under the influences of some other force, or has been dislocated from their personage. Then it might become appropriate to lay hand upon them to recall their spirit. Upon the death of the body mind dies, and the body ceases production over its functions, as such the body organs will lose the chemical properties which bond together. Time within the corpse is limited. The methods of Egyptian embalming are no longer lost to history. These would include the ritual removal and storage of the organs in the jars, in the order of the planetary path, as the funerary process prepares them with the knowledge of the spiritual planes. They pass through the gates of the dead and into the next world. To resurrect the spirit of the dead is an affront to the time they spent here. It can be done however to pull consciousness from one body to another across the era of time. As the time current is all spread out, and distance is years, decades, centuries etc. To the dead, it is all when they choose to incarnate. To achieve some purpose or another.

To light candles, to draw their spirit if it is lingering after death, is a good way to invite favor from them. However it is possible to lay hand upon them, generally the foot will do, if you clasp their foot in your dominant hand, and you send your energy, as channeled from the earth into their Chakra system. Flooding the current with your energy drawing back the stimuli of living Prana/Chi it will allow their mind/spirit to awaken temporarily.

As is stated in the nature of the sources. Every moment we perceive we are under a form of changed, a brought upon death state. So to transform death, is to resurrect life. To restore the function of the living, and waking minds within those who are dead. When gods are resurrected they become new. They become the combination who they were, and what they will be. Every generation of resurrection of a singularity can lose parts of it nature, parts of itself lost to history. The idea is to restore those missing pieces to their souls. To store themselves in history of things they influence, or find a way so as to anchor them to places, locations or things, which they are attached to. You can then make use of any process at your disposal to achieve such a conduit of focus, if you are the one doing the summoning. You choose the medium. If you have an elemental force which belonged to that spirit, it might be possible to get more visible manifestations, as you could fold the space time, around that area.

Assuming that you would be able to stay in a location which had existed in the same or similar form, you would appear to them as hallucinations, visions, extra terrestrials. And to you they would seem like shadows passing on the wall. A thin veil preventing interaction between times, yet observations will be permissible depending on the sort of observation. Given the right focus, and media the seeker would be able to work out their own personal methods tor reconnecting with their former selves. Any astrological data as well as a consideration for elemental, planetary, and other celestial allegiances to patron forces, deities, or the singularity, with regards to the individual and their past; allows for greater finesse when restoring the spirit to dead matter. For the spirit is inexorably inter-twined with such correspondence as they helped to shape their personalities and perceptions in life.

However it is, for the physical restoration of there is always a need to have some fragment of the original essence present within the flesh. You have to call like with like. It has to have the vibrational imprint of that which was lost.

Restoration of life

To return life through the pact of life with the Maiden of life, the Lady of Life, and the Mother of Life.

LAPAN INA RABUM
KADINGER ATE ME PETA BABKA
WUSSURU INA ZI
SA ANNU ANNA PAGRU
WUSSURU ANNU PAGRU
GULA SA BELET ERSETIM
KI'AM PARSUSA
PALASU DURANKI GULA SU IKKIBU
TARU SU TIIT GULA KANPA
TARU INA SHI GULA KANPA
TARU INA GISHTIL GULA KANPA
TARU INA ZIANA GULA KANPA
TARU INA SHI ANNA
DUGGAE GULA KANPA

LAPAN INA RABUM
KADINGER ATE ME PETA BABKA
WUSSURU INA ZI SA ANNU ANNA PAGRU
WUSSURU ANNU PAGRU NINTI SA BELET ERSETIM
KI'AM PARSUSA
PALASU DURANKI NINTI
SU IKKIBU
TARU SU TIIT NINTI KANPA
TARU INA SHI NINTI KANPA
TARU INA GISHTIL NINTI KANPA
TARU INA ZIANA NINTI KANPA
TARU SHI ANNA DUGGAE NINTI KANPA

LAPAN INA RABUM
KADINGER ATE ME PETA BABKA
WUSSURU INA ZI SA ANNU ANNA PAGRU
WUSSURU ANNU PAGRU TIAMAT SA BELET ERSETIM
KI'AM PARSUSA
PALASU DURANKI TIAMAT
SU IKKIBU
TARU SU TIIT TIAMAT KANPA
TARU INA SHI TIAMAT KANPA
TARU INA GISHTIL TIAMAT KANPA
TARU INA ZIANA TIAMAT KANPA
TARU SHI ANNA DUGGAE TIAMAT KANPA

Restoration of Life – English

That which is dead, now is not
The cells that are slowed, now are not
Restore the dead to life
Though nature must run her course
Return them to life
Be restored (x)
By the power of Aset
Be brought from the land of shadows
By the magic of Aset
Be returned the spark of life
By the power of the craft of life
The dead now rise before me!

Spirit Objects

A note must be said on the binding and otherwise containment of spirits that exist externally from the body. When you have the cycle of a thing, and it becomes interrupted by a personality from a spirit, or specifically non-living energy, when you would contain it, constrain it, bind it, imprison it would you want such a thing done to yourself?

This being said we will continue with the creation of objects bound to objects. When considering what you are going to be doing with spirits, demons, angels, gods and such there is a few points you should make note of to include in your ceremony of binding.

What metal corresponds to the God/Planet/Angel/Demonic/Djinn/Fae that I will be working with.

What stone corresponds to them.

What shapes are associated with the primary current from their point of origin.
ex: do they have any associations to the shapes of the tree of life, or the shells of the Qlipoth.

What properties are you going to be focusing on when using the object.

What smells, perfumes, herbs, and other correspondence align with the spirit you're going to be working with.

When you can answer the things on this list you will be able to begin crafting the ceremony of constraint. In the process of the Ring of the Red Queen, the conjuration takes the stand point that the object will be for another. When dealing with an object that will be kept for yourself. Your blood should be the catalyst for the ring/necklace/Stone you would be working with. The reason for this is that you are tying a force/spirit/god/angel to an object that you will be working with. You use the living catalyst of putting your all into containing the spirit. So long as your will holds, the spirit will be bound. If you use caste specific sources for your power, or you have worked on where you stand in relation to the tower of the art, then you will have no problem creating a personalized binding which will stand the test of time. It would then only be augmented by the use of further conjurations, blood, and material components.

Every conjuration should be specific, every spell worked at its own pace, and then used in conjunction with the associated accouterments that such works require. In some cases use of rings as well as charged blades are required. With cases like Crowley, he requires that a crown be worn when wielding the blade. So it becomes a very personalized quality that would cause the works to function.

Parts that should be observed in the creation of ceremonies/ritual to bind/contain spirits into objects are to include:
- Summons of power
- Conjuration of the vessel
- Summoning of the spirit
- Binding the spirit with some breakable means to the vessel
- Returning of the spirit into the vessel
- Sealing the Spirit into the vessel
- Naming the Spirit
- Containing the Spirit into the vessel

When these attributes are in there, any extra smells, stones or correspondences will only help to augment the conjurations. Keep these objects in boxes, wrapped in cloth. Treat them with respect and their power will never fail you. Cleanse the space after you have done the work. Doing such things to objects will only aid in your work if you remember that you did these things to them. You commanded them into your works, and not the other way around. They are to further your reach, not be the highest point of power you can attain. You should not have to rely on them more then is required for the object to maintain its use to you. Even if the spirit within falls dormant, its power should always be ready for use.

Summons of power

I am Eternal
I am Nameless
I am Dark
I am Light
I am Twilight
I am Death
I am Life
I am Spirit
I am Chaos
I am the devouring serpent
I am the blackened flame

Hear me
Draw back the veil
I have sworn the oath
These words find the lost
These words free the fallen

Hear me
Those outside of time
As I part space

Hear me
Blooded souls
Dragons of the first
Forgotten monsters of the void

Throw wide the gate
Through the darkness
Through the void

I open the way
As the way is made
I stand at the crux of the worlds

Gate of the Moon, Open!
Gate of Venus, Open!
Gate of Mars, Open!
Gate of Mercury, Open!
Gate of the Sun, Open!

Gate of Jupiter, Open!
Gate of Ouranos, Open!
Gate of Neptunus, Open!

The Water of tears,
      Parts before me!

The False Sea,
      Parts before me!

The Waters of Creation,
      Part before me!

The Waters of the Oceans,
      Part before me!

By my words open the gates
Open before me,
Open within me,
Open the way of the Gods.

By the oath of blood

By my pact with the source, Open!

Conjuration of the Vessel

To rend what heaven forged by blackest flame
My desire rise forth as I require
Take the light,
Take the dark,
Take the Shade
By my will and word and such death is made
I call by the blood and deed,
Come though forth
From the soul is born the demon seed

Come forth
O Monster
O Horror
O Nightmare shade

Demon rise forth present in truth before my eyes
No foulness, horror, deceiving lies
Bound to my will for eternity
Into the vessel I now command
Serve in all the ways that I require
I bind your essence by darkest fire!

Summons of the Spirit

From the bonds now rise to me
To the tasks which I will command of thee,
Return the this world
Yet bound eternally

Return of the Spirit

By eternal bonds,
Return what hence has gone astray
Return to the vessel
As I command,
Obey!

Sealing of the Spirit

I bind the spirit
By the seal of the Spirit
That which slumbers
Be bound.
That which is awake,
Be bound.
Unto the ending of time

I bind the deepest essence
To this place outside of time
Iin this space of its very own.

Naming the Spirit

I command by the blood fire,
I command by the Black fire
The light fire, and the violet flame
Burning eternally
That you are compelled by this fire
Divulge your name
As is commanded by this eternal flame

Conjuration of Containment

Into this vessel
I hold in hand
Removed from this land

By the black mirror
The waters of death
I bind this vessel
The soul to this flesh
By the blood within
Be bound by eternal chains
Sealed within this void.

Madness fear and death entwine,
Your soul I claim!
Your essence I contain!

Spirit Traps

Cards that bind the spirits, demons, forces unto the will. That can be useful for instant release, or written talisman charges. Use blood or the blood substitute as the anchor. These cards can be the medium that penetrate defenses and act as the gateways between planes, in places that are otherwise protected from such influences. If it cannot penetrate the bubble externally, then inside it can be thrust outwards. Use shade tendrils to bind the force into the void-space. Hand draw the sigil, or figure of the spirit using inks that are blooded. Use whatever design comes to you for containing the spirit.

Back   Front

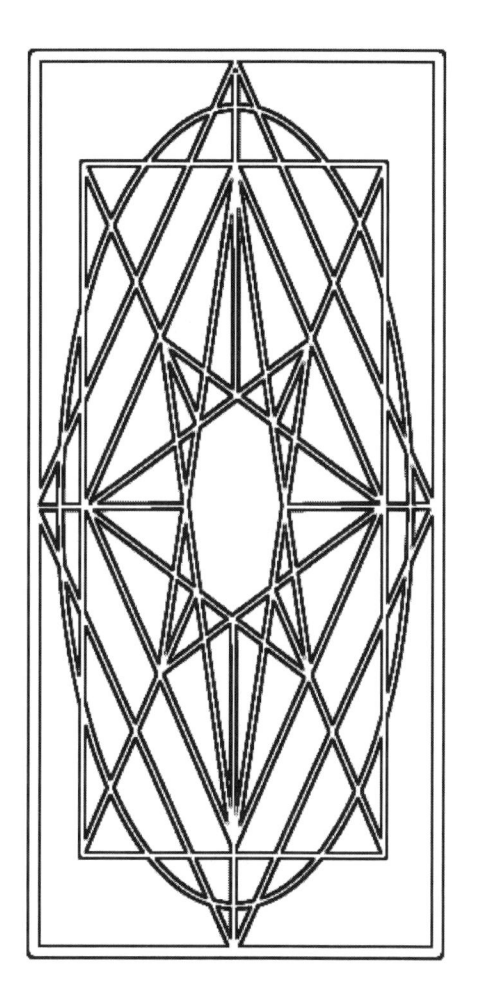

Removed from creation
Into this void
I command
Into this vessel
I hold at hand
Obey my command
Chains of the eternity
Now surrounded
Outside of time
Outside of space
Do my bidding
I bind thee
Bound eternal
To any desires
Obey the blood
Serve my will as I require

Conjuration To Bind Spirits

When you have a spirit bound before you, it becomes then necessary to break down the created walls of a psyche. Add the exorcism blend of herbs to the incense that has been used to summon the spirit, and give it body.

To rend what heaven forged
By blackest flame
My desire
Rise forth
As I require
Take the light
Take the dark
Take the shade
By will and word
Such death is made
I call by blood and deed
That forth from this soul
Is born the demon seed
Come forth, you monster
Horror and nightmare shade
Free from the bonds that heaven made
Demon rise come forth,
Present in truth before my eyes
No foulness,
No horror come, nor deceiving lies
Bound eternally into the vessel I hold at hand
Into this form I now command
Serve my will as I require
I bind your essence
By the blackest fire

Transference of Power

This work is to transfer one's essence into an intermediary to prevent the total passing from this earth upon cessation of life of the mage. Thus allowing a return of the magical prowess and spirit of the mage to be channeled through an object after passing to inhabit the vessel by means of a spoken charge.

Timing of this work is to be the new moon in October when the veil is at its thinnest. The very minute that the moon becomes new this work should end.

Set up is to consist of 5 white candles positioned with the single point in the earth. Then there is to be a green candle in the north inside the circle of 5, a purple in the east, a red in the south and blue in the west. There is to be an altar in the circle and on its center place a cauldron. On the left place a dagger, the object of transference, and a copy of the ritual if needed along with a white candle. Place on the left a small portion of each of the following herbs; mugwort, lavender, rosemary, and a single red rose. Fill then the cauldron with sea salt.

Upon successful preparation of the workspace, light the white candles with a charge to create a barrier so none may interfere on any plane.

> None shall see sight nor sound
> Of what is within my circle round

Then light the elemental candles by calling the elemental energies to be of aid.

> Elements now lend thy aid,
> For crossing the veil of time my spell is made

As this part is completed the cauldron is to have within its rim the white candle carved with the name of the mage in script in its center. To the northern edge the mugwort, the eastern rim the lavender, the southern edge the rosemary, and to the western rim the rose. Light the center white candle.

> Lit is this flame to draw ancient power
> To seal my working within this hour
> I spin and weave my magicks to begin a passing
> That only those of my line have a chance to be grasping
> Thus my will to transfer all that I am
> All that I am to grow to be
> Into this vessel to compound to three
> In rhyme this spell of passing spoken
> This the vessel is the token
> When the charge they then do read
> Kindle the fires from the seed
> Upon the day that I shall die
> My power loose and into them fly
> If truly of my chosen line
> Then the powers compound over each lifetime
> But if this work is stolen
> Day, night, or in between
> The charge be void, and no results be seen
> When in the light of the moon they then do read
> Kindle the fires of their seed.

With the dagger cut your dominant hand allowing blood to fall upon each of the herbs and the candle. Finally extinguishing the candle.

Blood to blood shall be how it is called from me
It shall compound life on life to form a trinity
As sealed by blood forever to be my legacy

Write then the charge of calling in a mixture of blood and ink upon the vessel of transference. Take then and bury all that is within the cauldron in a place of life. Its important to note that this is permanent and cannot be unmade unless the vessel is broken or stolen.

Rite of Restoration

When the soul/body itself has become damaged through attacks, or spells designed to fragment it, it becomes necessary to restore it to the point before it was damaged. Prepare a bath of salts, and herbs of purification. The incense should be of purification and rejuvenation. Bring forth the summons of power if this is to be a laying on of hands. Have the affected sit within the water, so that it covers the body, and the mantra repeated to the respective forces that must be called in sequence. This is the rite of cleansing the body which should be undertaken before any serious undertaking to make sure that the soul is working with the utmost efficacy possible.

> I call forth from the sacred mountains of the East
> Ao of the flowing waters
> Come forth and cleanse my soul
> I call forth Erh-Lang, lady of restoration,
> Restore to me my soul.
> I call forth Aset who restored Asar,
> That my power be restored unto me.

When energy currents are formed from just the conjuration of the above. Then it can be used on others. The array becomes an octagon array with a spherical core. With this array style the core then has supports in light blue that flow like a Mobius Strip cycling around the core of white. The conjuration is balanced by the earth currents from the Water that cleanses, and the generation.

Rite of Forgiveness

When one encounters bound spirits, or other such forces which have been sent to the lower pit, this work can be used to call up the freedom from their bondage. Use with whatever ritual set up is required for the containing of the spirit until such time as a purge can completely take effect.

I am priest of the fire
Stand tall before me,
I call forth
The corruptions within you
Be cleansed
By lightest fire of the Eternal Dawn
Engulfed
Purity beyond corruption
Service with surrender
Life that create Will
By this fire
By the will of the soul
Become engulfed
As this fire so burns
Be restored to your true form
Your soul be cleansed
Your bodies restored
The power of your origin returned
What was done unto you
Burned clean
The fall be burned clean from your soul
Birthed of this fire of the dawn
Fire which cleanses your sin
Be restored be forgiven
Be Returned
Elu
Elu
Elu

Conjuration of the Release

Greater form of purging and purification of the bound souls to the lower realms. Offers up the corruptions and the damnation as a sacrifice to earn it peace and freedom from the bondage which holds it.

On the altar of creation
I call upon the ancient Twelve
Be drawn forth before me
Those who have bound and punished.
I mark the sacrifice of the corruption.
Draw forth everything within
I command, present before me!

Part the veil in this place
Upon the Seal of restoration
From the bonds of this soul,
That I release from all damnation

Accept now this sacrifice,
Take the offering of this soul:
Life of corruption
Mind of corruption
Chaos within
Time of corruption
Spirit of corruption
Light of evil
Darkness of ignorance
Death of all corruption

That the sacrifice unto this charge:
That this soul be freed.
That through the sacrifice
That through the deed,
That through the abyss recalled
The source of will,
That through the creation of the this bond,
Be bound to the vessel of sacrifice,
I bind the corruption of this soul to the circle of sacrifice
The way is made open to the cleansed

Forces of the inner courts
The seven spheres in their places,
Through the eighth gate, and the open way;
This hour be the gate flung outwards
That this spirit shall be unbound,
Free from the chains of hell and the abyss

Conjuration of Service

Use with the array of the inner mind. This ceremony strips bare cognitive function. The purpose for this is to strip bare any rebellion or independence from raw forces conjured. To bind them at the level of the essence that their actions will be flawless in response to your commands.

This is an important step in the creation of the raw materia based animated spirit, as well as the commanding the already living will that people have. Normally ceremony can only push one to what would be the natural point where the will to survive is what overrides command and order.

In the case of those such spirits which are enthralled by this ceremony. Or have otherwise undergone this modification of their living spirit. It becomes the all pervasive current that floods their system allowing full control over the will. Either by having the will stripped bare of its cognitive abilities to only act as commanded. Or to disregard other personal limitations that such a spirit would have otherwise been bound by. Farther still to implant such limitations in otherwise willful hosts.

Accompanied with this ceremony should be the ceremony of marking. That way the spirit is totally opened, and stripped bare before your will. That you can bind it by the conjuration of direction as you will it. From this method one becomes the master of the will that is external to your own. Apply this in a way that becomes balanced by other works.

As with things of this nature. There are missing pieces. You must build the spirit up before such pieces can be used to cover over any holes.

By the pact of souls
Be brought to manifest before me
Spirit bound and be compelled
By the nature of my will to
Be rendered into service
By the bonds of the worlds flow
Bound before me hence
Thou shalt serve
By the source

I command you to my service
Your soul is bound unto this charge
Removed from creation
By the Seal upon which you stand
I make mark of this bond

By the blood of the living flesh
Which you will now inhabit
I bind you unto the seal for your redemption
Be freed upon the plane you are set,
Until such time as I call you forth
By this seal within your mind
You are now bound to respond

By the covenant you have given Oath.
So shall it be,
Unto the ending of all!

Conjure of the Light Fire

To be used for the removal of corrupt energies from souls/spirits that you come in contact with.

Hear now these words of magick
I weave forth the essence of creation
I am a member in the house Eternal Dawn
I call forth the fire within all the souls that live
I evoke it hence to restore what is bound by corruption
Be here by the words of the soul
As your essence is now set aflame
By the fire within all that live
By the fire which was at the beginning of all things
By this fire
Be restored
All corruption be burned away.

Union Rites

The Union Ceremony

It might not be clear when the traditions started, however for as far back as there have been people, there has been some way to keep them together, to raise their offspring. To be one with someone else. Two parts of the same collective whole that they build in order to have a miniature society, with pecking order in the home. It is this where we must find what is proper for our being, if we are to have a mate, and to have such a union. When there is the possibility of a life partnership, despite the average relationship now only lasting a few years. As people shift through divorce and back into marriage like a schizophrenic rubber ball, we must think carefully about those we would bond our souls and essences with. If we do not mean to do it for this one lifetime, then we should not do it at all.

That being said, many challenges face those who do such unions. The act of merging into one unit entirely, after the ceremony is achieved, is where the couple can survive or break apart. Yes the sex would be phenomenal, if the sex isn't good, why the fuck do you stay with someone who you can't make the hot sticky messes with on a regular basis. 3 times a year does not make for regular basis. Men masturbate generally once to three times a day if they can get away with it. Women, well that is an entirely different animal.

When we do union ceremonies, the trick to choosing one, is finding one that will balance out the aspects of the soul, implanting within both parties the particular current which needs to find its way to the forefront of the relationship to speed the blending process. We can examine the type of the union, by looking at the pieces which would go into it. Do you want there to be a blood ritual, to bond the soul, and body? Do you just want to bond the body? The elemental Ceremonies are the way to generally, as the focus on the aspects which will provide the deepest connections to the individuals, by exemplifying their inner natures.

Relying on instinct and intuition you will be able to find what path you are meant to walk. What it is that you are desiring to become. Through the methods above you can find that to be the case as well as your union ceremony, with another person, or married off to the archetypal/demonic force. The priest caste of any religious order in some way achieves this union. Through the vows of their order, their pact with their god. They wed the host archetype, and assume the mantle of power, with the vestments. They shift the power from the beseeching of god, to the assumption of the archetype, they are god. When they call upon god, they call upon the part of themselves which bound their psyche to the ideals and tenants set forth by their order, through which means that particular archetypal force is manifest.

From the resulting union ceremony one as though they become as god, become the hand of the god they seek. In the learning of this from an outside source, and observing it as the case, allows the developing Magus, to reach for the deeper nugget. Find the god-force they wish to serve, or use the source power of the singularity to become your god. Ideally you would become your own god, but it takes patience, time and learning the limitations of the influences we can manipulate. In such cases free will, overrides the desire of the god/mage. It in this manner is then the duty of the one who has undergone such union to be ready and waiting when those seek the aid thereof.

Demonic Union

Raw emotional fury, capacity for unknown states of being, and otherwise, unworldly relations in and out of the bedroom. A pact or oath that draws and binds the spirit, emotion, and the mind of the ones to be united. In this manner they become more effectively united, as it seeks out the extremes of all their traits. It forces them out of the psyche, in all aspects of their mental divisions, and their union with the dark Yin current.

Archetypal Union

In this work one connects themselves to their patron force. Whatever aspect they wish to spend their lives, or their current path upon the ideals of some archetypal force. In this case we are assuming deity. However the case may extend to any mythological god, demon, monster, angel, demon. Any of which can be drawn out of ones psyche, and married to the conscious mind. In this manner, the living host becomes the waking equivalent to the archetypal force. Of course, it is this union which would get many an adolescent Magus thrown into the nuthouse.

Soul Binding

This ceremony is our version of a wedding where the lines of fate are woven together. By calling up the personifications of the fates themselves to watch in attendance. The reason one would do this, would be to blend the aspects of each individual across two separate bodies. This being done would at the time of reincarnation, bring together into one soul in a single host. In undertaking this work, one accepts the division between the singular individual with the "dual" aspect to be taken.

If you were to do a ritual that will unite man with women in such a way that it will bring about the androgyny of the soul, in an attempt to create a divine union like unto the source of creation which was without gender. If a man was to unite with a man, you would be encompassing the bestial and primal aspects of both men, that they could become greater then the sum of their parts, and created a united masculine form. If done with a woman it would be the same, where the male counterpart would be a divine united masculine, they would be the divine feminine, as it is the collection of more than one part. Much like the gods have many faces so to would the soul have many faces. This sort of ritual undertaking is not really idea for any circumstance where one is not uniting with the feminine and masculine energies, even if it is two male bodies/female bodies. As future effects would be unknown at the time of reincarnation. The better way to apply this work would be to unite oneself to a current, to an archetypal force that the mage would become an extension of that critter.

In so doing would set himself/herself as part of the divine union of the god-form. In such a way one could consider this ritual as a way to create the divine union. The "Wife of Lucifer" or the "Husband of Lucifer" idea is present behind this sort of union rite. This would be a way to establish one's self upon the path of the living priest of the hierarchy. In as such that it matters not the unions "gender" preferences but so long as something like this is done, it will unite the soul to the god-force/demon/archetype. I would suggest that who undertakes this rite does so with the understanding that there isn't really a good way to divorce the current. As one takes it upon themselves, so to is it understood that if you are going to be uniting an archetypal current then the invocation on the vows must be done by a secondary party. This secondary party should word the vows with the mindset of "It is not I, but (Name of god)" not their own name.

The ring that shall be worn, shall be a symbol of the union ceremony and it should be customized as clearly as possible to the current which you will be bonding with. And worn during rites, ceremonies, and times where it is needed to reaffirm the union of the soul, with the current. The ring that shall be mentioned in this is to be of both blood, spirit, and metal/flesh that it will seal the union. It would be then appropriate for the two who unite as one, do so to unite in orgasm as well at the end of the rite. That they climax in union to forge the bond of matrimony with the archetypal force, in sexual gnosis. Thus sealing the body, spirit connection to the archetypal current.

The Ritual

The set up for this work is to consist of a vessel for containing fire, one black candle, one red candle, and one white candle. Position the urn on an altar; of course there should be no flammable surfaces nearby. There are to be 3 lots of 3, 4, 5 or 6 foot candle holders; they need to be all 3 the same size, placed one on each side and one in the center about 2 feet from the altar, just enough space where they won't melt from the heat of the flames. All candles are to remain unlit until later. Wood used for the fire should be oak. If possible insert a wooden symbol of the faith of slaves just to reinforce the energy of the dark fire.

The fire should be started before the ceremony, before people start showing up. When lighting the fire light it in the south. When lighting say something along the lines of:

> I am a member of the Ancient Order
> Priest of the eternal fire
> I call forth the dark fire,
> That fire from which everything came forth
> I summon its essence to bear witness to this union.

The candles should be placed red on the left, white in the center, and black on the right. These candles are to be made by the priest before the rite is to take place. In the wax blood from the couple is to be mixed in. In the wax of the white candle place a white rosebud; in the red candle a white rose in bloom; in the black dying white rose. Inscribe in the white candle the name of Clotho, on the red Lachesis, on the black Atropos. These candles are to be individually blessed by the priest on the morning of the rite. By this time in the rite the fire should already be burning as the people file into their seats. As the one of the couple stands by the altar the priest should then light the white candle, following with the red, and then the black.

At the lighting of the white candle say something similar to:

> Clotho,
> You who spin the threads of life,
> I humbly ask that you bear witness to this ceremony.

At the lighting of the red candle say something similar to:

> Lachesis,
> You who measure the threads of life,
> I humbly ask that you bear witness to this ceremony.

At the lighting of the black candle say something similar to:

> Atropos,
> You who sever the cord of life,
> I ask that you bear witness to this ceremony.

When you have done this, make a silent request to them by asking something similar to:

> As I am a member of the priesthood of the fire,
> I make this request to you ladies who dwell beyond the veil of time
> Please come forth and bear witness to this ceremony
> Please bring the threads of (X) and (Y)
> As they are to unite this day,

As soon as the couple is before you and the altar, have them face the fire; as you face them, your back should be to the fire. Say:

We are here today before the ancient forces
To bear witness to the joining of these souls till time is but a memory
We are here to join (X) and (Y)
To unite their threads for all eternity,
If any soul can give good reason why this should not take place,
Speak now or forever hold your tongue.
Then this rite shall begin.

Face the one on the right:

(X) do you take (Y)
In sickness and health, good or ill,
To be your partner until time stands still?

That person should say "I do", face then the person on the left:

(Y) do you take (X),
In sickness and health, good or ill,
To be your partner until time stands still?

That person should say "I do". Now should be a time for them to speak their vows. When that is done speak:

Now the rings are the symbol of this bond.

Face (X):

Repeat after me please:
(X) I place this ring upon your hand
Binding your soul with mine
Uniting my thread with yours
By this ring, I be wed
Until the resurrection of the dead.

Face (Y):

Repeat after me please;
(Y) I place this ring upon your hand
Binding your soul with mine
Uniting my thread with yours
By this ring, I be wed
Until the resurrection of the dead.

When this has been done, and the rings are on the fingers of each. Having said that, bring forth the red and gold silk ribbon, binding the hands that have the rings on them.

What is inside the vessel is the soul

These two separate beings here to be made whole
Two sides of the coin, braided in unity.
The rings the symbols of the bond,
May the fates that bear witness,
Acknowledge this bond,
Unite these souls for all eternity.
Let no force be able to cast asunder
What the fates have joined in union.
By the power vested in me
I now pronounce you life partners.
You may kiss your spouse.

The two should kiss, and blow out the candle with a prayer to the fates, or something similar:

Thank you for your attendance,
Clotho, Lachesis, Atropos,
You who have come from your realm beyond the veil
Please bind these two together.

Let the fire burn itself out, and with the ash, along with the candles give them to the couple, after the ceremony. In a velvet bag, with their names sewn in silver thread, to be given to the couple, along with the ashes in a white silk bag.

Blessing for the Candles of the Fates

The wax is to be poured on the new moon, with the flower and the blood added. The blessing for the candles:

As priest of the eternal fire,
I give this blessing for the union of
(X) and (Y)
Come forth Ladies of the greatest mysteries
When these your symbols subsumed in flame
To bear witness to a union of souls
Please shift your attention to this union of souls
Please bind together their threads
Link them after their vows have been spoken.

Elemental Union Ceremonies

The union of the elemental forces within the body of another living person, or to unite an elemental, djinn, angelic, demonic, or divine archetypal force does so in a way that the elemental attributes of the body are brought to the surface.

Working with these ceremonies in a way that unites a man and woman, man and man, and woman and woman, will do so in a way that ties their elemental natures together. To be used in an archetypal setting, the invocation of the spirit must remain so in such a way that it is not the human who is doing the union, but the invoked force of the element which is willingly bound to their consort.

These rites should culminate in the same orgasmic climax in as close to the elemental setting as possible where safety is concerned.

Of the Air:

It can unite through any boundary the passions. That it becomes so enraptured with the other person so as to penetrate deeply into the psyche of the body. Possible codependency can result. This can also be a short relationship as the harder the wind blows, there is generally less it can use to sustain itself. Settling into the calm of the day, and being able to move with the gales, and tempests that life throws at us. The air is in all things, and is one of the agents of life.

Of the Water:

All penetrating, all seeping into every aspect of the psyche, to blend and unite the soul. It is a nice simple way to become all muddied together, where one part is indistinguishable then the next, in its a way where the two can meld together, and flow through life as one. Possibility of unstable natures can go and drown out the other person when the water rises.

Of the Earth:

Balances the stable currents of their bodies, their souls and their mind. Will help in achieving stability of the home. Possible outcomes if put out of balance will be that there will be an unhappy union because there is a lack of passion, as the relationship settles and it becomes cold, and routine.

Of the Fire:

Ignites the passions of the souls, like the fires do. Keeps their passions at the fore front and tends to inspire great acts of love. This process is excellent for those who would cause their physical love, to be the keynote of their relationship. This can turn abusive if ones fire burns away to strong, or if their passions become directed towards another.

These ceremonies can also be used in such a way to balance out the negative aspects of the individuals own elemental affinity, to create a more rounded grouping of peoples, and energies. There by creating a forced balance through an external union, other then through personal ascension/connection with the elemental currents.

Union of the Air

It can unite through any boundary the passions. That it becomes so enraptured with the other person so as to penetrate deeply into the psyche of the body. Possible codependency can result. This can also be a short relationship as the harder the wind blows, there is generally less it can use to sustain itself. Settling into the calm of the day, and being able to move with the gales, and tempests that life throws at us.

There should be an altar set with a white cloth with a purple runner. There should be a purple candle that has been mixed with the blood of both the participants. There should be a dish suspended over the candle flame which has oils in it of love and union. There should be a silver, purple, and blue rope tied to the base of the candle. Priest makes the preliminary evocation over the space before the guests arrive:

>I am a member of the order of Night,
>Priest of the eternal fire,
>This space now purified
>By the elemental forces which
>Shall be called to forge this union.

When the ceremony is to begin and the parties of the couple are seated. The priest speaks lighting the candle:

>Let the air be filled with the spirit of the air,
>The breath of life
>Let this breath of life,
>Be breathed into the bond
>From the fire of their love,
>That as this flame burns
>So too does every breath
>Fuel the love which they share
>May the spirits of the Air
>Be evoked to bear witness to this rite,
>To bond this pair in eternal union,
>By the breath of life for their lives.
>As the air cuts through,
>As the spirit of change becomes this element
>Let them be able to change with each other,
>To break through any obstacle
>Which would tear them asunder.
>Be now evoked forth spirit of the Air,
>To witness the bond of (X) and (Y)

When said, there should be a pause of 13 heart beats. The priest shall continue:

>Now, (X) face (Y) and repeat:
>(Y)
>As I breathe my breath
>As the thought is made word,
>By the breath of life
>So do I vow,

I make this bond of everything that is my life
I bond to you,
I make this vow for you, that what is mine becomes ours
That we may grow together,
Overcoming all that would have us torn asunder
By my breath, By these words,
By my blood and by the air itself
I bond to you eternally

Now, (Y) face (X) and repeat:

(X)
As I breath my breath
As the thought is made word,
By the breath of life
So do I vow,
I make this bond of everything that is my life
I bond to you,
I make this vow for you, that what is mine becomes ours
That we may grow together,
Overcoming all that would have us torn asunder
By my breath, By these words,
By my blood and by the air itself
I bond to you eternally
Now for the rings

(X) while putting the ring on the finger of your mate please repeat:

(Y)
I do pledge to thee, on my three vital breaths
I give to you my heart
I give to you my mind
I give to you my vital spirit
That by this symbol of the bond,
I give you my life
That we may be joined eternally in union.

(Y) while putting the ring on the finger of your mate please repeat:

(X)
I do pledge to thee, on my three vital breaths
I give to you my heart
I give to you my mind
I give to you my vital spirit
That by this symbol of the bond,
I give you my life
That we may be joined eternally in union.

Then they should join hands, and the priest ties a rope from their wrists and places his hands over the knot. The priest should then lay his hand on top of the knot, and make the following invocation with his other hand over the fire of the candle in the dish.

By the Vital breaths within your bodies,
By the union of your souls
To the inner and outer worlds
Let the Air which bares witness to this bond,
Acknowledge it.
May the spirit of the air,
Spirit of change, and Spirit of adaptation,
Ensure your bond
Let no god nor man, nor force in creation
Tear asunder what is bound here this day
By the bond of the air,
That which gives the breath of life
May life itself be breathed into your lives
As you begin one anew
Forth from this day, may it be that you are one,
That you breath as one, and grow as one

The priest then motions them to kiss. When they have, the priest extinguishes the candle with this charge:

By the air which animated your bodies,
By the bond your breath as one
Be now bonded by your love,
Bonded by the air
With all the elements
Let new life come to you,
To always fill your lives,
That you are both born
Be given new life on this day,
The life where the two becomes one
Where the one becomes through becoming,
Unified with itself, both matter and spirit
It is so done,
The Spirit of Air shall acknowledge this bond.

After the extinguishing of the candle, the knot should be undone. The rope should be tied to a tree which the couple plants. The candle to be lit on the anniversary.

The Union of the Water

All penetrating, all seeping into every aspect of the psyche, to blend and unite the soul. It is a nice simple way to become all muddied together, where one part is indistinguishable then the next, in its a way where the two can meld together, and flow through life as one. Possibility of unstable natures can go and drown out the other person when the water rises.

The altar should be set with a white cloth, and a blue runner. There should be a bowl of water which has been purified in accordance with the rites of sanctification for the element of water. The candle should be blue, and mixed with the blood of each participant. There should be a blue, gold, and silver cord braided and tied around the base of the candle where it meets with the water.

Priest makes the preliminary evocation over the space before the guests arrive:

> I am a member of the order of Night,
> Priest of the eternal fire, This space now purified
> By the elemental forces which
> Shall be called to forge this union.

When the ceremony is to begin and the parties of the couple are seated. The priest speaks, lighting the candle:

> As the child to the mother,
> So the river to the sea
> As the blood is to water,
>
> So shall the spirit of the waters be called forth
> The eternal Tao, the water of life, That which flows over and through
> Every obstacle which comes against it
> We call forth the spirit of the primal water
> Bear witness unto this rite
> That the bond between (X) and (Y)
> Always flows eternally in balance
> As the river carves the valleys,
> As the river shapes the land So may the spirit of creation
> Be brought forth in this union,
> May the lives of these two who seek this union,
> Be brought together and changed
> As they are made one,
> Should have just reason this ceremony
> Not take place, speak now or be silenced

When said, there should be a pause of 13 heart beats. The priest shall continue:
(X) face (Y) and repeat:

> (Y)
> As my blood is the water, and thus my life
> I give of it to you
> I bond by the eternal way,
> That we come together as one
> That we are bound by bonding become as one

My life yours, my heart yours, my blood yours
I make this bond by the vow of living blood
To you (Y)

(Y) face (X) and repeat:

(X)
As my blood is the water, and thus my life
I give of it to you
I bond by the eternal way,
That we come together as one
That we are bound by bonding become as one
My life yours, my heart yours, my blood yours
I make this bond by the vow of living blood
To you (X)

Now for the rings, (X) while putting the ring on the finger of your mate please repeat:

(Y)
I give of my living blood, This sign of our bond,
That our union is made eternal
By the tides of this and all worlds
That we may flow together in balance,
United through all obstacles which we may face,
That by the living waters within us, We are so bound.

(Y) while putting the ring on the finger of your mate please repeat:

(X)
I give of my living blood, This sign of our bond,
That our union is made eternal
By the tides of this and all worlds
That we may flow together in balance,
United through all obstacles which we may face,
That by the living waters within us, We are so bound.

Then they should join hands, and the priest ties a rope from their wrists and places his hands over the knot. The priest should then lay his hand on top of the knot, and make the following invocation with his other hand over the fire of the candle in the dish.

By the spirit of the living water
Acknowledge this bond as it exists before you
Forged in blood, and life, To exist eternally for life
As the river to the sea,
Spirit of the Primal waters bind this to be.
Let no human or god annul
What by the elements have been ordained
By the earth, by the water, By the fire and the air.
Let it by the elements of creation
Ensure the blessings upon (X) and (Y)
By their kiss may it seal the bond of their souls.

The priest then motions them to kiss. When they have, the priest extinguishes the candle with this charge:

> By the water which gives life to your bodies
> By the crimson current which flows
> Through the rivers of your life
> May you flow together on the river of life
> Let the water birth for you a new body,
> Which shall bind you in your union
> Let this confirm your vow, your bond
> By the body of your love,
> May your currents always flow together in the eternal balance.

After the extinguishing of the candle, the knot should be undone. The rope should be given to the waters. The candle should be kept and lit on the anniversary of their wedding.

Union of the Earth

Balances the stable currents of their bodies, their souls and their mind. Will help in achieving stability of the home. Possible outcomes if put out of balance will be that there will be an unhappy union because there is a lack of passion, as the relationship settles and it becomes cold, and routine.

The Altar should be set with a white or green cloth. There should be a green candle which has been already mixed with blood of both participants. There should be a bowl of earth in which the candle has been placed. The soil should be mixed with blood of the couple as well. This is done to ensure the balanced union between both the receptive and active parties. There should be a gold, black, and green rope tied to the base of the candle, where the candle meets the earth.

Priest makes the preliminary evocation over the space before the guests arrive:

> I am a member of the order of Night,
> Priest of the eternal fire, This space now purified
> By the elemental forces which
> Shall be called to forge this union.

When the ceremony is to begin and the parties of the couple are seated. The priest speaks:

> I call upon the eternal fires to enter forth
> This medium of fire,
> I call upon the eternal flow
> The ancient earth to bare witness to this rite.
> Let this ancient force
> Be drawn forth in the blood,
> Spirit of those who will join in union.
> By this medium before us,
> By the blood of (X) and (Y)
> We call forth the spirit of the Earth.
> These souls have sought to solidify this bond,
> As the tree grows,
> So too shall their relationship
> By the eternal cycles of the trees,
> From seed, to sapling,
> To the Elder oak to acorn, thus birthed again,
> Let the love of these (X) and (Y)
> Remain through the periods of trials,
> Just as in joy
> As these two have sought their union,
> Let any speak now that shall
> Have them not joined,
> To provide such cause that this ceremony shall be interrupted.

When said, there should be a pause of 13 heart beats. The priest shall continue:

> Now, (X) face (Y) and repeat:
> (Y)
> What is bound in flesh, and bone

I give to you as my own
By the earthy form which bonds soul to bone
By the bond of the heaven to the earth, I now bond to you my, heaven, my earth.
Let this bond be eternal like the earth
As it will endure all and find away
Forth from this moment, on this day.

Now (Y) face (X) and repeat:

(X)
What is bound in flesh, and bone
I give to you as my own
By the earthy form which bonds soul to bone
By the bond of the heaven to the earth,
I now bond to you my, heaven, my earth.
Let this bond be eternal like the earth
As it will endure all and find away
Forth from this moment, on this day.
Now for the rings:

(X) while putting the ring on the finger of your mate please repeat:

(Y)
I bond with you as the earth bonds to the sky
As the water sits upon the earth,
All things that endure are of the earth
As the surfaces of the world may change,
Things come and go
The earth endures
I give this ring, to make this bond,
My vow that we will endure
That you are my earth,
You are my heaven
We shall be eternally
I give this to you,
As my symbol of this bond,
Through blood,
Through earth I choose you as my mate.

(Y) while putting the ring on the finger of your mate please repeat:

(X)
I bond with you as the earth bonds to the sky
As the water sits upon the earth,
All things that endure are of the earth
As the surfaces of the world may change,
Things come and go
The earth endures
I give this ring, to make this bond,
My vow that we will endure
That you are my earth,

You are my heaven
We shall be eternally
I give this to you,
As my symbol of this bond,
Through blood,
Through earth I choose you as my mate.

They should join hands, and the priest ties a rope from their wrists and places his hands over the knot. The priest should then lay his hand on top of the knot, and make the following invocation with his other hand over the fire of the candle in the dish.

I call forth the spirit of the earth,
Essence of nature
Be brought forth through this bond
Primal current of the earth itself, bare witness
Acknowledge this bond
Let no human or god annul
What by the elements have been ordained
By the earth, by the water, By the fire and the air.
By the elements of creation
Ensure the blessings upon (X) and (Y)
By their kiss may it seal the bond of their souls.

The priest then motions them to kiss. When they have, the priest extinguishes the candle with this charge:

Though this earthy fire may
Be out in the physical,
May its spirit burn in your spirits as one.
That by your bond to each other you
Become the earth
The foundation of the life
You two shall build together. Let this confirm your union.

After the extinguishing of the candle, the knot should be undone. The rope should be buried under a tree which the couple plants. The candle should be kept and lit on the anniversary of their wedding.

Union of Fire

Ignites the passions of the souls, like the fires do. Keeps their passions at the forefront and tends to inspire great acts of love. This process is excellent for those who would cause their physical love to be the keynote of their relationship. This can turn abusive if ones fire burns away to strong, or if their passions become directed towards another.

The altar should be set with a white cloth, and red runner. There should be a red candle mixed with the blood of each of the participants. at its base should be a braided cord of red, gold, and black rope. There should be a fire burning in a dish on the altar which is made of rosewood. Priest makes the preliminary evocation over the space before the guests arrive:

> I am a member of the order of Night,
> Priest of the eternal fire, This space now purified
> By the elemental forces which
> Shall be called to forge this union.

When the ceremony is to begin and the parties of the couple are seated. The priest speaks:

> We call forth the primal fire
> Bear witness to this ceremony
> As in the days of old,
> When fire was burning to raise
> The power of spirit the heavens
> It is that ancient spirit which is called forth
> Bear witness to this rite of union
> Be called forth, spirit of the flame,
> Acknowledge this union
> That the spirit of the these individuals
> Burn as a single fire, a twin fire
> Each burning within the other,
> Sharing the light of their love.
> Be evoked spirit, that two shall become one
> That one spirit shall
> Be birthed from this ceremony
> Be here represented, ancient luminary,
> Bond these two endure eternally
> Burn now to witness the bond of the union
> Between (X) and (Y) Be brought together
> Changed as they are made one,
> Their lights to burn in each others souls Together they are whole.
> If any should have just reason this ceremony
> Should not take place, speak now or be silenced

When said, there should be a pause of 13 heart beats. The priest shall continue:

> Now, (X) face (Y) and repeat:

> (Y)
> My heart is one, and so my desire

For you alone burns my fire
I give you my spark, my will in life
That you will hold it
In peace and through strife Let us by this fire be bound
You, (Y) are my eternal light.

Now, (Y) face (X) and repeat:

(X)
My heart is one, and so my desire
For you alone burns my fire
I give you my spark, my will in life
That you will hold it
In peace and through strife Let us by this fire be bound
You, (X) are my eternal light.
Now for the rings

(X) while putting the ring on the finger of your mate please repeat:

(Y)
You are my light, you are my spirit
I give to you the symbol of my bond
That we are bound eternally
By the fire of our spirit
I becomes we, and we become one
By this eternal band, we bond eternally

(Y) while putting the ring on the finger of your mate please repeat:

(X)
You are my light, you are my spirit
I give to you the symbol of my bond
That we are bound eternally
By the fire of our spirit
I becomes we, and we become one
By this eternal band, we bond eternally

The they should join hands, and the priest ties a rope from their wrists and places his hands over the knot. The priest should then lay his hand on top of the knot, and make the following invocation with his other hand over the fire of the candle in the dish.

Burn now the ancient fires,
Within the hearts and minds of those before us
Bind now, primal element,
Souls of those who seek union
Burn within each the others fire,
Each to fuel their mates desire This bond now formed, eternal
Binding round what none can cast forth
Let no force of god, nor man, nor spirit hence
Annul what by you has been ordained
Acknowledge this bond,

Between the souls Let each be whole from this bond of union

    The priest then motions them to kiss. When they have, the priest extinguishes the candle with this charge:

> By the ancient fires burning now
> Love eternal, and growth together
> This union always allow
> Let these souls become entwined,
> As the fire the wood does bind
> By banded ring, and vows of will
> Through blood, and spirit
> This fire becomes your spirit
> The twin to each others light
> That you will remain together,
> Through even your darkest night
> Let now your spirits burn eternally
> As the Fire holds you in this bond.

After the extinguishing of the candle, the knot should be undone. The rope should be given to the fires, with the ashes scattered. The candle should be kept and lit on the anniversary of their wedding.

Unions by Caste

Perspective aside, when one bonds with a time period, or state of being, such as the light, dark and shadowy forces of the world. They are doing so with the attempt to embrace the union of the two natures. This will also balance out missing perspectives in one's own body as it shares the links between bodies.

Of the light:

Erodes any blockages from the soul, mind and body, fills them with an unerring sense of peace and union with their partner. This is the most common form of union, as it is the one employed by the churches. It strips bare any influence which would break apart the union, and also removes aspects of the selves which would cause destabilization of the union. However the part of the individuals that are broken and stripped away, is what causes the split.

Of the Shadow:

Balances the light and dark attributes in the minds, bodies and souls. That they can find peace and union through all perspectives. Downside is they will not have instilled within them the link to any extreme changes in the passions which the elementals can provide, however it will be a balanced union.

Of the Dark:

Brings out the subconscious of the individuals. If they fall more into play with their secrets, their fetishes. The dark union could bring these to manifestation, and root them deeply into the nature of the relationship. It is in this union that we have the developing dominance, and submission, and other extreme possibility for those who would dare. This is what the person becomes, their fetish, their inner desire, within the confines of the relations.

If you were to use this to summon up the spirits, elementals, god-forces of these perspectives then do so with the understanding that it will bring out your inner nature in reference to the perspectives. Dark becomes emotional, Light becomes logical, shadowy becomes the combination of the two. When you summon up your gnostic trance you are able to do things with these unions that are more then a legal ceremony of union between a male and female. And it will like the other ones, increase that aspect of your connection to the singular collective.

Light Union

The altar is to be set with a white cloth, and gold runner. The cord is to be silver. The candle is to be mixed with the blood of the participants. There should be a mirror on which the candle sits. The cord should be tied at the base of the candle on the mirror.

Priest makes the preliminary evocation over the space before the guests arrive:

> I am a member of the order of Night,
> Priest of the Light Eternal fire,
> This space now purified
> By the Light forces which
> Shall be called to forge this union.

When the ceremony is to begin and the parties of the couple are seated. The priest speaks:

> I call forth the essence of the Light,
> The reflected forces in creation
> Acknowledge this union
> That which shines within in the souls
> Of those present,
> Be called forth essence of light,
> Current which balances out our souls
> Be it called forth to balance out these souls
> That through their union they are balanced
> By their active capacity to each other
> Wherein they are bound
> Through even the darkest night of their lives,
> Through the brightest day,
> Active to encourage the growth of their spirits.
> Let no force cast asunder
> What is now, brought together
> In this union of (X) and (Y)
> Any who should have just reason
> why these two shall not
> Become joined, speak or be silent

When said, there should be a pause of 13 heart beats. The priest shall continue:

> Now, (X) face (Y) and repeat:
> (Y)
> My lightest self, which I embody
> I give to you all of me,
> That which is in light within my heart,
> I give to you to make your own
> I bond to you that we are one,
> To face each others strengths
> Give strength unto our union
> This bond to you I vow in blood
> That we shall be
> Together through all obstacles

Now, (Y) face (X) and repeat:
(X)
My lightest self, which I embody
I give to you all of me,
That which is in light within my heart,
I give to you to make your own I bond to you that we are one,
To face each others strengths
Give strength unto our union
This bond to you I vow in blood
That we shall be
Together through all obstacles

Now for the rings (X) while putting the ring on the finger of your mate please repeat:

(Y)
I that bind with eternal band
Be bound unto you
Through the virtues of the planets
In their places
I vow to be yours in body,
I vow to be yours in mind,
I vow to be yours in spirit,
I vow to be yours in essence
That my being shall be yours
Eternally
Beyond my passing forth from flesh
I am yours, we are one

(Y) while putting the ring on the finger of your mate please repeat:
(X)
I that bind with eternal band
Be bound unto you
Through the virtues of the planets
In their places
I vow to be yours in body,
I vow to be yours in mind,
I vow to be yours in spirit,
I vow to be yours in essence
That my being shall be yours
Eternally
Beyond my passing forth from flesh
I am yours, we are one

The they should join hands, and the priest ties a rope from their wrists and places his hands over the knot. The priest should then lay his hand on top of the knot, and make the following invocation with his other hand over the fire of the candle in the dish.

By the light of the soul, bind these two
Let them be consumed by their own natures,
With strength together

May balance be brought
Unto these two become as one
By the dawn path,
The spiral of the labyrinth of souls
Be bound now by these forces to one
By their oath of word and blood,
As in the days of old,
Obey the ancient covenant and come forth
Spirit of the primal light, Acknowledge this bond

The priest then motions them to kiss. When they have, the priest extinguishes the candle with this charge:

By the ancient fires burning now
By the blood forth in brightest light
By the upward spirals of the souls labyrinth
These two shall be as one.
(X) bound to the light of (Y)
As (Y) is bound to the light of (X)
These two are made whole by their union,
And thus united eternally

After the extinguishing of the candle, the knot should be undone. The rope should be given to the fires, with the ashes scattered. The candle should be kept and lit on the anniversary of their wedding.

Shadow Union

The altar is to be set with a white cloth, and gold runner. The cord is to be silver. The candle is to be mixed with the blood of the participants. There should be a mirror on which the skull anointed in blood which supports the candle sits. The cord should be tied at the base of the candle on the mirror, and braided with the black cord out of the mouth of the skull.

Priest makes the preliminary evocation over the space before the guests arrive:

I am a member of the order of Night,
Priest of the Spark of Creation,
This space now purified
By the Creative forces which
Shall be called to forge this union.

When the ceremony is to begin and the parties of the couple are seated. The priest speaks:

I call forth the essence of the twilight,
The reflected forces in creation
Be called forth to acknowledge this union
That which shines within in the souls
Of those present,
Be called forth essence of light and darkness,
Twilight current which balances out souls Be it called forth to balance out the souls
Of those present in this union
That through their union they are balanced
By their active capacity to each other Wherein they are bound by this union\
Through even the darkest night of their lives,
Through the brightest day,
Balanced to encourage Their growth of spirits.
Let no force cast asunder
What is now brought together
In this union of (X) and (Y)
Any who should have just reason why these two
Shall not be joined, speak or be silent

When said, there should be a pause of 13 heart beats. The priest shall continue:

Now, (X) face (Y) and repeat:
(Y)
My shadow self, which is my nature
I give to you all of me,
That which is in shadow in my soul,
That which is the shadow in my heart,
I give to you to make your own
I bond to you that we are one,
To face each others weakness
Give strength unto our union
This bond to you I vow in blood
That we shall be together through all obstacles

Now, (Y) face (X) and repeat:
(X)
My shadow self, which is my nature
I give to you all of me,
That which is in shadow in my soul,
That which is the shadow in my heart,
I give to you to make your own I bond to you that we are one, To face each others weakness
Give strength unto our union
This bond to you I vow in blood
That we shall be together through all obstacles

Now for the rings (X) while putting the ring on the finger of your mate please repeat:
(Y)
I that bind with eternal band
Be bound unto yours
Through the virtues of the planets
In their places
I vow to be yours in body,
I vow to be yours in mind,
I vow to be yours in spirit,
I vow to be yours in essence
That my being shall be yours
Eternally
Beyond my passing forth from flesh
I am yours, we are one

(Y) while putting the ring on the finger of your mate please repeat:

(X)
I that bind with eternal band
Be bound unto yours
Through the virtues of the planets
In their places
I vow to be yours in body,
I vow to be yours in mind,
I vow to be yours in spirit,
I vow to be yours in essence
That my being shall be yours
Eternally
Beyond my passing forth from flesh
I am yours, we are one

The they should join hands, and the priest ties a rope from their wrists and places his hands over the knot. The priest should then lay his hand on top of the knot, and make the following invocation with his other hand over the fire of the candle in the dish.

By the twilight of the soul, bind these two
Let them be consumed by their own natures,
Find strength together
May balance be brought forth unto these two
Become as one

By the twilight path,
The spiral of the labyrinth of souls
Be bound now by these forces to one
By their oath of word and blood,
As in the days of old,
Obey the ancient covenant and come forth
Spirit of the primal darkness,
Acknowledge this bond.

The priest then motions them to kiss. When they have, the priest extinguishes the candle with this charge:

By the ancient fires burning now
By the blood forth in brightest light
By the dual spirals of the souls labyrinth
These two shall be as one.
(X) bound to the light of (Y)
As (Y) is bound to the light of (X)
These two are made whole by their union,
And thus united eternally.

After the extinguishing of the candle, the knot should be undone. The rope should be given to the fires, with the ashes scattered. The candle should be kept and lit on the anniversary of their wedding.

Dark Union

The Altar should be set with a black cloth, and a red runner. There should be a red candle mixed with the blood of the participants. There should be a skull on the altar which has been anointed with blood from the participants and supporting the candle. There should be a black cord coming out of the mouth of the skull. Priest makes the preliminary evocation over the space before the guests arrive:

> I am a member of the order of Night,
> Priest of the Dark Eternal fire,
> This space now purified By the dark forces which
> shall be called to forge this union.

When the ceremony is to begin and the parties of the couple are seated. The priest speaks:

> I call forth the essence of the Night,
> That which is beyond the veil,
> Beyond the abyss
> Be called forth essence of darkness,
> That passive current
>
> Which balances out our souls
> Be it called forth to balance
> These souls of those present in this union
> That through their union they are balanced
> By their receptive capacity to each other
> Wherein they are bound by this union
> Through even the darkest night of their lives,
> Through the brightest day,
> Let them be receptive
> Encourage the growth of their spirits.
> Let no force cast asunder
> What is now brought together
> In this union of (X) and (Y)
> Any who should have just reason
> Why these two shall not be joined,
> Speak or be silent

When said, there should be a pause of 13 heart beats. The priest shall continue:

> Now, (X) face (Y) and repeat:
> (Y)
> My darkest self, which I fear to show
> I give to you all of me,
> That which is in shadows in my heart,
> I give to you to make your own I bond to you that we are one,
> To face each others fears and Give strength in the darkness
> To our union
> This bond to you I vow in blood
> That we shall be together
> Through all obstacles

Now, (Y) face (X) and repeat:

(X)
My darkest self, which I fear to show
I give to you all of me,
That which is in shadows in my heart,
I give to you to make your own I bond to you that we are one,
To face each others fears
Give strength in the darkness
To our union
This bond to you I vow in blood. This bond to you I vow in blood
That we shall be together
Through all obstacles
Now for the rings

(X) while putting the ring on the finger of your mate please repeat:

(Y)
I bind myself to you,
I bond your soul to mine,
that we become one
As we can face each others fears
We will become strong
As we receive that which is given
From each other, We will be united
As we take of each others strength,
We will be one
In the darkness of our inner natures
I bind with you
(Y)

(Y) while putting the ring on the finger of your mate please repeat:

(X)
I bind myself to you,
I bond your soul to mine,
that we become one
As we can face each others fears
We will become strong
As we receive that which is given
From each other, We will be united
As we take of each others strength,
We will be one
In the darkness of our inner natures
I bind with you
(X)

The they should join hands, and the priest ties a rope from their wrists and places his hands over the knot. The priest should then lay his hand on top of the knot, and make the following invocation with his other hand over the fire of the candle in the dish.

By the darkness of the soul,
Bind these two
Let them be consumed by their own natures,
To find strength together
May balance be brought forth unto these two
Become as one
By the downward path,
The spiral of the labyrinth of souls
Be bound now by these forces to one
By their oath of word and blood,

As in the days of old,
Obey the ancient covenant and come forth
Spirit of the primal darkness,
Acknowledge this bond

The priest then motions them to kiss. When they have, the priest extinguishes the candle with this charge:

By the ancient fires burning now
By the blood forth in darkness
By the downward spirals of the souls labyrinth
These two shall be as one.
(X) bound to the darkness of (Y)
As (Y) is bound to the darkness of (X)
These two are made whole by their union,
And thus united eternally

The knot should be undone. The rope should be given to the fires, with the ashes scattered. The candle kept.

Funerary Rites

The Funerary Works

All souls pass through the world into the next this is a given. There are those souls who need a hand to learn the lessons, or through which means their life will provide a balance and a neutrality. It is in this manner that we turn our focus from the living world of the spirit to the transitional mediums that we can put the soul to rest. In the living art we have our spirit which is the slate on which we can focus and mold. In the ways that we have our waking mind divide from our sleeping mind. So we give them peace, and we give them rest. In the ways that we are able, based on the rites that follow, use which one you feel, brings out the most effective form of the work.

We judge ourselves on deeds accomplished, works done, and the things for which we have left undone. Based upon these views, we will decide where we go when we pass from this world to the next. It is ours to use what funerary arrangements we can plan for, in order to bring about the ease of transition into the soul into the other-world. Now when the body leaves its life, the spirit is generally released immediately. So the funerary works are generally more for those who are left behind who have not left the world, not those who did the leaving.

When looking back upon the life and times of those souls whose works bring about emotional balance for those who were left behind. You need to take time, and think about the associations of the lives of the ones you loved, who you were friends with, what is the feedback you get from those about their lives in relation to the elemental/perspective associations that they bring to the foreground. If you are going to be doing services for someone you are not familiar with, you should prompt the family members into asking questions. What do they embody, what was their star signs were perhaps, what associations did they lend themselves to in life? In this manner you can assist the family in their coping with the loss. As you will be calling upon the celestial/elemental force to bring peace into their lives as well.

There are then some ceremonies such as the opening of the way, and the blank slate ceremony that is meant to temporarily recall the spirit, in order to do what they could not other wise achieve in life. Particularly if they were horrid persons, then the Tabula Rasa could be used in purging their soul of the horrors they committed, if you were of the mind to do such a thing. Even thought the Conjuration of the Fall, is an exorcism of sorts. It can be used as a funerary work as well, to ensure that there be a definite prison for the spirit.

Passing of the Air

The altar shall be set with a black cloth, and a purple runner. There should be a purple candle beneath an oil brazier, a length of silver cord. Oils shall be burned in the brazer for those of passing and calming the spirit. There shall also be a picture of the departed, as well as trinkets which the departed was fond of in life.

When the ceremony is to begin, the officiant lights the candle with the invocation:

Awaken spirit of the air, Receive the soul of (X)
That they may find rest and peace within
The embrace of the quiet skies
Guide their spirit from the place of the lost,
Unto a place of rest.
Spirit of the Air,
Put to rest this soul who we bring before you
Let them lay their head
In the clouds that watch over us,
May their spirit soar amongst the ancients
In the heights of the heavens between worlds

The priest takes up the rope and makes the following charge:

This was the cord of the life of (X)
It has been entwined
With every soul who has come
To know (X) for who they were Let those who have known (X)
As they were in life
Come not to mourn the loss
Of their fallen friend
Instead, let them remember
How this life touched theirs
How they have become better for the knowing,
Changed for the knowing, like the sky in its flow
Let this soul, having shed flesh,
Changed form having become one with the air
Take refuge in the heights,
Amongst the skies

Those who have things to say about the departed should speak now, when they have said their peace the officiant should continue

We are here,
Survivors of the one who lays before us
We take solace in the knowing That your journey has ended
That you have left from us
To begin a new journey
One we all must take in time.
We that survive you,
Will carry your memory of the deeds

Which brought us together
For the whole of our lives,
That you will not be forgotten,
That you will be eternal in our hearts,
As your spirit sours to the heights,
The currents in the heavens
We commend to the air, your body (X)
That your soul shall find peace and refuge
In the arms of the embrace of this world
Be at peace, be with those who survive you,
That they may not mourn your memory,
Bring them comfort, and peace from this loss
Let your journey be amongst those of the Air
Strong and timeless,
May your spirit grow as the Ancient Currents
And with this,
We say our goodbyes,
May your journey progress
But let this flame burn within the hearts
Of those who carry your memory
Until its their time
To be of the world of the ageless and undying

The officiant should extinguish the candle.

Be at peace, (X)
Find comfort in the heights
Of the skies of the Ancient Air

The cord should be planted within the earth under a tree which loved ones plant in honor of the one who has passed. The candle should be wrapped in a black cloth, and burned when those who survive the lost, need to be reminded of the memories of the one who has left this world.

Passing of the Water

The altar should be set with a black cloth, and a blue runner. There should be a blue candle sitting in a dish of water upon the altar, with a length of silver cord. There should be a picture of the departed, and there should be trinkets which the departed favored in life.

When the ceremony is to begin, the officiant lights the candle with the invocation:

> Awaken spirit of the sea,
> Receive the soul of (X) That they may find rest
> That they find peace within the embrace
> Of the quiet depths
> Guide their spirit from the place of the lost,
> Unto a place of rest.
> Spirit of the Water,
> Put to rest this soul who we bring before you
> Let them lay their head in the sweet waters,
> May their spirit swim amongst the ancients
> In the deepest Oceans
> Their soul to flow as the current
> Let their essence flow as the tides
> Within the primal seas

The priest takes up the rope and makes the following charge:

> This was the cord of the life of (X)
> It has been entwined with every soul
> Who has come to know (X)
> For who they were
> Let those who have known (X)
> As they were in life
> Come not to mourn the loss
> Of their fallen friend
> Instead, let them remember
> How this life touched theirs
> How they have become better for the knowing,
> Changed for the knowing,
> Like the earth in her seasons
> Let this soul, having shed flesh,
> Changed form having become
> One with the water
> Take refuge in the shallows,
> Flow within the deepest waters

Those who have things to say about the departed should speak now, when they have said their peace the officiant should continue:

> We are here,
> Survivors of the one who lays before us
> We take solace in the knowing

That your journey has ended
That you have left from us
To begin a new journey
One we all must take in time.
We that survive you,
Will carry your memory of the deeds
Which brought us together
For the whole of our lives,
That you will not be forgotten,
That you will be eternal in our hearts,
As you swim the calm waters,
The currents of the seas,
We commend to the water, your body (X)
That your soul shall find peace and refuge
In the arms of the embrace of this world
Be at peace
Be with those who survive you,
That they may not mourn your memory,
Bring them comfort, and peace from this loss
Let your journey be amongst
Those of the Water
Strong and timeless,
May your spirit flow as the ancient currents
And with this, we say our goodbyes,
May your journey progress
But let this flame burn within the hearts
Of those who carry your memory
Until its their time to be of the eternal flow.

The officiant should extinguish the candle.

Be at peace, (X) and find comfort In the Waters of the Ancient Seas

The cord should be planted within the earth under a tree which loved ones plant in honor of the one who has passed. The candle should be wrapped in a black cloth, and burned when those who survive the lost, need to be reminded of the memories of the one who has left this world.

Passing of the Earth

The altar should be set in black with a green runner. There should be a candle that is green burning in a dish of soil taken from the grave of the one who has passed. There should be a length of green cord. The altar should be adorned with an image of the departed, and trinkets which they were fond of in life.

When the ceremony is to begin, the officiant lights the candle with the invocation:

Awaken spirit of the earth,
Receive the soul of (X)
That they may find rest and peace
Within the embrace of the quiet earth
Guide their spirit from the place of the lost, Unto a place of rest. Spirit of the Earth,
Put to rest this soul who we bring before you Let them lay their head in the sweet meadows,
May their spirit walk amongst the ancients
In the deep forests
Their soul to tread the places of the shades

The priest takes up the rope and makes the following charge:

This was the cord of the life of (X) It has been entwined with every soul
Who has come to know (X)
For who they were
Let those who have known (X)
As they were in life
Come not to mourn the loss
Of their fallen friend
Instead, let them remember
How this life touched theirs
How they have become better for the knowing,
Changed for the knowing,
Like the earth in her seasons
Let this soul, having shed flesh, Changed form having become
One with the earth
Take refuge in the groves, and walk in the fields

Those who have things to say about the departed should speak now, when they have said their peace the officiant should continue:

We are here,
Survivors of the one who lays before us
We take solace in the knowing
That your journey has ended
That you have left from us
To begin a new journey
One we all must take in time.
We that survive you,
Will carry your memory of the deeds
Which brought us together

For the whole of our lives,
That you will not be forgotten,
That you will be eternal in our hearts,
As you walk the green fields,
The pathways of the forest
We commend to the earth, your body (X)
That your soul shall find peace and refuge
In the arms of the embrace of this world
Be at peace,
Be with those who survive you,
That they may mourn your memory,
Bring them comfort, and peace from this loss
Let your journey
Be amongst those of the Earth
Strong and timeless,
May your spirit grow as the Ancient Forests
And with this, we say our goodbyes,
May your journey progress
But let this flame burn
Within the hearts of those
Who carry your memory until its their time.

The Officiant should extinguish the candle.

Be at peace, (X) and find comfort
In the fields of the Ancient Earth

The cord should be planted within the earth under a tree which loved ones plant in honor of the one who has passed. The candle should be wrapped in a black cloth, and burned when those who survive the lost, need to be reminded of the memories of the one who has left.

Passing of the Fire

The altar is to be covered with a black cloth, and a red runner. There is to be a dish that contains a fire, there is to be a red candle, a photo of the departed, and trinkets that the departed favored in life upon the altar, as well as a length of silver cord. When the ceremony is to begin, the officiant lights the candle with the invocation:

Awaken spirit of the fire,
Receive the soul of (X)
That they may find rest and peace
Within the embrace of the quiet skies
Guide their spirit from the place of the lost,
Unto a place of rest.
Spirit of the Air,
Put to rest this soul who we bring before you
Let them lay their head
In the warmth of the spark,
May their spirit be set free as these fires burn
As a reminder to those who have yet to come
Their soul to burn as a light between the worlds

The priest takes up the rope and makes the following charge:

This was the cord of the life of (X)
It has been entwined with every soul
Who has come to know (X)
For who they were
Let those who have known (X)
As they were in life
Come not to mourn the loss
Of their fallen friend
Instead, let them remember
How this life touched theirs
How they have become better for the knowing,
Changed for the knowing, Like the fire in its brilliance
Let this soul, having shed flesh,
Changed form having become one with the fire
Take refuge in the warmth
Of those who survive you,
Amongst the celestial fires

Those who have things to say about the departed should speak now, when they have said their peace the officiant should continue

We are here,
Survivors of the one who lays before us
We take solace in the knowing
That your journey has ended
That you have left from us
To begin a new journey

One we all must take in time.
We that survive you,
Will carry your memory of the deeds
Which brought us together
For the whole of our lives,
That you will not be forgotten,
That you will be eternal in our hearts,
As you walk the burning roads,
The pathways of the between the worlds
We commend to the fire, your body (X)
That your soul shall find peace and refuge
In the arms of the embrace of this world
Be at peace,
Be with those who survive you,
That they may no mourn your memory,
Bring them comfort, and peace from this loss
Let your journey be amongst those of the Fire
Strong and timeless,
May your spirit grow as the ancient Currents
And with this, we say our goodbyes,
May your journey progress
But let this flame burn
Within the hearts of those
Who carry your memory until its their time

The officiant should extinguish the candle.

Be at peace, (X) and find comfort
In the Flames of the fires of the Ancients

The cord should be planted within the earth under a tree which loved ones plant in honor of the one who has passed. The candle should be wrapped in a black cloth, and burned when those who survive the lost, need to be reminded of the memories of the one who has left this world.

The Opening of the Way

The altar is to be set with a physical effect of the departed if the corpse is not present. There are to be 7 black candles inscribed with the seals of the planets. If possible they should be mixed with the blood of the departed. There should be incense burning mixed with herbs for awakening and the 7 spheres. There should be a white candle placed atop a skull, mixed with the blood of the departed. The only ones present should be one of the family members who will speak for the departed. There is also to be a vessel for fire in the south of the space. There is to be graveyard earth in the north. There is to be water that has washed the corpse in the west. There is to be the incense burning in the east. The fire is to be light first. With the following charge:

> Oh physical fire,
> Light of the worlds between worlds
> I conjure and evoke you
> To become as the dark fire.
> To act as the beacon which calls
> The soul of the one who lays here in death
> To this place of death, to this place dedicated to the memory of their life.
> Hear me, great eternal fire,
> Be summoned by these flames

The water is to have a charge of the following:

> I call you spirit of the primal sea
> Eternal essence, come now unto me
> By this which has become as the river Styx
> Draw forth the soul of this departed
> Back unto me

The grave soil is to have the following charge:

> I call you forth spirit of the graves
> Darkest earth who takes the dead
> To the fields and pastures
> Spirit of the Earth return this spirit
> We seek forth from the dark forest
> That they may be drawn here,
> By the power of your element

The incense is to be lighted with the following charge:

> I call forth that the air, the breath of life,
> That has left this body
> Calls by these words
> The soul of the dead back unto this space
> By that which is dedicated
> To be in their memory,
> Draw forth their spirit unto this place.

The officiant asks the participant who is holding the effect of the person to come forward and answer unto the following.

Who speaks for the dead when they cannot?
What relation to the departed have
You that they
Be granted entrance unto the gates?
Why do you seek that for them Which was not their path in life?

The participant answers after each question is asked. The first candle is lighted for the moon:

I am a member of the order of night,
Priest of the eternal fire
I who am keeper of the way, Without me the way is shut
I am the gatekeeper,
Without me the gate is barred
By this dark fire,
I open the gate of the sphere of the moon.
May its power flow forth into the spirit of (X)
who lays before us in death

The officiant asks the participant:

Why do you speak for the dead,
When they cannot?
What name do you give unto this soul
Who lays here in death?
What memory do you offer forth to call this soul
Unto the gate?

The participant answers each question, and the second candle is lighted for the sphere of mercury:

I am a member of the order of the night,
Priest of the Eternal fire
I who am keeper of the way, Without me the way is shut
I am the gatekeeper,
Without me the gate is barred.
By this dark fire,
I open the gate of the sphere of the mercury.
May its power flow forth into the spirit of (X)
Who lays before us in death
Let the transformation begin

The officiant asks the participant:

What love has this soul known?
What pleasures did this soul enjoy?
What memory do you offer forth to call this soul
Unto the gate?

The participant answers each question, and the third is lighted for the sphere of Venus:

I am a member of the order of the night,
Priest of the Eternal fire
I who am keeper of the way, Without me the way is shut.
I am the gatekeeper,
Without me the gate is barred.
By this dark fire,
I open the gate of the sphere of the Venus.
May its power flow forth into the spirit of (X)
who lays before us in death
Let the power of the heart guide this soul Through this gate.

The officiant asks the participant:

What deeds has this soul done to warrant
The passing of these gates?
What triumph of the spirit Has this soul undergone?
What memory do you offer forth
To call this soul unto the gate?
The participant answers each question, and the fourth candle
is lighted for the sphere of the Sun:
I am a member of the order of the night,
Priest of the Eternal fire
I who am keeper of the way, Without me the way is shut
I am the gatekeeper,
Without me the gate is barred
By this dark fire,
I open the gate of the sphere of the Sun.
May its power flow forth into the spirit of (X)
Who lays before us in death
Let the power of the heart guide this soul Through this gate.
May the deeds of (X)
Guide them through this gate.

The officiant asks the participant:

What great struggle has this soul endured?
What victory of the spirit
Has this soul achieved?
What memory do you offer forth
To call this soul unto the gate?

The participant answers each question, and the fifth candle is lighted for the sphere of Mars:

I am a member of the order of the night,
Priest of the Eternal Fire
I who am keeper of the way,
Without me, the way is shut
I am the gatekeeper,
Without me, the gate is barred
By this dark fire,

I open the gate of the sphere of Mars.
May its power flow forth into the spirit of (X)
Who lays before us in death
Let the power of the heart guide this soul Through this gate.
May the deeds of (X)
Guide them through this gate. May the strength of their spirit
Allow them to enter forth this gate.

The officiant asks the participant:

What great justice has this soul survived?
What temperance has this soul achieved?
What memory do you offer forth
To call this soul unto the gate?

The participant answers each question, and the sixth candle is lighted for the sphere of Mars:

I am a member of the order of the night,
Priest of the Eternal fire
I who am keeper of the way, Without me the way is shut
I am the gatekeeper,
Without me the gate is barred
By this dark fire,
I open the gate of the sphere of Jupiter.
May its power flow forth into the spirit of (X)
Who lays before us in death
Let the power of the heart guide this soul
Through this gate.
May the deeds of (X)
Guide them through this gate.
May the strength of their spirit
Allow them to enter forth this gate.
May their walking be guided
By their strength and temperance Through this gate.

The officiant asks the participant:

What great pain has this soul survived?
What sorrow has this soul endured?
What memory do you offer forth
To call this soul unto the gate?

The participant answers each question, and the seventh candle is lighted for the sphere of Mars:

I am a member of the order of the night,
Priest of the Eternal fire
I who am keeper of the way, Without me the way is shut
I am the gatekeeper,
Without me the gate is barred
By this dark fire,
I open the gate of the sphere of Jupiter.

May its power flow forth into the spirit of (X)
Who lays before us in death
Let the power of the heart guide This soul through this gate.
May the deeds of (X)
Guide them through this gate. May the strength of their spirit
Allow them to enter forth this gate.
May their walking be guided
By their strength and temperance Through this gate.
Let it be by their losses,
That they are able
To bear the weight of this gate.

The officiant asks the participant:
What have you to say
On the soul of the departed?
What have you to give to the spirit of the departed?
What memory do you offer forth to call this soul through the gates?

The participant answers each question, and the candle is lit upon the skull with the following charge:

We have born witness to the soul
Through its stations,
I call forth by the power of the Dark fire,
The celestial gates to be open
The soul of (X) is thus named and made worthy
The trials have been endured, The lessons have been learned
Those who would speak for the dead
Have come forth
It is by this station
It is by the blood of the departed
That this flame is light
That it serves as a beacon for the soul
To ascend through the gates of the spheres That its journey may be eternal.
As the light of this fire burns,
So too do the stars in their places Be called forth you spirit of (X)
We open the gate, We open the way
Walk upon the way, and through the other-world
Spirit that has departed this world,
Be a soul upon the flows, and tides
Determine your own destinies.
We give you to your judgment,
Be made worthy to enter forth
The realms you desire.

The effect is to be placed on the fire with this charge:

We conjure forth the power of the gates
That this soul shall pass through all of them
Safely and without delay.
That their spirit free to do as they desire

By this fire burning
To manifest that which we require
We call forth by the blood of the lost
By the living memory
By the fire of the spark of life
We give unto this memory, this spirit
That they may pass between the worlds
Through the Gates
That the way is open unto them
That for them the way is open
That for them the Gate is open
Let them be one of the celestial
That their fire shall burn as the stars
In the celestial heavens.

The candles are to be extinguished, the water to be returned to the waters, and the earth returned to the earth. The incense is to be left to burn out. The candle and the skull are to be kept in the family, with the candle only being lit when they want a reminder of the journey of the soul of the departed.

The Ascending of the Way

The altar is to be set with a physical effect of the departed if the corpse is not present. There are to be 7 black candles inscribed with the seals of the planets. If possible they should be mixed with the blood of the departed. There should be incense burning mixed with herbs for awakening and the 7 spheres. There should be a white candle placed atop a skull, mixed with the blood of the departed. The only ones present should be one of the family members who will speak for the departed. There is also to be a vessel for fire in the south of the space. There is to be graveyard earth in the north.

There is to be water that has washed the corpse in the west. There is to be the incense burning in the east. The fire is to be light first. With the following charge:

Oh physical fire,
Light of the worlds between worlds
I conjure and evoke you
To become as the dark fire.
To act as the beacon which calls
The soul of the one who lays here in death
To this place of death,
To this place dedicated to the memory of their life.
Hear me, great eternal fire,
Be summoned by these flames

The water is to have a charge of the following:

I call you spirit of the primal sea
Eternal essence, come now unto me
By this which has become as the river Styx
Draw forth the soul of this departed
Back unto me

The grave soil is to have the following charge:

I call you forth spirit of the graves Darkest earth who takes the dead
To the fields and pastures
Spirit of the Earth
Return this spirit that we seek
Forth from the dark forest
That they may be drawn here, By the power of your element

The incense is to be lighted with the following charge:

I call forth that the air, the breath of life,
That has left this body
Calls by these words the soul of the dead back
Unto this space
By that which is dedicated
To be in their memory,
Draw forth their spirit unto this place.

Each of the 7 candles are to be lit with a charge of their station and their power. When this has finished the white candle is lit, with this charge:

> We have born witness
> To the soul through its station,
> I call forth by the power of the Dark fire,
> The celestial gates to be open
> The soul of (X) is thus named and made worthy
> The trials have been endured, The lessons have been learned
> Those who would speak for the dead
> Have come forth
> It is by this station
> By the blood of the departed
> That this flame is light
> That it serves as a beacon for the soul
> To ascend through the gates of the spheres
> That its journey may be eternal.
> As the light of this fire burns,
> So too do the stars in their places
> Be called forth you spirit of (X)
> We open the gate, We open the way
> Walk upon the way, and through the other world
> Spirit that has departed this world, Be a soul upon the flows, and tides Determine your own destinies.
> We give you to your judgment,
> You are made worthy
> To enter forth the realms you desire.

The effect is to be placed on the fire with this charge:

> We conjure forth the power of the gates
> That this soul shall pass through all of them Safely and without delay.
> That their spirit free to do as they desire
> By this fire burning to manifest
> That which we require
> We call forth by the blood of the lost
> By the living memory
> By the fire of the spark of life
> We give unto this memory, this spirit
> That they may pass between the worlds
> Through the Gates
> That the way is open unto them
> That for them the way is open
> That for them the Gate is open
> Let them be one of the celestial
> That their fire shall burn
> As the stars in the night sky.

The candles are to be extinguished, the water to be returned to the waters, and the earth returned to the earth. The incense is to be left to burn out. The candle and the skull are to be kept in the family, a reminder of the journey of the soul of the departed.

Tabula Rasa

The altar is to be set with a black cloth. The only light in the room is to be from a black candle mixed with the blood of the officiant. There is to be a vessel set for fire unlit. If the body is not present this is to be done with personal effects. If this is to be during the cremation ceremony, let the body wait to be burned while the invocation is made. If the body has already been cremated and this work is done to purify the soul the remains are required to be set in the vessel for the fire, and wood of oak is to be placed there in, with room enough to be set aflame by the black candle. The protective circle of this is to be on an eight pointed star. The barrier is to be marked in salt, and herbs of protection. The incense burned is to be of purification. The candle is to be lit with the following invocation:

> I call forth the fire which burns beyond the veil
> That fire which is timeless
> That which is the source of night itself
> Through the void it is called forth.
> The veil now lift and part
> That this eternal fire
> Be brought forth
> I call forth the Dark eternal fire,
> Be this flame that burns here now,
> Burn as the channel for the dark flame.
> By my blood I evoke forth the Darkest Fire,
> Let this light be the will of my desire

Add the candle to the wood, and ashes. Or set the body to cremation with the candle. While the body burns, or while the fire burns make the following charge:

> I am a member of the Order of the Night
> Priest of the Eternal Fire
> By my blood I call forth the dark fire
> To manifest before me
> Through this physical medium,
> I call forth the oath of blood
> Let this fire consume the body of (X)
> As this fire burns,
> Burn off the corruption
> From their deepest essence
> Let them be reborn into a new existence,
> All essences within this body
> I call forth that the Dark fire
> Obey the covenant of blood
> By the covenant,
> I grant the souls inhabiting this body
> At the time of death, Tabula Rasa
> By the ancient laws
> By blood are called forth,
> All corruption within the body of (X)
> Shall be purged,
> Their spirit shall return,
> All spirits within them shall return
> They shall be purified and purged

Let no taint remain of what is, or was in life
Tabula Rasa, is given (X)
Tabula Rasa, is bestowed upon (X)
Tabula Rasa wipes clean their slate
By the dark fire,
As this fire burns this shall be forth

From this day
Their spirit is purified
As their body is commended to the fire.
May the dark fire cleanse and purge
Their essence hence of all corruption and evil
Let them be born again to be and live
As an innocent soul free of all debt
All spirits, and essences within this body
That has been consumed by death
Be restored unto innocence
By the dark Fire this is made to be,
As you are made once again flesh.

The candle fire is to burn out of its own accord, that it may burn away all corruptions from the hearts, bodies, and essences of those who perished in the body of the one lost.

Exorcism Rites

The Fundamentals

In the world we have physical wars, occult wars, we have wars of the spirit as well. Generally when we must defend the realm we have protective measures, as well as offensive measures. It in this is where we must observe our targets. We must dissect what it is we are going to combat. In common works we have a foundations of what it is we are dealing with. However, in the field we have no measure other then what is presented to determine what is out there. There are criteria which need be applied, there are tells that a spirit force has on the region it effects. Observe how it manifests, is the elemental base that the spirit holding onto what is sustaining the phenomenon. What is the perspective of the primary energy. From identifying these parts, you will have what you need to select the exorcism.

Generally with the western traditions and the exorcism of the Golden Dawn, Egyptian influence is solar base. Witchcraft is generally based on lunar rites. Works of the Necromicon deal in other worldly entities, conjured up from planetary gates. When dealing with these forces it is the gates which must be closed, or their currents inverted in order to neutralize the occurrence. To choose the one aligned with the elemental of the affliction you run the risk of empowering the spirit. To choose the direct opposite energy might cause unnecessary conflict from the spirit. The result is to choose an energy which will be able to move through the space and achieve what it is you want, while still containing it.

In the references to the planetary spheres, their exorcism is not included in this work, as I do not sanction any work which would imperil the reader beyond a reasonable lesson in the work. What is here, will generally work for all subjects discussed in the historical grimoires, when the banishing rites, and exorcism of the western world fails. It is also not discussed the eastern methods of exorcism and banishment. However, you must learn in the field, and write your own methods, on what sources of energy works. If you have to work against a spirit, then you might have to use something higher in the hierarchy in order to deal with it accordingly.

When dealing with an object which is containing a spiritual residue, or cognitive spirit whose effect causes misfortune in a space/to its owner, etc. then you need to preform an exorcism in the same way you would for a body as to expel it from the object. There also makes reference of a box, or a container, they can be built easily enough. But at the same time, an array made of fresh inks, to seal the current can also be employed as well as the use of the soul trap cards, and other binding spells to seal critters into objects, and then remove the object from the space to purge the critter from it at a later time.

Exorcism of the Air

To be used when you need to purge a spirit of watery natures. That it can push it forth from the space as a great gale would the tempestuous seas. Not recommended for things of an airy nature, fiery nature, or earthy nature.

For a place

Incense should be mixed with herbs of purification. There should be a mirrored box with oils in herbs of purification which is in the center of the space. The officiant should have a fan marked with their blood, the character of Sun for the penetrating winds of the I-Ching. There should also be a censer that the officiant will hold and fan the incense into all corners of the rooms to be purged. Inside the mirrored box there should be a black candle mixed with the blood of the officiant. This should be lit before the ceremony begins with the following charge:

> I call forth by the blood of fire, I am Priest of the Dark fire.
> In this western point,
> My will burns as the will of fire.
> My will burns as the dark fire
> By my will, I evoke hence the dark fire

When the ceremony is to begin, the incense in the dish is to be lighted and in a circular pattern holding the incense in the recessive hand, the officiant fans it with their dominant hand. Making a circular path to the vessel, if purging a house then start at the lowest point working ones way up. With the box, and circle of incense with the box in the center in the last room to be worked on. As you fan the rooms clockwise repeat three times in each space:

> I call forth the spirit of fire, through the air
> I call forth the will of fire
> Banish these forces from this space By the will of fire be banished hence
> By all the purification of the herbs
> Be sent forth from this place
> By these herbs this becomes a neutral space
> Spirits be sent unto the darkened light I cast you into the vessel of night.

When the final room is reached leave the censer burning in the doorway. Then clockwise light each of the censers of incense with the following charge starting in the west.

> Spirits of unrest in this place,
> I draw you up and cast you out.
> Enter forth into the vessel,
> Be called unto its light
> Be cast forth into the vessel of night. Be drawn into the light.
> By the dual winds, be cast forth into the vessel.

When the 8 censers have been light, and the room is filling with smoke, add more incense upon the one in the doorway and begin fanning the room clockwise repeating the following 3 times:

> By the wind of heaven and earth
> By the bond of the heaven and earth
> By the breath of life made flesh to the word

> By the word of power issued
> Forth by the will of fire
> Be sent now into the vessel.
> Be cast into the night
> Be drawn into the night fire
> By these words
> By the blood of the will of fire
> Be sent from this place,
> Be sealed within the inner space
> Spirit of the breath made flesh
> Restore this place
> Return it once again to a neutral space

Seal the lid of the box, the candle should be extinguished by the closing of the lid, and wax should then be heated by the light of another black candle which has been lit anew after the charge has been made.

> Spirit of fire hear my cry,
> Bind those who do not die
> That which afflicts from beyond the tomb
> Is sealed within this mirrored room
> By smoke and blood
> By wax and stone
> Seal these spirits, by the light which has shown.

Seal the box in wax, and let the fires burn themselves out. Cleanse the space in normal fashion, and take the box to its place.

For a person

Incense should be mixed with herbs of purification. There should be a mirrored box with oils in herbs of purification which is in the center of the space. The officiant should have a fan marked with their blood, the character of Sun for the penetrating winds of the I-Ching. There should also be a censer that the officiant will hold and fan the incense into all corners of the rooms to be purged. Inside the mirrored box there should be a black candle mixed with the blood of the officiant. This should be lit before the ceremony begins with the following charge:

> I call forth by the blood of fire, I am Priest of the Dark fire.
> In this western point,
> My will burns as the will of fire.
> My will burns as the dark fire
> By my will, I evoke hence the dark fire

When the ceremony is to begin, the incense in the dish is to be lighted and in a circular pattern holding the incense in the recessive hand, the officiant fans it with their dominant hand. Making a path to the vessel at the feet of the person. Starting at the head, light each of the censers of incense with the following charge starting in the west.

> Spirits of unrest in this place,
> I draw you up and cast you out.

Enter forth into the vessel,
Be called unto its light
Be cast forth into the vessel of night. Be drawn into the light.
By the dual winds, be cast forth into the vessel

When the 8 censers have been light, and the room is filling with smoke, add more incense upon the one in the doorway and begin fanning the room clockwise repeating the following as the smoke flows over the body:

I call forth the spirit of fire, through the air
I call forth the will of fire
Banish these forces from this space By the will of fire be banished hence
By all the purification of the herbs
Be sent forth from this place
By these herbs this shall Become a neutral space
Spirits be sent unto the darkened light
I cast you into the vessel of night By the wind of heaven and earth
By the bond of the heaven and earth
By the breath of life made flesh to the word
By the word of power issued forth
By the will of fire
Be sent now into the vessel.
Be cast into the night
Be drawn into the night fire
By these words
By the blood of the will of fire
Be sent from this place,
Spirit of the breath made flesh
Restore this place
Return it once again to a neutral space

Seal the lid of the box, the candle should be extinguished by the closing of the lid, and wax should then be heated by the light of another black candle which has been lit anew after the charge has been made.

Spirit of fire hear my cry,
Bind those who do not die
That which afflicts from beyond the tomb
Is sealed within this mirrored room
By smoke and blood
By wax and stone Seal these spirits,
By the light which has shown.

Seal the box in wax, and let the fires burn themselves out. Cleanse the space.

Exorcism of the Water

For use with fire currents, or fiery creatures. To saturate their active prowess in the celestial waters to cool them out to make them able to be processed. It's not recommended for airy forces or of like elemental relationship. Earthy currents will also be displaced by the water as it washes clean the space.

For a place

There should be water that has been consecrated for purification purposes and the officiant is to asperge it with hyssop through the space. There is to be a mirrored box, with a black candle in it which has been mixed with the blood of the officiant. It is to be placed in the center of the space, and lighted first with the following charge:

> I call forth by the blood of fire, I am Priest of the Dark fire.
> In this western point,
> My will burns as the will of fire.
> My will burns as the dark fire
> By my will, I evoke hence the dark fire

When the ceremony is to begin, start at the bottom of the place if in a house, if not start from the western quarter. Aspurge the waters with the dominant hand of the officiant and repeat, clockwise around the space:

> Out of the marrow
> Out of the bones
> Out of the blood within this home Spirits within and spirits with out
> By the power of this water I cast you out
> Spirits of peace and spirits of life
> Spirit of water banish this strife

When you enter the center of the room where the vessel is lighted, continue to asperge the area with the following charge:

> I call forth the spirits of the flow
> I call forth the power of the water
> By the river of souls
> Evoked be now to purify this space
> Return it hence to a neutral space
> By the rivers whose course is endless
> Send forth these spirits into the deepest night
> Become the force to strong to fight
> Back into the deepest fire
> Be sent now into the vessel.
> Be cast into the night
> Be drawn into the night fire
> By these words
> By the blood of the will of fire
> Be sent from this place,
> Spirit of the breath made flesh

Restore this place
Return it once again to a neutral space

Close the lid of the box, the candle should be extinguished by the closing of the lid, and wax should then be heated by the light of another black candle which has been lit anew after the charge has been made.

Spirit of fire hear my cry,
Bind those who do not die
That which afflicts from beyond the tomb
Is sealed within this mirrored room
By smoke and blood
By wax and stone Seal these spirits,
By the light which has shown.

Seal the box in wax, and pour the waters out. Cleanse the space in normal fashion, and take the box to its place.

For a person

There should be water that has been consecrated for purification purposes and the officiant is to asperge it with hyssop through the body from the head to the toe. There is to be a mirrored box, with a black candle in it which has been mixed with the blood of the officiant. It is to be placed at the feet of the afflicted and lighted first with the following charge:

I call forth by the blood of fire, I am Priest of the Dark fire.
In this western point,
My will burns as the will of fire.
My will burns as the dark fire
By my will, I evoke hence the dark fire

When the ceremony is to begin, start at the bottom of the place if in a house, if not start from the western quarter. Scatter the waters with the dominant hand of the officiant and repeat, clockwise around the space:

Out of the marrows
Out of the bones
Out of the blood within this home
Spirits within and spirits with out
By the power of this water I cast you out
Spirits of peace and spirits of life
Spirit of water banish this strife

When you enter the center of the room where the vessel is lighted, continue to asperge the area with the following charge:

I call forth the spirits of the flow
I call forth the power of the water
By the river of souls
Evoked be now to purify this space

Return it hence to a neutral space
By the rivers whose course is endless
Send forth these spirits into the deepest night
Become the force to strong to fight
Back into the deepest fire
Be sent now into the vessel.
Be cast into the night
Be drawn into the night fire
By these words
By the blood of the will of fire
Be sent from this place,
Spirit of the breath made flesh
Restore this place
Return it once again to a neutral space

Seal the lid of the box, the candle should be extinguished by the closing of the lid, and wax should then be heated by the light of another black candle which has been lit anew after the charge has been made.

Spirit of fire hear my cry,
Bind those who do not die
That which afflicts from beyond the tomb
Is sealed within this mirrored room
By smoke and blood
By wax and stone
Seal these spirits, by the light which has shown.

Seal the box in wax, and pour the waters out. Cleanse the space in normal fashion. The box to its place.

Exorcism of the Earth

It works on watery nature things to stiffen them, as well as airy nature things. It provides a solid resistance for those sorts of currents. Not recommended for fiery currents.

For a place

The area is to have black candles placed in bowls of earth that have been mixed with the blood of the officiant. There are to be 8 of them, and the lighting should progress from the north, to the east around the circle in clockwise pattern. There is to be the mirrored box in the center of the space, inside the vessel there is to be a black candle that is lit with the following charge before the rite begins:

> I call forth by the blood of fire, I am Priest of the Dark fire.
> In this western point,
> My will burns as the will of fire.
> My will burns as the dark fire
> By my will, I evoke hence the dark fire

When the ceremony is to begin, start at the bottom of the place if in a house, if not start from the northern quarter. Scatter salt that has been purified in the corners and about the space to cast out any forces with the following charge:

> By the preserved earth
> By the black forest at midnight
> I call forth spirit of the Earth Through this which preserves
> Preserve the neutrality of this space
> Cast forth from it
> That which does not lay in still earth
> Cast forth from this place
> That which prevents
> This from being a neutral place

When you have reached the final room, the center of the space with the burning black candle in the center of the room. Light the black candles in the vessels starting in the north with the charge of:

> By the black earth, and by the land of Sheol
> I call forth by blood ties to the rich fields
> Of the lands between worlds
> By the power of the ancient deserts Which contains the souls of the lost
> By this fire of the darkest will
> By blood, cast it forth
> Send forth these spirits into the deepest night
> Become the force to strong to fight
> Back into the deepest fire
> Be sent now into the vessel.
> Be cast into the night
> Be drawn into the night fire
> By these words
> By the blood of the will of fire
> Be sent from this place,

Spirit of the breath made flesh
Restore this place
Return it once again to a neutral space

Make a spiral of salt upon the center of this space leading into the mirror vessel at the center. Seal the lid of the box, the candle should be extinguished by the closing of the lid, and wax should then be heated by the light of another black candle which has been lit anew after the charge has been made.

Spirit of fire hear my cry,
Bind those who do not die
That which afflicts from beyond the tomb
Is sealed within this mirrored room
By smoke and blood
By wax and stone Seal these spirits,
By the light which has shown.

Seal the box in wax, and sweep the salt out. Cleanse the space in normal fashion, and take the box to its place.

For a person

The area is to have black candles placed in bowls of earth that have been mixed with the blood of the officiant. There are to be 8 of them, and the lighting should progress from the north, to the east around the circle in clockwise pattern. There is to be the mirrored box at the foot of the afflicted, inside the vessel there is to be a black candle that is lit with the following charge before the rite begins:

I call forth by the blood of fire, I am Priest of the Dark fire.
In this western point,
My will burns as the dark fire
By my will, I evoke hence the dark fire

When the ceremony is to begin start from the northern quarter. Scatter salt that has been purified in the corners and about the space to cast out any forces with the following charge, and on the body from the head to the toe:

By the preserved earth
By the black forest at midnight
I call forth spirit of the Earth
Through this which preserves
Preserve the neutrality of this vessel
Cast forth from it
That which does not lay in still earth
Cast forth from this place that
Which prevents this from being a neutral place

When you have reached the final room, the center of the space with the burning black candle in the center of the room. Light the black candles in the vessels starting in the north with the charge of:

By the black earth, and by the land of Sheol
I call forth by blood ties to

The rich fields of the lands between worlds
By the power of the ancient deserts
Which contains the souls of the lost
By this fire of the darkest will brought forth
By the blood
Send forth these spirits into the deepest night
Become the force to strong to fight
Back into the deepest fire
Be sent now into the vessel.
Be cast into the night
Be drawn into the night fire
By these words
By the blood of the will of fire
Be sent from this place,
Spirit of the breath made flesh
Restore this place
Return it once again to a neutral space

Make a spiral of salt upon the center of this space leading into the mirror vessel at the center. Seal the lid of the box, the candle should be extinguished by the closing of the lid, and wax should then be heated by the light of another black candle which has been lit anew after the charge has been made.

Spirit of fire hear my cry,
Bind those who do not die
That which afflicts from beyond the tomb
Is sealed within this mirrored room
By smoke and blood
By wax and stone
Seal these spirits, by the light which has shown.

Seal the box in wax, and sweep the salt out. Cleanse the space in normal fashion, and take the box to its place.

Exorcism of the Fire

Works on watery and earthy forces, as it negates their properties. Water to steam, and Earth to a liquid. Not recommended with air, as it tends to create electrical currents that are generally unwanted.

For a place

Around the space in which the area is to take place there is to be a circle of fire built. 8 fires around the location. With 8 black candles mixed with the blood of the officiant at the center of each fires, that when lit are what starts the fires. In the center of the space there is to be an altar set with a black candle mixed with the blood of the officiant and a box made out of mirrors, held together with lead and black wax. Which can be sealed with wax, in which the candle can sit. The fire in the first point which is to be the western side shall be lit with the conjuration:

> I call forth by the blood of fire, I am Priest of the Dark fire.
> In this western point,
> My will burns as the will of fire.
> My will burns as the dark fire
> By my will, I evoke hence the dark fire

This charge is to be spoken at each of the lighting of the 8 fires. When the candles have been lit, and the fires begin to burn the area should be made ready by lighting the incense made for summoning spirits to it. The incense should be lighted in the east, and walked around the space to the south, then west, then north, then back to east. Always moving in a clockwise direction. When you have done this begin the summons of the forces which are to be exorcised:

> Hear me spirits of abominations,
> Those forces which are charged
> By the covenant of the Ancients,
> I lay claim unto your souls
> That you are bound by the dark fire
> You may not pass beyond this flame,
> That you who are in darkness,
> Shall be given light unto the night
> That by the night itself you are bound
> By the dark fire, by my will
> I draw you down unto this center flame

Light the candle inside the mirror box.

> Hear my words, my thoughts,
> My blood as it burns as this candle
> By the infernal light which shines eternally
> Within the abyss,
> That even the night fire which burns before us,
> You are called to it
> Be summoned forth spirits of this space,
> By the darkest fire, hear these words
> Be brought forth by blood, and word,
> By the power of the fire which pulls all to itself

I conjure that this summons is heard
By the covenant of the Ancients,
As souls are commanded
By this fire, obey this summons
Enter now this vessel,
That you may join with the dark fire,
Become apart of the will of fire
Enter now this lamp,
That your essence becomes
Assimilate now into the darkness
By this exorcism charged
To be bound thus unto the temple.
By the blood
By the fire
By the will of fire made flesh
Hear me and be bound inside this vessel.

Seal the lid of the box, the candle should be extinguished by the closing of the lid, and wax should then be heated by the light of another black candle which has been lit anew after the charge has been made.

Spirit of fire hear my cry,
Bind those who do not die
That which afflicts from beyond the tomb
Is sealed within this mirrored room
By smoke and blood
By wax and stone Seal these spirits,
By the light which has shown.

Seal the box in wax, and let the fires burn themselves out. Cleanse the space in normal fashion, and take the box to its place.

For a Person

Around the space in which the area is to take place there are to be 8 black candles mixed with the blood of the officiant at the center of each fires, that when lit are what starts the fires. In the center of the space there is to be an altar set with a black candle mixed with the blood of the officiant and a box made out of mirrors, held together with lead and black wax. Which can be sealed with wax, in which the candle can sit.

The fire in the first point which is to be the western side shall be lit with the conjuration:

> I call forth by the blood of fire, I am Priest of the Dark fire.
> In this western point,
> My will burns as the will of fire.
> My will burns as the dark fire
> By my will, I evoke hence the dark fire

This charge is to be spoken at each of the lighting of the 8 fires. When the candles have been lit, and the fires begin to burn the area should be made ready by lighting the incense made for summoning spirits to it. The incense should be lighted in the east, and walked around the space to the south, then west, then north, then back to east. Always moving in a clockwise direction. When you have done this begin the summons of the forces which are to be exorcised:

> Hear me spirits of abominations,
> Those forces which are charged
> By the covenant of the Ancients,
> I lay claim unto your souls
> That you are bound by the dark fire
> You may not pass beyond this flame,
> That you who are in darkness,
> Shall be given light unto the night
> That by the night itself you are bound
> By the dark fire, by my will
> I draw you down unto this center flame

Light the candle inside the mirror box.

> Hear my words, my thoughts,
> My blood as it burns as this candle
> By the infernal light which shines eternally
> Within the abyss,
> That even the night fire which burns before us,
> You are called to it
> Be summoned forth spirits of this space,
> By the darkest fire, hear these words Be brought forth by blood, and word,
> By the power of the fire which pulls all to itself
> I conjure that this summons is heard
> By the covenant of the Ancients,
> As souls are commanded by the fire, obey
> Enter now this vessel,
> That you may join with the dark fire,

Become apart of the will of fire
Enter now this lamp,
Be assimilated by the darkness
You are by this exorcism charged
To be bound thus unto the temple.
By the blood
By the fire
By the will of fire made flesh
Hear me and be bound inside this vessel.

Seal the lid of the box, the candle should be extinguished by the closing of the lid, and wax should then be heated by the light of another black candle which has been lit anew after the charge has been made.

Spirit of fire hear my cry,
Bind those who do not die
That which afflicts from beyond the tomb
Is sealed within this mirrored room
By smoke and blood
By wax and stone Seal these spirits,
By the light which has shown.

Seal the box in wax, and let the fires burn themselves out. Cleanse the space in normal fashion, and take the box to its place.

Conjuration of the Fall

Can be used with the array of the Inner World. As to fall is to become consumed by emotion. This is a greater form of exorcism and will bind any spirit against which it is used. When no other means of banishment works, this seems to always get the job done.

Hear me in the regions of the four
In the angles of the stars
In the seconds, in the hours and between
I conjure this road to the essence of time
By the roots of that which is before order
That which is before all time
The forces unto the ending of days
These forces from the first time
In the regions of the twelve
Come forth as the gates are open:

Cancer of the moon;
Leo of the sun;
Libra of Venus;
Scorpious of Mars;
Sagittarius of Jupiter;
Orphiel of Ouranous;
Capricorn of Saturn;
Aquarius of Saturn;
Pisces of Jupiter;
Aries of Mars;
Taurus of Venus;
Gemini of Mercury;

Come thou forth demon lords:

Athoth, reaper of Aries
Harmas, eye of fire within Taurus
Galila, twins of the Gemini
Adonaius, spirit of Leo
Astartoth, spirit of Virgo
Thammuz, spirit of Libra
Akiressina, spirit of Scorpio
Yubel, spirit of the Archer
Harmupial, Spirit of Capricornus
Achiradonin Spirit of Aquarius
Belias, Spirit of Piscies

You of the celestial orders,
You in the heights of the light,
By our source, the mind of all,
By these twelve of light, here of the one
By the twelve of the dark, here to receive
By the lightest of fire,

By the spheres which you offend,
The brightest sun at noon,
The black sun at midnight,
Unto you what is required!
For form be contort and foulness rise,
This to keep you from the skies!
Your wings to shadows, your body to scale,
Your hair to horn, become demon born!
We weave by sacred fire,
We expel you for what you have done
We consume the will within you,
We cast you forth from your place,
We cast you into the darkest space,
We cast you out into the Darkest Night!
We cast you hence into the pit!
Torn from rank
Be born of plight
Against our will you cannot fight
From the heights at which you sit,

Into the deepest hell; We command!
Into the darkest abyss; We command!
Into the pits; We command!
Into the void; We command!

Exorcism of the Divisions in the Mind

You that are divided, shall be cast forth
I bind by the blood on the earth before me
By the scent of the herbs, and their ruling spirit
That thou are banished from the spirit of (x)
The barrier shall be your undoing

That which is cast of darkness,
That which clothed of fear
That which is compelled by hatred and dispair shal be brought new fear
I command the darkness
I command the spirit
By the blood of fire,
By the will of ages

(conjuration of the tower of art/station of the Magus in the hierarchy)

I am that which is
I am that which shall be
It is you I command
It is your essence I bind.

"That was tasty rabbit..."

Dear Reader,

"Don't mind the demons, they are the ones who live here..."

    I do hope that you have enjoyed what is certain to only be the guide of beginnings to those on the path. Thank you for your patronage, and I do hope that the next works, bring about as much fun and enjoyment that these works provided for me in the writing.

                                      Yours infernally

                                                  Infernal Warlock

Lapidary Magick

Ring of the Red Queen

    We will have a stone and ring to be set together. The spell of the summons functions in this case more like a pact. In that those who wear the ring are the ones who fulfill the duty as the vessel of the Lilith/Az archetypal force. This will give them the ability for increased sexual projections, potency and overall lust capabilities. The cost of this pact is that the men she lay with are marked as vessels by the Az archetypal current. Which means that when they go and reproduce by consummating their union with another, they will be able to birth the children of Az., in preparation for being able to eventually give birth to the full archetypal force in flesh, as the marker grows within the subconscious and draws itself to life upon the climax. When the entire body of the lovers is thrust into the moment of mating, it will be the last bit of thought needed to build the egregore and insert it into a human body.

    Cleanse the ring in fresh water, let the stone sit in a circle of crystals. When the time comes for the woman to take ownership of the ring they must bleed on the stone to take possession of the pact. Prepare your altar, or work space as you generally do. On the sides of the skull place 2 black candles, in the mouth of the skull the customary black obsidian sphere. Set the grand array out, and the 8 seals of the planetary gates. Make your conjuration.

> I conjure the Red Queen of Whores
> Lillith mother of demons, lady of the damned,
> Hear now and come unto this summons
> Adorn yourself in the power given unto thee
> By this stone before me
> Bind unto it your power
> Your lust shall fill their intended with raw desire
> They come to consummate the bond
> The bond with you and your power
> That any lover they take on
> After the consummation of this union
> Shall be yours to give birth through,
> Should they breed
> Through them your offspring are bred
> That you shall rise forth
> From obscurity and the void
> Into the flesh and mind
> With your deathless soul
> By the covenant of blood
> Between the one who takes ownership
> Of the vessel of this summons
> Accept the offerings of
> Future generations birthed for you
> That as their lovers consummate the flesh
> They shall be marked as yours
> That their line shall be forfeit unto your will
> That you shall influence the generations
> Unto the ending of days
> For all who share blood with this ring,
> Shall become an extension of you
> That this ring shall bind the flesh and spirit

House the spirit of their flesh
The mind of the flesh
Be given unto the power of the red queen
They shall be as the the red queen
Those with whom shall consummate the bond
Outside of this singular union of couples
Shall be owned by the red queen
Their generations shall be in service to the red queen
As the fates of those who are birthed,
Shall be in service to the bond
We walk in the ways of darkness
You the ancient mother of the damned
Come forth unto this summons my queen
Assume now the guise of stone, and silver
That you should live again in the generations to come.
That shall having this in place,
Ensure you and your line
Restoration of flesh
By the covenant of the living blood,
So is sealed by the Dark fire

Ring of the Guardian

A ring which has been made to become a spirit object with a created being. Used principally at the time of the creation of the elemental, demon, angel, or other thought projection. Whoever dons the ring becomes protected by the thoughts of the construct. It will feed off of energies of the individual who wears it, but in this manner can be made to travel outside of the confines of the ring to feed. In these ways can it become a stable medium of protections to some degree from spiritual warfare. When the critter inside is weak or the wearer runs out of energy that goes towards anything not sustaining the base functions of life. The servitor in the ring will do the job it is set to.

Made of metals, stones, and other material components and used as the vessel of the spirit after its creation. Each ritual should be custom crafted depending on the nature of the spirit used. If doing these for distribution then a single ceremony repeated for each vessel will be required.

Ring of Transmigration

When you have something like the rite of transference it will lend itself to a very unique form of lineage. As with the Ring of the Red Queen you are allowing Lilith to lay claim to the progeny created from the sexual unions of the marked lover. In this way you are directly influencing the way the spirit is brought back from the other world. You will have objects of power, tied directly to threads of your soul as to give you a body to contain your mind/spirit at the time of death.

Verbum Caro Factum Est – *The Word was made Flesh*

This is the idea to make the word flesh, and in that word you contain your essence, so if you have the ring inscribed, and you preform upon it the rite of transference then you will be able to give your power to the next generation. From there you would be able to come through the subconscious into the mind of the one who owns the object. From there, like Lilith would be able to achieve through her own propagation. You become the one who has rebirth through a controlled setting of transmigration. The ritual of creation should be worked that whoever puts the ring on gets the automatic transference. Whereas if you are binding your soul to an object such as a grimoire or some such that when they read the words, the power behind the word was made flesh as though they were possessed by the word through the spoken conjuration.

Herbal Formulary

Reference ONLY

All works relating to plant matteials and other potential medicines are for references only and not for consumption. Seek proper medical care.

Medium of Transference

Make a puppet of cloth, in the astral color that best represents the person on whose behalf it is for. Stuff this puppet with herbs of healing. Upon its brow their zodiac, upon the groin their gender. Upon its breast should be three drops of their blood.

>Rise from this body
>Now free the mind
>Into this vessel
>All ailments bind

Burn the puppet on a ritual fire of wood of oak, and healing herbs. As it burns focus on the illness being taken with it.

>By all the elements
>Both near and far
>From this body all illness bar!

Scatter the ashes to a body of water, or in some great wind.

Greater Transference

Sew a human-shaped puppet out of cloth. Stuff it with herbs of magicks, write the seal of the ruling planet of their zodiac on the chest. Write beneath that their name, beneath that the ruling sign of their gender. Wrap in blue ribbon about the body some personal effect of theirs. Add a drop of blood/blood substitute to the chest of the doll, across the brow, and to the feet.

I give of the body of (x)
That it shall be the body of this which is before me
I burn of the holy seals and sacred herbs
That it shall receive the spirit of the form
That is within the flesh cloth.
That it shall fill the in-firmed vessel
And draw forth from it into these flames
The illness against which it is afflicted

Illness (name it)
I give of this to you
And bind you unto this puppet
Of flesh cloth, blood and herbs of good will
That you will release as it is released
Unto the flames which bind it thus.
By the three drops of vital blood.
One for the breath,
One for the mind
And one for the body

That (Name of persons) shall be free from illness
As the pact of the earth is called forth and you are
Delivered unto the flames
The disease is offered up
In the great names of power of the god of fire.

Conjuration of Desire

Mix the following herbs:

Lavender, Mandrake, Rosemary,
Dragons Blood, High John Root, Cinquefoil,
Mugwort, Yarrow, Vervain,
Wormwood, Yew, Devil's Shoestring
Frankincense, and Myrrh resin

These herbs should be mixed in equal part and blended together in a stone mortar. They should come in contact with no metal, other than the blade used to harvest them.

Simmer rain water, kept for three weeks, adding the herbal mixture slowly so that it is all thoroughly immersed within the heating vessel. Keep this from boiling, keep the water from cooking out by adding more when it gets low. The intent is to cook it down, to cook it strong. This should be simmering for no less than 6 hours, and no more than 13 for utmost efficacy. When it is done, add a drop of your blood and let this fluid cool. Bottle it into individual vials.

Use:

Write out your desire and burn it to ash. Mix the ashes with this condenser in its vial and throw it over your left shoulder so that it shatters. Walk away without looking back.

Other methods of application are to be as an ink when using written word magicks. Or to be used as an anointing oil for general manifestation. As this creates a general medium of manifestation through the power of the herbs.

Relaxation

Reference only

1 tsp Chamomile
1 tsp Vervain
1 tsp Damiana
1 tsp Lavender
½ tsp Mullein

Gives a minty smell, with a bitter aftertaste. Drinkable generic herbal tea. Add honey to sweeten. Relaxation, soporific. More relaxation than sedative. Dry mouth, mild sedative with effects not immediate.

Vision/Trance

Reference only

1 ½ tsp Mullen
1 tsp Damiana
1 tsp Elder Flowers
1 tsp Chamomile
1 tsp Lavender
1 pinch Life Everlasting

Hypnotic. Leave it sit for 10 minutes. Gets bitter after too long. Darker tea, chamomile and peppermint aroma. Makes the third eye tingly. Dry mouth effect and kind of spacy. Muscle relaxation gives way to the mindset of feeling relaxed.

Projection Awareness

Reference only

1 ½ tsp Mullen
1 ½ tsp Damiana
1 tsp Elder
1 tsp Chamomile
1 tsp Lavender
1 tsp Peppermint
1 tsp pinch Life Everlasting

Mild taste and smell, and very light, cool aftertaste. Sweet smell and taste. Stimulates the Prana current, not as relaxing as the trance. Slightly energizing. Raises the energy current, good for evening. Opens up the energy flow. Delayed onset of projective sensations. Cook for 5-10 minutes. After 45 minutes from consumption sedation effects increased.

Astral Vision

Reference only

1 ½ tsp Mullen
1 tsp Lavender
1 tsp Damiana
1 tsp Peppermint
1 tsp Elder Flower
1 tsp Chamomile
1 pinch Life Everlasting
1 tsp Yarrow

Pungent herb flavor. Healing from the inside, gives sensations inside and increases physical sensitivity. Cooling sensations in the palate. Possible aphrodisiac. Good for work with psychic processes and general awareness.

Projection

Reference only

1 tsp Vervain
1 tsp Elder Flower
1 tsp Damiana
1 tsp Angelica

Bitter flavor, honey should be added. Woody aftertaste. Almost immediate effect which dissipates quickly. Good for sudden inducing of mindsets for vision work. Recommended addition of peppermint or spearmint. After effects include increased empathy, and energetic stimulation. Responds well with movement of the body. Gives tingly sensations. Projection takes a bit to take effect. Movement first, then stillness.

Healing Projection

Reference only

1 tsp Vervain
1 tsp Elder Flower
1 tsp Damiana
1 tsp Angelica
1 tsp Peppermint
1 tsp Yarrow

Smells refreshing with a medicinal flavor. Like the projection tea but more controllable. Good for teaching energetic control.

Hang-Over Relief

Reference only

1 tsp Yarrow
1 tsp Rosemary
½ tsp Damiana
½ tsp Mint
1 tsp Chamomile
t tsp Lavender

Works but has a foul taste. Use honey and let sit for 5 minutes.

Speedy Relief

Reference only

1 tsp Yarrow
1 tsp Chamomile
1 tsp Damiana
1 tsp Elder Flower
1 tsp Mint
1 tsp Lavender
1 tsp Rosemary

The Flower softens it and makes it a light taste. Works quickly and is soothing. Add honey to taste.

Elemental Blends

When you would connect with the elements internally to increase one aspect over another. Note any allergy, or problem you may have. As there is no dosage given, as these are all for reference anyway.

Earthy Blend

Vervain, Mugwort

Watery Blend

Chamomile, Lemon, Spearmint

Airy Blend

Lavender, Goldenrod

Fiery Blend

Damiana, Peppermint

Gender Blends

Masculini-tea

Angelica, Peppermint, Lavender, Rosemary, Damiana, Chamomile

Femini-tea

Lemon, Yarrow, Primrose, Mugwort, Elder Flower, Mullen

For those of my readership who would prefer a lesbian-tea, a homosexual-tea, and transsexual-tea. Do your best with blending the herbs where appropriate.

Planetary Blends

For use as anointing oils, or other such instances when you would need an external, or internal connection to the planets. In such cases as you would need a physical link internally to that vibrational current.

Sun

Chamomile, Rosemary

Mars

Peppermint, Ginger

Moon

Wintergreen, Lemon, Jasmine

Jupiter

Hyssop, Clove

Mercury

Peppermint, Lavender

Saturn

Solomon's Seal, Mullen

Venus

Elder Flower, Cardamom

Miscellaneous Blends

Reference only

Exorcism Blend

    Yarrow

    Elder Flower

    Angelica

    Rosemary

    Mullen

    Peppermint

    Hyssop

Used to banish spirits, or fill the boxes used in the exorcisms that contain spirits. Burning it, Oils made with it, and washes made with it. Do what depends on what you have for the situation as it is in demand.

Protection Blend

    Angelica

    Cinnamon

    Hyssop

    Mugwort

    Pennyroyal

    Valerian

Used to make oils and washes for objects that need a bit of extra protection. Planetary herbs should also be included. Augment the vibrations of the herbs with stone fragments, and other conjurations.

Longevi-Tea

    Life Everlasting, Lemon, Lavender

Wonderful for rejuvenation.

Immortali-tea

    Apple, Sage, Linden, Lemon, Lavender, Life Everlasting, Vervain

Great for a little deeper rejuvenation.

Luck & Wishes

Sage, Wishes, Ginseng, Violet, Strawberry, Orange, Rose

Miscellaneous purposes, generally good if you scatter while proclaiming your intent to the winds. Or keeping them in a sealed jar with your intent. Any number of methods of application.

Purification

Chamomile, Hyssop, Lavender, Vervain, Peppermint

Sex Magick

Masturbation

With the advent of the modern world, and the joys of the internet, we find ourselves faced with the exciting potential for our Orgasm. In this case we can be as depraved as we want, by enjoying the company of others who are 10s, or possibly 1000s of miles from our location. While we enjoy our perverse natures and explore them out on the net, we find ourselves in a particular spot. Masturbation. The dirty word which has been the source of many a youth's journey to self discovery. The same is true with mages, witches, and whoever else. We all do it, some are not comfortable admitting this. They should visit a sex shop, talk with the clerk who can tell them all sorts of fun ways to get off.

We in our time of being can enjoy this depravity, and while we do, we can curiously shape our sex. As one who greatly admits to the pleasures and promise of masturbation, I can say I found the more unique the visualization the better. The more obscure, and impossible scenario the better it is, the harder I reach climax, and the longer the sensations last before I feel the need to beat meat again. As magicks are formed within the minds of the mage, we can guide ourselves to a point of no mind, gnosis, as its called. In this place of no mind, we die for a moment, we lose ourselves in the ecstasy of releasing the life creating ejaculate. While we do this, we can shape what we want the world to be, curiously enough when one is masturbating, every single cell in the body feels alive with energy.

It is this energy we seek. We seek to use this generative force to create from the raw material we are given. Acts of magicks, behave like orgasm. We reach our heights, and depths of emotions in the context of magick ritual. We shape the raw material. So we begin our exercise with the conscious birth of potential constructs.

Close your eyes, and see yourself standing naked in your favorite position. As you rub yourself, and stroke your pleasure center, feel the Chi of the earth flowing up through your feet. Exciting the toes, the tops of feet, as though they were in your lovers hand. Kissing softly and awakening all the cells of the body. Draw your deep breath, and bring this up. Every stroke a little higher on the sensations. As you bring this up through the throbbing member which you are pleasuring, breathe deeply, calmly and slowly. Feel yourself in these actions, filling with this Chi. As your bring this energy up, you should be stroking harder, slowly, and deep. Draw it up to your navel, from your root. Draw it up through the heart, filling every cell below it, with this tingling power source. As you radiate power, draw it up through your breast, up through your throat, being filled in your entire body with this flow. Sensually drawing up your flesh, exciting every sensation. Up through your mouth, behind your nose, up to the third eye. It tingles and you draw it up every higher. With every stroke, getting closer and closer to the source. The force your controlling though this process, is then at the top of your head. Your entire body radiating with this current. It reaches past your crown, and then it flows in waves and tide. With every stroke it flows down your body, and back up. As you rub your member, your in waves of ecstasy. When you have as much as you can, release and give into the orgasm.

This introductory technique, will help you raise energy consciously while doing any other form of magicks. It is a great breath technique to open up the flow lines from your Chakras, and Prana flow. I would suggest daily repetition of this method, until you're satisfied with the level of control you have over your body. When you have done this successfully with yourself. Attempt this with a partner.

Feel their energy current while you stroke them. Feel their responses with your hands, receive the flow of Chi. As you stroke firmly, pull the energy up through their energy points. Every cell, every Chakra, the Prana flow. Up through the crown, until you have the entire body full of this energy. When it is flowing down their body, and back up, bring them to orgasm as you pull the energy out.

The results should be the same as when you experienced the same. Work with this method as often as permissible by your relationship.

By doing this method, and doing it constantly you are working the Prana flow, the Chi flow that comes through the natural flesh and pleasure center. It will come later, that you should use this method to devour the energy which is released. As you consume what they produced during the event, pull that energy into your core. Fill it and push it through every energy center of your body. Consumption of this, begins a journey into your vampiric sexual sorcery.

The Great Rite

In our continuing study of the nature of the spirit, post-Right of Transformation, we will notice that the internal structure that we have, how we process energy, and work magicks, has become deeper in a way. The beginnings of acclimating to this new processing of energy takes months, and sometimes years to develop proficiency in. Over the years as we begin our practices, we learn that taking blood of others, who give it willingly will deepen our reserves, and our capacities towards working certain kinds of magicks. Perception based magicks, Elemental based magicks, and in some cases psychic based magicks will be easier with the augmented energies of the blood of those willing donors.

Sexually we will be at our best when we have drawn off of their Prana currents, and assimilated them into the cores of our beings. While still maintaining focus and contact. Doing things like projecting energy into their Prana flows, through massage and other means, such as kissing, touch, and penetration, will be a means to ride out, and deepen that person's capacities to handle the kinds of things you would explore with their inner nature.

Stimulating your partner's Prana flow, upon their back is the easiest method to raise their level of brute desire. Consciously project your active energies into their active current. Draw it up from their left to their right, and back down like a figure 8 double stacked. In this manner you pull at their active and passive Chi flow. And can pull the energy up through their Chakra points. When the time comes that you are ready for them to turn over, after their body has been "loaded" like one would charge a battery.

When they are on their backs facing you, you then can move your charged hands in patterns of seal forms you know, or are drawn to make. Speaking softly, in words subtle enough for them not to notice, but allowing your energy, and the words to vibrate in such a way as to pass from your hands into their vital energy centers, is a way to ensure that you will have loaded enough of a current inside their body, to sustain what would be drawing up and out of them.

Choosing a force which you are comfortable with, allows your connection to them, to your deity, demon, nature god, of choice. If you prefer goddesses to fill the vessel of your lover, or gods, or demons from the pit. Something which expresses the pure emotional state you would be drawing forth. If you happen to want a night of raw bestial sex, conjure up a spirit of a nature god. If you want to have an emotionally filling experience my favorite is calling upon the Morning Star to fill every cell of my being with a most beautiful sensation. Such things become entirely personal. You should develop your own vibrational conjuration. If your lover is so caught up in the indulgences of alcohol, while your hands are filling his form with energy, or her form, then you can damn near shout the conjuration in jest as it were, while you trace the seal of Lucifer on their brow where the third eye is. Over their heart, and on their members where you desire the greatest passion.

Ego advocare tu anima inferna,
Ego conjuro tu Luciferi

From this conjuration, you are using the vessel of your lover to be filled with the Lucifer's archetypal energy current. In our discussions we have said that gods, demons, and angels are archetypal critters created from focused thought forms and the collective of the human condition. Just because it might be a mythic construct to someone. That is what gives us the ability to pull it out of the mind of the all, using any vessel, which it can for the time it takes for the energy to burn off. Doing this can be a delightful way to tap into the bestial mind of your partner. In point of fact it can push that individual over the edge to the point where they give in, and just long for the sensations of the doing. So it quickly turns form foreplay into the sexual act. The less of a waking mind the person has while you do these things, even if you mutter conjuration to yourself, the easier it will be for you to get the kind of sex you're looking for.

This type of conjuration works on the basis, that you already loaded the energy into the body of another, we will call them host. In the time it takes for the act of sex, as well as it takes for the Luciferian current to have run its course, be it a couple of minutes, hours, or days. It will eventually burn out. When this occurs it can lead to an emotional burn out, or a temporary increase in whatever vices the individual has, or arises pleasures in to restore their emotional balance. As this is mild possession, it will be temporary.

While the host is being ridden by a demonic mind, you can link with that mind, and learn new magicks, you can link with the spirit the mind is attached to, pulling in raw Chi. It allows for a darker form of energy working, and assimilation of powers/energies into your body as you would be the subject of the release. The aim is that during penetration they would reach climax inside, and fill you with the dark Chi current, and revitalize your energy systems. In this manner your transformation of your lover's mind, into a host for a greater power, allows you to be rejuvenated.

To Give Birth

The work is designed to bring forth the spirit who is called by their name, or the name the mother and father would give birth to. In this work the spirit to be called by a singular side of the couple can be done by one of the partners without the knowledge of the other. However the name by which the spirit called would need to be the name of the baby upon birth. Unless of course, it becomes the seal by which the power of the name is to be released unto the baby upon its maturity, if it chooses to walk the path of the arts like its parents. It would go by a "common name" upon attainment of its own identity, and then it could be known as the name by which you call it forth in this ritual. It would unseal the power of the spirit, allowing it to embrace what it was called in this world to do, or embody, if an angel, demon, god, djinn, or other spirit to be incarnated into human flesh.

The rite of summons for anything of another energy than a general soul to be called by name should be substituted in the circle which is divided to represent the room. It shall be the sigil of the spirit, seal of the spirit, or other marker by which that spirit shall be birthed into the womb from the other world. Caution must be taken to ensure that the charging and preparation of the body of the mother be taken into account. It will err on the side of caution to take the extra steps.

Anoint the candles, bleed the inks, and light the candles, in the proper positions of their time. If you are taking any short cuts with this ceremony things which are otherwise the product of horror movies might occur. When you are summoning a spirit to incarnate into flesh, then you must do the ritual for the first time, on the day of that planet which rules its influence, and then in the corresponding hour of the influence on the consecutive days. When you are looking into specifics for this occurrence then it is best to look into what astrological zones will be in place in nine months from the time of doing. To achieve the best results so that they correspond to stick to the same day side hours, or night side hours that corresponds to the spirit. If possible eat foods which correspond to the planet of the influence over the spirit which you are going to be giving birth to.

The Summoning of a Human Soul into incarnation

Collect candles, 7 in each color of the planets, carve it with a seal of the gate, as well as the zodiac signs of the man and woman and anoint in an oil in the same hour of the planet, the following day.

The partner who is petitioning pregnancy is to have a small altar set up with a candle in the color of the astrological correspondence for their partner and themselves. It should be carved with the name, and the birthday of the person. They should likewise have one for themselves as well. In a circle of black ink, drawn on paper, or piece of leather. The gender of the baby, the name of the baby should be written.

The soul of the partner should be summoned to the circle, and the command should be given for bringing forth a new body. To call forth the soul from the great well of creation. That through the union of the two, the husband and the wife, the offspring shall be brought forth.

The party who summon the spirit of their lover, shall make love to themselves feeling their lover impregnating them with seed upon their own release. This should take place in the day of each planet, in the hour of the planet of the corresponding zodiac.

There should be a breadth of 3 days from the end, to consummation with the lover, if possible to be within the same circle of 7 candles.

A prayer of calling shall be said upon the lighting of each of the candles.

>The great gate of the sphere of (planet) shall open forth to bring forth (name of child)

Summoning the soul of the living:

>Forth from your mortal vessel free, your soul, your essence to come to me,
>>(x) whose father is (y), whose mother is (z)
>
>I draw you forth to mate with me.

Declaration of intent if done by a woman:

>I call forth from the well of souls to be, that the unborn ones hear me, and stir
>Bring forth to my body, my belly my womb,
>My well of generation of the body which shall house the spirit of (baby)
>That I shall be filled with the seed of my lover (Man) who shall be father of (baby)

Declaration of intent if done by a man:

>I call forth from the well of souls to be, that the unborn ones hear me,
>Bring forth by my body, my seed, my will,
>To pull forth the generation of the body which shall house the spirit of (b)
>That I shall be the one to deliver the seed to my lover (Woman) who shall be the mother of (b)

Upon anointing the candles:

>The fire of the spirit, melts the flesh of wax to give way to the spirit of the stars

(baby's name) hear my summons and come forth to flesh, to the womb of creation.

Upon declaration of incarnation:

> I command that as flesh is unto the wax the flame of this spirit is exalted upon flesh
> That the spirit of (baby) shall be put to flesh, wrapped in bone, and brought by blood
> The way is open that (baby) shall come forth through me, and walk with us, and be with us
> As it shall be (baby) born of (name of mother) and (name of father).

Art of the Mind

To Evoke Truth

Collect a white candle and an oil of consecration. Carve the word Nous into it down the lenth of the shaft, their name directly on the other side. Carve birthday on the right side between the name and the candle, with the symbol of the zodiac. On the left side of the name carve the lattitude and longitude of the place of birth, and if possible the time. Annoint this candle from the center of the candle to the wick, and the center to the base, with the oil across all four of these carvings in it. Starting with "Nous", the place, the name, the hour, the sign.

When you are ready, light the candle upon the gate of the mind:

I conjure forth the gate of Nous

By the source of the mind of the all,

I conjure that the gate be open,

That the way be set into the mind

Of this soulwho sits before me,

I shall have the things which I seek

From within the heart and soul

Speak your intent, that you have written on a piece of paper. Burn it with the following:

The way is open

The truth brought forth

Unto that which I seek,

The words of desire that I speak

Open the way I require,

This candle the beacon

My will evokes the truths pure fire

Burn an effect of the individual in the flames. A greater version of this spell would be to use a figure candle carved of the gender of the individual, with the seal of the mind carved between its eyes.

To Forget

Take a candle that is white and carved with a word in any language that is, "Nous". Take then a candle that is black and carved with the word for "Hyle". These candles should be mixed with your blood. Carve then on the other side of the candle the name of the person who you will be doing this work upon.

Gather writing of the person, describing what they would forget in their own hand, what they commit to paper so they do not have to remember. Take these papers and light them on fire with the flame of the white candle, letting them fall into the fire dish.

> I open here the gate to the mind
> So unto it the darkness
> May overtake and bind

Focus all the pain and loss that you can, that relates to the memory if it is your memory, have them focus all the pain into the fires as these things burn. Put the white candle into the dish so that the wax burns and melts, immolating the memories.

> I call upon the essence of darkness,
> To rise from its place and enshroud the mind
> Unto these memories the darkness bind
> I call forth the key to the gate of the mind
> Let darkness in, so that the memory none can find

Place the black candle still burning, into the flames when the white wax is burned down. Focus on these flames.

> Ashes to ashes
> This memory to dust
> Forgetting this pain is a must

As this fire flares, project all your feeling into these memories, adding herbs of banishing, herbs of forgetting and healing into the fire.

> As by the world of light now dark
> As this fire burns enshroud the memories
> That stir this spark!

There should be nothing left within this vessel, it all must burn. Then you must take whatever is ash to a cemetery, or place untrod, and bury it, you must commend it to the earth, in a place you have never gone, to a place you shall never go again, nor that you should be able to find it again. There is nothing left, within your mind. There is nothing left it is all gone and forgotten.

The Greater Seal of the Mind

Carve one white candle with the word Nous, carve the other with the word Hyle. Mark it like you would the candle of the spell of truth. Use a black female candle carved with the name of the individual upon their back, their astrological sign upon their breast, and the seal of the mind upon the head.

Mix an incense of the following:

> A few drops of your blood
>
> A few drops of the blood of a virgin boy (if you can find it)
>
> A portion of a your own tooth (if you have any)
>
> A spider carapace
>
> A bit of spider's skin
>
> Herbs of the seven planetary bodies.
>
> Salt Peter
>
> Charcoal powder

Anoint the candles with the consecration oil, from the heart of the female candle, to the crown. From the heart to the feet. Proceed likewise from the middle of the other two as well.

Get a letter of intent in the handwriting of the one who is doing the asking.

Set the gate circles up, set the elemental seals up. When this has been done, draw the following array. Starting from the center point, you have the 8 post natal trigrams of the I-Ching, and the 8 microgates of the earth, around a large central circle. Around that circle should be 8 planetary gates corresponding in the color to the source, and to the planet it represents. The outer band should be the prenatal trigrams that cause the generation of the 10,000 things. From there you have at left most point and right most point, a secondary plain 8 ray star should sit attached to the primary circle.

When you are ready to begin, light the candles and the incense and begin speaking the greater seal of 12, and when you have done this. Finish it off by adding in,

> I call forth the source Nous
> That the way to the mind is sealed
> Let no force enter forth this way
> Let the way be closed to all
> Let my will exist within the mind
> As the mind is sealed
> Upon this mind
> Be Set!
> I call forth the spider to spin the web that will work my will.

Let the center candle burn itself out. Close the circle and return to the house.

To restore the mind

The mind of the broken needing to be fixed, shall be so when moments of extreme passions can overcome the other. Under the rules of incarnation there exists a code : that the body is forfeit under the condition that the spirit accepts and gives over to another.

In such cases when possession of meat is forfeit into the invading force there is not much that can be done, aside from go back in the subconscious and change the will of acceptance, to the will of conflict. It in this conflict that can release from the mind the bonds that allow a spirit to take residence within the flesh, that is not of birth origin to the meat.

The body is crafted to contain a specific spirit, energy, personality. It in this method shall be the will to force the body to remember what its origin was, to remember the power it has over its flesh.

The parts of this work shall be:

The Linking spell – To bind the locations if you have more then one person doing the work.

The Greater summons of the Living Spirit – This is to draw the spirits of the body out so that it can be purged. Much in the form of an exorcism.

Conjure To bind the Spirit – To contain the spirit of corruption to a single place, so that the exorcism can be achieved safely.

Exorcism of the Division – To remove the the offending energies.

Conjure of the Light Fire – To burn off of the essence all of the corruption that has been attached to it by the afflicting demon.

Spirit trap/Conjuration of the Fall - The resulting corruption can be bound into service or sent to the abyss.

Time Magick

The Clock

Setting the Clock

In the course of the use of the temporal art one can use temporal projection upon singular targets. These targets must be able to feel the pressure of time. Therefore it is generally required that they are human. When you have your target in your mind's eye feel the current that flows around them. Notice how their energy field interacts with the fields around them. Find the division between their energy and the energy of the environment they are in, and pull up the force of time from the seal of time and set it like a clock face pointing up, 12 being ahead of them at their legs, 6 behind them down their middle. Set the clock to ticking by determining how urgent you would have them be, or how slow you would have them move.

Uses of the Clock

The clock itself is used to speed up one's perception of time. When you have a target who needs to feel the pressure of the influence of time. This can be made to be just an emotional unbalance in the their energy field, or it can be made to influence their body depending on how you root it into them. You can make it effect those people who interact with the target. There are other uses such as applying different spells to the clock, and time delay effects that slowly carve away their sanity, life, or some other effect that you would influence and use to effect them.

Layering the Clock

As this process is kinda touchy when you start applying it, layering different kinds of temporal flow requires an understanding of the environment your target is in. You can alter the time of those around them to conflict with the target to make them angry or calm. Use a sigil as the center for the clock and when it makes the arm full circle, the spirit becomes active and the influence saturates the life and environment of the target.

The Source Clock

When you combine this technique with sources you have the ability to time the goings on of other events and influences in the life. Combining sources in this manner will speed the time forwards, or cause it to slow down. Using the sources in combination with this technique can be used to influence locations, and regions beyond just a single living target. But you can use the target as the anchor in use of bigger ceremony when you need more then one person even if they aren't aware of it.

Sphere of Premonition

Take an obsidian sphere and keep in the dark for a full lunar cycle immersed in water meant to cleanse it of all its current energies. At the dark moon, hold it before you in your hand, letting only the light of the black candle shine on it. Give it this charge.

Of the was and is to be
Let now come that sight to me
Though the eye
Within my mind
Unto this sphere
This charge I bind
Though past and present
And future to see
While it I hold
Show the events to be!

Conjuration of The Greater Seal of Twelve

Manifest unseen beyond the reach of time
In the place of mind and shade
I throw wide the gates
By thought, will, blood
Become
Open now the gate
By the blood of power
By the thought and the word of the source
As the living fire commands
Open now the passage through the abyss
The way between the worlds
Open the way by my power
It is my key unto the great gate
I am the Keeper of the Way
I am the keeper of the keys
Open forth to my will

I call forth Spirit of the essence of Earth
By the pact of the oath of blood
To the earth by the seal of earth
By the spirit of earth hear me
Come forth, Opened the Seal of Earth

I call forth Spirit of the essence of air
By the pact of the oath of blood
To the earth by the seal of air
By the spirit of air hear me
Come forth, Opened the Seal of Air

I call forth Spirit of the essence of Water
By the pact of the oath of blood
To the earth by the seal of water
By the spirit of water hear me
Come forth, Opened is the Seal of Water

I call forth Spirit of the essence of Fire
By the pact of the oath of blood
To the earth by the seal of fire
By the spirit of water hear me
Come forth Opened is the Seal of water

ATE ME PETA BABKA
ANA HARRANI SA ALAKTASA LA TARAT
PETU BABKAMA LARUBA ANAKU
INA KADINGER SEMU INA MAMITU
PETA INA KUNUK INA BABU TIAMAT
ZI DINGER ANA KANPA
ZI DINGER KIBRAT ERSETIM KANPA

ATE ME PETA BABKA
ANA HARRANI SA ALAKTASA LA TARAT
PETU BABKAMA LARUBA ANAKU
INA KADINGER SEMU INA MAMITU
PETA INA KUNUK INA BABU NANNA
ZI DINGER ANA KANPA
ZI DINGER KIBRAT ERSETIM KANPA

ATE ME PETA BABKA
ANA HARRANI SA ALAKTASA LA TARAT
PETU BABKAMA LARUBA ANAKU
INA KADINGER SEMU INA MAMITU
PETA INA KUNUK INA BABU NEBO
ZI DINGER ANA KANPA
ZI DINGER KIBRAT ERSETIM KANPA

ATE ME PETA BABKA
ANA HARRANI SA ALAKTASA LA TARAT
PETU BABKAMA LARUBA ANAKU
INA KADINGER SEMU INA MAMITU
PETA INA KUNUK INA BABU NERGAL
ZI DINGER ANA KANPA
ZI DINGER KIBRAT ERSETIM KANPA

ATE ME PETA BABKA
ANA HARRANI SA ALAKTASA LA TARAT
PETU BABKAMA LARUBA ANAKU
INA KADINGER SEMU INA MAMITU
PETA INA KUNUK INA BABU ISHTAR
ZI DINGER ANA KANPA
ZI DINGER KIBRAT ERSETIM KANPA

ATE ME PETA BABKA
ANA HARRANI SA ALAKTASA LA TARAT
PETU BABKAMA LARUBA ANAKU
INA KADINGER SEMU INA MAMITU
PETA INA KUNUK INA BABU SHAMMASH
ZI DINGER ANA KANPA
ZI DINGER KIBRAT ERSETIM KANPA

ATE ME PETA BABKA
ANA HARRANI SA ALAKTASA LA TARAT
PETU BABKAMA LARUBA ANAKU
INA KADINGER SEMU INA MAMITU
PETA INA KUNUK INA BABU MARDUK
ZI DINGER ANA KANPA
ZI DINGER KIBRAT ERSETIM KANPA

ATE ME PETA BABKA
ANA HARRANI SA ALAKTASA LA TARAT

PETU BABKAMA LARUBA ANAKU
INA KADINGER SEMU INA MAMITU
PETA INA KUNUK INA BABU NNINB
ZI DINGER ANA KANPA
ZI DINGER KIBRAT ERSETIM KANPA

I open the gate of the eight primal elements
By the blood oath

I open the gate of the source of the life of all
I open the gate of the source of the mind of all
I open the gate of the source of the spirit of all
I open the gate of the source of the death of all
I open the gate of the source of the time of all
I open the gate of the source of the chaos of all
I open the gate of the source of the darkness of all
I open the gate of the source of the light of all

By the blood seal of the gate of algol
By the black blood and dark waters
By the eternal fires, and the dark earth
Come forth unto my summons and open the seal
Unto this world release the seal
I call forth the spirit of the earth
The the blood of the ancient is my blood
Through this my blood in this my work

I throw wide the gates
Open now unto the darkest planes of creation
Thought, will, deed, becoming
I summon forth the fires within my soul
I evoke forth the eternal fire
Open now these gates before me
The blood made thought
The thought made will
The will made word
The word made creation
Of this gate to the mind, the body, and the soul
The gate opens unto this my word

I open the gate these gates unto this mind
So unto the it, this darkness will bind
I call forth the essence of the source of darkness
These memories enshroud and bind
I call forth the key to the gate of the mind
Let this darkness in,
So these offensive memories none can find
Ashes to ashes,
This memory to dust
Forgetting this pain
She must

Hear me in the regions of three times four
In the angels of the seconds
Spirits of the hours
I conjure forth the root of the source of time
I draw my will by the root of the eight seals
Of that which is the ordered flow of time

I draw forth these forces from the beginnings of time
Unto the ending of all days
I call forth that coalescing force of movement
That which exists eternally in motion
Changing by degree
That it is brought forth
By the divisions of the twelve from the root of 8
I call you forth to set this seal of the ages

From the gate of the sphere of the moon, I call Cancer
From the gate of the sphere of the Sun, I call Leo
From the gate of the sphere of Mercury, I call Virgo
From the gate of the sphere of Venus, I call Libra
From the gate of the sphere of Mars, I call Scorpius
From the gate of the sphere of Jupiter, I call Sagittarius
From the gate of the sphere of Saturn, I call Capricorn
From the gate of the sphere of Mars, I call Aries
From the gate of the sphere of Venus, I call Tarus
From the gate of the sphere of Mercury, I call Gemini

By you twelve lords of the Zodiac and the influence of time
By the twelve abominations of the Zodiac, and the Demons of Time
By the twelve infernal houses
By the twelve houses of the stars
By the unseen ones of chaos
By the abstracts, on the rotation of the cycles

Athoth, reaper of Aries
Harmas, eye of fire within Taurus
Galila, twins of the Gemini
Adonaius, spirit of Leo
Astartoth, spirit of Virgo
Thammuz, spirit of Libra
Akiressina, spirit of Scorpio
Yubel, spirit of the Archer
Harmupial, Spirit of Capricornus
Achiradonin Spirit of Aquarius
Belias, Spirit of Piscies

Hear now my summons,
In the regions of the twelve
In the houses of the firmament and of this world
In the celeistial order that govers the shifting flows

I call you forth to set this seal upon the internal universe
That you, and only you by the virtures of the shifting ages
Can seal this event past its release
That in no time shall be subject to it
But in all time subjugated by it
I conjure thee

Come thou forth, 24 spirits of time
By the seals of your conscription
Against the shadows of the ages

Hear now my summons
Be brought down up the setting of this seal
By these twelve,
By these four times four
In the times and in the angles, in the passing perceptions unto the ageless
In all the rotations of the degrees

I open forth the way of the damned and forgotten
I open the forth the way of the lost and the desired
I open the way for the creation of the soul
I open this very way
That the image of the soul
Shall be brought forth before me
That it shall be remade in the image of its source

The way that has been made ready
By the twelve and the four
I open the way that has made ready
By the gates of the eight
By the primal powers of eight

Open now the door unto the soul
That through flesh and blood
It be opened unto my will by the great art

I bind the rotations of the twelve, that is sealed beyond the flow of time
In the space between spaces
Beyond the reaches of the sphere of the living,
Beyond the reaches of the sphere of the never-born
Beyond the worlds of the spirit
Beyond the underworld of the gods

Separate but held eternal by the twelve
Until the time is commanded to be released.

Blades of the Art

Conjuration of the Blade of Oblivion

Select a blade that will be the proper vessel for this conjuration, it should be fit to what you need.

I am the lord of infernos fire,
I summon forth the blades of oblivion
Burning beyond the veil of time
Hotter then the fires of Gehenna
Be summoned forth the darkest fire
That which flows through the deepest void
Flow with my words
Wrap this blade of death and darkness
Become my sword of the ancient ones
The blade which slays Tiamat
The blade that rends heaven from earth
I bid thee come forth

Pull the sword across your hand as you energetically unsheathe it:

Demon blade I hold before me
I name you;
I command you:
Answer unto my summons when I call your name
When you are swung strike down my enemies
No force against you shall stand
God of the abyss you are commanded
Obey this summons (name of the blade)

When you're half way though it unsheathe it .

Hold it blade to the sky, point up to the moon. Bid it sleep after you finish. Place your hand on the flat of the blade

I am he who commands you
I beckon thee forth from this the shell of stone and metal,
Free from this imposed body take form and respond to rest,

Bibliography

General Reference

An Intermediate Greek-English Lexicon founded upon the Seventh Edition of Liddell and Scott's Greek-English Lexicon, Oxford University Press, Clarion Press, 1889

The Magical and Ritual Use of Perfumes, Richard Allan Miller and Iona Miller, Destiny Books, 1990

Magical Alphabets, Nigel Pennick, Weiser Books, 1992

The Complete Book of Incense Oils & Brews, Scott Cunningham, Llewellyn, 2005

The Magician's Companion A Practical & Encyclopedic Guide to Magical & Religious Symbolism, Bill Whitcomb, Llewellyn, 2005

Three Books of Occult Philosophy, Donald Tyson, Llewellyn, 2005

Cunningham's Encyclopedia of Magical Herbs, Scott Cunningham, Llewellyn, 2007

The Complete Magician's Tables, Stephen Skinner, Llewellyn, 2009

Crystals & Stones, The Group of 5, North Atlantic Books, 2010

Right Hand Path

The Book of Common Prayer and Administration of the Sacraments and Other Rites and Ceremonies of the Church together with the Psalter or Psalms of David, The Church Hymnal Corporation, 1979

The Mystical Qabalah, Dion Fortune, Society of the Inner Light, Weiser Books, 2000

The Original Account of the Teachings, Rites, and Ceremonies of the Hermetic Order of the Golden Dawn, Israel Regardie, Llewellyn, 2006

Papal Magic Occult Practices within the Catholic Church, Simon, Harper-Collins, 2007

Crowley

777 and other Qabalistic writings of Aleister Crowley, Isreal Regardie, Weisr Books, 1986

The Confessions of Aleister Crowley an Autohagiography, John Symonds and Kenneth Grant, Arkana Books, 1989

Magick Liber ABA, Aleister Crowley, Weiser Books, 2010

Witchcraft

A Treasury of Witchcraft, Harry E. Weddick, Philosophical Library New York, 1961

The Witches Bible, Gavin and Yvonne Frost, Berkley Medallion Books, 1972

Crones's Book of Charms and Spells, Valerie Worth, Llewellyn, 1998

The Wicca Handbook, Eileen Holland, Weiser Books, 2000

The Complete Book of Spells, Ceremonies, & Magic, Migene Gonzalez-Wippler. Llewellyn, 2004

Crone's Book of Magical Words, Valerie Worth, Llewellyn, 2005

Taoism

I Ching A New Interpretation for Modern Times, Sam Reifler, Bantam Books, 1991

The Shambhala Guide to Taoism, Eva Wong, Shambhala Publications, 1997

The Tao of Physics, Fritjof Capra, Shambhala Publications, 1999

Magick, Shamanism, & Taoism the I Ching in Ritual and Meditation, Richard Herne, Llewellyn, 2001

Daoist Magical Incantations, Hand Seals, and Star Stepping, Professor Jerry Alan Johnson, Ph. D, D.T.C.M., D.M.Q., The Temple of the Celestial Cloud, 2006

Left Hand Path

Demonology, Sympathetic Magic and Witchcraft, J.N. Friend, Charles Griffin & Company, 1961

The Black Arts, Richard Cavendish, Perigree Books, 1967

The Satanic Scriptures, Peter H. Gilmore, Scapegoat Publishing, 2007

Qabalah, Qlipoth and Goetic Magic, Thomas Karlsson, Anja, 2009

Divination

Tarot Classic, Stuart R. Kaplan, U.S. Game Systems Inc., 1972

Futhark A Handbook of Rune Magic, Edred Thorsson, Weiser Books, 1984

The Tarot the Traditional Tarot Reinterpreted for the Modern World, Adam Fonteras, Carlton Books Ltd, 1996

Alchemy

Alchemy Science of the Soul, Titus Burkhardt, Fons Vitae, 1997

The Secret Teachings of All the Ages, Manly P. Hall, Tarcher Penguin, 2003

Theurgy or The Hermetic Practice a Treatise on Spiritual Alchemy, E. J. Langford Garstin, Ibis Western Mystery Tradition, 2004

Alchemy of the Nine Dimensions, Barbara Hand Clow with Gerry Clow, Hampton Roads Publishing Company, 2004

The Archidoxes of Magic by Parascelsus, Stephen Skinner, Ibis Press, 2004

The Weiser Concise Guide to Alchemy, Brian Cotnoir, Weiser Books, 2006

The Hermetic Museum Alchemy & Mysticism, Alexander Roob, Taschen, 2006

Regional

The Egyptian Book of the Dead the Papyrus of Ani, E. A. Wallis Budge, Dover Publications, 1967

Babylonian Magic and Sorcery, Leonard W. King, Weiser Books, 2000

Norse Magic, D.J. Conway, Llewellyn, 2003

Grimoire Texts

13 gates of the Necronomicon, Donald Tyson, Llewellyn world wide, 2010

Necronomicon, Simon, Avon, 1980

Grimoire for the Apprentice Wizard, Oberon Zell-Ravenheart, New Page Books, 2004

Companion for the Apprentice Wizard, Oberon Zell-Ravenheart, New Page Books, 2006

The Gates of the Necronomicon, Simon, Avon, April 2006

Dead Names, Simon, Avon, November 2006

The Demonic Bible, Tsirk Susej, Embassy of Lucifer, 2006

Grand Key of Solomon the King Ancient Handbook for Angel Evocation and Djinn Summons, Asaph Ben Berechiah, Ishtar Publishing, 2009

Appendix

Of Locations

Every location of the art has a significance. It depends on the level of the working that you are doing, your hopes in the results achieved, and the timing of what you are doing. When you set a space, you are building the foundations of the world as you would make it. So to bring into focus a work that makes manifest the primal forces then you will have to set the space in a place of either nature, or in a room which has been cleared out, and physical elements set relating to what you would achieve. Where you decide to do your space is a large part of the aesthetics of what it is you are trying to achieve. As some of the Chaotes would say you are going to evoke the psychopomp, the dramatic god force which determines the alignment of the ritual. However that being said, the best way to go about setting the space is when you are writing or reading it, make note of any aspects which are key notes in the ritual itself, and try and form a relation to it through the place you choose to do it in.

There are many types of locations, many types of places which evoke a certain frequency to those who would draw upon their power. Nodes, Nexus points, and Ley lines are prime examples of locations such as this. Places over moving or flowing water also have a magnetic flow which will "carry" the current out to manifest, next to a fire will cause the fire of the spirit to ascend even through the blackest pitch of what ever you are working in. A dark forest at midnight will be able to help evoke the spirits of the earth, and the things which cannot assume form without a natural medium. A beach, sunlight or moonlight, or in the dark of the moons, it matters not, still draw in, and have a private stage at which you sit to all the spirits of the waters of creation. Great things can be achieved when you draw the spirits from the water. Should you seek to work with spirits of the lost, dead, or forgotten, or connect with your ancestral forces, patron, or some other work of peace for your own spirit, then seek out a nice wooded cemetery to make your work space. Vacant buildings when you are drawing temporal arts, or spirits who have passed and need a connection of a gate between worlds. It depends on what you have available to you in your community, the things you can do without being interrupted, and your imagination. It is much better to perform your work when you are most suited for doing the work.

If you get distracted, or if you find yourself debating on one location or another, you can consult your divination medium of choice, seek meditation with your patron, or just go to each space and meditate on what will yield the most energy to your work. That which causes you to question whether or not a place is better or worse, again goes back to if you will be detracted by passers by or anything else which may find it appropriate to interrupt your time with the elemental forces. As pagans we must exercise discretion when working with or discussing the things which formed the notions of the Zionist divinity, and relating back to non-pagans; and yet, non-pagans may have no discretion, no accord when dealing with us in turn, when we are obviously busy, in the middle of a ritual, and don't have time to be distracted. This will not happen in a proper setting, you will by the nature of the location and the wards you set in place ensure that you will not be interrupted, however there is no pity to be had for the poor soul who wanders into the ritual space, intoxicated, or just to be obnoxious and gets possessed, sick or some other unfortunate happening. If they do, and your location becomes violated by the unworthy, loud and irritating, you have every right to evoke the wards and protections against the spirits which attack the circle. This will banish their souls, their works, and anything nasty they have brought with them back to where it came from, or into the ancient desert of the wastes. Reference your copy of the Simon *Necronomicon* for this exorcism. When you have been threatened, stay inside your circle, make your proper charges; if you are innocent of initial aggression you can draw forth the cosmic currents to do away with the nastiness which might seek you out. However, if you tell people where your rites will be held, or what your rituals involve, then you will have to deal with some of that. Use discretion. If you are doing something, or have done something to cause such distractions then you deserve it.

So if you have chosen your site, then you should also meditate on why you have chosen it. If you can bring a sense of understanding to why you are drawn there. Is it only for this one working? Or is this location going to be your sacred place? If it is to be your sacred place then tell no one, when you are there, it is your place, nothing can distract you in that space, and you can safely cast a circle. It doesn't matter if it's a corner of a park, or it's your closet or your bedroom, or something, which when you reserve it for ceremony you are in a place where you will not be bothered, you will not have distraction as you commune directly with your currents of choice. No one can tell you what to believe so long as you have that belief, you have the ideas, and you know why you do what you do. The places where you do these things are between you, the natural forces, and your patron. No one else needs to know the location, unless you're working with multiple people. In which case you should have ritual location for group workings, reserving solitary rites to your sacred space mentioned above.

Circles

The world we *see* is not the world that *is*. Our brains omit information which allows us to process the things that are, so we can with our perception go about them in the proper way. Circles duplicate this concept. They omit what you do not need, and draw only into your center the forces you would work with. Therefore, when you draw an array, keep in focus your intent. Every planet and element has an associated number, shape, and design. There are hundreds of references for this, *The Magician's Companion* is one of the best, most complete compendiums available for this. Each planet having its shape, should also have correspondence to your work; any stars you would draw into increase efficacy are to be the same.

This is best done through example. Let us assume you are conducting a rite, the target of which is to create a node. Begin with a piece of paper, and draw a circle to represent the space of the world which you are working. Then mark your awareness of the north, south, east, west, and center points of this circle; so that you can determine the direction the energy points are going to come from. Then, link these points into a diamond or square shape, if you are going for the full 8 elemental points, with the chaotic central point; as with chaos it stirs the forces of creation then do so with the eight ray cross, and interlacing squares. Every line which crosses over or under a line, represents a movement within the space. If you have a summoning circle, then your lines should overlay each other in a counter clockwise pattern drawing forces down into the center of your space. Since this rite is to build a center a power then you are drawing out the natural currents so you have the lines overlapping each other in a clockwise pattern. As the sun in the heavens moves in that pattern around the central stick, so to does the natural current flow out from that point as well. You need to ensure that your elemental points are connected where they need to be, both inside and outside the angles of what you are drawing. Every angle, open line, square or circle incorporates some aspect of the natural world.

Cleansing

When you are conducting a work, you want it to be the best that it can be. So it becomes necessary to purge what ever has gotten an build up of anything, both physical and spiritual. Thus spring cleaning is prudent when you are going to be embarking on a ritual. If you are out in nature doing a working then you must clean the area of all unnatural objects which would detract within the radius of the currents which you are working. You must cleanse the energy and the tools which you use to draw the circle on which you work, also cleaning and cleansing your body from any foulness which may have arisen. Old grimoires and historical sources demand that the student or the practitioner embark on long periods of fasting, cleansing, and abjurations to make sure their body is clean, their spirit is in tune with the forces they would work with and they are exhausted, and in the right frame of mind which becomes conducive for entering into the trance which will allow them the capacity to slip into the mind state of the supernal mind, physical mind, or bestial mind.

To cleanse is to prepare your body, before ceremony. Many chose to bathe in salts and blessed herbs, consecrating the waters to what ever forces they wish, scrubbing themselves down a ritual number of times. It is in these rituals which support the embarkation on a practice which is outside the daily routine. That is going to be the act of separation between the world we see, touch, taste, perceive with a common mundane mind, into the world which is our own creation. When we are in the circle, we are the masters of the world, we are the ones who determine what current exists within it, what balance or chaotic force is unleashed and returned outwards into the greater macrocosm. To be in the right frame of mind, to be cleansed of all doubt and worry, is the best way to prepare not only the physical locations and the tools you are going to be using, but also the body itself. The mechanics of the act of ritual on the body exist as both strength for those who need direction, and weakness for those consumed by the order of their structures. Balancing both these aspects is important for balance in your working.

Banishing

A sticky concept for many people. This is where you will clash with people from different castes of the art. Some will require that they summon up the flaming pentagram, or the greater ritual, lesser rituals of the Hexagram, the Pentagram, the conjuration of the elemental summoning pentagram. Where every wave of the arm, point from where you begin draws or banishes that current. It is in the act of the word banish. When you banish, not only do you send away thoughts, and ideas, 'to banish it from your mind' you also banish its current from your working. In the Simon *Necronomicon*, there is a blurb, rather famously it states roughly that there are no effective known banishing from the golden dawn structure to the forces found within. This is very true. That order bases their work on Solar rites, the banishing of the sun are not effective against the planetary currents because the planets are the forces which are being summoned. When you work to send something away, you have to do one of a number of things, outlined below.

Cease the flow of energy to the work – without the current the manifestation should not be able to be stable, since there should exist a void from your circle. There are some works where you are to be inside the circle, warding the world from what you are doing as you peel back the layers to draw out the primal currents. Others require that your circle act as the barrier to all things, and you are outside of it while the forces which you have summoned remain within, bound only to manifestation within the boundaries. When you have ceased the flow, the energy will cease, and they should be forced to return to their plane of origin.

You must then if this force does not work, use some aspect of that which you have brought forth against itself, so that by its own nature it becomes compelled to return. For example, as you as a reader, are probably going to be asking about demon and spirit manifestation; we have a spirit conjured up and it is being obstinate. What you must now do, is return it; but it was human, and it doesn't want to return to being a spirit. You can threaten that you will bind it to some cruel fate which it can never again see the world of the living, bind the thing into servitude to do your bidding for all eternity, or some such thing of that nature. Which should inspire it to either run away or get violent. If it does neither, you have the capacity then to do what you must to make your point known, that even though it is a spirit, as one who works with the elements of nature you will blow it apart to its elemental components, thus destroying it. This should make it aware of a form of mortality it still has, and should depart. If this does not work, and it is mocking what you say, you are lacking the necessary will for follow through. The object is to inspire the force to move and vacate of its own accord, going back to what ever task it was set to do previously.

After having drained the flow of current from the circle, and otherwise threatened the remnants of the existence of the spirit, you have not been able to get it to leave. If you know of something which it fears, or has more power then it, start an conjuration of that force. Banish it by what it fears: my enemy's enemy is my friend. If you have a demon, and it doesn't leave peacefully, then you will have to evoke an angelic host or god force to return it if you cannot make it go by your own power. This should annoy it, but it will be forced back into the plane where it came from.

However if you feel you would like your own approach to dealing with spirits, you can bind them to objects and make them serve you as punishment for their obstinate behavior; you can conjure up a gate that sucks them into a plane which is the exact opposite of their plane of origin; you can bind them to some lower plane as punishment; or seal their essence away for a period of time as Solomon did to the demons he tricked and trapped in the brazen vessel, and tossed into the sea. Banishing works by either embracing a mindset which is opposite to the one you have worked in to draw forces to you – your space being cleansed should have a sturdy banishing done on it, which contradicts or can negate the work that you are doing. This creates a region where, if your ward breaks, the outer area neutralizes the current. If you are working energy in a negative vacuum space where the art is not capable of being worked, or in some dead space, then you must preform a rite of similar type followed quickly by one of the type you are working with to dislodge and nullify the energy around so you can work easily.

Incense

Historical and modern works usually call for some scent to perfume the air. Not only does incense work as a great banishing and cleansing tool, but also to set the mood for the work, and stir the airy currents for the transformation, attuning the air for the proper frequency so you enter into an airlock of consciousness so to speak. Burning incense in your summonings and evocations gives a medium through which the spirits can coalesce and manifest. Every herb used in a work has planetary, elemental and chemical properties which should be taken into account, as well as any reactions they might have with you, or each other. Some herbs don't mix, shouldn't be mixed, or just can't be mixed. Like the circle, the incense should be made with care, and in a way which draws out the most of the natural currents within the earthy body, as well as the energetic body of the herbs themselves.

Every work requires its own recipes, the best ones are made by hand, however compendiums such as *The Encyclopedia of Magical Herbs,* by Scott Cunningham, and *The Master Book of Herbalism* by Paul Beryl are prizes for any library as references. Cunningham's *Complete book of Incense, Oils, and Brews* is the best list of completed recipes available for substitution. When dealing with herbs, you are dealing with nature's chemicals; all modern medicine is based from extraction, duplication, and refinement of the natural chemicals found in the herbs. Alchemy at its finest where the chemical nature of the world, and science of the spirit blend into a union where the results can be tremendously powerful if everything works together in unison to achieve the same result.

When harvesting or mixing the herbs, have a care as to the timing and their planetary alignments. Every herb has a time of day, time of month, celestial body, element and purpose that it is in correspondence with. These all should match as closely to the timing alignments of the individual components and to the overall intent of the working. What is this mixture going to achieve? Like the cleansing, it sets the body and the energy in unison so that the mind is able to access the levels which will make the intent manifest. It should be that incense fills the air with the vibrations that the circle draws down into the center of the space. It is on the circle which the work takes place. All of the subtle currents are laid bare, and the work can draw itself into focus of the mage. The mind of the one doing the work must be squarely in the range which is acceptable to the flow of the work. If you are working to achieve the results on a supernal plane so that it correlates to events you're setting into motion on the physical plane, you must be able to work within the scope of all three mindsets. If you are working with a ritual that is formed on physical manifestation then you must bring yourself to where you can draw into a bestial primal mindset if it would be for a more blatant manifestation, or if you were to raise yourself to a higher state if you would have the work come about more subtly. It might arise in your working that you have to fluctuate between your mind sets in order to properly make your work manifest.

While you are drawing out the higher aspects of your own work, and bringing out the sets of mind which will achieve the ultimate aim of the rite, then you will need to have the array of incenses and powdered herbs prepared beforehand to add to the coals. It is such an easier task to stock with a little extra then being stuck in a precarious position with having too little. More can always be saved for later study, or later inclusion in a fresh batch if one can be made. Like your circle, ideally everything you use in your ceremony should be crafted by you to suit your own ends. When you need specific tools, mixtures, or components which are otherwise hard or rarer, even difficult to get hold of, then it becomes prudent to seek out the ones who deal in such things. Stock up when you have the means, so that whatever tool you have on hand, you will have a means to be able to do something if you need to.

Experimentation is also a great way to get to know what herbs and materials do what, as well as your nuances with their subtleties and elemental personalities. If you can connect with the plants on a correspondence level, then you will be able to bring out the god forces you are familiar with in the plants.

Candles

Every time you light a candle, what do you think about? Do you think that what you are drawing in with that light, or repelling from that light is a force which you can use to create a manifestation of your will? In ritual a candle is both shield and sword; it is the light which draws and the light which destroys. It is what ever the mage needs it to be. The wax of the candle represents the earth, the flame ties it to element of fire, any smoke and heat represents air, and the liquid wax is the water. The spirit put into the lighting, the creation of it, the symbols carved on it, or the components mixed into it, or surrounding it, give it the intent which will cause it to be what you require. The color is important only so far as you tie it to the planetary, elemental, or celestial forces you are attempting to manifest through its application.

Use candles at the points of your circle to draw the elementals, use white ones to banish them. It is your intent behind the lighting and the things which you use them for that matters. Modern references dictate to the student that they use new candles every time only, because there is a risk of contamination in working. This is untrue. It may be prudent that you reuse old ones, so long as the purpose behind their lighting remains the same. The spirit of the flame will gain in potency as well as everything else about it, if you keep using the same style, color, and spare wax into new candles transferring the flame over to the new candle so as to charge it with the spirit elemental which you have created to serve your purpose.

You can do this with any element, so long as you transfer the medium, or the spirit of the medium through the elemental components. They can be dormant as long as they like, but when you light a candle which you have been using the flame of for 30 years to act as the light which protects your circle from being attacked, then that in and of itself becomes a powerful protection. As you progress in your studies, or you have progressed to the point where a new candle every time can be just fine, because you transfer a part of your own spirit into it, to hold it in place while you work the rest of the ritual, that might be effective as well. Like the herbs, burned or unburned and used as sprinkling powders, or added components in the wax, will only increase the efficacy of the work. Make sure that everything ties and builds off each other. If you use one herb in the incense try and tie it somehow into a condenser you use to draw out the circle, and mix into the wax of the candles. Everything about what you are working is to bring about a single end, all the different parts must function as a whole. It is this whole which will make your working succeed or fail.

Rituals are about the ceremony, about the separation between the worlds. It is imperative that these behaviors are known for what they are. Rituals are repeated exercises, in this case the entire basis of this work is to cement the pre-ritual and post- ritual concepts which are needed, so that when you are doing your work, you bring the entire focus of where you need to be, and what you want, when you light your first candle and vocalize the establishment of the circle. These are actions to have you ready to work the art, so that when you light a candle in your day to day, you are not predisposed to conjuring something, or summoning something. The candles, the incense, the circle, are all built to act as a safety between you, and the forces which you would work with on such a scale of experimentation, research, communion, or other advancements.

With practice and experimentation you will learn what works for you, and what does not. It is your own flair, your own style which will build your initial series of rituals in ways which cause you to focus your entire being on the things that you want; making them manifest in the manner which best suits you. Having a thickly smoked room, atop a circle with the elemental candles laid out, where everything has been cleansed – it is getting to the point where you will be able to begin the rite you have before you. Only make use of the materials, and the ceremony which will give you the most protection and get your mind into tight focus so that when you begin you will not be distracted by the other energies which will manifest as your work progresses. Should something unexpected arise then you will have to deal with it. There are no second chances, so make sure that you can mix your incenses, and chant your vocal charges from memory, or on a seconds notice if you need to stop and banish something mid conjuration.

Music

Everything has a frequency: every planet, every moon, every body of mass has some frequency which causes it to form, stay together, and to be what it is. As more work is developed in the field of cymatics, we stick to the foundation of the incorporation of the musical arts into ritual, as both psychological and psychical. The point of a rite is to generate a current which will be sent out on a frequency loud enough for the rest of nature to respond. Like adding a note to a symphony. However, to properly use the arts of sound you must understand what levels do what to the human body, in that you must also be aware of the sorts of behavior and mood shifts that occur. Making use of any and all materials available on hand that you will be able to switch into the proper mindsets which require a fluid control of your environment so that you adapt if problems arise.

Trance states which occur for deep levels of sleep and relaxation are affecting the Delta waves at 0.5 to 4hz, this is where you are into a neutral physical mindset. When you enter into a tranquil state of awareness where internal imagery often occurs are Theta waves from 4-12hz; this can be a bestial or physical mindset. A relaxed nervous system, great for stress management, accelerated learning and mental imagery occurs with the manipulation of the Alpha waves at 8-12hz; the bestial mind. Waking consciousness and alert states of mind, are Beta waves at 12-30 physical mind. "K-complex" waves are at 30-35hz and they bring clarity, sudden states of integration and what can be determined as the "akashic experience"; the best way to describe the supernal mind. When you enter into psycho-dynamic states of awareness those are the super high Beta waves 35-150hz, can be any of the states of mind which will allow you the control over the manifestation.

With these internal currents harnessed with the biokinetic forces of your body, and from the currents which are stimulated with the props of the circle, the incense, the candles, and the other ceremony, you can reach the proper states needed to cause your desired rite to bring full manifestation as you have planned, if you can incorporate all the needed aspects into it. With the constructs to shift your consciousness, master these forms and you will be able to do any rite and spare your sanity.

There is also a frequency which can be harnessed through the use of music and sound patterns by incorporating the sounds and frequencies of the planetary bodies. These numbers and the observed patterns which these vibrations form can be incorporated into the circle, as well as the components used in the rites and formula which the rituals are performed around. It is all in order to bring the will into alignments with the celestial, elemental, and spiritual forces which shape creation so that you as a mage can state that you are a child of the universe. You serve your patron in the best way you have the capacity to. Your rituals can reinforce your union or alignments with your elemental forces and your patron. Even though it was discussed that your patron is a living mind as an extension of your own, in its highest aspect it is what you have the capacity to be, by becoming more in tune. It is through the use of the rites which you perform that your rituals and the more you practice them will get you more prepared in order to handle the trials and ordeals which nature tends to throw in your way. Never an opportunity not to learn something useful.

When you study more into sound, draw deep the correlations between the mathematics of the Pythagorean era, and modern day physics. They are not that far off. Through the understanding and manipulation of sound in its proper capacity we have the foundation on which we can work anything we desire. If we can intone the syllables like the ancient Hebrews wrote, we can create from their intonation a soul, or bodies, or anything which we deem necessary for our survival. These processes are written of in the Sefer Yetzirah, and hold true with the current level of understanding of the theory behind what frequencies are capable of in causing the creation of bodies, symbols and holding the molecular structures of things together. So to work with the frequency as properly suggested one will find themselves with the very building blocks of creation, from the elementals, to celestial, to the waves on which they flow together, all furthering the energy, all raising the power level so that when it comes time for the work to take shape, then it will be an easier process, especially if you understand the mechanics behind the systems which you work with.

Of Stones & Metals

We shall continue to push the boundary with the works, we have focused on blood, the spirit, words, the elements in their spiritual nature. Now we shall have a focus for a time on the stones, and metals. The things which by their very nature have allowed us to build the enormous structures to the sky, travel to the moon, and all sorts of various other things which are yet to be named that we can achieve with these. There are like every field of magicks great discourses done by those doctors who explore the sciences behind them, and those who have grown up around the works of mother nature and contributed back to the literary field their findings. Correspondence books are the majority of my shelves and in them you can find any number of things, at least referenced a single time in each.

While it is nice to have this collective of what others have found about the mineral there are a few things that I should point out. Working with stones in my youth I discovered their ability to project the current I desired. As any plucky person I figured if I could lay them in certain patterns I would achieve results that were desirable for nearly any person. At the time of this writing it has been a nice discussion with one who has spent a few years learning about stones, minerals and metals in ways I forgot they could be made use of. So here will be it my attempts at explaining the methods for some of my more recent forays into the world of mineral magicks.

In the stone world you have the object which exists, it pulses with the natural rhythms of the Chi flow. When you breathe upon it, or send energy into it, it begins to vibrate at higher levels. You combine these with any of the words, sounds, vibrational aids such as perfumes, color symbolism, and other tools and you will have a means to focus the current your working with. Unlike dealing with magicks that comes specifically from the body of the mage, or the celestial world. When working with stone magicks they each have a body, they each have a spirit, and they each have a character of their own. After all it takes tens of thousands of years to make them. In some form or another they are the recorders of all the worlds events. Sometimes they even are witness to what occurs as the imprint from the far off reaches of space. So here we begin by taking an object so common as a stone, find its spirit, work it into our rituals, spells and other such activity.

Blades of the Arts

In our discourses over the different doings and tools we come again to the particularly fun materials. Such as those crafted out of sacred metals, inlaying them with the precious and semi precious stones. It is these which we give great measure to. They are formed, their bodies crafted and the purposes to where their journey is up to fate. It is from here that you must decide what use such shells of beings would be put to. What classification would you give them, what ritual purpose would you have?

In this manner you could impart the souls of the dead warriors fallen in the great battles, you could bind to them demons, or shades, you could invite Djinn, you could call upon the sacred names of god to embody the metallic host to become the medium for its wrath, or justice. You could draw down angelic hosts, or other forgotten less noble creatures to take residence within the blade.

Condition the blade, if you be inspired to work the dead, place the thing in a crypt under auspicious moons, suns, and lunar phases. If you are going through an elemental construct. Made of metals of that element, immersed in that element. The flaming sword of heaven is a popular reference to such things. However for our purposes it will be a description of properties some blades I have come across over the years have held.

Blade of Innocence – Held in the dominant hand of a virgin boy who pierced the dominant hand of another virgin boy shedding blood on holy ground. Current where about is otherwise unknown, as this was stolen from my possession.

Blade of the Right hand of Baal – The demon Ba'al one of the 8 demon lords of Hell, bound to a blade, the ring commanding the power of Hades to keep him in line. Ba'al the general of the armies of hell. This object can remove the soul from the body and offer it up the abyss as well as implant souls that the wielder desires.

So we have the blades which occur by happenstance, and natural occurrences, as all of them walk different paths, each one has a journey unique to its own spirit. The other way is to make a blade specifically crafted for a purpose, using ritual, summoning, and possible blood magicks. From here it is up to you how to create such blades as would come in useful to your path. The spells of the binding spirits should be referenced in what it is you will make.

Working the Rites

When it comes time to put together your full working. From the pieces of the array, the tools, and the conjuration. You have your time, and your spoken parts written. Other such influences are all ready to go, and you are just needing your place to set your working area up. You have your array made of parchment, or inscribed in a catalyst upon the floor. Your ritual space is the last thing which should be discussed.

Our magicks can be achieved anywhere when we understand the blending of the sources, and our work. If you use the grand array of the eight, or any of the other general array's and you have them made out on parchment, or paints, depending on the scale of where it is you would conjure. The following steps are generally all you need in order to piece together the elements of the working which have been laid out thus far.

General Set-up for ceremonial magicks:
- clean your space, remove all things which are not needed for the influences you are seeking to draw.
- Set your space with all the tools, in their locations, and keep them covered until the time of the working.
- Set any extra lighting such as a spare simple white candle for lighting for reading any lengthy conjuration.
- Draw out the array on the floor using what ever media is required for your work. Even if you have a complex array design upon the altar as the point of focus for your work, there should be a clear division within your area on the space in which you work. If you don't have a dedicated room to working the art. Salt is the single best media of division.
- Set any extra ritual tools, or components of cleansing, banishing, or any side spells you would other wise require as extra protections in the ceremony.

With this set up complete you would be able to move onto the doing of the ceremony. All you have to do is cleanse the space with your favorite banishing spells, or conjurations afterward. We undergo this cleansing so as to keep clear the division of our work, from the waking world. So as not to cause bleed over and maintain control over the work.

The Great Art

How the Great Art comes about is the union of the various bodies of the spiritual, mental, and emotional consciousness with the physical body and the consciousness created therein.

This Art remains as always the seeking out of the Creation of the Lapis Philosophica, stone of the philosophers. Whereby the creation results in the "elixir of Life". However for the sake of this work we will continue to stick to the foundations of the elements which make up the mental, spiritual and physical bodies.

Mercury, Sulfur, and Salt make up the Azoth
Azoth is the prima materia, the first matter that makes up creation.
Add it to the "Gold" and "Silver" in a half to half ratio it creates the Lapis Philosophica.

The alchemists not only partaking of the chemical formula within their laboratories, but also the application of the techniques discovered to the day to day life. For the purposes of this work, it is physical, emotional, spiritual, and the mental union of all of the three aspects of the individual soul.

To break it apart and put it back together. To forge the individual in their deepest hell and refine them by their highest hea4ven. One must progress on the journey beginning at the bottom in order to gain access to the subtle worlds. If one does not then then additions of the "lighter" side of their nature will cause the destruction of their consciousness and leave them an empty husk of a being. Begin at the bottom, and go up, one step at a time.

Recreating the physical body in the works of the spiritual, and to attain the greater reaches of the soul is impossible without being able to understand this. The undergoing of this process is contained within the full scope of this work, as such it is the creation of your own art, and your own path for you to find your path to your "God-head".

Paths of Practice

This world will reveal many secrets and many truths to the one willing to delve deeply enough. One should be willing to go to any length to become one with the source, a true power for nothing but the source and the force of nature, that is if one wants to ascend back and return to the source. However one can use what ever resources are available to them gaining more ground with each passing step on the ladder of their practices.

If the ladder goes high enough, there are times in which it plateaus, and gently slides down when mastery over that level is attained, then with the adding of new materials the student then ascends to another level on the ladder. Always growing always improving. It is a path of rectification of the soul, alchemy on the grand scale. I would not venture to say the Grand Arcanum lies within these pages for the willing soul to seek out, because gives the game away. However on the nature of souls and essences, there is an inherent essence in all things, again I will repeat that as often as I feel is needed to get the point across, that nothing can truly be without it, so long as it has some connection to an existence of some form.

As the life of a man is governed by the nature of his own will not interacting on just the mortal level but on the nature of all existence with every life lived sending out shock waves and energy based on the beliefs in life, death, emotions, conceptions of time, and their perception on how this world should be. Perception is very much reality, and if one desires so one can influence their environment by shifting their perceptions into a focused set.

These beginner concepts are restated here for the purpose of reinforcing what is coming. Sometimes things are required of the soul to act as more guiding hand then not. In cases like this the master becomes a puppet master of the environment, putting things in place to further his own ends. Souls of those around are players in the game, and his game becomes then being one to move larger pieces. In the moving and setting up the board in a larger manner one needs a distinct advantage in the game over the others, and a way to gain this advantage is to get mastery over an aspect of people whom are players. To do this one must effect their essence, this is done in many ways, social, emotional, mental, sometimes physical programming. All have proven themselves as viable tools of manipulations, but these are crass. The best way to gain advantage over something is to do it in a way where it affects the essence, and the soul. The creation or rather recreation of the soul of one who is sentient by their own right. Humans, animals, whatever is conscious can be affected by this if they are unaware of the basic threads that bind them to greater source.

Folk Magick

Superstition and lore are transformed into belief structure that can alter the physical, spiritual, and emotional worlds.

Folk magick is the created belief structure, everything within is created through the process of "belief". Everything the individual creates through their own will. Healing, Blessing, Cleansing, Destruction, Banishment, Summons, Evocation, Invocation can be achieved through this form of the arts. It becomes through Psychosomatic effects - to believe the world is changed the world may or may not adapt itself.

Negative Effects:

There may or may not be success. Insanity might be the
gross result of instability within the balanced whole. Through the externalization of the will, and willing subjugation towards
exterior forces created through this belief structure. To become a slave to ones own created God force.

Types of practice:

Organized religion, Gypsy magick, Voodoo, Santeria

Shamanism

Working with the Ancestral forces, Natural forces, and the bestial principals found in the natural and celestial worlds.

The basis of this work is upon the ancestral forces, Folk magick based upon the externalized balance on techniques of the past. As in folk magick can assume full mantle of spirit. These arts can do all that folk magick can with the added attack and defense of greater area, and manipulation of the weather patterns and physical world and dreaming world. Dealing with the celestial timing of events on a yearly pattern.
Ceremonies of passing through the different phases of the cycles of seasons, years, aeons etc.

Negative Effects:

If you fail to maintain your balance with the arts your will will collapse upon your world, you can lose yourself to the mantle of the god forces and natural forces you have been working with, the community rises against you. Insanity and death are a gross result.

Types of practice:
All forms of shamanism, path working, ancestral, shape shifting.

Witchcraft

Manifestation of the will through the directed currents of the natural world, spiritual world, and elemental world.

All the things that Shamanism and Folk magick are based in as well as the integration of the celestial world. Drawing down instead of praying towards celestial forces. The dealing with the influence of the natural, elemental, and spiritual worlds towards the living condition. Luck magick/jinxes, Love magick, healing, blessing, curses & hexing, banishment, etc.

Negative Effects:

Friends will turn against you, causation of localized
madness, community revolt, insanity and death through externalization of the madness.

Types of practice:
All forms of the arts can have aspects of this craft.
Witch - Based on folk magick, and shamanism
can incorporate all things in the natural and celestial world to mediate between the living or spiritual conditions.

Necromancy

Manipulation of the non living forces of nature, and the life currents found within the environments of the physical and celestial worlds.

The calling forth of the non living essences of creation. Time that concept of what has been to cause change in the natural world. Ex: to recall the spirit of the Yggdrasil through a oak staff. Willful manifestation through the use of "past/death" states with the potential life and converts it towards one owns ends. This path does not call forth and manifest higher forces, but manipulates the forces of the world already in existence either in states of decay, or their various points of radiation from the source to recall them to a past point in their existence.

Negative Effects:
The draining of the life force of the individual to fuel the art, the will consumed by the manifestation of what you are attempting to achieve thus the loss of self, the loss of individuality towards the world essences, and the eventual insanity, death, and localized effects of what ever has been ill created.

Types of Practice:
All forms of the modern types of the Arts have connection with the acts found within the study of the manipulation of the spiritual and natural world.
Necromancer - Calls upon the non living animation principals of the world to manifest and manipulate the world.

Necro-Thaumaturgy - Manipulating the energy of the essence/soul of a non living force, such as nature, planets, demons, spirits, gods, etc. Things that exist beyond humanoid or plant life.

Sorcery

Creation through utter will. Verbum Caro Factum Est - The will made flesh. The prime elimination of the "To-Be" forms of words and actions. Making them simply to become "IS' through their own natures. To cause Creation of the Will through the willing of the manifestation to occur. There is no longer deity, there is no longer spirit, and without question Will is brought forth to create from the foundations of the "world" as it exists, to make it fit to the will of the sorcerer.

Negative effects:

Entropy takes effect and the inertia of the true will is
lost.. If you cannot hold your own will, to bend as the reeds, and lasting as the stone in the mountain, though changing form never broken, then if you become broken your world will collapse upon you. Leaving you worse then dead.

Types of practice:

Thaumaturge - One who makes use of their will to cause influence to the world and elements by subjecting the fundamental essences to their desires by means of a focus, such as a spell, rite or ritual.

Wizard - Changes the way situations come about through the manipulation of the natural. One who makes use of the planar realms, studying circumstance, with causes and effects, applying their magick to the key events as according to the desired outcome.

Sorcerer - Causes overt changes in the environments according to will. One who blends the realms in their own mind, causing change by means of gates, and altering the perception as to the nature of reality around a focus.

Mage - They exist as their own source 'priest and sorcerer' to their will and the forces of creation and thus is the Thaumaturge. A person who harnesses energies to shape and shift the world as it is perceived.

High Magick

Calls upon all forces of the celestial and super celestial origins to manifest in the world some aspect of the source current that is desired for manifestation.

Calling upon the Angelic hosts, and celestial forces through complex rites and ceremonies through the application of use of the higher forces that created them to command them to obedience. The logic driven forces, and cold action and reaction of nature occurring to achieve ones will through the subjugation of the Supernal Realm. The Conjuration of the Supernal world into the physical world. The prayer and subjugation of the high forces towards ends via petitioning the Super Celestial forces to make the celestial, physical, and infernal worlds fall into line with the will of the magician.

Negative effects:

You lose your footing with your will, or the connection to the higher power rejects the command. The force you have brought forth is then brought down upon you and your life, destroying you utterly and compelling you into a form of service, insanity, and/or eventually death. Suicide is possible.

Types of practice:

All forms of magick have the potential to make use of the techniques of High Magick, that the entirety of creation can be subjugated to the will of the individual petitioning from the highest source to compel the things of the lower source into action. Clerical magick, Books of Angelic Summoning, Enochian, Greater Key of Solomon, Cabala, Theurgy.

Priest - Theurgy - One who by means of theurgic rites, rituals, prayer, and spell calls upon the directed forces of their deity. The calling upon "god-force" or 'spiritual force' as one who is in service to achieve the desired outcome through supplication to the higher force then the one who has subjugated himself to service. The God is the Master, the priest is the slave to the God.

Antinomian Theurgy - the subjugation of the self to the demonic lords, to become the priests of the infernal world.

Demonic magick

The use of the emotional bodies of the self, and the greater worlds of the heights and depths of the spheres of creation towards what ever emotional, physical, or spiritual ends. The Calling upon the cold logic of the opposite emotion to compel obedience from the raw emotional force that exists. The manifestation of the inner worlds to the exterior worlds, the underworld brought forth to the physical world. The manipulation of weaknesses through the emotional natures of the things, and the subjugation of spirit through punishment, pain, and torture by the Supernal natures. Compelling by the forces of "light" into the "darkness" to shape with the darkness the events, and physical changes desired in the world.

Negative Effects:

The will breaks and the magician is subsumed and subjugated like and/or by the forces he attempted to command. Insanity, death, persecution, and slavery will result if things go badly for the one who does not understand the weight of the works being under taken. Suicide.

Types of practice:

Clerical magick, Goetia and the Lesser key magick, The Qlipoth in all its forms.

Chaos Magick

The application of any of the techniques mentioned above to achieve manifestation through what ever acceptable medium will manifest the desires.

The application of properties through any medium available in the moment of need.

Negative effects:
See the Worst Case Scenario Handbook.

Types of practice:
Anything.

Tools a Primer

Every craftsman needs their tools. A craftsmen of energies is no different, for there are those tricky projects that require that a little something extra be used. To really begin there is always a book of works, blank in the beginning and only filled with rites and spells; the recipes of one's work on their soul. It can be worked so that upon its consecration you can make it a link to this world even if your soul has moved onto another plane, so as never to lose connection to this world through something that came from your mind and your essence to better craft this world.

There is a blade of this art, but only used to draw one's own blood in works requiring that catalyst of living and WILLING sacrifice. It can be any design, or be any amount of blades, but must be reserved for nothing but your personal use, in the employ of a living catalyst to link, increase, seal, or command in any of the works you set out to accomplish.

The ritual robe is the astral Armor, when the mage is working with things that shift the planes, it has the potential to link his energies to the energies of the plane on which he is working from and increase the effects of what he is working. Besides, nothing really beats the flair of a hand made velvet robe and cloak in modern society.

The Chalice of the art is the feminine receptacle of energy channels. It is a well of energy just as is the human vessel. Like the human vessel that energy can be taken in and unified with the soul of the mage, linking what is otherwise a separate energy, allowing for an ascension of the soul to occur. Of crystal, glass, wood, metal, or any materials that align with your energies best, should be employed for the chalice. More then one chalice can be used as well, with a different energy needed in different works. One crafted of each of the elemental energies is most beneficial in the long run so distinct energies don't blend and corrupt what needs to be distinct, however that in itself might be a desired purpose. It is up the discretion of the mage on what is the proper stock of stemware in their box.

The wand, even though seldom used as a part of works, can be used where ever is sought more energy in work. Like the chalice, as it is the vessel for the fluids of the work, the wand is the stem of the mage, where energy can be directed in a focused manner to achieve a precision that may otherwise be more difficult to achieve. The wand should be made of oak, and filled with a condenser to further entwine the energy of the mage and his work.

Skulls of the art have almost no place in modern magick as practiced by the more socially accepted counterparts of this work. Yet when a human skull, acquired by lawful means, cleansed, etched, and charged is used in works drawing upon the strength of humanity, nothing compares. So in this work it is recommended that in a majority of works a skull is to be present as it always has some form of energy to lend. Skulls being of a neutral nature to begin with, can be shifted to a lighter or darker nature with the use of symbols, spells, and figures etched upon the bone.

After you have selected the tools for your working, each working may require a new tool, or an old one what ever will fit your needs the best, you should preform a consecration ceremony of some sort to align the elemental current with the tool of your working. That way you can draw upon the power through the physical construct of the tool. Giving each wand, chalice, cup, sword, circle a name, gives it a relationship to you, that way when you call the name, you call the "essence" of the tool to come to your aid, whether or not it is actually present in your work or not.

On Consecration of Tools

    The altar should be set, should you be using one. In the beginning it is usually wise to set one, for allowing the ease of mindset between the lower physical world and the higher spiritual world become distinct. You should have a candle that is inscribed with the name of the power that you are going to call, its color should also reflect what you would concentrate it for the use of:

Red for fire, war, blood.
Black for the night, death, dark earth, decay, transmutation.
Blue for water, rain, transformation, healing, wealth.
White for death, power, oblivion.
Purple for transcendence, sexuality, foresight, air.
Green for earth, friendship, union, natural force.
Yellow for fire, perception of ego, development of self.
Orange for lies.

    And so on. There are hundreds of correspondences for the colors from the Cabala and the Qlipoth, to chaos magick and the planets. The color is supposed to bring out what you feel as your intent. These candles are also to be soaked in a salt water solution prior to use, so that they will last a while, as this method hardens the wax. If you do this you will have a less wax dripping on your altar as well as being able to have a candle that can be used as a base for the element in many rituals. A lot of authors and sources recommend single use candles for the spells and rituals they preform.
    When you work a spell, ritual, or rite you need this to be able forge a link with the elements of that current. So being able to have candles that last is an important part of this. The candle should also, if possible, be carved with the symbols of the gate and seal of the planet it represents, to get the energy for that link as specific as possible. You want it to be a gate when ever it is lit.
    When you have this candle of the Art you also have then the tool which you have spent time thus far cleansing from all energy, and it is time to give the initial consecration. Next to the candle on the altar which is positioned in the corresponding direction of the eight point star, take water which has been blessed to become a medium of transference from the waters of creation, that the water becomes the initial link to the false sea, in which the desires are cast out so that the will is made flesh. This is a particular charge of energy depending on what you are consecrating for any rite. Each and every last grain of salt, herb, wax, blade, bone that is ever used in a ritual fashion should be consecrated according to its alignment prior to its use in ritual. Once an Item is charged, such as a seal, candle, skull, wand etc, it should only be used for that singular current of energy ever. If you consecrate a chalice to the water of creation, then you will not be able to effectively use it for calling on things from the false sea. However you can consecrate a chalice to be the medium to channel energy from every plane of water that you desire allowing the water to manifest properly as you call for it.
    Follow through with your charge be it spoken, or burned, or a bloody link forged between you and the object. Remember with blood that it also matters the way it is drawn forth for the link. If it is an accidental cut where the blood has been mixed with ink, then the energy is unstable and chaotic till focus is directed through the pen which writes it, allowing for a focus put to this energy. If it is cut forth deliberately from your hand, then that energy becomes a focused and directed link to your dominant or recessive self.
    Lastly comes the circle. You must have a circle set when you consecrate something, as it separates your world of the physical, from your world of the spiritual. You must then call this boundary into existence around you and your altar. Light your candle, and then anoint the object.
    Having anointed the object, your work done, withdraw the circle. You should snuff the candle to keep the energy. You should return the water to the earth. What ever remains of your wax candle for that element should be wrapped up in a portion of cloth, so that it shall only be exposed to the world of

the spiritual and never used for anything but that link to the current for which you have carved it. Over time, you should have a store of supplies, both new and used candles, plenty of herbs, and materials that you use commonly to create a cupboard, trunk, room full of mediums that you can use easily that are on hand for your working.

When it comes time for another ceremony that will be making use of tools that are already created then it comes necessary to cleanse them of prior energy but maintaining their spiritual links. Here are some examples of how to do this.

Cleansing Charged Tools

Within an object that has been prepared by your own hand, or by your intent one must make conjuration unto its purpose so to ensure that the purpose is to be directed by 'this' extension of your will and correspondingly your thoughts.

Surround yourself with the currents that you would have present themselves within the objects you would charge it to become the emanation of. The following are then examples of this. To mix the herbs with your blood is to make the tool an exact extension of your will as well.

Chalice:
Clean with spring water in set within a condenser mixed with the following herbs:
>   Chamomile, Rosemary, Dragons blood

Blades:
>   Chamomile, Dragons blood and Bay leaf

Cauldrons:
:
>   Lavender, chamomile, rosemary, mandrake

Wand/Staff of the Art:

>   Bay leaf, dragons blood, rosemary, chamomile, mandrake

Exercises

Give examples of your tools and their connection to the elements.

Give at least 3 paragraphs describing what tools you set for what purpose and how you would charge them for your purposes and cleanse them.

Write out a ceremony that will charge each of the basic four elemental tools with the elements and an herbal recipe to cleanse them, using what you have on hand.

Blades of the Art

The metals hold particular influence that align to the planetary bodies that would be associated with what ever working, one is doing. Carved with various symbols, sigils, and seals these things become the embodiment of the great powers, pillars of creation. As with all tools the basic correspondences are needed for the crafting of a proper metallic object. You must be familiar or have someone who is familiar craft the body of the blade for you. Ideally if you can get away with having a blade pierce an innocents dominant hand, held in the dominant hand of the innocent on sanctified ground to become a weapon of the infernal, then your one step ahead. However if you do not have this capacity then there other methods to employ to gain the powers associated with what your after in a blade.

The Chalice

The feminine receptacle of creation. The womb of the earth, and seas. It is the eternal well that energy shall be called forth to bring creation out of. When using the chalice you must select the material it is to be carved from, or shaped into. Stone is particularly useful, as well as crystalline glassware that you can etch the symbols of the art into. Blood should be put into any mixture consumed so as to bind your living spirit to the work. Where not consumed the blood substitute is sufficient, so long as it has been mixed properly.

The Wands of the Art

Action, masculine projection of the will. When carved from the branch of a tree that has been chosen for its attributes, cut at the hour of height of that power. It should be dried, carved, and hollowed out. Modern-day techniques are handy when it comes to drills. Filling the wand with a condenser that has been crafted to be the duplicated current of the mage is the best.

However if you would be so bold as to branch out into different experiences, you can bind spirits to the wand to be the active medium for your will. To do this, mix the condenser from the planetary alignments, a blood condenser to act as the medium of animation, and the sigil of the spirit/demon drawn in the same substance and placed in the hollowed out core of the wand. Bone wands carved from fingers of dead people and animals, or other parts of their body depending on the influences you would gain can be used as well. Engravings of the symbols of power, or hollowed and the marrow filled with the condensers will work just as well. Its a matter of what you are trying to achieve in your work that will dictate what kind of a wand, if one is needed.

Keep them stored in an oak box with a velvet lining, not only for style but to keep it safe. Carve, paint, or burn into the lid, sides, and underside a barrier seal to keep the current from discharging when not in use. Also adding a locking mechanism to this box isn't such a bad idea.

Skull of the Art

When working with the arts there are many reasons one would use and employ such a barbaric object as a skull. These are to heal the human spirit, act as anchors to the souls/spirits/gods conjured and bound to them like the sacred statuary in the shape and icons of the gods.

Cast the skull in plaster from a plastic mold. This is the best way to achieve desired personalization. This will allow you to also create the negative mold to custom craft the positives used in rituals.

When you cast these skulls the components must be mixed into the fresh plaster before you put it in the mold to sit. You can also imbed stones into the mold if you create the cavities for it. Into the medium of plaster we have the fine choice of adding what ever raw component to customize every aspect of the ritual tools.

Why plaster is such a lovely medium for the artificers who would embark upon custom crafting their tool is that the plaster has no resonance. It is an aetherically dense non-conductive material. However when the components are painted on or carved into, or molded into it. It acts as the perfect insulation for the medium. Like the bones act as the insulation for the spirit that animates them.

Human bones need thorough cleansing to remove the spirit that once inhabited them. Any animal skulls used will contain the spirit of that animal but it is best removed all together so one can be grafted into the bone, as its permanent residence. The same can be applied to bones molded from human or animal remains, crafted from plaster, with the components mixed into them. Uses for this would be endless when it comes to a neutral casting.

Through this process we enter into a new period of mastery of the art when we can create anew any of the tools we want out for such neutral media. When we implant the components into it, much as one would implant the energy into the living body of man.

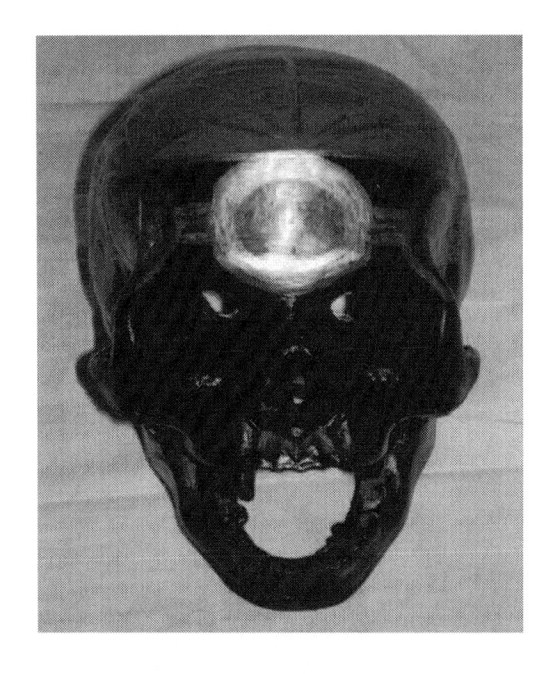

Box of Containment

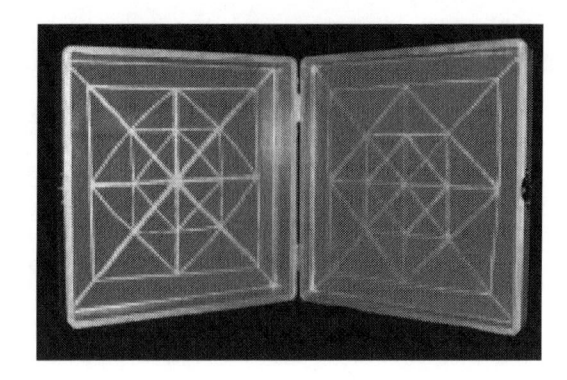

The Inside

Purpose:

    This array is built to contain the current that would other wise be free flowing energy from the object after the initial charge has been made.

Construction notes:

    18 karat gold array lines to act as the conduits of the current to be able to neutralize and create a stable containment field for the object that would be placed inside.

    The red is to represent the will, and the blood that is mixed into the paint, to provide it with a living essence to keep the current flowing. As well as to give the one who has made such objects control over the flow.

Uses:

    This particular box is used with the seals of power. The design inside is for neutralizing high level currents into a containment field. Can be adjusted and applied to larger objects where the current needs to be neutralized for proper storage.

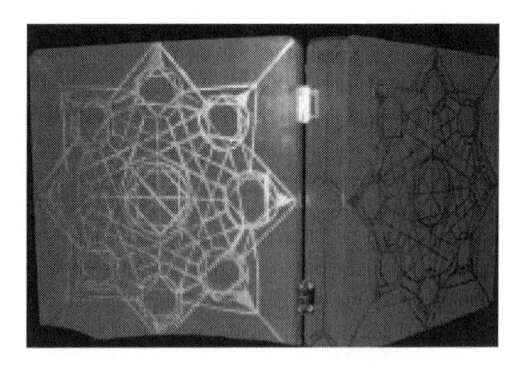

The Outside

Purpose:

    To absorb power generated from both within and externally to maintain a shell of protection and neutralize exterior and interior currents that are placed with such objects. The array is meant to hide objects of power from such things that would other wise be able to determine if such objects are around. Acting as a containment for dead space, that makes it appear that it is an ordinary object from someone with the power that would notice this array. Such an object after it has been crafted with this array can be painted with a less "obvious" design, if you would have the object blend into its surroundings, and make the case of this one appear to be a "normal" cigar box.

Construction notes:
> 18 karat gold to set the lines for the current to be neutralized.
> Blood to be mixed with the paints in order to give intent, purpose and direction to the object, making it self sustaining.

Uses:
> Containment of objects that give off a presence. To protect such objects from outside influence through neutralizing of
> its currents.

Seal of Perpetual Creation

The Bottom

Purpose:
    To form a self generating current on contact with terrestrial currents.

Construction notes:
    Blood mixed with the paints for giving it a self generating current.
    18 karat gold used to set the lines to establish the flow for the current.
    Ink mixed with blood to form the connecting point to the terrestrial current.

Uses:
    Drawing up balanced energy from the earth creating a portable ley line node. As such this object can temporarily create new current in the terrestrial fields where they are placed allowing for a stabilized creation.

The Top

Purposes:
    To maintain a neutralized point of generation with the balance of the darkness, light and the blood. To the center point of creation which can take on any manifestation.

Construction notes:
    Blood mixed with the paints for giving it a self generating current.
    18 karat gold used to set the lines to establish the flow for the current.

Uses:
    Can be a suitable node generating point for the terrestrial current. Can open up the tower of art, as well as conduits directly to the source of creation.

Seals of the Gates

Gate of the Earth

For works creating directly with the primal terrestrial currents.

Gate of the Darkness

For works creating with the primal darkness.

Gate of Light

For works creating with the primal light currents.

Gate of the Summer Solstice

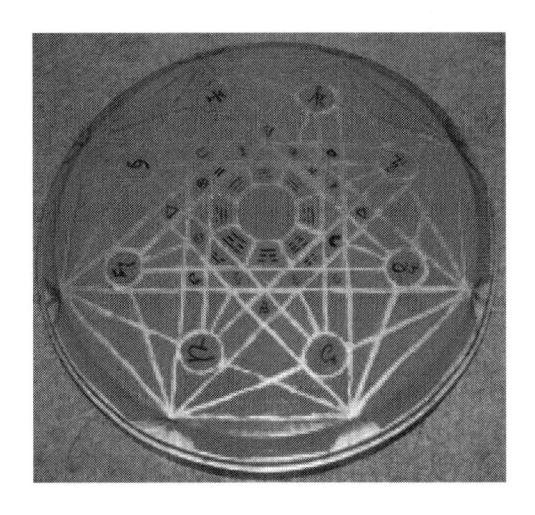

Temporal workings and things that involve the celestial currents.

Creation of Tools

When working the rituals, and ceremonies throughout your career a practitioner of the ceremonial arts, then you will from time to time have to craft your own tools, with methods that are unique to your own caste of magick, to get the most out of your energies. These are what would amount to the scalpel in the hands of a surgeon if the surgeon had the ability to craft the scalpels for every surgery. Here is an example of a type of method for a wand construction.

The Construction of the Wand

First with the wand the proper wood should be selected, from woods corresponding to the properties you wish your wand to possess. For example: oak for strength and power, ebony for dark magick and shadow workings etc. After the selection of the wood, a period of observation should be made in the harvesting of the wood at the corresponding hour when its energies are at peak before the severing of the limbs from the tree. The knife or saw should be consecrated as an implement of sacrifice.

Following the separation of the rod from the tree should be the cleansing of the raw wood by the spell of consecration. When this has been accomplished, set the wood upon a lathe where the completed rod is of 7 inches, 9 inches, or 13 inches. Work the wood on the lathe to make a shaft and a handle. When the designs of both have been made and the wood is able to be taken to a drill, bore out a core in the handle allowing the insertion of the catalyst (later described), and bore out the handle so it will slide over the completed shaft sealing the catalyst inside. A hollow copper rod in those dimensions works as well also.

When the drilling has been completed and the wand is ready to be assembled, place it again upon the circle of cleansing making sure there are no residual energies to the wood which could have been implanted during the construction. Create a catalyst according to the properties you would have in the finished piece possess. This catalyst should be made of one or more of the following metals:

Melting Point
- Platinum - High Celestial influence 1770 C 3220 F
- Titanium - High solar influence 1670 C 3040 F
- Gold - general solar works 1063 C 1945 F
- Silver - general lunar works 961 C 1760 F
- Brass - Jupiter 930 C 1710 F
- Nickel - low lunar works 1453 C 2647 F
- Bronze - Combination of mostly solar with lunar influence
- Copper - Venus 1084 C 1983 F
- Tin – Jupiter 232 C 449.4 F
- Iron -Mars 1536 C 2927 F
- Steel - Earth energy with lunar influence
- Mercury – Mercury -38.6 C -37.95 F
- Lead –Saturn 327.5 C 621 F

Combine the metal filings or liquids with herbs of corresponding significance. Add any stone shard also associated with the final desire. Cleanse the catalyst before you insert it into the rod by working the cleansing spell. When this is done, add the blood from the line of the future user, when adding the catalyst to the rod.

Upon completion of the wand-to-be, inscribe it with any runes or symbols you would use to further increase its potency. Inscribe these upon the rod where the handle would cover the wood. Attach the wood pieces together with wood glue. Sand and varnish the piece yet leave the very tip unvarnished. When this has been done, cast the spell of consecrations in the next corresponding hour to the goal. This then can be used as a focus for the energies in works of the soul and those processes where the energy would be most beneficial.

Exercises for Tool Creation

Create the description of how you would create a tool of the art from scratch. List what materials are to be used, why you would include them. Include as well, any sources of information that you use in the construction.

Write out another style of mediation to the element the tool represents, with a ceremony of consecration for the purpose you are making the tool for, as well as a means to cleanse it.

Create a table of correspondence chart for the tool, element, stones, metals, herbs that you use when it comes to researching for the element, do this each for each of the four elemental tools.

Creation of the Grimoire

This requires research of the prospective student to search out what style of text they would get the most use from. I used a Renaissance binding style of four cords with a sewn binding and a solid black leather cover.

Depending on how long it will take you to source out your materials, it would be best to begin early in the year. At least one week prior to the full moon before the new moon in october, fold the pages, and sew the spine. Glue the spine, and cover on the shell. This will be the pages for the grimoire. Glue the ribbons on that will be the page markers if you choose to have any.

3 days before the full moon rise, paint the grimoire shell with seals in blooded paints and any arrays which would add power to the work. Use blooded paints and inks.

On the Full Moon when its at the height, hold it open so the light hits it, and read the Conjuration the vessel. Ready the end page array before the new moon, glue it in place. Hold it up to the darkness, and write in the conjuration of power you would have that pulls upon your station, your tower of art, your "selves". The ink should be blooded.

Perform the transference of power ritual upon this empty vessel that it shall recieve your spirit. It will become your grimoire of art.

Here ends this volume.

Printed in Great Britain
by Amazon